EVALUATING SOCIAL PROGRAMS

DONALD E. CHAMBERS
School of Social Welfare
The University of Kansas

KENNETH R. WEDEL
School of Social Work
The University of Oklahoma

MARY K. RODWELL
School of Social Work
Virginia Commonwealth University

ALLYN AND BACON
Boston   London   Toronto   Sydney   Tokyo   Singapore

Series Editor: Karen Hanson
Series Editorial Assistant: Deborah Reinke
Production Coordinator: Marjorie Payne
Editorial-Production Service: Chestnut Hill Enterprises, Inc.
Cover Administrator: Linda Dickinson
Cover Designer: Suzanne Harbison
Manufacturing Buyer: Megan Cochran

This book is printed on recycled, acid-free paper.

Library of Congress Cataloging-in-Publication Data

Chambers, Donald E.
    Evaluating social programs/ Donald E. Chambers, Kenneth R. Wedel,
Mary K. Rodwell.
    p. cm.
    Includes bibliographical references and index.
    ISBN 0–205–12907–2
    1. Social service—Evaluation. 2. Evaluation research (Social
action programs) I. Wedel, Kenneth R. II. Rodwell, Mary K.
III. Title.
    HV41.C43 1992
    361.6'068—dc20   91–14023
        CIP

Printed in the United States of America
10 9 8 7 6 5 4 3 2 1   96 95 94 93 92 91

Contents

Preface

We have been dissatisfied with program evaluation books on several counts: many do not keep up with controversies in their field, and some are written with selective biases that exclude attention to rival positions. Often they use examples that highlight a few major, national, multi-million dollar "successes" in evaluation research (the national Head Start evaluations, the national guaranteed income studies—e.g., SIMDIME—etc.). But these, interesting as they are, are on a scale that makes them nearly irrelevant to most local or state human service evaluation efforts. This book hopes to correct those problems by actually highlighting the disappointments in the record of program evaluation (as well as its workaday successes) and presenting fair-minded versions of the major methodologies, the main controversies, and a review of the major solutions proposed. There is no doubt that all the answers are not yet in, and so we wish to present our own answers for readers to consider, some of which are seeing print for the first time here.

We believe that this is a sound way to proceed. It is unlikely that a consensus on a general solution to these issues will emerge very soon, and students, direct practitioners, and administrators alike must be prepared to make some decisions on their own about how to pursue their program evaluation responsibilities. It is to this specific end, therefore, that this book is directed. We are attempting to provide readers with sufficient grasp of the controversial issues that they can choose their own courses. This means that we are sacrificing some depth in favor of breadth. Of course, buried in the depths of these controversies are philosophical problems of exquisite complexity, but we do not deal much with arguments at that level, as interesting and important as they are.

Our primary intent is practical, so we take pains to consider how the controversies and the proposed solutions answer the practical demands of the working lives of social work and human service practitioners and administrators. Thus, we wish to consider methods in the sense of teaching the reader appropriate criteria for choosing from among several method options. While we will speak of specific types of methods by way of illustration, we are not writing a "how to" handbook; rather, our aim is to give sufficient detail to prepare the reader to make choices, and then to provide a bibliographic bridge to answer questions of the very specific, "how-to" type.

The issue of dealing with coverage of specific methods in a book for the education of administrators and practitioners is not easy to resolve. Of major importance is the matter of prior preparation. Methods here can be so complex that they require doctoral level work and research experience as well. Most can be grasped with a typical, good undergraduate social science background. The human service and social work practitioner/administrator audience and its students, for whom this book is intended, are required to have only the latter, so we have compromised on the issue of coverage of methods and technical issues in that direction. We have assumed that students and readers will have completed course work in a fundamental undergraduate research course.

This book is addressed both to present managers of human services, programs, and social work, and human service professional practitioners who deal directly with consumers—and to students who will occupy those roles in the future. Among managers, our concern is particularly for those whose organizational roles place them between top-level policy makers and "street-level bureaucrats" or professional practitioners. We believe that, while not identical, the middle manager and the direct practitioner have convergent needs for program evaluation skills and a viewpoint on the field. Both are responsible for conducting program evaluations of some kind and so must be prepared to make choices about methodology, methods, use of scarce resources (e.g., practitioners' use of time) and must employ skill in interpreting results. In addition, no matter what role a person occupies in an organization, successful organizational life demands the ability to exercise influence, if not power. To do so effectively demands keeping in mind the perspectives of all the other players. It is no less true for social program evaluation roles. Practitioners should be better able to make evaluations of how programs work for them, and administrators should be better able to involve practitioners in their program evaluation ventures, if they each understand the other's role, self-interest, and problems in the evaluation enterprise.

Finally, both will have much responsibility for its implementation, and on that account practitioners and middle managers have more influence than they often realize (or use, as a matter of fact). All experienced top-level policy makers know that they are ultimately at the mercy of their operating staff when it comes to information about operating programs. Some believe that the consequence of this is so important that, beyond the decision as to whether the organization itself exists, ultimate control lies in the hands of implementers. In order for both practitioners and middle managers to make program evaluation work for their own purposes, they need a clear grasp of the issues and a solidified viewpoint to work from. Of course, human service program middle managers often have responsibilities for evaluation research that go beyond those of the direct practitioner. We believe that this middle-management responsibility has a special character. That is, it is seldom that program managers themselves design and implement a comprehensive program evaluation; rather, their responsibility is more likely to be along the lines of

1. Interpreting the findings of evaluations and their implications for the programs or policies for which they are responsible,
2. Writing contract specifications for evaluations—what central questions the evaluation is expected to answer; what design constraints are to be observed; from an organizational and political point of view, what factors are crucial to measure, etc.,
3. Evaluating whether evaluation contract proposals, external or in-house, are complete and adequate to the task for which they are intended.

These middle-managerial responsibilities are the ones we have most in mind when writing the book. This is expressed in the selection of examples and in setting the level for the discussions of method.

However, this book on program evaluation does not concede that evaluation research is the sole concern of administrators at the policy and program level. In the first place, all direct practitioners in social work and the human services should routinely be able to construct procedures that give them a fix on the outcomes of their own work with clients. Those evaluation procedures, the single subject designs, and client self-report measures that they often entail are important, and this book deals with them in explicit, practical terms. This book is also directed toward the need of practitioners to involve themselves in the evaluation of the whole programs in the context of which their practices occur.

Practitioners must be prepared to shape and influence the design and implementation of evaluations at the overall program and policy level. They need to be concerned with both product and process—especially process, or they will cede to others the control of important aspects of their professional work. Experience shows that there is no reason to assume that the effect of program evaluations will be necessarily benign or that it will always be in the best interests of clients. Left to its own devices, the program evaluation process is an unguided missile whose effects are never quite predictable. On that account, we believe it is just as important for practitioners to be prepared to participate in the planning of evaluation research at the program and policy level as it is for them to be able to conduct small-scale studies of their own practices.

We hope that this book differs from those currently in print on several accounts. Special attention is paid to evaluating implementation and program designs via a separate chapter solely devoted to that subject. There is some agreement in the field that one of the major shortcomings of two decades of evaluation studies is the tendency to take program designs, their intervention concepts, and their actual implementation for granted. Hence the term *black box* research. That term refers to studies that attribute outcomes to an independent (causal) variable assumed to be in the design—in place and actually operating to influence results—but with no actual data to validate the presumption. One reason for this shortcoming is the relatively crude state of our art, indeed even our inexperience in translating theory into a set of actual activities that are sufficiently explicit to be consistently implemented by sets of practitioners or staff members.

Experience shows that that important task can no longer be neglected in evaluation research. First, we may get stronger conclusions about program effects, for some authorities think it is a major reason for "no effect" findings in evaluation studies. Clearly, under conditions of seriously compromised implementation, even positive, well-documented outcomes cannot be legitimately attributed to the influence of the program. That is not a trivial case, because it can prevent replication of useful, positively evaluated demonstration programs. The problem is fairly simple—findings cannot be expected to be reproduced at will, when in the original experiment we cannot be certain that the causal process was ever put in motion.

This book remedies this shortcoming by presenting a step-by-step method for accomplishing a translation of the more general theoretical ideas into a program design. Program designs are written, and graphic schemes identify the crucial factors and conditions minimally necessary for the theory to work in the way it was intended. This method also includes a way to account for the compromises with theory that have been required. This approach is somewhat akin to what Peter Rossi calls the "theory-ridden approach." We also present methods of monitoring (observing) the actual organizational behaviors and activities that go into the implementation of the program design. We present a review of the present literature on this aspect of implementation. We believe we have useful and unique things to say to program managers who are faced with the problems of monitoring implementation on small to non-existent evaluation budgets.

Most books have not included serious attention to the fact that two, quite different, perhaps even contradictory, evaluation methods exist in the field. The traditional and dominant method is quantitative. The "newcomer" is qualitative. We include generous attention to the qualitative approach and its associated methodology in devoting Part Three exclusively to qualitative approaches. Finally, we believe this book is also unique in devoting a systematic attention to newly emerging official standards in the social program evaluation field. Although there are discussions of ethics in some evaluation books, none that we are aware of combines a discussion of ethical standards with a review of legal issues (including professional liability) in evaluation research and the relatively new professional standards for evaluation research published by the Evaluation Research Society. Since, universally, those who conduct evaluation research come from training in some other discipline whose professional standards seldom refer to program evaluation, it is the Evaluation Research Society standards that are relevant.

CHAPTER ONE

The Program and Policy Evaluation Field

History, Types of Evaluation, Leading Controversies, and Some Agreed-upon Practice Wisdom

This book is about evaluation research. Its main concern is how to obtain a rounded picture of the operations and effects of social programs and social policies. We will address the key questions of how they "work," whether they do what they are supposed to do, and, if so, for whom, to what extent, and with what unwanted side effects. We will want to be generic in our consideration of social programs and policies. Thus, we intend to make reference to programs and policies that deliver welfare benefits to both the poor and the rich, educate genius as well as the mentally disabled, provide health care (and sometimes disease) and distribute justice as well as the mail. We believe that, although differences among them are important, many of the problems in determining their effects are shared.

It is important for those new to this field to understand that the evaluation of social programs and policies has created a new enterprise, a program evaluation "industry." It has its own journals (perhaps as many as seven), recognizable sectors, and sub-specialties. And, there are two trade associations—The American Evaluation Association and the Educational Evaluation Society—complete with annual meetings, a newsletter, an advertising budget, and local chapters. In fact, the evaluation enterprise is ubiquitous. It is, by now, sufficiently influential so that, on some occasions, the findings of large scale evaluation projects sometimes shape the discussion of U.S. welfare program expenditures.[1] Although there are few program evaluators who work on them, those large projects are important to the field because they are often influential in shaping social program technology and standards. There was a

1

time when the evaluation of social programs and policies was an obscure corner of the local health, welfare, and/or educational bureaucracy. At stake were simply the affairs of a small group of client-consumers plus a few professional or bureaucratic careers. To be sure, there are times when it is still only that, and, even so, it is important to those folks. But there are also occasions when the social program evaluation enterprise stands close to the heart of current issues and national preoccupations, and that is always exciting.

In order to understand the present state of this field, one must have some historical perspective: the key actors, the economic, political, and sociological events that together make up the general historical context out of which the program evaluation field grew. Let us now turn to that.

A Brief History of Social Policy and Program Evaluation in the United States

Early Roots: Two Enduring Lessons from the First and Second Generations of the Practice of Program/Policy Evaluation

First lesson: The response to the findings of social policy and program evaluations is not invariably positive In 1845 the reaction of the Board of Education of the city of Boston to the results obtained from the first-ever use of printed tests to assess how well its students were doing was to discontinue giving the tests when they all too clearly revealed the students' low performances (Travers, 1983). Killing a messenger who carries bad news is not news, of course; in fact, it has a certain familiar and contemporary ring. History teaches us that public policy is often unresponsive to empirical findings: facts alone are seldom responsible for changing things in desired directions, and, although it is surely possible to imagine worlds where that is the case, it is unlikely that it is the one we currently inhabit. That is an extremely important idea readers should take note of because it speaks about one of the important ways in which program and policy research differs from other kinds of research.

Second lesson: History reveals that large-scale political events drive the development of program and policy evaluation research For example, the development of various educational tests and measurements grew rapidly after 1917 when the need arose to screen Army inductees for service in World War I (Worthen and Landers, 1987, p. 3). Although some of the very first attempts to assess the effectiveness of public social policies and programs occurred in education, they did not all occur there. The evaluation enterprise has often been an instrument of widely varied social and commercial purposes. In the 1920s psychology and sociology were put to use in evaluating work productivity. Industrial psychology arose as a major embodiment of that trend. Studies of factors effecting productivity at the giant Western Electric industrial plants were large, ongoing, and widely known. Western Electric's Hawthorne plant was one of those sites. Some students may recollect that name (the Hawthorne effect) as one given to a "contaminating effect" memorialized by Stanley and Campbell as a technical problem for experiments involving human subjects (1966). In fact, we will discuss that very issue later in this book.

There were other well-known examples of the influence of large-scale events on social program evaluation. During World War II, sociologist Samuel Stauffer and his student, Robert Merton, developed the beginnings of a type of sociological research centering on experimental and survey methods as they studied the effectiveness of military programs that taught soldiers how to fly warplanes. Nor should we leave a discussion of the early roots of this field without referring to the flowering of advertising and mass communications following World War II; one of its main tools was what has come to be called *market* or *consumer research*, an important instrument in the evaluation of products and consumer response to them. A huge and profitable industry developed out of this effort. Along with it, a mass survey technology developed, and, as it concerns sampling and measurement, it has found many applications in social policy and program evaluation research.

The Golden Age: The Third Generation of Program/Policy Evaluation

President Lyndon Johnson's "Great Society" programs of the 1960s involved massive expenditures in the service of social interventions of all kinds. It introduced program and policy evaluation to a degree that was, clearly, out of scale in relation to earlier times. Even though the New Deal programs of the 1930s' depression era were probably of equal size, relatively speaking, they had little in the way of an evaluative component. A crude technology was available so, if not in the New Deal, it is reasonable to ask why were there no evaluation efforts until the Great Society programs of the 1960s.

One important factor was the development of a particular mind-set in both Congress and the upper echelon of the presidency: the management-by-objective (MBO) style of Robert McNamara, secretary of defense during the Kennedy presidency. Touted as the "whiz-kids," MacNamara and others were recruited into government service from the higher reaches of the post-World-War II industrial management sector.[2] No doubt they had been important players during the 1950s when the United States became, perhaps, the wealthiest and most widely industrialized country the world had ever known, and they were widely respected because of their association with that era. MacNamara's installation of the MBO style in the defense secretariat was an influence not only over military but domestic spending as well. By the time the Great Society programs were proposed, Congress was reasonably familiar with its basic concepts: clarity about desired outcomes, managing people and resources toward their realization, and directly observing whether objectives were obtained.

Congressional mandates for the evaluation of the Great Society social programs were built into its enabling legislation and appropriations from the very start. The Head Start program, various welfare/work training programs, school lunch and Food Stamp program expansions are all examples. This is the era that saw the passage of the Civil Rights Act of 1964, the Coleman Report studying the effects on children of equality of educational opportunity in U.S. public schools, the Elementary/Secondary Education Act of 1965 (ESEA), and Title I federal funding of educational programs for the economically disadvantaged—the most costly federal program for education in U.S. history. All of these programs are important in the history of the program and policy evaluation field since it was the first time that funding became widely available for systematic evaluation. If this was the "golden age" of the program and policy evaluation enterprise, its golden eggs were the congressional appropriations that funded it.

Nor was this all. Following or coincident with the Great Society legislation, the federal government began to institutionalize its commitment to funding social program and policy research for its own in-house use. The General Accounting Office (GAO) began (routinely) to do special studies evaluating social program outcomes, a responsibility going well beyond its original function as fiscal auditor and certainly beyond traditional accountancy boundaries, however conceived. The GAO is a part of the executive branch, note, and responsible not to Congress but to the president. As it became clear that the GAO tended to interpret findings in ways that (unsurprisingly) reflected the interests of the incumbent president, Congress concluded that they needed to establish their own evaluation research operation where research into public program operations and outcomes could be conducted under their control. Skeptics might say that Congress wanted a mechanism by which it could bias evaluation findings towards their own interests, of course. It took the form of the Congressional Budget Office (CBO) and began operations in the late 1970s. Its first Director was Alice Rivlin, a person with a long professional practice in program and policy evaluation and the author of an important early program evaluation text (Rivlin, 1974). Later, and in the same mood, Congress also established their Office of Technological Assessment (OTA) to give them their own capacity for evaluating some of the highly technical effects (and side effects) of modern industrial medical and scientific products on which they are asked to legislate. Note that all three of these efforts are large in scale and require sizeable annual appropriations.

Finally, but certainly not least, this golden age in the field of social program and policy research was capped by the founding of the large private and quasi-governmental research institutes and foundations. There are similarities among them but, also, several important differences, so it is useful to distinguish at least three sub-types:

1. *Profit-making corporations.* One example is the Westinghouse Corporation whose evaluation subdivision did, among many other things, a series of very expensive evaluations of the Head Start program. These evaluations played an important role in determining the size and character of its operations over the years. Other examples are Abt Associates, Midwest Research Institute, the Rand Corporation, and Mathematica, Inc., to mention but a few. Mathematica, Inc. was a major actor in the design and analysis of a large-scale guaranteed annual income experiment (for example) involving thousands of recipients and conducted over several years in New Jersey, Iowa, Denver, Seattle, and elsewhere. This set of experiments is a leading example of a government actually trying out major program innovations in policy before committing them to legislation. Examples of very high dollar and politically important social experimentation (that are conducted by for-profit corporations) are becoming more frequent—for example, the national educational voucher experiments.

2. *Private nonprofit corporations.* These entities operate without, or with few, public funds. The Ford Foundation with its huge private endowment is one example, illustrating that non-profits also fund actual program operations as well as conduct research. Their evaluation enterprise is often an outgrowth of interest in social program operations. Other types are clearly the reverse, since their main interest is in the research effort itself.

3. *Quasi-non-governmental organizations.* "Quango" is the handy British acronym for these organizations, which are "quasi" only in the sense that, while private and nonprofit, they would not be likely to exist at all without public funding. The Institute for Social Research at the University of Michigan is an example. These university-based and other nonprofit research institutes have, in an important way, developed out of the history of the program evaluation field. They were often initiated by University faculty interested in these questions for academic reasons and given state budget support as "seed money," but they have always been funded largely by federal grant dollars. They compete directly with the private, profit-making sector described above for some of the largest public program and policy evaluation contracts; although, in almost every case, they are, overall, smaller in scope and budget. For example, the Institute for Research on Poverty (IRP) at the University of Wisconsin has conducted extensive and well-received research on the economics of a wide variety of social welfare transfer programs. Social security retirement and disability, the Low Income Energy Assistance Programs, Food Stamps, and child support policies and programs are some examples. Their program and policy proposals on child support were the basis of the Wisconsin state legislation for such a program, and their initial research findings evaluating its effects were a prominent factor in the recent, important Congressional changes in the federal child support system.

After the Boom Comes the Bust: The Years Since 1980

With the election of Ronald Reagan to the presidency and strong fiscal conservatives to Congress, there began a major effort to dismantle the social policy and program structure developed in the United States since the New Deal years of the 1930s. It was determined, broad scale, and very ambitious. Although its general structure remained very much the same, there were major reductions in social program expenditures in all sectors of the social welfare institution in this country; one consequence was a major reduction in federal funding for the evaluation of social programs and policies. While the GAO, the OTA, and the CBO remain, contract funding for new demonstration and pilot programs and for monitoring of ongoing programs was greatly reduced. There are some exceptions, among which the continuing commitment to research on Head Start and the effectiveness of work-training programs and policies are prominent, both of which have a great following in Congress. It is notable that funds for the evaluation of the new workfare programs passed by the 1988 Congress are meager.

Bright Prospects for the Future: Fourth Generation Program and Policy Evaluation

This is an exciting and propitious time to enter this field. Much is happening. The newcomer will find great controversy, whose wider implications are quite radical and more profound than the immediate concerns in evaluating social programs and policies. It is not a field for those who are looking for single answers, since, for the big questions, there are always several answers, each more or less compatible with the view of at least one recognized authority. An ongoing debate between respected authorities almost always makes for a lively field.

One of those debates involves no less than an idea that comes near to questioning the validity of the way contemporary western civilization understands itself: are the basic presuppositions of science correct? That is, is empirical science an adequate way of knowing about the world and, in particular, about the human condition? Since research evaluating social programs and policies began by using scientific methods and still rely primarily upon them, it is an issue of great interest to this field. After all, if modern empirical science is suspect as a basis for investigation, then it brings the justification of expenditures on social program and policy research expenditures into question. And, it raises the question of what the alternatives are, if indeed we have lost faith in empirical social science. Actually, this whole issue is part of a great modern critique of science, its uses, and what the idea "truth" really amounts to. Let us call this critique by the name now most frequently given it, the *post-positivist critique* (House, 1982). As the reader will discover later in this chapter, one reaction to this abundance of skepticism is the development of a type of social program evaluation called the *constructivist approach*, a more qualitatively oriented research method that is very different from traditional quantitative empirical social science. Those new to the field should find these methodological contrasts interesting.

Not only are there new qualitative methods to learn about but a new respect for quantitative findings as well—findings from some of the "mega-evaluations" of large, well-known social programs or policies. A leading example is the study (several, actually) on the impact of the Head Start program. Head Start, the reader may recall, is the federally funded, locally operated preschool program for preparing low income and/or minority children for entry into elementary school so that they are equally well pre-pared in reading and number skills and can compete with middle-class children. Originating as one of the main set-pieces of the 1960s' poverty program, it has survived over the years, despite opposition and alternating cycles of generous and starvation funding. Some of those cyclical changes have been due to congressional response to the conclusions of large-scale program evaluations which have examined its performance relative to its legislated objectives. One of the questions these evaluations asked was, "Do low income children exposed to Head Start really do better compared to middle-class kids" (i.e., better than non-Head Start enrollees)?

The Westinghouse Report, using large and nationwide data, showed that Head Start children, in the main, *did* do better in the first grade but that those gains rapidly vanished the next year. At first that finding was accepted as a reason to severely restrict or even close down the program. The next round of program evaluation results produced different conclusions: indeed, the gains Head Start produced for preschool children remained intact over several years. Those conclusions are now widely accepted. Later, when almost all social programs underwent Reagan era excisions, Head Start was never seriously threatened.

There are other examples of this new confidence in the findings of social policy and program evaluations. For example, much attention has been given to the studies of the effects of a small guaranteed annual income as a strategy to relieve the social problem of poverty, one called SIMDIME, for example (Skidmore, 1983). It is an important policy—some have proposed it as an income maintenance alternative to very costly traditional programs, like Aid to Families of Dependent Children (AFDC) and Supplementary Security Income (SSI). Despite some methodological shortcomings, these studies cre-ated great interest because of their surprising findings. Despite a guarantee of income from the government, most primary wage earners still worked at their usual pace (that is, they reduced work effort by only a trivial amount). That finding contradicts the most basic economic premise about economic rationality—that people work mostly for money. How it is to be interpreted has generated considerable debate.

The debate about the usefulness of traditional quantitative science for program and policy evaluation purposes is not difficult to characterize, though we will not deal with it thoroughly at this point. Instead, because of its importance, whole sub-parts of this book will be devoted to it in such a way that each side of the argument receives a fair hearing. Accordingly, Part Three concerns the most traditional and thoroughly developed way of conducting the evaluation of social policies and programs, the quantitative approach, while Part Four concerns the most recent innovation, the qualitative approach. In the next section of this chapter we will speak in more detail about the different approaches to research on public social programs and policies.

Types of Social Policy and Social Program Evaluation

Out of the history discussed above, a number of different ways of doing what is called program or policy *evaluation* have developed. Note carefully that, whatever they are called, evaluation types are very different, so that categorizing them is not easy. One of the earliest ways of distinguishing among evaluation types was via the use of terms like *formative* and *summative*. These terms are still used in the literature. A *formative evaluation* is one in which the emphasis is on service delivery processes—they were called *formative* because the purpose of the evaluation was to assist program implementation—to form the operational activities of the social program. A *summative evaluation* was to assess the outcome of social program activities—to find out to what extent the program achieved its objectives (Patton, 1978). Their purpose was to *sum-up* the achievements of the program, hence the term *summative*. This older distinction, although important, is probably no longer adequate to describe the rich variety in evaluation types. We need a different way to classify evaluation types, and it is that to which we now turn.

Considering that social programs have many different aspects, let us speak of research on each aspect as a different type of evaluation:

1. *Studies of program outcomes*. One aspect of a social program or policy is its objectives; therefore, we can speak of one type as being concerned with *evaluating* whether intended objectives are actually achieved. This type is nearly identical with what was earlier spoken of as summative evaluation. Note, however, that it is a broader concept, including pre-implementation modeling of the extent to which the program design is likely to impact the social problem (estimations of effect that are made even before the program begins, based on theoretical projections or prior research and program experience).

2. *Studies of cost-effectiveness/cost-benefit.* Another aspect of a social program is its cost; therefore, we can speak of *evaluating* the costs of obtaining those outcomes, either in relation to doing nothing at all or in relation to alternative intervention programs.

3. *Implementation studies.* Another aspect of a social program or policy is its actual program operations or activities; therefore, we can speak of *evaluating* whether the program design has actually been put into operation. Note that this is a main part of the concern of the formative evaluation type. Implementation studies also include what are frequently called *feasibility* studies, the study of the practicalities in implementation, prior to actual implementation and *evaluability* studies, the study of a program's readiness to undergo evaluation and profit from its findings.

4. *Consumer satisfaction studies.* We can also speak of *evaluating* the immediate reactions of program consumers to program processes or operations (consumer satisfaction studies, application, the effect of waiting periods, appeals on take-up rates, etc.) and consumers' net judgments of outcomes and usefulness in relation to their problems and circumstances.

5. *Needs studies.* Finally, though certainly not the least important, there is an aspect of social programs and policies that concerns the incidence of human need in populations; thus, we can speak of *evaluating* the extent to which some important human need exists in the surrounding community population (*needs studies*), a need that some social program might be relevant to reducing.

This list is of great importance for future human service practitioners and/or administrators because it alerts them to the first question all program and policy evaluations should begin with: "What is it that this evaluation is to accomplish for us?" Although it is amusing to imply that an expensive and serious organizational effort could somehow not bother to keep in mind why it was doing something, the idea is based on the actual experiences of evaluators, and is not just the product of an overactive imagination. Nor is this idea peculiar to the public sector, since it is as frequent in profit-oriented business as it is in the public sector. Our list of evaluation types is important as a preventive to these sorts of organizational comedies. It describes the available options for focusing a program evaluation. Taken together, recollection of these options should help evaluators keep in mind exactly what question it is that they will need to answer. However, note that these options are also a range of choices about which type of evaluation to pursue. What follows are some principles about making choices among evaluation types.

Principle: Choices Among Evaluation Types Should Be Based on the Questions One Wishes to Answer

The list of evaluation types is itself an occasion to recall an important wisdom. This list should not be used as a Chinese menu from which pieces can be chosen for eclectic, delightful variety. Each option is costly, time-consuming, and will provide answers to only a limited range of questions. It should be obvious that a study of whether a program is adequately implemented cannot yield information that bears on the effectiveness of the program—or vice-versa. It is embarrassing to report that, in actual fact, ordinarily intelligent people make this mistake. Notice also that there is a certain logic to the order in which different types of evaluation should be done. It shouldn't be a mystery that a needs study should precede an implementation study, which itself should precede an outcome study. Unfortunately, it appears to be a mystery in organizations that routinely ignore this advice. Of course, even beyond these reasons, the choice of a particular type of evaluation at a particular time is important—evaluation funds, like everything else in our imperfect world, are always in limited supply. A wrong (expensive) choice of one type of evaluation at one stage is likely to rule out the right choice at another time, precisely because of lack of funds.

Principle: Types of Evaluation are Specific to Organizational Self-Interest

The choice of evaluation types may sometimes be based on its potential for creating a particular public or private image. Different types of evaluation appeal more directly to some than others simply because the work a person does in an organization may be facilitated by a particular type of evaluation. Among the most obvious examples of more or less understandable self-interest, consider top-level administrators whose responsibility includes *dividing up money* among programs: it seems likely that they will be partial to studies of program outcomes, since they produce a database upon which they might rationalize decisions—which programs get how much or little and which might be discontinued since they are doing no demonstrable "good" at all. And, of course, that type of manager will be interested in cost studies as well. Also, won't staff members whose tasks are to make professional judgments be partial to studies of consumer satisfaction and program implementation (human service practitioners in general and middle-managers, or "street-level" bureaucrats, specifically)? Such studies speak about the reactions of clients to program processes and can tell practitioners and middle-managers something about the immediate effects of what they do. After all, it is program effort that middle managers manage, and they are naturally interested in how much effort went into which activities.

There is an important principle to grasp here, one that can predict the cooperation and good will of agency personnel toward a program or policy evaluation project. Since evaluation ventures typically require cooperation, this principle suggests occasions for doing one rather than another type of evaluation. It also suggests when additional rewards for administrators who control program evaluations are not only a good idea but (perhaps) essential if one wants to obtain any (useful) data at all. Note that the cooperation and good will of front line practitioners or staff is usually just as essential, as we will discuss at a later time in this book. Let us be quite clear: what is being said here is that the political agendas of the organizational actors as well as those of the evaluator must be entered into the earliest decisions about evaluations in the planning process.

Principle: Program and Policy Evaluations are Always Political in Nature

By now the reader should be aware that the evaluation enterprise is filled with political agendas. It should be no surprise, actually. Program evaluation has to do with fact gathering in the context of organizations. Organizations are very political: there is "turf" to protect, loyalties and other long-standing personal relationships to look after, and there are always careers and economic survival to think about. These are not the ordinary, newsworthy politics of the legislative variety—intellectual issues, public morals, votes, and the next election. Rather, these politics are the kind that are internal to organizations, politics spelled with a lower case "p," the politics of authority, sexual relationships, and small groups.

Thus, fact gathering is never a neutral activity in organizations. Organizational players often resist, in unpredictable ways, the process of evaluating a social program. Sometimes the resistance is for good (that is, understandably rational) reasons: facts can negatively or unpredictably effect the working lives of persons, close personal friends, and the groups to whom persons and friends are organizationally loyal.

Of course, organizational players can respond to proposals to evaluate a social program or policy quite positively, as something useful to their self-interest and work tasks. They may think that program evaluation ventures can provide important information to assist management decisions and/or to better understand the ongoing impact of programs on clients. Or, they may expect program evaluation ventures to be opportunities to demonstrate their executive, management, or program design prowess. Given these competing and contradictory expectations of evaluation projects, it is possible that an evaluation proposal can trigger large-scale organizational combat (sometimes mortal) between those who want to forward the evaluation and those who want to stop it.

So far as we know, no program evaluation venture has ever suffered from over-emphasizing these principles in its planning stage.

Actually, our list of evaluation types is not complete, since it ignores an important type. Let us now turn to a discussion of the differences between quantitative and qualitative approaches.

Quantitative and Qualitative Types of
Program Evaluation

At the most simple level, this distinction refers to differences in research processes. While the terms *quantitative* and *qualitative* are not always literally accurate in describing differences in research process and approaches, they capture such an important part of the distinction that we cannot resist the temptation to use them. The distinction is not only important in its own right, but also because some of the leading controversies in the program evaluation field center around paradigm differences that these types represent. In the next section, which deals with leading controversies in the field, we will discuss the issue of paradigm differences.

It is clear from our earlier sketch of the historical context that social program and policy evaluation developed out of a quantitative tradition in social science. Its early practitioners were concerned with quantifying such diverse things as school achievement, work production, and the nutritional effects of welfare programs. Ordinarily, the effort was conceptualized, quite consciously it would seem, in imitation of an empirical laboratory science. The hope was to use the obvious and persuasive power of scientific method in the service of bettering the human condition—laudable, no doubt. This imitation of physical science required, among other things, the derivation of hypotheses in advance, quantitative measures, and an arena in which to perform controlled experiments. The hypothesis was to be tested with data that was organized in such a way as to give good opportunity for falsification. In the scientific experimental arena, the world was to be viewed as rational, as basically accessible to understanding by rational means. And, it was assumed that parts of the world could be extirpated from the whole and studied to good effect, independently.

Twentieth-century social science itself developed out of a heavily quantitative version of this conception of science. It tended to think of science and scientific progress as laboratory science, using a "house building" metaphor—laboratory experiments gradually documented facts which then added up to theories, both adding "building blocks" to a "scientific edifice" (representing all of human knowledge) (Gordon, 1964). It was an "edifice" built from bottom up. "Grounded" was a common phrase.

It is understandable that social scientists were impressed with the idea of laboratory science, for, after all, the laboratory experiment is a marvelous invention of great power in validating human knowledge. Among other things, it allows the creation of empirical worlds that would otherwise remain entirely in the realm of human imagination. Some theoretical ideas can only be tested in imagined worlds and some can be too expensive or time consuming to search for real-life examples. They may be important for the test of a theory, but they can also be so rare as to be exotic: flightless ducks, bird-eating insects, nonspeaking human cultures. While some imagined worlds just can't exist in "real" life—humans walking in a gravitationless sphere—some could, given sufficient human energy and resources. When that is true, the findings of laboratory experiments become a marvelous source for innovation in everyday life. It is marvelous because it suggests that the capacity of the human specie for adaptation is (theoretically, at least) limited only by its own imagination. It is conceivable that some social programs and policies could be adaptations like that.

An example is the Guaranteed Annual Income experiments. There is no conceivable natural example of a condition in which common workers have a guaranteed wage. After all, isn't mother nature infamous for requiring that most human beings work for a livelihood? The only way in which this imagined possibility could be tested was to construct an experiment in which such a guarantee was actually given to real people so that results could be observed. That was done in several sites over a period of a number of years, and, indeed, the results were startling different from expectations and have strongly influenced public opinion in the intervening years.

A rather strict quantitative approach to the evaluation of social policies and programs was developed out of an oversimplified quantitative conception of laboratory science. A. J. Taylor's *industrial psychology* is a single but important example, since it provided a ready-made metaphor for a quantitative approach to social policy and program evaluation. The industrial production metaphor stands easily beside empirical science: the steps required to create a production line are roughly analogous to those required to create a laboratory experiment. Continuing that metaphor, social programs could be viewed as industrial production lines: social program staff were production workers, their product was reading-writing-arithmetic skills, or the elimination of child abuse incidents, or the reduction of dysfunctional behavioral patterns of the chronically mentally or developmentally disabled. The manufacture of those products was accomplished by a process conceived to be under the total control of production workers doing identical replications of the process.

The ultimate criterion of the merit of a production line is the creation of the most product at least cost. It necessitates a focus on outcomes and on quantitative measures. Note that the terms *most product/least cost* require quantities, by definition. Much of the standard language found in the evaluation literature carries the mark of that metaphor speaking as it does of program specifications, performance standards, designs, program inputs and outputs, etc. In an experimental laboratory metaphor, the evaluation of social programs and policies looks at each social program as a type of experiment, a test of some hypothesis about how the world can be changed. It looks forward to the numbers generated by the test to see if they are useful in making decisions about whether that hypothesis is or is not supported—that is, whether the program (or some of its parts) should be expanded, contracted, or closed down.

The qualitative approach to the evaluation is quite different, using very different preferences about research process, a whole different metaphor for developing knowledge, and thus a whole different set of assumptions about the nature of knowledge, discovery, and the surrounding world. While it is surely an oversimplification, we can say that the qualitative approach emphasizes the development of knowledge based on observation of wholes rather than parts—in particular, the observation of relationships between parts. The operating assumption is that the nature of things in the world, including and especially human beings, is believed to be dependent upon their context, upon what they are currently related to (Lincoln and Guba, 1985). Thus it is as important to observe context as it is to observe the thing itself. It is crucial for the qualitative observer to observe relationships and whole things rather than parts extirpated from the whole.

Although qualitative approaches do not reject quantification altogether, they surely restrict its influence. They advise observers to quantify in the service of description rather than for analysis of causation. It is important to know how many of a thing there are, but that alone will not determine the investigator's understanding of why a thing is like it is or how it works. The qualitative observer is most interested in describing processes and in obtaining direct, common language judgments of what various reporters thought those processes accomplished. For example, while a quantitative researcher will be vitally interested in the number of social program participants who accomplish preset, formal (perhaps legislatively determined) objectives, a qualitative researcher will be more interested in taking the objectives of the working staff and clients who are enrolled as problematic: what are they, and, in particular, what are the differences among them, and how do they depart from formal, legislated goals, or the kind of goals found in policy manuals.

They will be particularly interested in how those differences have interacted with each other as well as the consequences of those interactions. They will not seek to measure precisely any of that; rather, the data gathered will be common language reports from those who have experienced it. Hypotheses will not be conceived only at a time prior to the investigation; rather, they may be reformulated during the process, and, in fact, new ones may be added if they appear fruitful. The analysis of the data will not proceed statistically but by the search for patterns, trends, and commonalities among the reports received. Validation will proceed by what qualitative researchers are fond of calling *triangulation:* i.e., finding (or not finding) different reporters saying the same thing.

It seems fair to say that the qualitative process is quite suspicious of generalization; in fact it is hardly interested at all. While a qualitative investigator may wish to sample by category in order to be sure that data from important types was included, probabilistic sampling or the attempt to be quantitatively precise about the error entailed in generalizing from one site or setting to another is counter to its basic assumptions about the nature of discovery. It is probably not overreaching to say that the qualitative approach assumes that what is important to discover is uniqueness, not commonality. Thus, it would be unlikely to consider generalizability to be of much importance.

There are a number of different kinds of qualitative approaches, and perhaps the oldest member is ethnography, the traditional method of anthropological investigation. It is to be found in some form within nearly every social science, most particularly sociology and psychology, but including political science and economics as well. The method was developed by early anthropologists in studying pre-industrial peoples when early anthropologists needed a method by which to systematically investigate the incredible variety they found: in patterns of authority, kinship, property, gender relations, symbols, religious experience, etc. When taken together these constitute much of the meaning of social life. It is that "shared meaning" that anthropologists generally view as constituting human culture which is the central objective of their study.

Ethnography relies heavily on direct observation of interactions between people being observed. Ethnographers do not so much *interview* as they observe everyday behavior in which people may, indeed, talk. The belief is that through the observation of this everyday behavior and conversation that interpretive meaning is provided for the observer, whose goal is understanding what is happening, analysis and interpretation are derived from words and behavior. Ethnography is quantitative in the sense that scaling, precise measurement, and metrics may enter, but are not essential to, the drawing of conclusions. It is qualitative in the sense that its measuring instruments are, in the ordinary case, the judgments of its observers—ethnographers-on-duty, so to speak.

Another type of qualitative method is *constructivist inquiry*, a method whose recent advent has provoked widespread discussion and whose most vocal spokespersons are Egon Guba and Yvonna Lincoln (1986; 1989). Some would say that constructivist inquiry was developed out of discontent with the product of quantitative inquiry and as a counter-reaction to it. Beginning in the late 1970s and extending to the present, many reviews of what the social program and policy evaluation research effort have produced have been quite negative in their conclusions.[3] William Dunn (1982) is but one example: "Those very sciences that owe their origins to practice rarely produce knowledge which enlarges our capacity to improve that practice" (p. 84). Massive concessions about the utility of social program research were made even by authorities whose reputations were (in important ways) built on the advice they offered about how those investigations should be conducted. Donald Campbell (1982), long considered a leader in this area, responded to William Dunn as follows: ". . . my willingness to use dialectic concepts in describing the scientific method (which I do in print here for the first time) may be regarded as making a major concession to Dunn's point of view" (p. 118).

Campbell has made further concessions about the ability of social science research: "There is no purified, validated social science from which we can derive sound principles for social engineering" (p. 121).

Like other qualitative approaches, constructivist inquiry proceeds from very different assumptions from those of standard empirical and quantitative laboratory science, that is, those differentiating kinds of assumptions we described above: concern with wholes rather than parts, intrinsic-nature-as-dependent-upon-context, reliance upon direct investigator observation, and the rest. Constructivist inquiry has developed its own standards for validation and its own vocabulary for the research process (Guba, 1986). Although it shares much with ethnographic method in these regards, it differs in seeking to describe events in the absence of commitments to pre-existing theory. Although it would appear to have an even more radical commitment to the dependence of "truth" on social meaning, actually it prefers to think of theory as grounded in and limited by the explanations of the human subjects from whom it receives reports. It would leave validation of conclusions, data, or theory to human subject judgment in a way that ethnography would not permit. Ethnography is, after all, basically an academic enterprise and designed to produce conclusions which can be debated by those other than the observed subjects. Constructivist inquiry would not, basically, agree with that objective.

There are a number of other qualitative methods of general interest that are sometimes quite unique, though we cannot discuss them here at length. One example is *Service Delivery Assessment* (SDA), described by Michael Hendricks as a method of monitoring service delivery methods via qualitative methods. SDA is intended for use by upper echelon decision makers, uses small samples, and makes extensive use of observer judgments (1981).

Major Problems and Controversies in the Field of Social Program and Policy Evaluation

Vigorous controversies have always swirled through the literature of the social program and policy evaluation field. It seems that there is no idea so fundamental that it cannot be, and frequently is, attacked with abandon. Here we will consider the four fundamental problems and controversies we believe are the most widely debated. The reader should notice that these arguments mirror debates in the academic social sciences in general. They are vigorous in the applied field since they (occasionally) determine action and expensive choices in public affairs. The fundamental problems and controversies considered here will be: (1) the paradigm problem, (2) the measurement problem, (3) the implementation problem, and (4) the utilization problem. We will not try to resolve these problems here, since solutions are what the rest of the book is about. Our objective here is simply to give the reader an introduction to the dimensions. We will begin with the paradigm problem, since its main elements will be familiar from the discussion of the differences between quantitative and qualitative evaluation types just concluded.

The Paradigm Problem

A discussion of differences between the quantitative and qualitative types of approaches to policy and program evaluation comes down to a discussion of the paradigm problem, since their differences revolve exactly around that issue. On that account we will not review it again in detail but rather recollect only its main outlines so that we can focus on a related controversy: whether quantitative and qualitative can be used together simultaneously so that their best features can be brought to bear on practical evaluation problems.

Recall how the paradigm for quantitative inquiry was said to be drawn from the paradigm for traditional laboratory science. It assumes a world in which it is, at least theoretically, possible to understand everything. It is a world in which (in principle) the nature of things is so stable that they can be separated into parts which can be closely examined apart from their original context; a world whose fundamental features can be replicated by the investigator so that factors of interest can be introduced and removed at will so that the effects of so doing can be observed. Hypotheses about results-to-be-expected are constructed in advance, and, while the direction of findings is important (positive/negative), the numerical match of findings to expectations is the crucial test of validity—the important results of investigation are expressed in numbers. The paradigm anticipates that the conclusions of inquiry can be generalized to a "real world" to the extent that the laboratory (or quasi-laboratory) conditions can be replicated there. Thus, while an experiment begins by attempting to shape the laboratory world in such a way as to replicate the "real world," in applying laboratory conclusions to the "real world," it is quite the opposite: The attempt is to constrain the "real world" in order to replicate the laboratory conditions there!

A fundamental feature of the modern science paradigm is its capacity for self correction (at least within its own paradigm): The virtue of an experiment is the extent to which it allows for results contrary to expectations, contrary to those expected if the hypothesis is correct. Subsequently, any test of the hypothesis that turns out differently can refute it once more, and, thus, a self-correcting feature is built into traditional science. As it is usually expressed, all truth is subject to verification (by data), and, since verification is never final, all truth is subject to revision. Another fundamental feature of this type of modern science is control over the phenomenon to be understood. The paradigm demands preoccupation with measurement, with numerical results, with advance predictions, and with replication of findings as a measure of that control.

The paradigm for qualitative inquiry could hardly be more opposite. It assumes a world that is only partly understandable by rational investigation, a world in which the intrinsic nature of the parts of a thing are determined by their surroundings. Thus, hypotheses about how things are related to each other can not be stated in advance, only observed in their natural setting. It assumes change to be a constant condition so that inquiry under this paradigm is characterized by a preoccupation with growth and development in natural settings. Since important changes are not changes in degree but changes in kind or type, the concern is with changes in "state," as in a physical change from a liquid to a gas or solid. Such changes, at the moment of change, are best described qualitatively—as in "yes it is"or"no it isn't"—and it is probably not possible to describe those moments in numbers (though of course the consequences of such changes might be best described numerically). The paradigm is nearly silent with respect to generalization of findings, application beyond the original site of discovery. The focus is on presenting findings in a form that is useful there, and not in other places, where it is presumed that, since context is different, processes and, indeed, forms themselves would be quite different. Fundamental features of qualitative inquiry, particularly the version known as constructivist inquiry—are its preoccupation with description, and direct observation of social action in its "natural" context. Emphasis is placed on collecting multiple interpretations of the meaning of actions and events (Dorr-Bremme, 1985).

One of the important controversies in the field is whether these two paradigms can be used together to direct policy and program evaluations. Some see it as an attractive possibility that would capitalize on the strengths, the best and special features of both. Early advocates were Cook and Reichardt (1979). By now there seems to be some consensus, even among advocates, that the integration must be done with careful attention to what is meant by integrated methods. At one level, integration can mean the side-by-side use of qualitative and quantitative method, each for the purpose of answering a fundamentally different question. Thus intended, integration would generate fundamentally different results; the hope would be that when the two different kinds of results were thought of together, even richer interpretations would occur. For example, many think that qualitative methods are especially well suited to the description and analysis of social program and policy processes, while quantitative methods are especially well suited to the study of policy and program end-products (Judd, 1987). A study which integrated the two (i.e., used both) would be expected to enrich its conclusions by having available two different kinds of results—results about process and results about the final end-product. Integrated methods can also mean taking observations of the same variables by both quantitative and qualitative methods. About that there is less consensus and less experience (Kidder and Fine, 1987,

p. 623). Actually there are not many evaluations that use multiple methods. A 1985 study of published evaluations shows that only about 11 percent have, and although no one knows the extent to which that sample models the whole picture, it seems unlikely that it would be dramatically larger than the 11 percent figure (Lipsey, Crosse, Dunkle, Pollar, and Stobart, 1985).

There are others who are not sanguine about the possibility of integration, particular about proposals that are not careful about exactly what is meant by integrating or multiple methods. They would say that quantitative and qualitative methods, in whatever version, are based on fundamental assumptions that are not merely different but diametrically opposed to one another. After all, the matter of different assumptions about the relationship of the investigator to the subject, the goal of inquiry, and the nature of the relationship between facts and values are discernibly nontrivial issues. J. K. Smith says this in a straightforward "... for now, the differences appear more notable than the possibilities for unification" (Smith, 1987, p. 50).

There is yet a third viewpoint on multiple or integrated methods (Reichardt and Cook, 1979). The main architects of the leading form of qualitative inquiry, Guba and Lincoln, conclude that quantitative methods have become outmoded by *fourth generation evaluation*. By that term they mean social program evaluation in a qualitative mode, "... focused not on objectives or decisions but the claims, concerns and issues ... of stakeholders" (i.e., those whose self-interest is put at risk by the evaluation).

> *Fourth generation evaluation is neither a competitor nor a replacement for earlier forms [of evaluation], it* subsumes *them while moving the evaluation process to higher levels of sophistication and utility (Guba and Lincoln, 1986, p. 85).* (emphasis ours)

It is not altogether clear what Guba and Lincoln intend by the term *subsumes*, but it is important, since it is at the heart of their position about the use of multiple methods. Taken literally it asserts a far-reaching claim that they have invented a theory of investigation that not only covers all of traditional science, a competitor hundreds of years old, but also its younger off-shoot, social science, as well. They would appear to be asserting that a constructivist research approach accomplishes simultaneously the objectives of what is traditionally considered quantitative and qualitative methods (Guba and Lincoln, 1989).

Let us turn now to another controversy of interest to this field, the measurement problem.

The Measurement Problem

While it is not always a pleasant characterization, some would say that evaluating social programs and policies is mainly about judging the effects of social engineering—that is, about the effectiveness of an attempt to manipulate human responses. Precisely because the subject is the human being, social science has a problem some other sciences do not have: there are special complications in studying human beings and other living things. This must be given special emphasis here, since it has important practical consequences for how one proceeds in evaluating social policies and programs. The nub of this controversy seems to come to this: in ways that rocks and stars don't, human beings and other living things react to being studied. It creates enormous difficulties in interpreting measurement data, i.e., how to distinguish between what is the reaction of interest and what is simply a reaction to being studied.

If the reader would like to imagine the frustrations reactivity poses for a scientific researcher, consider a geologist who found, upon investigating a strata of rock, perhaps one exposed by an excavation for a new road, that it changed its shape depending on whether it was being looked at, what instruments were being used to measure its thickness, and even, what kind of conversation geologists were having when measuring it. When we ask the reader to further suppose that the rock strata exudes a peculiar substance when it is poked and prodded, no doubt they will wonder whether they have strayed out of a textbook and into some unusually weird science fiction script. But that is the point: indeed science-fiction plots often involve the idea of living things appearing in unexpected shapes. It is that presence of life—of constant response and adaptation (reactivity, in short)—that creates such enormous, some would say insurmountable, problems for those who would attempt to construct its measure.

There are those who are not at all daunted by these problems. They would insist that the characteristics of living, reactive things have long been profitably measured (fish populations, monkey behavior, the responses of microbes), and, since those measurements have been the basis of important discoveries, the measurement of human qualities should not pose insurmountable difficulties.

Their opponents would respond that those successful scientific ventures have nearly all been concerned with non-humans. Measuring human qualities has complexities that distinguish it from measurement problems with regard to the qualities of other living things. One measurement difficulty peculiar to human beings occurs when, often enough, the only way to get a reading of some types of responses is to ask the subject under study. Interpreting the data that emerges from asking is not always straightforward. Unfortunately for scientists, it is a human quality to actively and continuously manage the impressions they are making on others. People sometimes edit what is said to others to create an impression of social conformity— e.g., what is reported is what the subject thinks others would believe should have been the case rather than what was the case. Or, contrariwise, people edit what is said in order to create an impression of, say, mildly attractive social deviance, of daring-do, or of independence of spirit—any of those things that are different from ordinary, tedious social conformity. While most of us might prize that kind of variability, many believe that it is a nightmare as a subject for scientific measurement and nearly impossible to sort out when interpreting measurement data.

Of course, the problem is not just the measurement of the attributes of living things, though that is surely difficult enough. It is further complicated by the fact that there are limits on human experimentation. Death, permanent injury, and great pain are simply unacceptable consequences to determining the experimental truth of things. [That does not exhaust the argument, of course, and the interested reader might turn to E. R. House (1982) and Stephen Tuolmin (1977) for further discussion and other references.]

The Implementation Problem

In order to understand the implementation problem, we will first need to sort out some terminology. Simply considered, social policies are ideal prescriptions for action, and social programs are their concrete embodiment. Formally, social programs exist solely for the purpose of carrying out ideals and solutions in the real world. The specifications for the shape of social programs are derived, in important part, from the concepts and meanings of terms in policy statements. (We will give over a whole chapter to the large problem of how to construct them.) Taken together, those program specifications constitute the program design. But there is yet another level of the "real life" form of a social policy, the implementation level, where the tasks specified in the program design are actually carried out by real, live people working in active organizations.

A whole new literature on implementation has been developed in the last five years. Prior to this time there was not much in the literature concerned with the problems of installing social program ideas in ongoing organizations. It was generally assumed that the authority structure inherent in formal organizations was sufficient to implement a program design. It didn't seem far-fetched to assume that, if activities are ordered, they will, in fact, be carried out. But insuring that staff people and administrators do carry out orders in the intended way, consistently, and consistent with the spirit of the general policy from which they are derived has turned out to entail mountainous difficulties.

A set of *program specifications* for social programs should contain fairly exact descriptions of actions to be taken at specific times, by specific people, under specific conditions. Specifications are based on a theory. For example, the theory below. Here it is proposed that episodes of physical child abuse occur because mothers (note the sexist bias) have themselves been physically abused as children. Among other consequences:

- Mothers have learned physically abusive responses to children as expected maternal behaviors.
- Mothers have no internal psychological model for the mothering of their own children, having been deprived of a positive identification with such a mother from whom they could have learned it.

A program design derived from this theory might propose, for example, that "at-risk" mothers learn non-abusive responses and a positive identification with a mothering adult. Here is an (over) simplified example of a design for a, now common, social program used to reduce severe physical abuse of children. Assuming certain definitions of mothering and of *non-abusive responses*, the program design might propose the following:

- Straightforward teaching or demonstrations to the mother of non-abusive responses to children under a variety of common circumstances
- Direct physical contact and the development of an intense emotional relationship between a potentially abusive mother and a staff member such that all those things meant by mothering could actually occur and mothers could develop an internal mothering model

The list is important because it contains the program specifications. Evidence of their existence is evidence of program implementation: gentle physical touch, warm and reassuring spoken words, providing food and warmth and even shelter, exercising authority (establishing standards of behavior, expressing disapproval, withholding rewards, applying sanctions, etc.). The program specifications actually must state explicit behavioral standards for actions like those above. Staff must express them if it is to count as an implementation of the design (and thus of the operationalization of the theory). The program specifications would also establish explicit, quantitative performance standards for "how much" and "when." To the extent actions met those standards, the program would be considered implemented and vice-versa.

A theory-derived program design, program specifications, and performance standards are essential if the social policy and social program enterprise is to be considered as having anything to do with a scientific enterprise.[4] They are essential because each is necessary to the derivation and testing of the hypotheses that lie at the heart of science. So constructed, every implemented social program is a test of some hypothesis.

The implementation problem is that there are so many ways in which actual operations can fail to come up to the standards or specifications, even though designs, specifications, and standards can be precisely defined. Aside from common problems resulting from ordinary human failings (staff carelessness, incompetence, ignorance, or simple disobedience), just consider the problem of *non-standardization* of treatment in programs providing not material benefits but human services—marriage counseling, community support services (for the chronically mentally ill, for example), home-making services, problem solving, referrals, and client-advocacy are just a few examples. Usually employing many practitioners, consider how difficult it would be for a program manager to insure uniform implementation of a program design over time, in different practitioners, different clients, different program sites and sub-parts. In the example given above, in order to implement the program to standard, practitioners would have to express "gentle physical touch," "reassuring words," "expressions of disapproval," and "establish standards of behavior to be followed" so that they:

- Were applied by a practitioner in the same way to the same client over time
- Were applied by a practitioner in the same way to different clients
- Were applied by different practitioners in the same way in a single site
- Were applied in the same way in different sites in which the program was implemented

That is, indeed, a daunting list, and anyone who has conducted a professional practice within an organization knows how difficult it would be to meet such expectations.

Of course, this is not the only kind of implementation problem. Let us mention only a few. First, there is the problem concerning *which* variable in the theory is "best" to focus treatments upon. Theories about the human condition, if they are to be of any explanatory value at all, have large numbers of causal factors linked together. That is only to say such things as, for example, that divorce cannot by itself be said to *cause* juvenile delinquency, nor that some sort of exotic maternal bond could, alone, be said to *cause* schizophrenia. While it is satisfying to move toward a more complicated way of understanding, it does create a problem—when it comes to acting on a ten factor theory, one is constrained by practicality to choose less than ten on which to focus influence in the desired direction. No program staff or individual practitioner can possibly deal with anything more than a small number of factors at a single time—plus or minus seven at the most, an experimental psychologist might say. A part of the problem is that social theory generally lets us down here, for theory about the physical things of the world usually simplify matters into manageability or else specify the relative importance of causal factors.

Unfortunately, there is no theory known to us and used for social program designs which specifies, in advance, the relative importance of its causal antecedents in a way that would allow us to choose one over another. The fact of the matter is that program designs are usually created from an arbitrary, opportunistic, or practical choice of a few among many causal factors. Program designs focus on mothers rather than on fathers of abusing children since they are available under threat of court action; designs focus on worker motivation rather than job availability because, under certain conditions, employees can be delivered into a classroom and employers can not be. Almost all discussions of the relationship between causal ideas and practical interventions stress the need for causal variables to be open to manipulation, practical, etc. What is usually not mentioned is the frequent negative correlation between the openness of a causal factor to influence and its relative power to make a difference. Indeed, it would seem that it is extremely difficult to design simple human services that make important or lasting differences to people in need.

Second, there is the problem of serious internal organizational resistance to program implementation, perhaps outright sabotage. Third, there is the common problem of fiscal shortfall where a social program is underfunded to the extent that it could not possibly achieve its objectives nor any important part of them with the resources at hand. And finally, there is the problem of latent organizational objectives—the program design as implemented is transmogrified into one which is used for any number of latent personal or professional objectives of staff and administrators, not to mention being used in the service of straightforward organizational survival rather than explicit human services delivered to clients. Its staff positions can be used for employing redundant or incompetent staff, for symbolic purposes ("look, we are paying attention to your type of problem, we have this program in operation"), etc.

The Utilization Problem

In the short history of the evaluation research enterprise it became painfully evident early on that research findings were not being utilized in the shaping of social policies and programs. Patton notes no less than four official and influential public sector reports that came to this conclusion as early as the late 1960s (Patton, 1978). Nor has utilization appeared to depend on the quality of the findings or the care with which the research was conducted. The problem has continued nearly unabated. Here are only a few expert judgments:

- . . . *the impact of research on the most important affairs of state was, with few exceptions, nil" (Deitchman, 1976, p. 30).*
- . . . *it has proved very difficult to uncover many instances where social science research has had a clear and direct effect on policy even when it has been specifically commissioned by government (Sharpe, 1977, p. 45).*
- *[Despite using new approaches] . . . the influence of evaluation on program decisions has not noticeably increased. Even evaluations that have tried conscientiously to abide by the traditional [remedial] advice have had indifferent success in making evaluation the basis of decisions (Weiss, 1988, p. 7).*

Such conclusions are disorienting to the whole field and the problem continues to this day. It would seem to be an entirely noncontroversial idea that the very best scientific study and empirical fact should be used as a basis for b، the formation and reform of public policy. Nonetheless, while it would be too much to say that the evaluation enterprise never effects social policy and programs, there is no substantial disagreement with the conclusion that for over two decades its effectiveness has been disappointing, and that when it is influential, it is in a diffuse and nonspecific way (certainly not along the lines of a single evaluation result influencing a single organizational administrator). Further, new approaches have not made important differences.

Perhaps it is Carol Weiss who has studied and written about the utilization problem more than anyone else. The main line of Weiss's argument is that the problem isn't that evaluation results don't get used at all; they do, but in a way different from what we expect. Weiss believes that current conceptions of the way evaluation findings will effect a decision-making process are excessively simple-minded. That is, nearly two decades of literature in this area has stressed the importance of tailoring evaluation research precisely to the questions of one single decision-maker or a very small group of decision-makers. Weiss's contribution is to notice how widely dispersed the authority for organizational decision making is, and how political the exercise of that authority is:

> . . . it is not the . . . benevolent despot who uses evaluation [findings] to improve the program. Rather, evaluation findings come into currency among many groups and interests involved. . . . Multiple groups have a say and policy is the resultant of conflicts and accommodations across a complex and shifting set of players (Weiss, 1988, p. 8).

Weiss is fond of Lee Cronbach's (1982) notion that evaluation is at its best when it facilitates negotiation among organizational decision-makers.

This viewpoint acknowledges the real-life complexity in researching organizational life. Among these elements are, of course, entrenched organizational resistance to change and unbending personal and career self-interest that is threatened by research which promotes the possibility of change. In addition, organizational management often cannot make it clear to themselves what information they really need. It shouldn't be a surprise, therefore, that evaluation efforts often don't provide it. And in fact, Weiss says, real-life decisions require such a wide scope of information that no evaluation project could ever provide it all. The advice to us is that we have expected too much from evaluation in believing that it should often yield, directly, program reformulations and "go or no-go" policy decisions. Rather, evaluation results find their way into the ongoing (political) dialogue about public policy by shaping the minds of leading actors and in shaping the terms of the public and semi-public discourse. It can be an important contributor to the political negotiations *that form* public social policy. Program improvement objectives for evaluation are much less substantial in her view. Weiss believes that all those problems can, at some level, be overcome and that evaluation research in its present form has a considerable future (Weiss, 1988). (Naturally some

program and policy evaluations are purchased for very
very specific policies and programs, not for the policy and
nity as a whole.)

se who disagree. Michael Patton is a good example. Patton
believes that the problem of utilization is ultimately due to fundamental
problems in the way evaluation research is conceived. Thus, ". . . what is
needed is a comprehensive approach . . . within which individuals involved
can proceed to develop an evaluation design with a built-in utilization component appropriate to *the unique circumstances* they encounter" (Patton, 1978).
That need for "uniqueness" moves Patton away from conceiving social program evaluation as a standard form of empirical, scientific study. Patton's
wisdom was to observe that since it is the scientist-evaluator who controls the
study (the "experiment"), it is bound to answer *their* questions, not the
questions of those who administer the social program—on that account it
should be no surprise to us that evaluation findings are not utilized by
administrators.[5]

Patton's first order solution is to relinquish control of the evaluation
project to those who are going to use its findings; they should control the
definition of the problem to be researched and (a more radical suggestion)
they should also control the methodological choices to be made. Methodology
is not value-free, Patton argues, so that such choices can only be made by
taking political and ideological positions. For example, if nothing else, the
choice of what is *important* to study is essentially a value-laden choice, and not
a purely scientific one, as Max Weber argued more than a century ago (Weber,
1862). That is certainly obvious in the political-organizational arena in which
most social program evaluation lives and works. Since the end-users are the
ones who must live with the consequences of these choices, only end-users,
and not technicians, can legitimately make them. The technician's role is to
assist with those choices, but not to make them.

Endnotes

1. See for example, Skidmore, F. (May 1983). *Overview of the Seattle-Denver
income maintenance experiment final report.* Office of Income Security Policy, Office of the
Assistant Secretary for Planning and Evaluation. U.S. Department of Health and
Human Services. Washington, DC: U.S. Government Printing Office. For a survey of
some other positive and useful results of evaluation research from very different social
program areas, see Bloom, H. S., Cordray, D. S., & Light, R. J. (1988). *Lessons from selected
program and policy areas,* New Directions for Program Evaluation Series, #37. San
Francisco: Jossey-Bass.

2. For other details about the intellectual history here and "the professionalization of reform," see Friedman, L. (1977). The social and political context of the war on
poverty. In Robert Haveman (Ed.), *A decade of federal antipoverty programs* (pp. 28–29).
New York: Academic Press.

3. For a handy, concise, (and excellent) presentation of the points of view within the controversy, see special issue of the *American Behavioral Scientist, 26*(1), 1983; Cronbach, L. J. (1982). *Toward the reform of program evaluation.* San Francisco: Jossey-Bass; Patton, M. Q. (1978). *Utilization-focused evaluation.* Beverly Hills, CA: Sage Publishing Co.; Rossi, P., & Wright, J. (1984). Evaluation research: An assessment. *Annual Review of Sociology, 10;* Lipsey, M., Crosse, W., Dunkle, J., Pollard, J., Stobart, G. (1985). The state of the art and the sorry state of the science. In D. Cordray (Ed.), *Utilizing prior research in evaluation planning,* New Directions for Program Evaluation Series, vol. 27 (pp. 7–28). San Francisco: Jossey-Bass; Gilsinan, J., & Volpe, L. (1984). Do not cry wolf until you are sure: The manufactured crisis in evaluation research, *Policy Science, 17,* 183–194.

4. Note that the implementation problem is presented here *within* a quantitative evaluation research framework. It can be fruitfully approached through a qualitative method, and we believe that such a method is particularly compatible with it.

5. Patton is also concerned with consumer judgments, of course. Because our topic is a discussion of the problem of the utilization of evaluation findings by program personnel and decision-makers, we are not emphasizing this view on the subject here.

References

Bloom, H., Cordray, D. S., & Light, R. J. (1988). *Lessons from selected program and policy areas.* New Directions for Program Evaluation Series #37. San Francisco: Jossey-Bass Co.

Campbell, D. (1982). Experiments as arguments. *Knowledge: Creation, Diffusion, Utilization, 3*(3), 327–337.

Cook, T., & Reichardt, C. (Eds.). (1979). Qualitative and quantitative methods in evaluation research (vol. 1). Beverly Hills, CA: Sage.

Cronbach, L. J. (1982). *Toward the reform of program evaluation.* San Francisco: Jossey-Bass.

Deitchman, S. (1976). *The best laid schemes: A tale of social research and bureaucracy.* Cambridge, MA: MIT Press.

Dorr-Bremme, D. (1985). Ethnographic evaluation: A theory and method. *Educational Evaluation and Policy Analysis 7*(1), 65–83.

Dunn, W. (1982). Reforms as arguments. *Knowledge: Creation, Diffusion, Utilization, 3*(3), 82–104.

Freidman, L. (1977). The social and political context of the war on poverty. In Robert Haveman (Ed.), *A decade of federal anti-poverty programs* (pp. 28–29). New York: Academic Press.

Gilsinan, J., & Volpe, L. (1984). Do not cry wolf until you are sure: The manufactured crisis in evaluation research. *Policy Science, 17,* 183–194.

Gordon, W. (1964). *Building blocks of human knowledge* Unpublished manuscript, Washington University, St. Louis.

Guba, E. G. (1986). What have we learned about naturalistic evaluation? *Evaluation Practice 8*(1), 22–43.

Guba, E. G., & Lincoln, Y. S. (1986). The countenances of fourth-generation evaluation: Description, judgment and negotiation. Paper presented at Evaluation Network Annual Meeting, Toronto, Canada, 1985.

Guba, E. G., & Lincoln, Y. S. (1989). *Fourth generation evaluation.* Newbury Park, CA: Sage.

Hendricks, M. (1981). Service delivery assessment: Qualitative evaluations at the cabinet level. In N. L. Smith (Ed.), *Federal efforts to develop new evaluation methods* (pp. 5–24). New Directions for Program Evaluation Series #12. San Francisco: Jossey-Bass.

House, E. (1982). Scientific and humanistic evaluations. *Evaluation studies review, volume 7* (pp. 15–26). Beverly Hills, CA: Sage.

Judd, C. (1987). Combining process and outcome evaluation. In *Multiple methods in program evaluation* (pp. 23–42). San Francisco: Jossey-Bass.

Kidder, M., & Fine, M. (1987). Qualitative and quantitative methods: When stories converge. In *Multiple methods in program evaluation* (pp. 57–75). San Francisco: Jossey-Bass.

Lincoln Y. S., & Guba, E. G. (1985). *Naturalistic inquiry.* Beverly Hills, CA: Sage.

Lipsey, M., Crosse, W., Dunkle, J., Pollar, J., & Stobart, G. (1985). The state of the art and the sorry state of the science. In David Cordray (Ed.), *Utilizing prior research in evaluation planning,* (pp. 7–28). New Directions for Program Evaluation Series, vol. 27. San Francisco: Jossey-Bass.

Patton, M. (1978). *Utilization-focused evaluation.* Beverly Hills, CA: Sage Publishing Co.

Reichardt, C., & Cook, T. F. (1979). Beyond qualitative and quantitative Methods. In T. Cook & C. S. Reichardt, *Qualitative and quantitative methods in evaluation research.* Newbury Park, CA: Sage.

Rivlin, A. (1974). *The evaluation of action programs.* Boston: Allyn & Bacon.

Rossi, P. H., & Wright, J. (1984). Evaluation research: An assessment. *Annual Review of Sociology, 10,* 331–352.

Sharpe, L. (1977). The social scientist and policymaking. In Carol Weiss (Ed.), *Using social research in public policy making.*

Skidmore, F. (May 1983). *Overview of the Seattle-Denver income maintenance experiment final report.* Office of Income Security Policy, Office of the Assistant Secretary for Planning and Evaluation. U.S. Department of Health and Human Services. Washington, DC: U.S. Government Printing Office.

Smith, J. (1987). Quantitative versus interpretive. In *Multiple methods in program evaluation* (pp. 27–51). San Francisco: Jossey-Bass.

Stanley, J., & Campbell, D. (1966). *Experimental and quasi-experimental designs for research.* Chicago: Rand McNally Co.

Travers. R. (1983) *How research has changed American schools.* Kalamazoo, MI: Mythos Press.

Tuolmin, W. (1977). Psychic health, mental clarity and other virtues. In T. Englehardt, Ed., *Mental health, philosophical perspectives* (pp. 50–58). New York: Reiderer Publications.

Weber, M. (1946). Methodology and the social sciences. In *Max Weber: Essays—sociology* (pp. 180–195). Oxford: Oxford University Press.

Weiss, C. (1988). Evaluation for decisions. *Evaluation Practice, 9*(1), 7, 9, 12.

Worthen, B., & Landers, J. R. (1987). *Educational evaluation.* New York: Longman, Inc.

CHAPTER TWO

Ethics, Legal Issues, and Professional Standards in the Evaluation of Social Programs

Introduction

Ethics, legal issues, and professional standards are a much neglected topic in the standard evaluation research literature. It is Joan Sieber's opinion that "... there is virtually no literature on the ethics of program evaluation" (Sieber, 1980, p. 52). We agree. A good many textbooks on the subject have no indexical reference at all to ethics. (See, for example, the 1985 edition of the widely used Rossi and Freeman text, *Evaluation*.) The most recently published book on program evaluation to come into our hands (1988) contains twenty-two separately authored articles on program evaluation but, as far as we can tell, has no reference at all to ethics in any of them (Weiss and Jacobs, 1988). Few texts have any reference to legal issues, much less to accepted professional standards such as those of the American Evaluation Association or the Joint Committee on Standards for Educational Evaluation.

Books and journal articles provide no solution when they note the problem of ethical obligations and professional standards but fail to set out ethical principles or describe the state of the debate about them. It seems to us that the debate should be both vital (and troubling) to anyone interested in either evaluation research in general or the continuing everyday ethical drama of (how shall we call ourselves?) professionals-in-drag who earn their living working within organizations. The worst case is the trivialization of ethical issues. Here is an example concerning the issue of client confidentiality:

> First, confidential information must be kept confidential. Some information in files may even be damaging to the person's social and financial affairs . . . release could open the

> *evaluator to legal suits in extreme cases . . . the evaluator would [then] look unprofessional and the loss of credibility might result in their being denied access to records the next time.*

And, if one follows the advice of the reference in the index, here is the *complete* discussion of the issue of "informed consent":

> *A service provider trying an approach supported only by uncontrolled studies often does not inform the client, patient or trainee that the treatment is new and not thoroughly understood. Nor does the service provider seek to obtain informed consent from a client, patient or trainee as an evaluator would when conducting an experiment (Posavac and Carey, 1980, p. 233).*

We would like to present a reasonably full review of the issues and the state of the debate about ethics in research as well as to inform readers about closely related and derivative matters—legal issues and professional standards. We are particularly concerned with ethical issues for we believe that we have a responsibility to call practitioners to a moral duty—to make its presence unmistakable even if we cannot always make its precise outline crystal clear. It is our view that ethical issues are not, somehow, an optional consideration for practitioners. We do not believe that they can be entirely reduced to a matter of "It all depends on your point of view," nor so individualistic that nothing of importance can be said to practitioners and students collectively. Ethics and professional standards must be of importance to the field if it is to consider itself a professional calling. After all, an ideological and service ideal distinguishes a profession as much as its possession of arcane knowledge. That service ideal also requires practitioners to analyze its agreement with their own motives and actions. Further, self-interest can be marvelously subtle so that "Testing one's policy choices against one's own . . . ethical premises precludes unconscious inconsistency or subconscious hypocrisy" (Fetterman, 1987, p. 443).

We believe that there are good reasons for the neglect of ethical issues in research; it is not just a matter of sheer intransigence. While discussion of the issue can be found in classical texts, it wasn't until the shocking revelations of the vicious and inhuman Nazi medical research at the Nuremberg trials following World War II that (with one exception discussed below) ethical codes for research saw the light of day. In fact, the Nuremberg Code coming out of those trials was ". . . the first major curb on research in any nation" (Faden and Beauchamp, 1986, p. 154). Ethical codes for the conduct of research are indeed a feature of the 20th century. Of course we should consider that while scientific research involving humans is, no doubt, ancient, it didn't become common (in the United States, for example) until the middle 1950s (Faden and Beauchamp, 1986, p. 151). The Nuremberg Code was born out of a concern to prevent the repetition of the injury, disability or death that occurred in the Nazi experiments as a result of their scientific research. We won't dwell upon those grisly details here beyond recollecting to readers that the experiments used groups of people the Nazi government chose to consider as racially inferior and stigmatized—Jews and gypsies in particular—and experimented with the effects of jaundice and spotted fever virus, as well as with the effects of drinking gasoline, being immersed in ice water, etc. The Nuremberg trials were a "... watershed event ... and changed forever and always how we would view the involvement of human subjects in scientific research" (Faden and Beauchamp, 1986, p. 153). The Nuremberg Code had ten principles, informed consent and the like, and, though inadequate from the point of view of the present day, it served as a model for a number of subsequent professional and governmental ethical codes published during the 1950–60 era (Faden and Beauchamp, 1986). One of the truly grand ironies of the whole subject of research ethics standards and governmental regulation is that "... no other nation appears to have had such morally and legally advanced regulations" concerning the control of human experimentation and the use of innovative therapies in medicine as those that were promulgated by the Health Department of the Third (Nazi) Reich and were in effect at the time of the Nazi research experiment-atrocities (Faden and Beauchamp, 1986, p. 154)! In fact these may have been the very first official public regulations ever to deal with informed consent in any detailed manner. Anyone who is willing to rest the responsibility for the protection of human subjects entirely with government and the public sector ought to consider that fact carefully.

Beyond the fact that it is a fairly recent endeavor to take ethics in research seriously, there are other reasons why it has been a neglected issue. One such reason is that of ethics, by nature, is difficult to think about—there is nothing easy here. The ordinary terms in ethics are often ambiguous, sometimes arcane, and surely subject to multiple interpretations. Just to begin thinking about them, some basic philosophical assumptions must be laid out. And it turns out that they often seem arbitrary, suspiciously traditional, culture-bound, or hopelessly authoritarian. Few fit the adjectives that we would ordinarily like to use for knowledge that we prize: hard, factual, logical, valid, systematic. And finally, the last straw, for many there seems to be no clear test for the certainty of ethical conclusions. Taking all that together, perhaps the wonder is that anyone would bother discussing it at all.

However, we have a special reason to pay close attention to ethical standards in this book. We consider its primary audience to be professional practitioners working within an employing organization and assigned some task that involves policy and/or program evaluation tasks. We conclude that they have a special set of ethical problems (Bailey, 1965). Our argument is that any professional working for a public organization has, by that fact, an ethical duty to promote the best possible programs and policies for client-consumers. Since no social program we know of is perfect, all professionals working in such conditions must be advocates for program change—at some level and to some degree. While others may not agree, we believe some professional obligations are morally superior to most organizational obligations, and particularly so when client-interests conflict with organizational self-interest (Becker, 1967). We believe that condition is particularly relevant when program change is debated, since status quo is usually argued as being in the best interest of organizational "stability." In that situation the ethical obligation of the professional can be to the client's interest as over and against the interests of the organization. And that is only one of the special ethical problems professionals have when working in bureaucratic organizations.

Of course there may be other reasons for the obscurity of ethical discourse in evaluation literature. We speculate that the preeminence of the free-enterprise, for-profit research corporation in the evaluation research field has a certain, if not determinant, bearing on the matter. From the perspective of some who would seem to be able to speak for that perspective, it seems clear that some topics do not raise the same ethical issues for those practitioners as they do for those working in a not-for-profit organization (Warwick, Meade, and Reed, 1975). For example, one such author, in a book devoted to practice standards for program evaluators, disapproved when he found that well-known authors in the field were advocating the notion that there were conditions under which evaluators had a professional responsibility not to evaluate a program (whether the potential value of an evaluation justified its cost or whether a good job could be done with the resources at hand, for example).

> . . . in my long experience with RFP's [requests from the government for proposals], I can recall only one where we refused to propose because we felt the work required was unreasonable from the standpoint of the resources available.
> Standard 5 [of the Evaluation Research Society professional standards for evaluators] argues that agreement should be reached at the outset on whether the evaluation is likely to produce information of sufficient value, applicability and potential to justify the cost. . . . (In) my many years of [contracting for] government evaluation work I can think of no instance where this issue was ever raised. If the government goes to the trouble to issue an RFP, it is hard to imagine that a company will ask the government if it really wants to do the evaluation . . . in the RFP situation one does not raise questions about the value of the work or whether there is enough potential . . . to justify its cost (Carter, 1982, pp. 39, 42–3).

That viewpoint must imply that the ethical issue of how to handle requests for help with an evaluation that should not be done is simply not discussable in a profit-making context. The implicit rationale seems quite clear: to do so would jeopardize the maximization of profit, and, after all, that is the reason for the existence of profit makers. We suspect there are other such ethical issues as well, issues that would work contrary to maximizing profit. And, while we will not belabor the issue, we disagree that maximizing profit is or should be the priority value consideration; in fact it cannot be so for professionals, all of whom ascribe to human service as the paramount obligatory ideal. Note carefully that it is not profit itself that is wrong here for professional practitioners, the problem is with prioritizing and maximizing of profit as the highest ideal.

Ethics in Conducting Evaluation Research

Important Concepts and Distinctions Relevant to Ethical Issues

Distinguishing ethics from values, professional standards, and the pursuit of the truth Ethics are standards for behavior, standards for the conduct of human affairs. The emphasis here is on behavior. Note that the concept *values* is closely related to ethics. If we follow Kluckhohn in thinking of values as "... conceptions of the desirable," ethics are standards for behavior and values are the conceptions of the desired from which those standards are derived (Kluckhohn, 1950, p. 380). When authors speak of ethical premises they are usually speaking of value premises, from which specific ethical behaviors have been derived. Professional standards have a dual concern— behaviors that are unethical or (ideally) ethical and professional behaviors that provide the effective service to people or that represent substandard practice.

Of course it is true that any professional behavior that doesn't represent the "best way" to serve people is probably unethical in the sense that it is an ethical responsibility to be competent; however, that obscures an important difference between professional standards and professional ethics. Their difference lies in the source from which they are derived. The source of professional standards is some (presumably) scientifically validated knowledge statement about causal effects (a change in variable x changes variable y), while the source of a professional ethic is some value statement about what is desirable for people (x is by definition good for all people).

The difference is important, because a professional can be one without necessarily being the other. Consider an architect may be an unethical scoundrel who takes money from building contractors to look after their interests when his ethical obligation is to pursue the interests of the building owner who pays his architectural fee. Such an architect might still build buildings that are stunningly creative and never fall down. It is only rarely that competence effects being ethical, in fact. While some might say that if one is competent, being ethical is easy, it probably only attests to how little the speaker knows of the ways of the world. Being ethical is a matter of choosing morally "right" actions, being a professional who works within professional standards is being a competent practitioner who (on current definitions) uses scientifically verified generalizations to guide practice.

It is also important to appreciate the difference between ethical standards, standards for professional practice, and standards for the pursuit of the truth. The difference between the latter two may be obscure for those who consider themselves professional researchers, since, in that case, the latter two are probably identical. It is not hard to understand why such a distinction might seem obscure to them, for their professional practice is, precisely, the pursuit of the truth and (should be) nothing else. Our objective is not to pursue that question (which is actually very knotty and may even be full of imponderables) but rather to clarify that there are those whose professional calling does not entirely fit that description. It is to those people that this book is primarily addressed. In fact the ethical obligations of the professional practitioner-researcher (or administrator) are more complex when they are conducting research. At that moment they are doubly responsible: responsible to the ethical premises of the researcher-at-work and to the professional practitioner-at-work.

In order to give some perspective on this issue, let us listen to those who don't, for a moment, think this is true. Baron and Baron, for example, say that "The only difference between the objectivity required for an evaluator and a scientist, as we see it, is that because the temptations to fall from grace are greater in evaluation than in traditional research, we must be more self conscious" (Baron and Baron, 1980, p. 89). Baron and Baron approach ethical standards as ". . . principles which brook no compromise or exceptions once they are established . . . universal and absolute" (Baron and Baron, 1980, p. 88, 89). The best definition we can find for the Barons' concept of ethical standard is ". . . those principles of honest practice and scientific procedure . . . generally congruent with . . . strong consensus" (Baron and Baron, 1980, p. 94). Baron and Baron contrast ethical standards with methodological standards that offer, as examples, standards that might be constructed for choosing research designs or statistical methods.

Although we would all wish for a simpler world and a simpler time, where ethical standards could stand as ultimate, absolute timeless principles, it simply does not seem to be the case. At least it is not the case in the world of program and policy evaluation research, though, of course, it may be true in the world of laboratory research. Even though we cannot speak of that world at first hand, in the nature of things it seems unlikely. What are the counter-examples that we are speaking of? First, ethical standards may lead us all into dilemmas where meeting an ethical obligation toward one person entails being unethical in some strict sense toward another person. Or ethical standards may actually conflict with one another so that both may not be met simultaneously. Ethical obligations entailed in the best way of truth-seeking may simply not be possible given the context within which the policy and program evaluation enterprise commonly operates. For example, the best (and so, presumably, the most "ethical") way to pursue a given question may involve inquiry into organizational secrets that no organization interested in survival would be willing to reveal. Thus, while we believe that the following advice given by Baron and Baron is certainly ethically sound, it may be too simple a counsel of perfection in coping with the complexities of research in the natural life of an organization:

> [evaluation researchers need] something like the Hippocratic Oath for physicians: a search for the truth and let the chips fall. . . . If that cannot be done, the evaluation should not be done (Baron and Baron, 1980, p. 88).

Later in this chapter the reader will find a subsection which speaks about the issue of the ethical dilemma and its importance.

In an attempt to resolve this problem Baron and Baron make a distinction between ethical and methodological standards.

> Whereas ethical standards should be universal and absolute, we believe that methodological standards should be particular and relative. . . . [Thus, with] methodology, we are dealing with decisions constrained both by situational realities about what is possible and by the state of the art in regard to new research design, theory and statistical approaches (Baron and Baron, 1980, p. 89).

However, we can't make this difference stand on its own two feet when it comes to applying it to the research situation. To us, the ethical standards they set out for truth-seeking scientists sound very much like methodological standards for professional practitioners doing research: "use initially favorable and unfavorable informants," "observational times scheduled on the same basis," "assess both intended and unintended effects" (Baron and Baron, 1980, p. 88). These sound very much like routine methodological standards to us, though they surely aren't as technical as some of their other examples of methodological standards.

Types of Moral Principles

We have made the point that ethics are themselves derivative, that is, they come from value principles to which people ascribe. Most people believe that those moral principles themselves have a source. Feldman (as well as a good many others) identify three sources for those principles: intuitionist, utilitarian, and contractarian (Feldman, 1987). Although it may not be precisely exclusive nor altogether exhaustive, it captures much that is valuable. The heart of the most commonly used source, the intuitionist, is a non-rationalized choice of some small number of values or principles which are simply defined to be most good. Its essence is individual choice: on faith. A main feature of the intuitionist approach is the idea that no rationale is required for the basic justification of ultimate moral principles—it may be a product of non-scriptural revelation or enlightenment, an interpretation of a scriptural statement, or simply an intuition. Most people would agree that "Thou shall not kill" is

a basic moral principle; although there might be many attractive rationaliza-
tions which justify its morality, the fact that it is a precept of Mosaic law is
sufficient justification for people for whom it is an accepted rule.

In contrast, the source of the utilitarian moral principle is a ratiocination,
a reasoned conclusion from the fundamental idea of what is "the greatest good
for the greatest number." It is specifically not scriptural, revelatory, or a
product of intuitive enlightenment. It is the product of a particular way of
reasoning about what is good for human beings. The standard of judgment is
itself an abstract principle, "the greatest good for the greatest number." Unlike
the intuitionist source, it is complicated, since the utilitarian must jump some
difficult hoops: what is "the good," what is the "greatest good" among them,
and who is to be included when counting the greatest number. The con-
tractarians, John Rawls most prominent among them, are also ratiocinators,
using logical processes (as well as imaginative constructions too complex to
detail here) to choose ethical premises from among values which concern how
people can best live together. Rawls' favorite is a sophisticated version of
another (ultimately) hebraic commandment—do to others as you would have
them do to you (if you were in their same place), "being sure that in doing so
everyone's liberty is maximized and if any favoritism is shown it must favor
the most disadvantaged" (Rawls, 1971). We believe that, ultimately, all types
of moral principles are intuitionist; that contractarianism and utilitarianism
are distinguished only by the use of a deductive logic that places them at one
remove from the intuitive choice of the phrase, "greatest good for the greatest
number," as a guiding moral principle.

Ethical Premises in the Protection
of Human Subjects Document

An example of a set of ethical premises are those contained in the *Basic Ethical
Principles Underlying the Statement of the National Committee for the Protection of
Human Subjects in Biomedical and Behavioral Research*. It seems clear that these
ethical standards for the protection of human research subjects also have a
basically intuitive source. It speaks of three fundamental ethical "principles":

1. *Beneficence*: the avoidance of unnecessary harm and the maximization of
   good outcomes
2. *Respect* for autonomy and freedom of persons and non-autonomous
   persons
3. *Justice*: equitable treatment and representation of subgroups within
   society

The phrases that follow the concept name are the ethical premises. They have
quite direct implications for the behavior of those who are responsible for

evaluation research. "Maximizing good outcomes" implies many ethical obligations for those who conduct evaluation research. Among them are:

1. The responsibility to conduct research that has promise for improving social programs and policy implementations and to disseminate its findings upon completion
2. A guarantee of their personal competence to pursue a particular investigation
3. Responsibility for protecting the right of research subjects to give voluntary informed consent

Respecting personal autonomy means taking responsibility for procedures in regard to informed consent—For example, procedures that avoid coerciveness and stick to the ethical principle here: full disclosure of the known consequences of a treatment and/or clear disclosure of the unknown or untried. The justice standard refers to such ethical obligations as: not studying subjects more than is deserved, choosing subjects precisely from among those who will be benefited, and making it clear to potential participants in a study with random assignment to controls that it is possible they may be in a no-treatment group.

Ethical Issues in the Program and Policy Evaluation Enterprise as Different from Laboratory, Biomedical, and Behavioral Research

The Protection of Human Subjects document is of supreme importance with respect to the ideals it pursues. Note, however, that it was conceived mainly out of a concern for physical science and medicine. The research enterprise that the document envisions, therefore, is either a modern research laboratory or a setting contrived to be as close to a laboratory as is possible, given the subject of the research and the chosen methodology. The social program and policy research enterprise is, for better or worse, fundamentally different from laboratory research because (fortunately, we would say) it is shaped by its subject, which, in turn, (necessarily) shapes its methodology. Its subject is the life that is lived on at least three levels simultaneously. One is the life of those who are in need. Another is the life of, say, the street-level bureaucracy (staff people) interacting with consumers—life on the boundary between the human service organization and its client-consumers. And still another is the life within the organization itself—the internal and external, social and political life of street-level bureaucrats and line superiors interacting with staff administrators and executives; the life of those who live on the boundary between the organization and the power structure of the society.

We believe that there are ethical issues that come out of each of these three levels. The Protection of Human Subjects document, however meritorious in other ways, cannot go far enough in covering the issues of concern to the peculiar type of research enterprise with which we are concerned here. It does concern one aspect: the rights of human subjects or clients of human service agencies who are involved in evaluation research projects. Thus, we will consider the Human Subjects document as integral. We will also wish to be concerned with the other subjects of evaluation research; therefore, we will give special place to the ethical issues arising out of the political and social character of the evaluation questions to be answered. And, we will want to be concerned with ethical issues that arise out of the political, social, and, yes, human character of the organization that is so vital a part of the subject of evaluation research.

Ethical Dilemmas

Finally, before we turn to a discussion of ethical issues themselves, it is important for the reader to understand that it is a mistake to limit consideration to ethical issues one at a time, as if they always stood in splendid isolation from each other. In fact, they often do not, and their interactions can be of the greatest interest. Consider that a professional may be called to two moral duties simultaneously: think of the physician who is ethically responsible to preserve life but is faced with a situation where, to preserve the life of a mother, she must endanger the life of a foetus-child in the womb. Nor is it only physicians who must confront literal life and death situations: consider the situation where a personal counselor who is ethically responsible for the confidential revelations of a client hears a serious death threat from an emotionally disturbed client. And, of course, it is not only life and death matters that entail serious ethical problems; it is usually other interests that are involved: financial, property, reputation, access to markets, privacy, etc.

The point of these examples is to illustrate the concept of *ethical dilemmas:* situations in which ethical behavior toward one client or person necessarily entails unethical behavior toward another, or in which pursuing one ethical standard violates another (Johnson, 1985). Compared to coping with or making decisions about single ethical issues and their application to real life, ethical dilemmas represent an entirely different level of difficulty for the professional practitioner, a difficulty that should be given standing in any discussion of ethics. They are of special human interest because they often involve a certain tragic element—the tragic choice between the interests of (or, indeed, the life of) two equally appealing human beings. Inevitably they are of special interest to ethicists and professionals alike because they have the potential to make clear the relative importance of ethical premises, one compared to the other, or even serve as a dialectic out of which arises an entirely new ethical premise.

The concept of ethical dilemma is useful in other ways as well. One of the problems in dealing with ethics is to avoid what has been called the *counsel of perfection*. The issue is not to counsel the avoidance of ethical perfection or even that it is somehow not desirable, rather that given the fact of dilemmas, all ethical standards cannot always be simultaneously achieved in the messy world of human affairs. Counsels of perfection would be, shall we say, "victimless crimes," were it not for the fact that they can sometimes be the most unwelcome of gifts—a serious and important but impossible task. On that account the counsel of perfection can be off-target, totally demoralizing to precisely those who are most inclined to take ethical obligations seriously. Sieber, in an otherwise splendid review of ethical issues in program evaluation, gives advice about being ethical that borders on the counsel of perfection because, in our view, it reads as if she did not consider the possibility of the ethical dilemma. For example, she advises: "And, to be ethical is to anticipate and circumvent such [ethical] problems" (Sieber, 1980, p.53). If some ethical problems involve the kind of dilemma discussed above, some ethical problems simply cannot be anticipated and circumvented. And, on those occasions, Sieber's advice is a counsel of perfection.

With these concepts in hand the reader is now better prepared to entertain a discussion of ethical issues that have a certain relevance for policy and program evaluation research. We would make no claim that these issues are all those that are relevant; we would only claim that we believe they are among the most important. We will consider them as single issues first, just for purposes of clarifying their nature, and then, at various points, we will turn to their interaction, or dialectic, with other ethical issues so that we can (following our own advice above) consider specific ethical dilemmas as well.

Ethical Issues in Protecting Individual Research Subjects

While our priority topic is ethical issues that are uniquely pertinent to the evaluation of social programs and policies, we will briefly review some current ideas about the ethical responsibilities of social experimenters and data gatherers in general. The skeptic might say that social science research produces such "weak knowledge" that its dangerousness to research subjects couldn't be much of a problem compared to biomedical experimentation. That fact is acknowledged by many (Faden and Beauchamp, 1986). However, there are important exceptions to the usual benignity of social science research, and some examples have occasioned concern, if not the kind of public outrage that has greeted some biomedical procedures. It is important to review them so that the reader can see that, however unusual or benign, questionable ethical practices can be an issue in social research.

Faden and Beauchamps review this issue, and one of their dramatic examples is the mid-1960s' research of Laud Humphries, in which addresses of customers of a homosexual "tea-room" were obtained surreptitiously (by following them out of the public restroom and jotting down auto license numbers) (Faden and Beauchamp, 1986, pp. 173–79). Posing as a health officer, Humphries then called at their homes for the purpose of obtaining data about their social status and other details of their personal life (Humphries, 1970). Then there is Zimbardo's Mock Prison at Stanford University (1973), an experiment that the investigator terminated early because the (student volunteer) jailers became intolerably brutal and abusive to the volunteer inmates (Zimbardo, Haney, Banks, and Naffe, 1973).

There is also a set of psychological experiments which may be the most famous since the Russian experimentalist, Pavlov, found a way to set his dog to salivating at such an incredible rate. In the early 1960s, Yale psychologist Stanley Milgram advertised in the New Haven (Connecticut) newspaper for research subjects. He then involved them in an experiment that tested a hypothesis about how much (or how little) psychological pressure it took to get people to administer a painful (even possibly fatal) electric shock to another person (Milgram, 1963). Even though the person who was being given electrical shocks was an actor faking pain and discomfort, and there was no possibility at all that the impressive apparatus could produce such a shock, the ethics of that experiment have been debated for twenty-five years (Burt, 1979). A clear consensus among psychologists has not yet emerged. Nor, in the opinion of some, is the type of experiment Milgram did forbidden by the latest revision of the guidelines for federally funded research for protecting human subjects.

Those who believe the experiments were unethical argued their case in two quite different ways. First, there is the beneficence argument: it is unethical to put research subjects into a situation which might generate irreconcilable guilt (by methods described earlier) because it is a serious and undeserved harm to the unwary (Baumrind, 1964). Second, there is the autonomy of persons argument: it is unethical to deceive others about the aims and purposes of affairs you ask others to be involved in such that they are unwittingly involved in something they might refuse to do given full knowledge (Kelman, 1967).

Informed Consent

There are other examples of exceptions to the general benignity of social science research—some of great relevance to program and policy evaluation research. It turns out that one of the main ethical issues involved in these relevant exceptions is informed consent. For example, informed consent is almost always at issue when research subjects are captive audiences: i.e., children in foster homes, institutional residents, like underage school pupils, nursing home residents, mental hospital patients, and literal captives, such as imprisoned felons. Such persons are not fully autonomous, being under the authority of others—some more, some less of course. Since they cannot literally run away from a persevering experimenter, the reader can see how they are particularly vulnerable to unethical manipulations by experimenters. Research evaluating the effectiveness of such programs may plausibly trespass on the rights of such persons. Obvious examples are behavior modification programs with mentally ill, retarded, or behaviorally disturbed children. For example, most people believe there is some period of time that is too much time for a child to spend in solitary confinement isolated from peers (a time-out procedure) and constitutes personal harm that is unethical. The fact that it is done for a virtuous reason, such as protecting other children from aggression, may be beside the point.[1] Another example is the psychic pain, produced at will by a therapeutic manipulation of peer group disapproval, that might be termed unethical if sufficiently severe. Again, that its objective might be therapeutic may be irrelevant.

Those examples seem intuitively convincing, and perhaps that is because one empathizes with a person experiencing pain who has no effective way of withdrawing from the situation. That is why the informed consent issue is so important here: if the person freely gave consent to involvement in such a treatment, the reader's sense of injustice would probably not be offended. We assume that ordinary people can give consent and can be sufficiently well informed to judge their own self-interest. An important consideration is how *informed* consent must really be. Here are the standards generally invoked: consenters must have enough information (facts about what the treatment entails, its probability for helping, and its known maximum negative and positive consequences), consenters must comprehend the meaning of those facts, and consenters must give consent voluntarily, without any implicit or explicit coercion (Faden and Beauchamp, 1986). One important aspect of voluntariness is the consenters' knowledge of their right to withdraw from the research project and of how to exercise it (Diener and Crandall, 1978).

It is important for those involved in program and policy evaluation research to be clear that it is not only institutional residents who fit the notion *captive audience.* Certainly any citizen whose survival is dependent upon a cash, credit, or in-kind welfare benefit is not totally free from the authority of others. The test for captive audience is embedded in the answer to the question: are conditions in a person's life such that it is either socially or financially very costly to refuse involvement in a research project? Do others hold power such that the prospective research subject could imagine the possibility of reprisals against them if they refused to participate? (Whether the probability for the reprisal is actually great is probably not germane.) Affirmative answers to those questions raise the possibility that such a person cannot give free consent to involvement and, thus, creates an extra ethical responsibility for the staff of a research project. One of the ways to meet those extra responsibilities is, for example, to simply increase the number of opportunities for the person to refuse involvement. Another is to be sure that all persons are clear about their right to refuse. The most effective way, of course, is to construct the system by which research subjects signal agreement and refusal so that it is clear to the choice maker that no one could ever know who participates and who doesn't.

While the concept of informed consent seems justified intuitively, explicit rational justifications for it can be easily summarized. Their history is short in view of the fact that research on human subjects in the United States was not common until the middle of the 20th century (Faden and Beauchamp, 1986). The earliest and most common basis for settling ethical questions, including informed consent, was the notion of beneficence: that is, the obligation of professionals to control imposed risks. It is expressed in the common professional caveat: "above all, do no harm." With regard to informed consent, the argument would assume the form of statements such as the following: it is ethical to withhold information that creates needless anxiety. It appears that this standard way of looking at consent issues with regard to discussing treatments of various kinds with clinical patients was imported, en toto, to deal with the consent issue in recruiting or selecting research subjects.

However, there has been increasing discomfort with the obvious shortcomings of using the beneficence rationale to deal with the informed consent issue. Lately something of a consensus has emerged that the rational justification for informed consent should rest, instead, on the notion of enabling autonomous choice of persons involved as research subjects (Faden and Beauchamp, 1986). Ultimately this idea rests on valuing respect for personal autonomy—that is, incursions on persons' rights to decide that their own fates should be protected, not abridged. The concept here is an aspect of root values such as *self-determination,* and that should be no stranger: some human service professions, particularly social work, and some applied social scientists share a commitment to essentially equivalent values (Gordon, 1964). Of course, while that perspective on informed consent is more cognitively satisfying, it is not entirely user-friendly: the meanings of root values such as self-determination are sometimes ambiguous or difficult to flesh out (Faden and Beauchamp, 1986).

However, one does not have to be somehow opposed to civil liberties to sense that there are occasions in which a dedication to informed consent works at cross purposes with obtaining quality research data. Anthropologists who regularly use participant observation as a research method (who, indeed, can probably safely be said to be responsible for having brought it to its present state, if not for inventing it), are best at describing that. Noting that most of the discussion of ethics in social science research envisions the biomedical laboratory as a context, Murray Wax believes that the ethical issues for research done "in the field" are substantially different (Wax, 1980). Though we believe that the issues arising in the biomedical laboratory context are relevant, we concur with Wax this far: ethical issues are quite different and perhaps even more complex in research in the context of what we shall call *natural settings*, that is, environments where the pursuit of knowledge for its own sake is not the primary objective for the main action. Such environments are what Wax has called "bounded wholes," where members have certain things in common, like an organizational life, a hierarchy of authority, perhaps a moral code, and a dialect or special set of terms used in their everyday lives (Wax, 1980). We believe the environment that is typical of those studied in program and policy evaluation research is much like that.

The problem for program evaluators and the evaluation research enterprise is that an ethical commitment to the notion of informed consent of research subjects runs counter to conducting research in (or into) such a setting. Although the practical problems of a laboratory researcher focus around reproducing the phenomenon of interest inside laboratory equipment so that it can be observed at will, quantitatively, and precisely, the practical problems of investigation in natural settings are very different. Here is Wax's ever-so-literate description:

> *The task of a fieldworker is to enter into the matrix of meanings of the researched, to participate in their system of organized activities and to feel subject to their code of moral regulation. . . . [it] is a complex interaction between researcher and hosts . . . in a process of exchange or reciprocity and so it cannot be assimilated toward the model of a biomedical experiment where the researcher is free to outline what is to be done to the passive subjects (Wax, 1980, p. 273).*

The question of informed consent takes on an entirely different set of meanings in this context in comparison with a biomedical laboratory context. In a natural setting, research becomes an unfolding process in which the role and status of a researcher continues to change as a function of many things— trust, for example (or external environmental factors). Thus, the degree to which organizational life is revealed to the researcher is a function of trust, of familiarity, of low stress in the environment, etc. A standard consent form is nearly irrelevant to this kind of research subject since it could never be truly informed: neither the subject nor the investigator could at any given time know in advance what might be said about which kind of things, issues, or other persons. Informed consent is actually more of a process than an event, a process which continually expands and contracts as a function of factors such as those discussed above. As Wax says ". . . consent becomes a negotiated and lengthy process—of mutual learning and reciprocal exchanges—rather than a once and for all event" (Wax, 1980, p. 275). Describing field research as involving a development of a primary personal rather than a secondary contractual relationship, Wax says:

> *In primary relationships, consent is not contractual but developmental: it is a process not a single event. . . . During good fieldwork . . . deepened relationships . . . offered the opportunity to perceive and understand more: [therein] in a sense, consent is broadened in scope (Wax, 1980, p. 282).*

Endnote

1. The use of behavior modification examples should not be taken as an indication of our belief that there is something generally unethical about it. We choose it mainly because we can assume that most behavior modification procedures are relatively uncomplicated and generally familiar to most readers. Indeed, experience seems to show that they often raise ethical questions, but we suspect that is due not to an unethical nature but precisely because the technology can be so powerful. No one bothers to worry about the ethics of weak interventions, a point we made earlier, relevant to social science-based interventions in general.

References

Bailey, S. K. (1965). Ethics and the public service. In R. Martin (Ed.), *Public administration and democracy* (pp. 283–298). Syracuse: Syracuse University Press.

Baron, J. B., & Baron, R. M. (1980). In search of standards. In R. Perloff and E. Perloff (Eds.), *Values, ethics and standards in evaluation* (pp. 85–99). New Directions for Program Evaluation Series, #17. San Francisco: Jossey-Bass.

Baumrind, D. (1964). Some thoughts on ethics of research: After reading Milgram's "Behavioral Study of Obedience." *American Psychologist, 19,* 421–423.

Becker, H. S. (1967). We must decide whose side we're on. *Social Problems, 14,* 239–248.

Burt, R. A. (1979). The Milgram experiments: The rule of objectivity. In R. Burt (Ed.), *Taking care of strangers.* New York: Free Press.

Carter, L. (1982). The standards for program evaluation and the large for-profit social science research and evaluation companies. In P. H. Rossi (Ed.), *Standards for evaluation practice.* New Directions for Program Evaluation Series, # 15. San Francisco: Jossey-Bass.

Diener, E., & Crandall, R. (1978). *Ethics in social and behavioral research.* Chicago: University of Chicago Press.

Faden, R. R., & Beauchamp, T. L. (1986). *A history and theory of informed consent.* New York: Oxford University Press.

Feldman, D. (1987). Ethical analysis in public policy-making. *Policy Studies Journal, 15*(3), 441–460.

Fetterman, D. (1987). Guilty knowledge, dirty hands and other ethical dilemmas. *Human Organization, 42*(3), 214–224.

Gordon, W. E. (1964). Basic constructs for an integrative and generative conception of social work. In G. Hearn (Ed.), *The general systems approach.* New York: Council on Social Work Education.

Humphreys, L. (1970). *Tearoom trade: Impersonal sex in public places.* Chicago: Aldine Publishing Co.

Johnson, P. (1985). Ethical dilemmas in program evaluation with family court related clients. *Evaluation and Program Planning, 8*, 45–51.

Kelman, H. C. (1967). Human use of human subjects: The problem of deception in social psychological experiments. *Psychological Bulletin, 67*, 1–11.

Kluckhohn, F. (1950). Dominant and substitute profiles of cultural orientation. *Social Forces, 16*(2).

Milgram, S. (1963). Behavioral study of obedience. *Journal of Abnormal Social Psychology, 67*, 371–378.

Posavac, E. J., & Carey, R. G. (1980). *Program evaluation: methods and case studies.* Englewood Cliffs, NJ: Prentice-Hall.

Rawls, J. (1971). *A theory of justice.* Cambridge, MA: Harvard University Press.

Rossi, P. H., & Freeman, H. E. (1985). *Evaluation: A systematic approach* (3rd Edition). Beverly Hills, CA: Sage Publications Co.

Sieber, J. E. (1980). Being ethical: Professional and personal decisions in program evaluation. In R. Perloff and E. Perloff (Eds.), *Values, ethics and standards in evaluation,* New Directions for Program Evaluation Series, #17. San Francisco: Jossey-Bass.

Warwick, D. P., Meade, M., & Reed, T. (1975). *A theory of public bureaucracy.* Cambridge, MA: Harvard University Press.

Wax, M. L. (1980). Paradoxes of "consent" to the practice of fieldwork. *Social Problems, 27*(3), 272–283.

Weiss, H. B. , & Jacobs, F. H. (Eds.). (1988). *Evaluating family programs.* New York: Aldine-De Gruyter.

Zimbardo, P. G. (1973). On the ethics of intervention in human psychological research: With special reference to the Stanford Prison experiment. *Cognition, 2*(3), 243–256.

Zimbardo, P. G., Haney, C., Banks, W. C., & Jaffe, D. (April 8, 1973). The mind as a formidable jailer: A Pirandellian prison. *The New York Times,* section 6, 38–60.

CHAPTER THREE

Legal Issues and Professional Standards in Evaluation Research

Professional Standards

Professional standards for evaluators are important to practicing professionals in several ways. First and foremost, such standards should produce the very best kind of evaluations, and such evaluations should create program benefit and service improvements as well as locate ineffective human service programs so that doubt can be cast on continued expenditures. However, for any profession there is only a loose couple between practice standards and the quality of professional practice, so we should view that claim with some skepticism. But, whatever their status as tools of professional upraising, these kinds of professional standards will undoubtedly be the first criteria by which evaluation practitioners will be judged, should their professional actions or judgment ever be called into question. A few examples should suffice: in the unhappy event of showing cause as to why an employee-evaluator was discharged, in documenting why an evaluation contract was terminated, or (worse) why it was not paid for upon completion. Professional standards can be used in court to convince a judge why a suit for contract non-performance, malpractice, or breach of confidentiality should be settled in favor of their client and against the practitioner(s) or their employers. Although it is not inevitable that the judiciary must use the professional standards developed by professional associations as criteria, judges may be reluctant to construct their own standards when others are available, sanctioned, and ready-to-hand.

Standards for evaluation practice have not been around very long. The Evaluation Research Society (ERS) published its *Standards For Program Evaluation* in 1982. The ERS standards can probably lay claim to being the most authoritative in the evaluation enterprise, even though there is another older set. The very first standards to appear were those of the Joint Committee on Educational Evaluation. There was some competitiveness between the two. A former chairperson of the Joint Committee took exception to the ERS venture in standards, arguing against their publication on the grounds that they overlapped with those of the Joint Committee and would contribute to ambiguity in the minds of those who would have occasion to use them (Stufflebeam, 1982). While the ERS committee acknowledged its debt to the ideas embedded in the Joint Committee standards as well as those published by the U.S. General Accounting Office, they persevered, feeling justified, since the Joint Committee standards were intended primarily for educational programs, and the GAO standards primarily for impact evaluations. Peter Rossi dissents, commenting that the ERS standards seem to serve a somewhat selfish organizational agenda. Nonetheless he accepts the legitimacy of the ERS standards on the grounds that they are needed, since they are concerned with a much broader spectrum of evaluation types and substantive fields (Rossi, 1982). Those who have examined both conclude that on basic issues there is little basic divergence between them (see Cordray, 1982, p. 70, 73 and Table 1 for example), so we will use the ERS rather than the Joint Committee standards as exemplary and as a main focus for discussion in this text. Of course, some might feel differently since the . . . Joint Committee (not the ERS) was accredited by the American National Standards Institute (ANSI) as the only group accredited to set evaluation standards in the United States . . .* Perhaps some might be persuaded by that but we aren't; it is the purpose of this accreditation body (which only accredits accreditation agencies) simply to judge whether a particular set of standards is sensible AS A SET OF STANDARDS. But, of course, the issue isn't whether the Joint Committee or the ERS standards are good as standards, rather which set of standards is arguably better than the other. The American National Standards Institute claims no pre-eminent authority in any field, and certainly not in this field where there is so little accepted wisdom. Actually we are tempted to view the decision of (ANSI) to accredit the Joint Committee standards as the body to issue evaluation standards in the United States as evidence of poor judgment: doesn't it seem dubious to take the position that standards for evaluating educational programs should be appropriate as standards for a evaluating social programs like, say, food stamps or child sex abusers? The problem is that so much is different: research designs, measures, theoretical bases and ability to control the research environment are only a few examples.[1] Finally, it is the case that the federal General Accounting Office (GAO) evaluation standards still refer to the ERS standards and, plainly, most of our audience will be doing evaluations which are (ultimately) funded from U.S. Treasury dollars.

*Personal communication from James R. Sanders, Chair of the Joint Committee on Standards for Educational Evaluation. 4–2–91 and 4–30–91

Finally, readers should use this whole matter about whose standards should prevail as strong evidence that there is no strong convergence on standards in this field. And in that spirit, though we believe that the ERS standards are superior to those of the Joint Committee, what follows below is basically a strong critique of the ERS standards. We conclude that the reader needs to understand the controversial issues on standards and that for that particular purpose, ERS standards are particularly well suited.

The ERS Standards are controversial for what they say, as well as for what they do not say. We will review and summarize the basic standards and then analyze both the objections of their most trenchant critics as well as the replies of their most committed followers.

Notice that the ERS committee proceeded in a tentative way and certainly can't be faulted for a radical stance—they took some pains to say that these standards were an "initial formulation" and "subject to . . . revision" (ERS Standards, 1982, p. 11).

Basic Assumptions Underlying the ERS Standards

First let us look at some important assumptions and structures made by the committee that constructed these standards for program and policy evaluation. First, the ERS Standards Committee (1982) framed the scope of their subject by setting out six different categories (types) of evaluation activity. They are types commonly referred to in the evaluation literature, well known to evaluation practitioners, and certainly not controversial:

1. *"Front-end" analysis*—evaluation activities that characteristically occur prior to implementation of a social program, often those relevant to decisions about whether the program should be implemented at all; for example: needs studies, program design, studies of operational feasibility, etc.
2. *"Evaluability" assessment*—gathering information and making observations that go into making a decision about the readiness of a program or an organization for a formal evaluation process
3. *Formative evaluation*—making observations about an ongoing program in order to make incremental modifications for its improvement (including small scale field trials or demonstrations)
4. *Impact evaluations*—observations, usually systematic and formalized, to determine outcomes in relation to pre-specified program goals in order to make major decisions about program continuation, expansion, or contraction
5. *Program monitoring*—observations to determine whether the fit between program activities and some preconceived program design service is being delivered to particular target populations or groups in compliance with policy or funding constraints
6. *Meta-evaluation*—the collation of results from a number of evaluations to draw summary conclusions about a program design type or general programmatic

solution to a social problem; the secondary analysis of a single evaluation to review the soundness of its findings

Setting forth types of evaluation was an important move for the committee, legitimating a broad scope for evaluation activities (some might say too broad), a corrective to the common misconception of program evaluation only in terms of impact (outcome) assessment. It also lays a basis for later assertions that the standards will apply differently to different types. Here (and later) the standards legitimate (indirectly) non-experimental types of evaluation. Note that the standards refer to case studies and clearly expect that option to be exercised in making decisions about an appropriate evaluation type (ERS Standards, 1982, p. 13). However, judging from the terms in which the ERS Standards discuss impact evaluation, it is clear that for this purpose the Standards call for a quantitative method and some type of experimental or quasi-experimental comparisons (ERS Standards, 1982).

Second, note that the standards are "simple admonitory statements," that is, they are expressed as statements about what practitioners should do, not about what practitioners must do. The Standards make three additional points in this regard:

- The standards are not exhaustive since they cover neither legal requirements nor government regulations.
- A judgment about compliance with the standards requires the consideration of the context in which the evaluation took place.
- A "reasonable person" basis for judgment is specified when decisions about compliance with standards are being made: i.e., ". . . what an informed, disinterested party would consider reasonable and appropriate in the circumstances" (ERS Standards, 1982, p. 11).

Third, underlying the ERS standards is a notion about what a good evaluation should include. The standards are organized around this idea, that is, the fifty-five standards are stated under one or another of these headings. Lincoln (1985) believes that the serial order listing implies some notion of standing for distinct "phases" (p. 251):

1. Formulation of the evaluation
2. Structure and design
3. Data collection and interpretation
4. Communication of findings and disclosure issues
5. How results can (should) be used

Fourth, the Standards assume that external, "independent" program evaluators generate the most credible evaluation product, at least where an impact evaluation is concerned. That is, an evaluation that is concerned with providing information for major decisions about program continuation, expansion, or reduction, evaluations of perhaps the greatest consequence, require external, "independent" evaluators (ERS Standards, 1982, pp. 9–10).

Standards for the Formulation Phase of an Evaluation Project

The twelve standards for this phase require that the formulation of an evaluation project contain a clear idea of what is to be done, how it is to be done, the purpose of the venture, and what constraints are expected to be in operation (ERS Standards, 1982, p. 12). For example, the standards are clear that the information needs and expectations of users and decision-makers should be taken into account, the type of evaluation should be specified, and its cost as well as appropriate alternatives should be estimated. Note that the standards specify written agreements prior to the beginning of the project on certain key issues:

- That the evaluation proposed ". . . is likely to produce . . . information that will justify its cost"
- Program objectives
- Need for cooperation of key staff or community members
- Financing required for its completion
- Limitations on public access to data
- Time schedules for project completion
- Obligations and involvements of all parties

Standards for the Design and Structure of an Evaluation Project

The ERS Committee standards do not take a position on the types of designs that are to be preferred. They impose little constraint on the type of research approach, referring to both qualitative and quantitative styles as well as experimental and quasi-experimental types. The Standards require that the following aspect of evaluation designs and structure be clearly detailed and rationalized:

- The procedures by which the effects of nontreatment are estimated (note, implying the need in impact studies for a no-treatment comparison group)
- Sampling and measurement methods

Standards for Data Collection and Preparation

The standards are quite stringent in their concern for the reliability and validity of the measuring methods and instruments used in an evaluation: estimates of reliability and validity estimates are not only to be given but are to be ". . . verified under the prevailing circumstances of their use" as well (ERS Standards, 1982, p.12). The standards require that documentation of "source, methods, circumstances and processes" of measurement procedures be maintained (ERS Standards, 1982, p. 12).

The ERS committee standards are concerned for the protection of both research subjects and research data. The standards state that measuring methods or instruments that entail adverse risk should be subject to independent review and warn about the importance of informed consent of data givers (ERS Standards, 1982). Evaluation practitioners should be aware that there are several standards which imply that it is the evaluation practitioner who is responsible for handling and storing data in such a way as to prevent unauthorized use or access or unrecoverable loss through catastrophic events (ERS Standards, 1982).

Standards for Analysis and Interpretation of Evaluation Data

The standards are explicit in requiring that evaluation practitioners be prepared to bring up-to-date analytic methods to their work. The standards ought to lead consumers of the evaluation product to expect that analytic procedures will be specified in advance and adhered to subsequently (ERS Standards, 1982). "All analytic procedures, along with their underlying assumptions . . . , should be described explicitly and reasons for choosing them clearly explained" (ERS Standards, 1982, p. 15). The usual cautions in applying statistical methods are embedded in the standards (e.g.: ". . . appropriate to properties of measures used . . . ," etc.). Of special interest is standard (#37) requiring estimates of both "statistical *and practical significance* of findings." Evaluation practitioners should take notice that here, as in a number of other places, the standards call for considerably more documentation than is probably consistent with current practice. Of special interest is the standard referring to the fact that "data analysis should be sufficiently documented so that it is replicable" (ERS Standards, 1982, p. 15).

Standards for Communication and Disclosure

The ERS standards here are primarily concerned with the clarity and completeness of statements by which evaluation findings are expressed. They are explicit in requiring a statement of the relative importance of findings and feedback to "... those who contributed [data]." The standards come out clearly on the side of maximum openness of research findings to the general public: "... *the evaluator should serve as the proponent for the fullest, most open disclosure*" (ERS Standards, 1982, p. 16).

Standards for the Use of Evaluation Results

According to the ERS standards, it is the evaluation practitioner who is responsible for anticipating and preventing misinterpretation and misuse of evaluation information. Note especially that the standards give official recognition to the issue of policy and program side effects, assigning the evaluation practitioner the responsibility of bringing potential side effects (positive or negative) to the attention of relevant audiences. The evaluation practitioner is also responsible for maintaining a clear distinction between findings and policy recommendations on the one hand, and on the other, keeping a clear distinction between their role as evaluator and as advocate (ERS Standards, 1982).

A Critique of the Standards

It is a daunting and probably dangerous task to write a set of professional standards. All the more so in a field where there is so little settled wisdom. We believe that the committee who drafted the ERS standards should be congratulated for an earnest and intelligent effort and for the courage to set out, forthrightly, a set of positions that they knew would draw criticism from all sides. Indeed it has. In what follows we will try to summarize those criticisms, draw out the basic issues, and comment on their practical importance for the everyday work of the evaluation practitioner.

1. The Quantitative-Qualitative Methodology Issue

The ERS Standards tiptoe gently around current controversies in the field about the merit of the various methods of evaluation. In fact, the Standards do not speak of general methods or approaches to evaluation, but of *categories* of evaluation. By that term they seem to intend something like the purposes of evaluation. For example, the categories used by the Standards contrast needs studies with formative evaluations and impact evaluations. Used this way, the classification scheme has a certain merit, because it allows an easy way for the Standards to make the point that the type evaluation used should be fitted to the purpose of the effort. It is a useful point, no doubt.

While the ERS Standards are silent on the quantitative/qualitative methodological controversy, we believe that they are quite biased toward quantitative approaches as the most powerful way to evaluate the impact of social programs. While the Committee authors appear to have tried to avoid any methodological bias, they have not succeeded on the following counts:

- Many standards are expressed in terms that assume a quantitative approach.
- There is only a single clear reference to a (basically) qualitative method, i.e., the case study (ERS Standards, 1982, p.13). Most serious kinds of programmatic decisions (that is, program discontinuance or program expansion) are expected to result from an impact evaluation using a quantitative method and one or another form of experimental or quasi-experiment design (ERS Standards, 1982, p.19).

Other knowledgeable commentators have read the ERS standards and have also concluded that they have an experimentalist, quantitative bias, so we do not believe that it is just our own narrow opinion. Yvonna Lincoln says:

> *Words like non-treatment, sampling reliability, validity, generalization, replicable . . . leave little doubt as to which methods are thought to possess most power (Lincoln, 1985, p.252).*

While the standards mention case studies, evaluators who wish to use a non-quantitative, non-experimental method will find no ERS Standard by which the methodological adequacy of a qualitative study could be assessed (Lincoln, 1985). Lincoln believes that the ERS Standards express a preference for:

- A particular and singular purpose for evaluations: data on "cause-effect" relationships rather than data on simple description by participants in the social action
- Evaluations structured to serve the interests of those identified with the program (administration and practitioners) as over and against those whom the social program serves (clients and consumers)
- More or less "value-free" as opposed to "value-explicit" evaluations (Lincoln, 1985, pp. 252–253)

Evaluation practitioners should be aware that it may not be difficult for a disgruntled contract-giver, employer, or colleague to make a case that an evaluator's practice is outside of professional standards if, for an impact study, they proposed an evaluation method which used a substantially qualitative or nonexperimental methodology. Let us imagine, for a moment, how a legal mind might go at constructing such an argument that a qualitative strategy was nonstandard profession practice:

- The Standards document does not even explicitly recognize the existence of such a method known as qualitative or nonexperimental.
- Such methods are not just controversial, clearly they have no wide support among active, competent evaluation practitioners.

One respected commentator in the field, Richard Berk (1982), notes that "The Standards can be seen as demanding that nontrivial deviations from conventional approaches require extra justification; the burden of proof falls on the innovator" (p. 63). All of that should serve as fair warning to the adventurous or the unwary.

Attention should be drawn to the fact that various types of evaluators were disproportionately represented on the ERS committee that constructed the Standards. We note that four of the nine members of the drafting committee were then employed by (or were retired from) large research corporations—the Educational Testing Service was well represented with three of four such in their employ. Other members include two who were employed by the U.S. General Accounting Office (GAO), one by a state Office of Mental Health, and one held a full time University faculty appointment. We believe that it is important to think about whether the basic self-interest and viewpoints of these various evaluation practitioners are homogeneous. Indeed we think not; we believe that it is no stretch of the imagination to believe that their points of view are fundamentally different. All members of this committee were certainly qualified to construct evaluation standards, but reading them seems always to bring to mind a private-sector research corporation contracting with the federal government for a large-scale evaluation. No particular committee member somehow had a particular personal interest at stake, but it is quite natural that they should formulate standards for practice in terms that are relevant to their own experience. It stretches credibility too far to be asked to believe that career line biases and the experiential frame of reference of those drafting standards would not be reflected in the ERS standards. It is not that ERS standards biased in this way are intrinsically wrong, just that they are not right for all whose practice will be judged by them.

It would go a long way to cure the problem if the ERS would draft addenda to the standards that recognize and apply to the particularities of other aspects of the evaluation enterprise (the on-staff evaluator, the state or local level evaluator, the academic in evaluation roles). This would recognize that large-scale federal evaluations are important and widely influential, both substantively and normatively, on the whole evaluation field, but are not coterminous with it either.

2. *The Internal/External Evaluator, Objectivity and Credibility*

The ERS Standards take the general view that evaluation is done for officials who are the primary client of the evaluator. Note that standard 17 refers to them as the client, explicitly. However, there are others who are effected by evaluation process and findings, particularly benefit and service consumers. The Standards mention consumers only once in the entire document. Lee Cronbach is right to say that this short shrift is inconsistent with a document that also insists that all "... parties to the evaluation" are to come to a mutual understanding about its nature. The basic problem here is that the notion of public interest as a factor in the evaluation process and product hardly appears in the ERS Standards at all (Cronbach, 1982, p. 52). Actually, that bias should be no surprise, considering that the ERS Standards were constructed by a committee whose majority was comprised of those whose interests and experience lie in the realm of large, profit-oriented corporate professionals.

That fact has another unfortunate consequence. Since the majority of the ERS Committee can be described as professionals who practice in the role of "independent (non-agency staff) evaluators," it calls into doubt the credibility of statements in the ERS Standards to the effect that external, "independent evaluators" produce the most credible product. It is called into doubt since it obviously has the potential to serve the career self-interest of the majority of the committee who constructed the standards. The reason that consequence is unfortunate is because there is no way to resolve the doubt that is created about the motives of the committee members whose interest this statement serves. It is an important issue. The committee may, in fact, be correct, but the doubt about self-interest can only be resolved by some judgment of motive— always a dubious judgment. Had the ERS taken care to see that the career self-interest was better balanced, the credibility of standards such as this one would not be in doubt.

The ERS Committee did not serve its public well by not making clear that even independent evaluators themselves are aware that the conclusions of evaluation research done by external contractors is not, somehow, that distant, that devoid of intrinsic self-interest. There are always the next and future contracts to be considered, and few organizations, public or private, receive future contracts from contractors who tell them things they don't want to hear. Evaluation practitioners working for large corporate private research and evaluation enterprises know that. For example, Launor F. Carter (1982), retired vice-president of a for-profit evaluation and research firm, quite rightly points out one example of how supposedly objective evaluators have, in fact, clear self-interest that seriously biases evaluation results: one way in which government agencies pursue "certification," Carter notes, is by obtaining evaluation results from "supposedly impartial" university-based researchers.

Just as it doesn't seem too much to say that there are university-based researchers who are willing to do that to serve their own career opportunities, it doesn't seem too much to suppose that corporate research practitioners may well do the same thing.

Some argue that external private contractors are in some ways actually less free than many internal civil servants. Private contractors, after all, are in the business to turn a profit, and no one could reasonably expect them to act against their fiscal best interest. Of course, internal evaluators, who are civil servants, are not always paragons of enlightened altruism in these regards, since every civil servant has a career to be pursued and protected and thus much of the same argument above applies to them as well. However, we think the contrary argument is just as sensible—that if there is any difference, contrary to popular wisdom, it could favor the civil servant who is ordinarily protected against losing a job only because of expressing plausible opinions about the failings of a public program. And, in this decade at least, an honorable tradition is developing for civil servant whistle-blowers whose courage other civil servants might wish to emulate—especially those with a professional calling as well. The King cannot automatically have the head of a civil servant only because of personal disloyalty. On the contrary, if external private research contractors, big or small, have discovered a way to tell the King that he is naked, it certainly is a well-kept commercial secret.

The wisdom here comes to the fact that it is folly to believe that any evaluator, in whatever role or circumstance, has some kind of corner on objectivity. All ventures which seek to render evaluative judgment are fraught with subjectivity from beginning to end. The best safeguard for utter enslavement to it is devoted and public attention to multiple perspectives and systematic observation, two issues which we will discuss at some length in a later chapter.

3. The Weaknesses of the Standards as a Statement of Professional Obligations

Since the standards are billed as admonitory statements, we believe that they are only *obligatory ideals:* ideals meant to guide, perhaps ideals so rarefied as to mitigate the practitioners' obligation to them (McGuire, 1982). Not only do the Standards explicitly say that they are "simply admonitory" but the operating verb in all the Standards is *should,* not *must.* The word *must* does not appear in the document at all as far as we can see. Obligatory ideals do not specify so particular a path that it is easy to decide whether a given instance deserves praise or punishment. These professional standards are not, properly, standards at all; rather, they are exhortations to evaluation practitioners to do good. Nor is this just our own narrow opinion; Launor Carter (1982), a long-time evaluation practitioner/administrator and former vice president of a large private evaluation and research firm, seems to share this view. While

Cahn (1982) and the ERS Standards' own subcommittee on legal implications of the Standards are less exercised about this matter than are we, they do agree: "... the purpose of the Standards is for guidance and education" (pp. 90–91). Nor is Lee Cronbach (1982) exercised about this matter. In fact he takes an opposite view, one which we feel obliged to report here even though we disagree. Cronbach believes that he knows precisely why the committee adopted standards that are more symbolic than real and argues in favor of the importance of such symbols as over and against firm Standards that would be normative and constraining. Cronbach's argument for professional standards that are not standards is that:

- Standards might "institutionalize mere [non-substantive] conventions" and when they do they stifle experimental creativity.
- Non-substantive standards can become false marks of excellence.
- Standards can keep "superior technology from coming into use" and are typically designed to restrain trade (as in professional certification requirements).
- Standards are likely to be political compromises and thus will not accurately reflect an important substantive professional issue.

The argument is clear. We will leave it to the reader to debate the issue and formulate their own position. We believe that Cronbach is wrong to think that these standards are, somehow, non-substantive conventions. Conventions they may be, but it is not non-substantive to assert (for example) that specifications for evaluations must always be written, results must show practical as well as statistical significance, and that the fullest possible public disclosure of evaluation results is the responsibility of the evaluation practitioner. Perhaps Cronbach cannot avoid experiencing evaluation as a nationally known expert, so that he may be sufficiently autonomous that it would never occur to him to act in these ways. Few evaluators can conduct their practice in this way, and almost all of us can recollect violations of these standards.

So, even though the ERS Standards seem to us to be commonly violated and thus their assertion an effective stroke for the improvement of practice, at the level of ideals, we believe that most of the issues dealt with by the ERS Standards are actually non-controversial, other than the non-explicit issue about the relative merits of quantitative-experimental vs qualitative methodology. Practicing evaluators we know, for example, would all support common ideas like these contained in the Standards: an evaluation proposal should be embedded in an explicit, written contract that specifies what is to be done, how, and why; major players should agree that those specifications agreed upon will yield worthwhile information; data analysis should use up-to-date methods; data access should be specified and protected, etc. We do believe that the Standards ignore some important issues.

There is some merit to Cronbach's argument on standards; there are some practice ideals that would be better left as symbols rather than as minimum standards. There is an easy way to accommodate the Standards to that idea. The ERS Committee could follow the lead of some state bar association codes for professional conduct: split the Professional Standards into two sections, one on absolute obligations and one on ideals that are desirable but not mandatory or are strongly conditioned by circumstance. ERS could still do that rather easily in subsequent revisions.

Finally, with respect to the weaknesses of the standards, the document makes a significant concession when it says that the Standards don't "encompass . . . [all] the *accepted norms* for professional and corporate conduct . . ." with regard to evaluation practices (*underline ours*) (ERS Standards, 1982). What other "accepted norms" might there be that the committee knew about but did not pay attention to? Note that the Standards document is not referring here just to all those norms controlled by others that it could not hope to summarize: e.g., norms embedded in law or in government regulations, say, on contracting practices. A professional standards document that will not tell or give a set of general guidelines to practitioners so that they can know when they are outside of normative practice seems crippled in the extreme. Could it be that the above statement is (cryptically) intended to refer to the fact that norms for qualitative, non-experimental methodology are not included?

4. A Strong Standard for Evaluation Measurements

The document sets a standard for the reliability of measures and measuring methods that seem to us to be little followed in practice. It could mean, literally interpreted, that reliability estimates should nearly always be redone in each evaluation project. The standards say that reliability of measures should be ". . . verified . . . under the prevailing circumstances of their use." We interpret that to mean, for example, that even though a particular measuring device has been widely used, a new reliability study (however modest) must be done whenever previous reliability estimates are (for example) based on program participants that are different in things like age, social problem, geographic area, cultural factors, etc. How "different" is an important "difference" is not specified by the Standards, and that leaves the practitioner at somewhat of a disadvantage.

Be that as it may, it is certainly true that the Standards are technically and substantively correct in asserting that the reliability of measures is quite specific to time and place. In fact, we do not raise this point to quarrel with it, only to mark for readers how much more seriously it is taken here compared to what we think to be the common practice in evaluation research. Actually, we would encourage the ERS Committee in its strict interpretation of this technical issue since it is more than a mere technicality. It is not merely technical at all, since it is well known that the most likely consequence of poor reliability of measures is to systematically obscure positive findings, (not the reverse) (Rossi and Freeman, 1982). One of the most constant (and accurate) criticisms of evaluation research is that, more often than not, its findings show no effect; is it therefore possible that lax attention to the reliability issue is one of the major causes?

5. Documentation Required By the Standards

It is clear that the Standards require considerably more documentation than appears to have been the usual practice in evaluation research. Evaluation practitioners should take note of specific documentation now required by the standards: documentation of

- *Source, methods, circumstances and processes of measurement procedures (ERS Standards, 1982, p. 12)*
- *Data analysis [procedures] sufficiently documented so that it is replicable (ERS Standards, 1982, p. 15)*

Note also that written agreements are unequivocally required prior to the beginning of the project on certain key issues (that the evaluation proposed is likely to produce information that will justify its cost, the objectives of the program to be evaluated, need for organizational or community cooperation, financing matters, time schedules, public access to data, obligations and involvements of all parties) (ERS Standards, 1982, p. 12).

Because the Standards do not distinguish between Standards for a private independent evaluation research contractor and an evaluation conducted by in-house staff employees, we cannot be clear whether the standards for such things as written agreements and documentation apply to organizational employees as well. Standards for most professional practice are general standards, applying wherever practice occurs, if one thinks of professional standards for, say, medicine or architecture. We see no obvious reason why that should be any different for the practice of evaluation research. If it seems odd that an organizational employee would have a written contract with the employing agency about a particular task, that is only to emphasize how much less professional autonomy is usually given to evaluation researchers who work in an organization as compared to other professionals like physicians who work in an organization. While it would seem odd to imagine an organizational chief executive officer ordering a physician what treatment to administer to a sick employee, it probably wouldn't seem odd to imagine the CEO ordering her program evaluation staff how to design a project! We conclude that the standards for written agreements and documentation are excellent, and that they should help create a good context for evaluation research. Applying those standards to in-house organizational staff simply makes clear to all concerned that employees' professional obligations are not superseded by administrative convenience or custom.

6. New Emphasis on the Interpretive
Responsibilities of Evaluators

The Standards assign many responsibilities to the evaluator, not all of which the ordinary evaluation practitioner might expect. For example, the Standards are explicit in holding the evaluator responsible for estimating the practical significance of findings. That is not always a straightforward matter and calls for the use of considerable judgment as well as science. There are important and vexing questions to consider in making that kind of judgment. For example, for what purpose, with regard to what group of people, and under what particular circumstances is the practicality of findings being judged. The Standards are quite explicit in holding the evaluator responsible for alerting relevant audiences to the existence of potential side effects (unintended, we presume). Such an action is sometimes, perhaps often, a very political (and sometimes daring, we might add) act. Finally, the evaluator is the one who the Standards hold specifically responsible for taking a stand as advocate for the "fullest, most open disclosure" of evaluation findings (conditioned of course by existing contractual constraints or governmental regulations). Once again we believe that it is right for the ERS Standards to assert these obligations, and we applaud them for a forthright, ethical, and moral stand. We wish to alert evaluation practitioners to them, however, since they could be overlooked by the unwary.

Finally, the Standards use strong, clear words to say that it is the evaluator's task to guard the privacy of data, observe disclosure constraints, and even see to it that the data is not destroyed by natural disasters. While a private evaluation contractor might well have sufficient control of an enterprise to make it reasonable to expect that responsibility to be met, an organizational staff member may not. Building security and data storage (or storage of any kind) is usually an item of much tedious and even delicate organizational negotiation, in which evaluation staff may not ever participate.

7. The ERS Standards Curb the Evaluator
Acting in an Advocacy Role

The Standards come out quite clearly against evaluators serving as advocates of either ideas, programs, or personnel. In doing so the Standards have to adopt an empiricist viewpoint that would insist on the ability of the evaluator as a detached, disinterested observer of a social program or policy. Standard fifty-five is clearly of that sort. This position is clearly consistent with the general lean of the ERS Standards in the direction of a model of evaluator function as a disinterested, dispassionate scientist.

8. The Standards Focus Obligations on the Professional,
Not the Organization

Launor Carter (1982) criticizes the Standards for leaving in the dark the obligations of organizations who give contracts out—an important point, for, if evaluators have obligations, so must those who contract with them or employ them to do their evaluations.

9. How Influential (Important) Will the Standards Be?

Not much, Carter says—the for-profit evaluation corporations will ignore them if they create expense, unless government agencies take them to heart. There is no acknowledgement by Carter (for the profit sector) of the profit sector's responsibility to support standards that would generate the best evaluations! (Carter, 1982). There is no guess on Carter's part about whether government agencies will take the Standards seriously.

However, Carter (1982) has an important suggestion about how to make the ERS Standards potent: convince the Office of Management and Budget (OMB) to include a simple phrase in its standard boiler-plate government contracts alluding to the necessity for the contractee to follow ERS standards. There is no indication that the ERS ever followed up on that as far as we know. More people worry that the Standards will be so influential that they will discourage innovation. Lee Cronbach (1982) was not very concerned about that, but Richard Berk (1982) is. Berk thinks that the Standards are too assertive for the state of the art. He worries about the effect of standards under conditions when we cannot answer the following questions about what is right with respect to evaluation technical procedures: What if nobody knows? What if nobody knows but some think they do? What if it is only possible to know in theory? (Berk, 1982, pp. 60–61). We think those are important issues that should be taken seriously in any discussion of professional standards in this area.

One of the reasons the Standards won't be as influential as they could be is because there are useful technical guidelines upon which there is some considerable agreement and on which the Standards remain silent. In fact, Berk (1982) lists ten such guidelines, all probably better and more clear than many of the statements found in the Standards. They are stated at a level of generality that we don't think would discourage particular innovations. For example:

- *"Analysis of attrition should be routinely undertaken and reported."*
- *"Results based on a priori model specification should be clearly distinguished from results based on post hoc models and exploratory analyses" (Berk, 1982, p. 64).*

David Cordray (1982) thinks the standards are a useful description of good evaluation process but unlikely to be influential until they improve evaluation practice. That could best be done by some mechanisms for review procedures (pre-release, in addition to ex post facto, summative review). Implicit in his criticism is disapproval of the assumption of the ERS Standard that the informational needs of the evaluator's client is the main audience. Here Cordray does not intend to consider how ERS Standards might be used in litigation, but it is clear that professional standards and standard setting organizations often enter into that arena.

> *Once the ERS adopts a code of conduct with some specificity, it should expect the number of such requests . . . [for identifying expert witnesses, amicus curiae briefs, etc.] . . . to increase and it becomes obliged to honor them (Cahn, 1982, p. 86).*

However, the ERS Standards' own subcommittee on legal implications of the standards makes it quite clear that the standards are so general in nature that it is unlikely that ". . . evaluators who voluntarily adhere to them will be subject to new legal liabilities related to malpractice issues" (Cahn, 1982, p. 91). That is not to say that the situation will always remain that way, for the Subcommittee has also said:

> *. . . if standards have some [greater] specificity, they offer best evidence in a court of law concerning appropriate practices for a profession. If the ERS adopts additional codes, the likelihood that evaluators will be involved if malpractice cases occur will increase . . . (Cahn, 1982, p. 94).*

Let us now turn to the subject of legal issues and how they do or might impact evaluation practice.

Legal Issues in Evaluation

Litigation has come into the evaluator's work-a-day life. Evaluators have been sued, apparently, even though there aren't as yet many specific cases to be cited. Perhaps the best known example, though not an actual suit, can be found in the *Social Science Quarterly* (Bonjean, 1980). The letters to the editor and authors' replies found there (Newman, Musheno, Levine, and Palumbo) include a threat by the Institute for Community Design Analysis to file a five million dollar suit against this journal, apparently for publishing the conclusions of an evaluation that one of the parties believed to be erroneous and thus damaging to the Institute. The article in SSQ concerned the (lack of) effects of a program which the Institute had designed and conducted. Newman believes that the published report later had a significant influence on Congressional appropriations and thus was responsible for ". . . depriv[ing] hundreds of thousands of residents of public housing of one of the few mechanisms that has shown any promise of reducing crime in low income communities" (Newman, 1980, p. 324). The questions around which litigation turned were common enough. Was the whole intervention theory really tested in this research? Could the effect of one type of program input be disentangled from others? Was certain pre-test data clean of program effects, and exactly what was legitimate to include on the cost side of a cost-benefit calculation? We cannot discover what the ultimate outcome of that encounter, was but it is plain that journals in the evaluation field consider legal implications to be of sufficient importance to warrant publication of a few (though not many) articles on the topic.

We are indebted to Thurston for concise advice about legal issues in evaluation practice. Our discussion will rely on his outline of the four main legal issues in program evaluation practice: defamation, contract performance, malpractice, and breach of confidentiality (Thurston, 1984). Each have important particulars, so let us take some care to sort them out.

Contract Performance

Almost all evaluation practice done by private practitioners necessarily involves some kind of contracts. Certainly the ERS Standards (and most active practitioners today) advocate explicit, indeed written, contracts. Consider a contract to perform the evaluation of a social program or policy system as a set of agreements about what is to be done, how it is to be done, who is to do it, and when it is to be accomplished. Its essence, like any contract, is to represent a meeting of minds on issues of importance. Evaluation practitioners should be aware of the fact that there are certain minimal elements behind an enforceable contract (and the reader should think a moment about how a contract that is not enforceable is hardly of any use at all). Those elements are: the mutual assent of parties to the contract, a meeting of minds about it, and an offer and an acceptance (Thurston, 1984). Those elements lead Thurston (1984) to specify the following guidelines for things to be included in an evaluation contract:

- An identification of the parties involved
- The type of evaluation desired
- The price
- The time of payment and completion dates
- The nature of the program to be evaluated (p. 18)

That list is not exhaustive, since there could be other important agreements that should be set out in writing, but minus these basic terms, the contract is considered "unformed." Thurston (1984) expresses what we believe to be an important point here. When there is debate over the interpretation of a term or in the absence of sufficient specificity, professional standards can be used to fill the gap. Custom and prevailing usage (practices) can perform the same function. In fact,

> where custom and usage are inconsistent with professional standards ". . . the courts will probably treat custom and usage . . . as more important than professional standards" (Thurston, 1984, p. 19).

Evaluation practitioners should also know that, loosely speaking, unless money (or something of value) changes hands, there is not an enforceable contract. Note also that oral agreements can be as enforceable as a written contract, though written contracts (where they exist) always have precedence over the oral contract, according to Thurston (1984, p. 19).

Malpractice and Confidentiality

While it seems too obvious to mention, it pays to keep in mind that professional malpractice is always judged against some applicable standard. Where evaluation practice, or any other professional practice for that matter, is judged to be below prevailing standard, a case could be made for malpractice. For example, the ERS Standards could be an important bench mark in this regard. We believe that it would be wise for evaluation practitioners to use the ERS Standards as a guide in this regard and certainly to resort to them where malpractice is threatened. It is quite possible that the ERS Standards do more to protect professional practitioners than they do to protect the consumers of the profession's product. That is commonly the case with professional standards of all sorts, and it is certainly an irony, since overriding public interest of any set of such standards is to protect the profession's clients. One of the problems caused by a set of practice standards that are as wobbly-kneed as the ERS Standards is that they can work to protect wrong-doers; bad practice can probably use one of its vague provisions (or lack thereof) for vindication and for protection against suits for malpractice.

A breach of confidentiality between an evaluator and a person providing data to an evaluator can be pursued through a malpractice charge, according to Thurston (1984, p. 21). The information that staff members have to give about organizational operations, about how important data was collected, about the existence of relevant documents can be of great importance to an evaluation. And, when such information is sometimes given under conditions of confidentiality, it is Thurston's opinion that, in general, the law supports the notion that privacy ought to be protected (1984, p. 21). While being threatened with a malpractice suit on account of a breach of confidentiality is not the common experience of evaluators, Thurston thinks it is a possibility, and that it would behoove practitioners to be quite careful about giving assurances of confidentiality to those who give them information, since the evaluator's ability to keep that promise is not always easy. Information which contributes to negative conclusions about an organization arouses hostility, naturally enough, and staff members who are believed to be instrumental in contributing to its revelation are likely to be the target of organizational revenge. That kind of revenge can be sufficiently damaging so that redress from the evaluation practitioner might be sought.

Sometimes it is even the case that the source of some kinds of data cannot really be disguised, despite the most earnest attempts—organizations may be too small or access to data systems sufficiently limited that a process of elimination will easily reveal those who are responsible. We believe that evaluators have a responsibility to foresee that kind of difficulty. Finally, evaluation practitioners might wish to consider carefully the fact that it is quite unlikely that they could keep a promise of confidentiality if a court of law sought the identity of sources. It is sobering to consider Thurston's advice in that regard: evaluators cannot protect sources any better than can journalists, ". . . short of being willing to go to jail in contempt of court when asked by the judge to identify them" (Thurston, 1984, p. 21).

Defamation of Character

To *defame character* means to injure a person's public reputation in some way. There are two general types of defamation of character: *libel,* which refers to the written form, and *slander,* which refers to the spoken form (Thurston, 1984, p. 15). With regard to evaluation practice, defamation of character would most likely take the form of characterizing a person so that it reflects negatively on their capabilities in their profession, employment, trade, or business. Thurston says that the characterization must be in the form of a statement about what the person does in the course of their occupation, it must be clearly connected with them in particular, it must be publicized by the defamer to a third party, and it must result in some damage. Note that public officials and "public figures" in general are not given protection against defamatory statements (Thurston, 1984, p. 17). Public officials are often those who are involved when the evaluator is considering whether the results of an evaluation might be construed by some person to be defamatory. Of course, defamation of character can be established if some kind of intended malice can be shown. Although it shouldn't have to be said, evaluation practitioners should know that they are liable to legal suit if they make statements that could be interpreted as defamatory and are in possession of information that they know is actually false, or if they have expressed serious doubts about the truthfulness of a statement but proceed without verifying its validity. Thurston (1984) believes that would be considered a "reckless" disregard of professional responsibility (p. 17).

Defamation of character suits can be defended against in several ways. If the person who believes they are defamed has approved of the statements, it is assumed that consent was given and no defamation can be charged. The generalization lawyers commonly make is that truth is always a defense against a charge of libel or slander. There can be nothing slanderous, libelous, or defamatory about a statement that is clearly true. It is important to be aware that the burden of proof is upon the one who is defamed, of course. Thus, it appears to be the case that where evaluation practitioners draw conclusions about social programs that others find offensive or downright defamatory, their main recourse must be upon the strength of their research findings—if they are not strong, then, of course, potentially libelous conclusions shouldn't be drawn.

One of the interesting kinds of principles of immunity against being charged with defamation is one which may apply particularly well to the situation of evaluation practitioners: the principle which gives qualified immunity to those who provide "fair comment and criticism" to things in the "public domain," such as books, legitimate theatre, and art shows. Thurston (1984) notes that to date there has been no case that specifically involved evaluation research and was pursued along those lines. On the face of it, most evaluators would probably agree that the public would profit by fair, "public" comment and criticism of public social programs in exactly the same sense in which it profits by an unfettered and public critique of books, theatre, and art shows.

Endnote

1. The Joint Committee Standards were clearly constructed with educational programs in mind: how could it be otherwise when (a) the title, of course, proclaims these standards to be . . . For Evaluating Educational Programs; (b) the members of the Joint Committee that oversaw the construction of the standards were appointed by twelve organizations, all but one having terms like "Education," "Teacher," "School," or "Curriculum" in their official titles.

References

Berk, R. A. (1982). Where angels fear to tread and why. In P. H. Rossi (Ed.), *Standards for evaluation practice* (pp. 59–66), New Directions for Program Evaluation Series, #15. San Francisco: Jossey-Bass.

Bonjean, C. (September 1980). On the costs of publishing evaluation research. *Social Science Quarterly*, 61(2), 329–332.

Cahn, J. (1982). Legal and government implications of the ERS standards for program evaluation. In P. H. Rossi (Ed.), *Standards for evaluation practice* (pp. 83–96). New Directions for Program Evaluation Series, #15. San Francisco: Jossey-Bass.

Carter, L. F. (1982). The standards for program evaluation and the large for-profit social science research and evaluation companies. In P. H. Rossi (Ed.), *Standards for evaluation practice* (pp. 37–48). New Directions for Program Evaluation Series, #15. San Francisco: Jossey-Bass.

Cordray, D. S. (1982). An assessment of the utility of the ERS standards. In P. H. Rossi (Ed.), *Standards for evaluation practice* (pp. 67–81). New Directions for Program Evaluation Series, #15. San Francisco: Jossey-Bass.

Cronbach, L. J. (1982). In praise of uncertainty. In P. H. Rossi (Ed.). *Standards for evaluation practice* (pp. 49–57). New Directions for Program Evaluation Series, #15. San Francisco: Jossey-Bass.

Evaluation Research Society Standards Committee. (1982). ERS Standards for program evaluation. In P. H. Rossi (Ed.), *Standards for evaluation practice* (pp. 7–20). New Directions for Program Evaluation Series, #15. San Francisco: Jossey-Bass.

Lincoln, Y. S. (1985). The ERS standards for program evaluation: Guidance for a fledging profession. *Evaluation and Program Planning, 8,* 251–253.

McGuire, D. (1982). Obligatory ideals. *Commonweal, 38,* 362–368.

Newman, R. (1980). Letter to the editor. *Social Science Quarterly, 61*(2), 324.

Rossi, P. H. (1982). Editors notes. In P. H. Rossi (Ed.), *Standards for evaluation practice* (pp. 3–6). New Directions for Program Evaluation Series, #15. San Francisco: Jossey-Bass.

Rossi, P. H., & Freeman, H. E. (1982). *Evaluation, a systematic approach,* 2nd Edition. Beverly Hills, CA: Sage.

Stufflebeam, D. L. (1982). Next step: Discussion to consider unifying the ERS and joint committee standards. In P. H. Rossi (Ed.), *Standards for evaluation practice* (pp. 27–36). New Directions for Program Evaluation Series, #15. San Francisco: Jossey-Bass.

Thurston, P. W., Ory, J. C., Mayberry, P. W., & Braskamp, L. A. (1984). Legal and professional standards in program evaluation. In *Educational Evaluation and Policy Analysis, 6*(1), 15–26.

CHAPTER FOUR

Needs Studies

The word *need* evokes many different meanings. Expression of need appears early in the infant human vocabulary, and continues to represent a significant component of human communication throughout the life processes. Psychological theories have been built around the concept of need. Economic dynamics can be explained, at least in part, by the notion of need. Social programs are based on assumptions of client need. Given these broad and encompassing features of need in the grand scheme of human behavior and social interaction, how can we place a viable handle on the idea of need for the purposes of needs studies? Our first step is to sort out usable definitions to guide us in the process of need determination.

Webster's Dictionary (1975, p. 768) gives the definition of need as "1: necessary duty: OBLIGATION; 2 a: a lack of something requisite, desirable, or useful, b: a physiological or psychological requirement for the well-being of an organism; 3. a condition requiring supply or relief: EXIGENCY; 4: a lack of the means of subsistence: POVERTY." For the purpose of our discussion, the meaning of need stated above in definition 2, 3 and 4 appear to have particular relevance. We are concerned with the identification of conditions that give rise to actions that may improve the functioning of individuals and groups within society. In some cases our attention is devoted simply to the documentation of a condition; as in a systematic inquiry into the number of homeless in a given community. In other cases, needs studies represent a consideration of that which is lacking or required to bring about change, as in a determination of special in-home care needs for the elderly. In either case, however, we are concerned with improving the human condition.

Conceptual Dimensions of Need

The concept of need is ambiguous and intermingled with implications for life-sustaining biological, emotional, social, and spiritual processes for preservation and development of the human organism. In this regard, needs can be thought of as necessary for: survival, growth and development, self-fulfillment, and ultimately for life ending processes. However, the conceptualization of need goes well beyond the individual organism to a consideration of community and societal processes as well. Collective as well as individual decision making is required in the expression and meeting of needs. A typology of needs offered by Bradshaw (1977) helps to conceptualize the interplay between individual and societal action in terms of needs. Four types of needs are described:

1. *Normative need* is determined when a standard is established and comparisons are made between the standard and what actually exists. When an individual or group falls short of a desirable standard, a need is said to exist. An example would be the poverty level, as determined by the standard of income required to sustain an individual or various sized family groupings.
2. *Felt need* is based on the perceptions of the individual experiencing need. It is equated with want, and may be biased evidence of "real" need when an individual is not fully informed, unable or reluctant to ask for help, or is thought to be inflating experienced need.
3. *Expressed need* is felt need turned into action. It is equated with demand, and represents existence of need based on those people who demand a service.
4. *Comparative need* is determined when individuals or groups receiving a service are used as a referent point for similar individuals or groups who do not receive the service. It is a measure of the existence of need based on the similarities of conditions and characteristics of those receiving a service, as for example in comparing populations and services provided in rural and urban areas.

McKillip (1987) adds an important dimension to the concept of need as the value judgment that some group has a problem that can be solved.

A conceptual approach taken by Gates (1980) further helps to expand on our understanding of need from a social science perspective. The conceptual framework includes: (1) the psychology and the sociology of need, (2) the economics of need, and (3) the political economy of need. The psychology of need is represented in needs of individuals and ranges from basic survival needs to needs for achievement and self actualization. Sociology of need is represented by the presence of cultural differences among groups in society as, for example, in the reality of the extended family role in child rearing. The economics of need deals with consumer and/or producer wants (needs) and aggregate consumption patterns represented in supply and demand. However, a distinction is made between needs and demands; *needs* refers to a client's interest in or preference for a certain service, and *demand* refers to concrete decisions made and actions taken related to meeting needs (Conner, Jacobi, Altman, and Aslanian, 1985). While the concept of need is alien in macroeconomic theory, the notion of need nevertheless has economic implications, as in policy initiatives to increase or decrease consumption through subsidies, tax credits, marketing, price controls, rationing, etc. The political economy of need is represented by social institutions that establish and implement social policies relative to need, as in a state legislature determining rights to services for special groups such as the mentally retarded and developmentally disabled.

Assessment of Need

Following from this brief conceptual overview of need, we next consider working definitions of needs assessment for *front-end evaluation* in the human services. Needs assessment can be defined as orientation to action. *Needs assessment* is defined as "systematic appraisal of type, depth, and scope of problems as perceived by study targets or their advocates" (Rossi, Freeman, and Wright, 1979, p. 82). Needs assessment may also imply a standard or norm to be considered. *Needs assessment* is "the difference between the extent of a condition or need in a given population and the amount of service provided to meet that need" (Mayer, 1985, p. 127).

Identifying Needs

Needs assessment may occur at different levels in the social welfare enterprise. As shown in Figure 4–1, needs may be identified for assessment activities as occurring in four broad categorical levels. First is the individual or group needs level. Much of what occurs in social program needs assessment is concerned with the needs of individuals or groups as clients or potential

---

FIGURE 4–1 • *Needs Levels*

Individual/Group Needs
    Food
    Shelter
    Social services
Organizational Needs
    Technical assistance
    Organizational development
    Training
Community Needs
    Neighborhood development
    Services coordination
    Funding
Societal Needs
    Social problem identification
    Demographic indicators
    Social policy analysis

---

recipients of social programs. The needs assessment purpose is client oriented. Needs assessment at the organizational level may also be concerned with the needs of individuals or groups, such as in the case of training needs for certain personnel. The emphasis is on a particular facet of organizational functioning as opposed to needs of those who are or may be recipients of organizational services. Community needs studies may represent a focus on individual/group needs, but usually in broader context, that is, they are community oriented. An example would be a needs study sponsored by a United Way Agency to determine community-wide social problems and special need groups. At the societal level, needs studies take on an even broader scope. An example would be a needs study to determine current needs for low-income housing at a given point in time. While our attention in this chapter is directed more to the concerns with needs of individuals and groups as clients or potential clients, similar methodologies are often employed in individual organizational, and community or societal needs studies.

The program evaluator will find it useful to gain a perspective on the nature of need being considered. Is it a natural need, such as in the case of biologically determined needs: food, shelter, security, or medical condition? Is it a need which has been created such as in the case of unsanctioned social behavior? A further categorization of needs emerges when needs are seen as manifestations of specific social problems. Jansson (1984) provides a categorical scheme based on various forms of deprivation. These forms of individual/group level needs are presented in Table 4–1. The consideration of needs as deprivation brings up an additional delineation useful to consider in the planning stages of needs studies. Does need arise from a clearly determined cause, or factors which sustain the need and/or block the meeting of need? With regard to this dichotomy, Mayer (1985, p. 129) suggests that sustaining and blocking functions can be identified initially through literature search for theoretical frameworks that have been developed for understanding a condition in question. An example would be discriminatory hiring practices blocking affected individuals and groups from achieving full employment potential.

The above sets forth a broad scheme for initial thoughts in the identification of need and scope or level for needs assessment inquiry. Next we consider application of the research technology common to the subject areas covered in this book, as it applies in the case of needs studies. First considered are the issues derived from the quality/quantity dichotomy.

Need Technology

It is doubtful that we can come to an agreement on the definition of an area of need, a general description of the need identified and level at which a needs study could occur, without further considerations. Take for instance a case of

TABLE 4-1 • Selected Forms of Deprivation

Material Resources Deprivation	Developmental Deprivation	Physical Deprivation	Interpersonal Deprivation	Deprivation of Opportunity	Deprivation of Personal Rights
Inadequate income	Various forms of mental illness	Various forms of physical illness	Marital conflict	Lack of education	Lack of basic civil rights (voting, free speech, due process)
Inadequate food	Developmental disabilities	Addictions to alcohol and other toxic substances	Destructive child-parent relations	Lack of access to social services	
Inadequate housing	Bereavement and other crises	Malnutrition	Loneliness	Lack of access to medical services	Lack of equal access to employment and promotions
Inadequate or blighted community	Lack of challenging work	Handicaps	Lack of adequate recreation	Lack of access to employment	Lack of equal access to services
				Lack of "survival skills" (e.g., knowledge of employment markets and job-related skills)	Commitment to mental or other instututions in absence of procedural safeguards

Source: Jansson, B. S. (1984). *Theory and practice of social welfare policy: Analysis, processes, and current issues.* Belmont, CA: Wadsworth, p. 8. Used by permission.

need based on the "material resources deprivation" of "inadequate food" as listed in Table 4–1. For the sake of discussion, let's consider such deprivation for older persons (age fifty-five or over) confined to their own homes. First is the recognition that the definition of *adequacy* is a value-laden and highly subjective concept without further information. We can easily pursue this matter by clarifying whether we are talking about amounts of food available, nutritional value of food consumed, regularity of food intake, and so on. Regardless of which criterion, or multiple criteria, we choose, it will still require the use of a standard to fully define what we mean by adequate. Following our example further, we can specify adequacy of food for older persons by following the standard of minimum daily requirements suggested by the Department of Agriculture. Title III-C of the Older Americans Act uses this standard in policies for provision of meals to older persons in congregate settings and those confined to their homes. Our example reveals how a standard helps to determine, in qualitative terms, what we mean by adequacy. In fact, needs assessment could be undertaken to gather information that would assist policy makers in making determinations for setting such standards. In the case of our example, a standard becomes a dividing line between adequacy and deprivation. Given the above standard, we are now in a position to quantitatively enumerate needs based on a study of a given population of older persons. Our attention is now directed to basic technical issues that arise in the quantification of needs.

While we can now consider the matter of measuring needs, it is important first to consider an important intervening factor. In reality, the measurement concerns an enumeration of conditions from which numerical estimates of need can be drawn. An assumption is that meeting a need will, in fact, also alleviate a condition assumed undesirable. Gates (1980) points out that it is entirely possible that the same condition can be alleviated by meeting one of a large variety of different needs. "The effect is that needs cannot be measured directly; instead, one first enumerates conditions, one then establishes relationships between the various needs that, if met, will alleviate those conditions, and then one enumerates needs" (Gates, 1980, p. 119). The adoption of quantitative methods for enumerating conditions upon which estimates of needs are based also requires that the needs assessor confront common problems in measurement of need variables. The reader is referred to Chapter Nine of this text for a discussion of common problems that will be confronted in social research measurement activity.

Methodology in Need Studies

A number of methodological approaches have been developed for application in needs studies. In the discussion which follows, the various methodologies are grouped according to whether the emphasis is qualitative or quantitative in nature. Approaches in both groups have been found useful, and the application of one or more particular methodologies will vary according to factors associated with time, cost, feasibility, level of precision required, etc. The various qualitative methodologies will be discussed first.

Qualitative Approaches

Key informant Key informants are used in both qualitative and quantitative approaches to needs assessment. The focus in this section will be primarily on the use of qualitative data gathering techniques with key informants, while later in this chapter we will cover quantitative techniques that also utilize key informants for data sources.

Key informants are persons who are asked to provide critical information which will contribute to an understanding of need. The key informant approach rests on the assumption that identifiable individuals or groups of individuals possess information about certain social conditions, hence need indicators. Usually the persons who would be selected as key informants have some firsthand knowledge of the condition under study, or in some cases perhaps they have even directly experienced the condition. Individuals normally sought out to serve as key informants include policy makers, those currently engaged in service delivery, users of services, and others who are in a position to regularly communicate with persons who experience given needs. Potentially, key informants may represent groups as divergent as elected public officials to bartenders. Logical sources for key informants include: public officials; social program administrators and service giving personnel; clergy; school administrators and teachers, health care personnel; law enforcement personnel and other community leaders.

While key informants may directly supply the data which constitutes the needs study, they can also serve as intermediaries for data sources. In the latter instance, key informants provide needed information that is then refined for inclusion in further inquiry, often in more quantitative approaches to needs assessment. An example would be the use of key informants to identify critical uses in a social condition which, in turn, serves as input in a needs assessment survey.

An initial step in the key informant approach involves the identification and selection of key informants. A purposive selection process is often preferred and can be quite effective when it can be based on known factors, such as availability of informants, time they may be willing to give, and resources required to reach informants. This is particularly the case when the key informants are used as an intermediate source in the collection of needs data. When greater precision is required for purposes of reliability and validity in use of key informants, as in the quantitative approaches discussed later, special effort will be necessary in securing informants—such as in the use of sampling technology.

Several techniques are available for securing information from key informants. Personal interviews have the advantage of interactive communication between needs assessor and informant. Face-to-face contact allows for clarification of questions and answers, though it can be time consuming and more or less costly. A high participation rate can often be achieved through carefully planning to interview key informants. Telephone interviews can also be successful, though much depends on the informants' knowledge of the authenticity and purpose of the assessment. The telephone interview works best when the key informant has prior knowledge of the needs study and/or the caller. Another popular technique is the mailed questionnaire. The data received from a well-designed questionnaire can result in ease of comparison and clear delineation of key informant choices among posed options. The major drawbacks to the mailed questionnaire with key informants, as in other areas of social research, are cost in preparation of questionnaire documents and mailing expenses, relatively low response rates, and limitations to data collection imposed by questionnaire format. In general, the more information requested by a mailed questionnaire, the less likely a high return rate. Multiple use of these techniques can be very productive. For instance, a brief mailed questionnaire with a follow-up telephone interview is often quite useful. Another suggested approach is the reverse: the brief telephone interview followed up by a personal interview or mailed questionnaire.

The key informant approach allows for considerable flexibility in the amount of structure to apply to the process. For some occasions it is desirable and appropriate to leave the structure completely exploratory and open-ended. In many cases, particularly when it is decided to utilize a mailed questionnaire, some minimal structuring will be beneficial.

Open-ended questions yield information about individuals' stated impressions, attitudes, and personal experiences. They are particularly useful in exploring ideas about needs and probing for background information, especially in the case of telephone and face-to-face personal interviews. Thoughtful, qualitative, open-ended interview questions are worded in language that:

1. Permits the respondent to take whatever direction and use whatever words he or she wants to convey an answer
2. Is understandable
3. Gives a clear indication of interviewer neutrality
4. Is sensitive
5. Probes deeper in the interview process
6. Establishes a two-way flow of communication
7. Allows the interviewer to maintain control of the interview (Moore, 1982, pp. 169–179)

Recording of data during the key informant interview is a critical detail. Tape recording and transcribing are popular alternatives. Note taking is considered essential even when other recording methods are employed, for the following reasons:

> Notes taken during the interview can help formulate new questions as the interview moves along, particularly where it may be appropriate to check out something that was said earlier; and taking notes about what is said will facilitate later analysis, including locating important questions from the tape itself (Moore, 1982, pp. 179–180).

Immediately following the interview, summarization of data and reactions to the interview process are recorded in preparation for data analysis and interpretation.

Open-ended questions may also be combined with structured questions in mailed questionnaires or for interviews with key informants when more specific or comparable data is required. The use of combined fixed-alternative and open-ended questions is discussed further under the topic of needs assessment surveys.

Some follow-up on the key informant approach is suggested. In general we can expect the informants to value a note of appreciation for their efforts. Additional advantage can be gained through further participation of the key informants. This is particularly so when the initial data provided by informants serves the intermediate purposes mentioned above. Warheit, Bell, and Schwab (1977) suggest that, as an extension of this approach all of the informants can be brought together to discuss the findings of the study. Follow-up of this nature can provide a dynamic setting for further insights into needs being addressed.

Case study   The case study approach in needs assessment involves an analysis of circumstances currently known or readily available about a particular social condition in a particular locality or situation. A case study represents an attempt to understand underlying causes of a condition, and the sustaining and blocking factors involved as roadblocks to improvement. Through an understanding of the facts associated with a particular case, generalizations can be made to similarly affected individuals and groups. A case may constitute a single individual or family, small representation of such individuals or families, a social agency, or even a community. Regardless of the specific elements of the case, the process is similar. Through an understanding of needs from a case, generalizations can be made to a broader collective.

A major advantage of the case study is its economic appeal. Generally, a case study approach can be relatively inexpensive if adequate information is already available. A disadvantage to the case study approach is the error factor that may occur when generalizing from the specific to the general. An example would be in using the case study to determine needs of the small family farm to project the needs of small family farmers generally. It is extremely difficult to control the many intervening variables that play a role in determining the fate of the small family farmer. Another example would be with the homeless. A case study can be very insightful in helping to understand some of the dynamics that are involved in the condition currently being described as homeless, but which fall short in representing basic needs of all who are afflicted by the condition. In sum, the case study approach is seldom adequate by itself as a needs assessment method, but in combination with other methodology it can be a very useful qualitative addition.

On-site visit Related to the case study discussed above, the on-site visit approach is another qualitative method that is useful in gaining insights about a particular social condition. Too often program evaluators have prepared paper needs assessments without ever viewing firsthand the dynamics of the subject under observation. The on-site visit can be an early exploratory approach to needs assessment, or as with other qualitative approaches discussed here, it can be structured more for purposes of collecting specific data. An example of an on-site visit for purposes of needs assessment would be to spend a day observing the processing of contacts at a helpline service agency. The needs assessor will pay particular attention to how requests are received, how they are handled, the information collected and recorded, and referrals made. This approach begins with the notion that, through basic observation, it will be possible to gain insight into the nature of requests, and from such observations initial hunches about the condition under study developed.

As in the use of case study, this approach is most often made effective in combination with other methodologies in needs assessment. Although some social conditions do not lend themselves to an on-site visit approach, in many cases this method can be invaluable in defining and understanding needs. A chief advantage of the approach is that it is relatively cost efficient and easy to arrange. The on-site visit alone, however, is seldom adequate as an approach to make concluding generalizations about needs under study.

Semi-structured groups Semi-structured groups provide information sources on social conditions as need indicators through informal group processes. Here we are using the term *informal* to indicate that while some structuring is necessary to initiate the group process, the interaction of group members is relied on as an information source. The two popular techniques of semi-structured groups for needs assessment are the *hearing,* and the *forum.* The hearing approach will be discussed first.

The hearing, or more commonly referred to as public hearing, has become popularized through efforts to increase the participation of consumers and interested parties in many public social programs. Title XX (Social Service Block Grant) social service programs, for instance, greatly expanded the use of hearings to involve social service clientele. Although there is usually a basic purpose for holding a hearing, the absence of more formal constraints of structure allows informal group processes to arise. One outcome of the hearing is a source for information that can be useful to the needs assessor. The use of this approach is economical, since the hearing is typically scheduled for more over-arching purposes and does not require any special arrangements. In other words, it is taking advantage of a group meeting that has already been set up. Another advantage is that it brings a group of persons affected by the social condition together in one place, and often the needs assessor can interact with individuals in addition to observing the group process. On the more negative side, hearings can often be dominated by one, or a few, vocal individuals who may represent narrowly based interests or concerns. The hearing can be an important source of information, but it is seldom sufficient as a single approach to establish a set of needs. Often it will aid the needs assessor in a determination of the tone set by a social program and reveal expressed unmet need as perceived by persons affected by existing programming.

The forum approach is a semi-structured group meeting designed to illicit information from individuals about the needs and service patterns of extant programs that provide for need. The forum may range in dimension from a small group of interested persons concerned about a particular social problem to a community wide forum. In any case, the forum is designed around a meeting or series of meetings to which individuals are invited and asked to express their beliefs about social conditions and the needs they perceive to exist. The process involves structuring the session(s) around key issues, yet allowing latitude for spontaneity in the group interaction.

Usually it is desirable to publicize the forum and encourage attendance from representatives of individuals and groups who might share a concern in the condition under study. Use of mass media, announcements at social agencies, and mailed announcements can be especially helpful in advertising the forum. In the case of the community forum, all segments of the community's population should be encouraged to attend.

While a forum can begin in a large meeting, such an environment is not conducive to the open interchange desired. An opening large meeting can provide the structure to state goals and objectives of the forum, ground rules, basic information sharing, assignment to smaller group, and other logistical tasks. Following such an opening session, small groups are formed for the purpose of group interaction which will lead to desired information sharing and expression of perceived needs. Depending on the number of persons involved and other relevant variables, a large initial forum meeting may not be called for. A strategically located meeting or meetings can be planned, so that small groups are allowed to begin interacting with a minimum of front-end structuring.

Many group dynamics techniques are available to move smaller groups along on the task of expressing beliefs about needs. A particularly important activity is the recording of ideas, attitudes, and perceptions of those participating. To assist in this process, a comprehensive recording schedule is suggested, with special attention to a listing of all suggestions made by participants. A final step is a summary of suggestions regarding needs identified, with a special notation of items accorded a high priority. A checklist of priorities can be provided to each person at the end of the session with the instructions to return it to the forum sponsor. Warheit, Bell, and Schwab (1977) offer a sample schedule for the collection of such information regarding the perceptions and suggestions of those attending a community forum as presented in Figure 4-2. Their example involves a survey of the mental health needs of a community, and includes a computerized coding procedure.

The forum approach is relatively easy to conduct and inexpensive to carry out. It has the advantage of bringing together divergent viewpoints and the opportunity to distill the information afforded through group process. Further, it has the added advantage of involving concerned citizens who may be a lobbying force when efforts are undertaken later to bring about measures of reform or desired service provision. The forum approach is not without some major disadvantages as well. First, it is often difficult to bring together a significant number of knowledgeable citizens who truly represent the various segments of effected or concerned individuals and groups. Another significant disadvantage is that, as in the semi-structured hearing discussed above, it can be very difficult to keep groups on track, and to keep them from shifting from positive efforts toward problem solving to general gripe sessions. A further disadvantage is that the involvement of individuals (especially current social agency clients) in the forum may heighten their expectations for an unrealistic change in current conditions. Finally, it should be remembered that information derived through the forum can be highly impressionistic, difficult to analyze in a systematic and comparative fashion, and lacking in so far as it may fail to tap a truly representative attitude toward the expression of needs. As in the case of the hearing, the needs assessor can rarely afford to rely entirely on the information gained from the forum, but it can be a very beneficial supplement to other needs assessment approaches.

Structured groups   Structured groups provide information sources on social conditions as need indicators through more formal group processes. By formal, we mean that such groups are purposefully structured with selected individuals to accomplish goals and objectives set out by the needs assessor. In recent years numerous group dynamics techniques have been developed which have been applied to needs assessment through the structured group. Several of the more commonly reported approaches to structured groups for

---

FIGURE 4–2 • *Community Forum Interview Schedule*

	Column	Code in Office
	1–4	_____
		ID Number
	5	___ Card No.
1. Location of Meeting:		
_____	6–7	_____
	8–9	_____
2. Date of Meeting:		
Day _____ Month_____ Year_____	10–11	_____
	12–13	_____
	14–15	_____
3. What Is Your Race?	16	_____
1 White		
2 Black		
3 Other _____		
4. What Is Your Sex?	17	_____
1 Male		
2 Female		
5. What Was Your Age on Your Last Birthday? _____	18–19	
6. What Do You Consider Your Main Job or Occupation?	20–22	_____
_____		
Describe by Title and Kind of Work		
7. Every Community Has Individuals Who Are in Need of Mental Health Services. About What Percentage of the People in This Community Would You Estimate Are Receiving Some Form of Mental Health Service?		
_____ actual percentage	23–24	_____
8. What Additional Percentage of Individuals in the Community Need Mental Health Services But Are Not Receiving Them?		
_____ actual percentage	25–26	_____

FIGURE 4–2 *Continued*

	Column	Code in Office
9. In Your Opinion, What Are the Most Pressing Mental Health Needs of Those Living in Our Community?		
	27–28	
	29–30	
	31–32	
	33–34	
	35–36	

10. In Every Community, Some Groups of Persons Have More Mental Health Needs Than Others. From the List Below, Please Rate the Needs of Those Living in This Community:

	Much Above Average	Some Above Average	Average	Some Below Average	Much Below Average	Column	Code in Office
a. White Men	1	2	3	4	5	37	
b. Black Men	1	2	3	4	5	38	
c. White Women	1	2	3	4	5	39	
d. Black Women	1	2	3	4	5	40	
e. The Young	1	2	3	4	5	41	
f. The Middle-aged	1	2	3	4	5	42	
g. The Elderly	1	2	3	4	5	43	
h. Rural Residents	1	2	3	4	5	44	
i. Small-Town Residents	1	2	3	4	5	45	
j. City Residents	1	2	3	4	5	46	

	Column	Code in Office
11. What Kind of Services Do You Feel Should be Provided to Meet These Special Needs?		
	47–48	
	49–50	
	51–52	
	53–54	
	55–56	

Source: Warheit, G. J., Bell, R. A., and Schwab, J. J. (1977) *Needs assessment approaches: Concepts and methods.* Washington, D.C.: U.S. Government Printing Office, p. 111.

use in needs assessment activities are discussed below; they include focus groups, nominal groups, and Delphi groups.

Focus groups   Focus groups have been popularly used as a technique to determine advertising strategy, attractiveness of new product lines, and consumer preference for products and services (Advertising Research Foundation, 1985). Focus groups for needs assessment in the human services can be composed of representatives of the proposed target population, or be representatives of citizens with special knowledge about the social condition under study. Small groups are structured to provide a dynamic environment in which participants interact with one another to give shape and definition to needs, and, through an interactive process, check the validity of one another's reactions.

The components of a focus group are fairly simple and easy to apply. The structure and expected processes for a focus group of representatives made up of target group members are outlined in the following:

1. *A moderator or moderators are given responsibility for leading the discussion, and to assist group participants focus on the problem under consideration. Participants are generally encouraged to respond in their own terms, although the moderator helps to keep group discussion on track.*

2. *Participants (usually eight to ten) are selected to represent the target population under consideration. Group composition should be homogeneous enough to allow for free interaction among participants. Depending on the circumstances, it may be preferable that participants be unfamiliar with each other in order to maximize creative expression.*

3. *Participants are encouraged to be creative and express feelings as well as ideas about needs in sessions lasting up to 90 minutes. All members of the group are encouraged to participate, and interaction between participants is encouraged.*

The focus group approach has the advantage of being relatively inexpensive. It can serve as a source of information on the target population members' perception of need, either in place of, or supplemental to, individual interviews and quantitative approaches to needs assessment. Tape recording focus groups offers the possibility of double checking first impressions on the expression of need. The disadvantages lie in questions about validity and consistency in responses to need. In this regard, the needs assessor is encouraged to address the issue of validity by examining whether the focus group is measuring what it proposes to measure.

... *if you conducted focus groups to gain perceptions on a potential program, did the focus group procedure really provide perceptions on this program or were the results artificially developed by the interactions of group participants (Krueger, 1988, p. 41).*

It is often preferred to conduct a series of focus group meetings with different participants, and to utilize the focus group in conjunction with other needs assessment approaches.

For more information on focus groups, the reader is referred to Krueger (1988), VanGundy (1988), and Greenbaum (1988).

Nominal groups   The nominal group technique (NGT) developed by Delbecq and Van de Ven (1971) serves to help overcome superfluous group dynamics of more unstructured groups in program planning activities. NGT allows for idea generation and evaluation of idea content with a minimum of adverse group dynamics content. As in the focus group, NGT can be used with clients, key informants, citizens, or service providers or others assembled to identify and examine conditions or problems and associated needs indicators.

In preparation for the group interaction of NGT, premeeting activities include: (1) formulating and pilot testing (with group leaders) of the question to be raised, (2) assembling required supplies such as flip charts, index cards, paper, etc., (3) preparation of meeting room, with adequate number of tables for subgroups, and (4) training inexperienced group leaders (Moore, 1987, pp. 25–26).

The time required for a nominal group meeting is generally from an hour and a half to three hours in length. Nominal groups can be created from a larger audience of individuals or, at a minimum, as few as five or six individuals. The separate steps required for conducting a nominal group process are briefly outlined as follows:

1. Participants are divided into subgroups of five to nine participants around a table, and a subgroup leader is given responsibilities for guiding the group process.

2. Individuals are allowed time to react to the question (need statement) through a silent idea generation period. Participants are asked by the subgroup leader to give responses to the question with short written phrases before any verbal interaction takes place.

3. A round-robin reporting of ideas takes place among subgroup participants. Ideas are recorded on newsprint for participants to see, though discussion is discouraged at this point.

4. Open discussion and clarification are allowed among subgroup participants, with the leader encouraging participants to ask one another the thinking behind ideas reported.

5. A ranking of ideas is accomplished by combining the judgments of each subgroup participant. Subgroup participants privately rank their favored ideas (usually the top five) on index cards, and the composite of rankings are reported on newsprint.

6. An opportunity for further clarification may be provided and another round of ranking conducted if there appear to be particularly divergent individual rankings in the previous step.

7. Rankings for the subgroups are combined, and a report of aggregate rankings is reported for the entire group.

The end product of the nominal group process is a priority ranking of answers to various need analysis questions.

The advantages of the nominal group are similar to those for the focus group. The nominal group is relatively inexpensive in terms of efficiency, and can be a particularly effective way to process the wisdom of key informants. Even though special efforts are made to structure out unwanted group dynamics, limitations, as with the other group approaches discussed here, may be factors. Taken alone, the outcome of nominal groups may be suspect as to validity of results.

For further information on the specifics of nominal groups, the reader is referred to Moore (1987), Ulschak, Nathanson, and Gillan (1981), and Delbecq, Van de Ven, and Gustafson (1975).

Delphi groups   The Delphi group approach has received popularity as a means of multiple-source forecasting on a wide range of social and environmental subjects. It is an interactive, structured group process based on the use of several rounds of written questionnaires that give the participants feedback on what others say and why they differ in their opinions. As typically applied, the Delphi approach differs in one fundamental respect from the other structured group approaches discussed here. The group interaction in Delphi is through written anonymous exchanges, not face-to-face interactions. On each round the participants are permitted to change their previously expressed opinions on the basis of feedback from other participants' responses on previous rounds. Usually, at least three rounds are required. After the final round has been completed, a summary of the groups' conclusions/recommendations is prepared.

The minimum and maximum number of participants required for a Delphi group is not fixed. However, less than five participants or greater than twenty would suggest problems in the balance of responses in the first instance, and manageability in the latter.

An outline of the basic steps for a three-round Delphi investigation is paraphrased from VanGundy (1988) in the following:

> 1. *A question (or need statement) is developed by a work group conducting the Delphi technique that can be clearly understood by the group members, and later the panel of experts.*
>
> 2. *Respondents to serve as an expert panel are selected and contacted. They should reveal a sense of personal involvement or interest in the question, have knowledge about the situation, and be motivated to participate. A nomination process is used to recruit and select respondents, usually from a target population of well-known, knowledgeable individuals.*
>
> 3. *Based on the question (or need statement) in step 1, a questionnaire is developed and tested with the panel of experts. The initial questionnaire poses the broad question to the respondents, and usually allows for open-ended responses.*

4. *The results of questionnaire #1 are summarized in such a way that they can be understood clearly by the panel of experts in the second questionnaire. The work group conducting the Delphi technique records responses on index cards, sorts the cards into common categories, develops consensus on labels for each category, and prepares summaries reflecting the content of the categories.*

5. *Questionnaire #2 is developed using summarized responses in questionnaire #1. The focus of the second questionnaire should be on identifying areas of agreement or disagreement, opportunity to clarify meanings, and establishing tentative priorities placed on topics or solutions. Panelists are typically asked to rank or reveal agreement on items presented in this round. Following the testing out of questionnaire #2 with a group on nonparticipants, it is then mailed out to panel participants.*

6. *The results of questionnaire #2 are analyzed, with special attention given by the work group to determine if the information provided will help towards arriving at an agreeable outcome, make alterations needed in the questioning process, or deciding if the process should be terminated.*

7. *Questionnaire #3 (if the process continues) is developed using summarized results from questionnaire #2. The intent of questionnaire #3 is to pull together the entire Delphi process. The questionnaire is again tested with nonparticipants, and mailed out to the panelists.*

8. *The results of questionnaire #3 are analyzed as in the previous round, and a final report is prepared. The final report typically contains a review of the original question, goals of the Delphi process, procedures used, final results, and, if possible, any actions taken as a result of the Delphi group technique (pp. 325–326).*

Variants of the Delphi group may be applied in efforts to achieve the overall goals of this structured group approach. Included are variations in the number of rounds used, the questionnaire format, and the structure of the expert panel. An abbreviated Delphi procedure called the *mini-Delphi* is particularly useful when order-of-magnitude estimates are called for (Helmer, 1976). In the mini-Delphi a significant amount of anonymity of the regular Delphi process is abandoned and the expert panel is assembled in the same room. The procedure for using a mini-Delphi is outlined as follows:

1. *Each panelist is directed to independently and secretly write down an estimate of the quantity in question. Responses are collected and collated, and the resulting distribution is displayed before the group. Specific responses are not identified by the panelist giving the response.*

2. *A brief debate takes place, and panelists are given the opportunity to defend relatively low or relatively high responses.*

3. *Each panelist is directed to once more vote independently and secretly. Responses are collected and again collated; the median of responses is accepted as the group's consensus (Helmer, 1976, p. 15).*

The Delphi group approach is flexible and relatively inexpensive to carry out. A chief advantage of Delphi over the other structured group approaches discussed here for needs assessment is that it is designed as an interactive method to avoid face-to-face intimidation and group think dynamics. Another advantage is that it is possible to involve participants in a group process where resource constraints preclude face-to-face interaction; participants in the Delphi may potentially be from throughout the nation, or worldwide.

The Delphi group was developed for the purpose of forecasting, and therefore emphasis is more on the future than with other structured groups. Its use as a needs assessment method need not be limited by that feature, but it is probably safe to say that it has a more proven track record in considering a projection of future needs.

The Delphi group used alone raises similar validity issues as discussed with other structured group approaches. There are also some technical disadvantages with the Delphi. While it can be ego flattering to be asked to participate in a Delphi group, the commitment to see the process through may be difficult to sustain for a length of time. When one or more participants drop out, reliability for the approach is threatened. The full process of planning, developing a questionnaire, selecting and contacting participants, processing response, and compiling results makes this the most time involved of the structured group processes discussed. Consequently, it may lose the advantage of being relatively inexpensive to conduct if opportunity costs are taken into consideration.

For further information on the Delphi group, the reader is referred to McKillip (1987), Moore (1987), and Linstone and Turoff (1975).

Quantitative Approaches

Services inventory Services, or resource inventory, is a method for determination of services and/or resources available to a designated population. The purpose of the services inventory is to document type and scope of services currently available, overlaps, underutilization, and gaps in services available or delivered. It is concerned with who provides what to whom. In many respects the services inventory can be thought of as a mix between the qualitative and quantitative approach; we treat it here as quantitative because of the strong emphasis on enumeration of quantifiable data, such as number of services delivered, etc. However, qualitative issues will appear in any attempt at services inventory.

While services inventory is not usually a means to directly assess need, it is important as a means to overview the environment or *suprasystem* for a given target population with a specified geographic location. If such knowledge is not currently known to the needs assessor, a strong argument can be made to undertake a services inventory before other needs assessment methodology are employed.

In order to begin an inventory of services, it is first necessary to consider an appropriate classification system for the target population categories, service provider categories, and service categories. While it may be necessary for the needs assessor to develop a classification system, several schemes are available which may be adaptable or provide models for the construction of a classification system to fit the situation confronting the needs assessor. Considered here are three general models or schemes for classification: the comprehensive community planning model; the client functioning model; and the service program attributes model.

Perhaps the best known and most widely used classification system representing the comprehensive community planning model is the United Way of America's UWASIS II: A Taxonomy of Social Goals & Human Service Programs (1976). UWASIS hierarchically arranges programs and service aggregates in relation to either interdependent human and social service goals: optimal income security and economic opportunity; optimal health; optimal provision of basic material needs; optimal opportunity for the acquisition of knowledge and skills; optimal environmental quality; optimal individual and collective safety; optimal social functioning; and optimal assurance of the support and effectiveness of services through organized action. A second level in the taxonomy identifies thirty-three different categories of services systems, each of which is aligned with a major goal. A third level in the taxonomy identifies 231 specific services, each aligned within its appropriate parent service system. Finally, the service level is subcategorized into some 587 specific programs, each directed toward the achievement of an objective.

Client functioning classification models start with an attempt to categorize according the to level of problem, rather than according to the solution to the problem, as in UWASIS II. One of the most widely known examples in the human services is the *Diagnostic and Statistical Manual of Mental Disorders* (DSM III-R) (American Psychiatric Association, 1988). DSM III provides an elaborate listing of standardized problem areas in mental functioning, and provides a basis for categorizing mental health problems. Other classification systems of individual functioning attempt to categorize problems according to physical disabilities, levels of educatability, job skill levels, etc.

The quantification of needs by levels of client functioning can be particularly useful in matching specific areas of need with current levels of service provision. The resulting information will be used to identify overlaps, underutilization, and gaps in services.

Service program attributes models for classification represent an additional information source useful to the needs assessor. The list of possible attributes for inclusion in such a classification system will vary according to situational circumstances. However, it is possible to identify some of the more obvious attributes that will concern the needs assessor. Eligibility criteria for services are usually an important factor for consideration. Service capacity indicators such as presence or absence of waiting lists for services is another variable that can be useful information. Also of potential interest to the needs assessor is whether fee structures for services are present, and how they are administered. Such information can be useful in identifying the characteristics of service provision, assess the capacity of agencies to deliver services, and, if increased demand is anticipated, the expansion requirements. However, Moroney (1977) cautions that "these sorts of data reflect demand and measure only the tip of the iceberg as far as need is concerned. The population that comes into contact with human services agencies is probably different from the nonuser population, and it is conceivable that these very differences determine service utilization" (p. 144). Given these words of caution, service capacity data, as well as data on other service program attributes, can still provide useful information that, when combined with needs estimates, moves the needs assessment process toward resource allocation decisions. As mentioned above, a particular advantage of the service inventory approach is that it provides an "overview" for the needs assessment process. Although the service inventory will not provide data about the prevalence of unmet need, when integrated with other approaches, it greatly assists in an understanding of services currently available to current target population groups. Overall, a service inventory can be relatively inexpensive if required data are available and accessible. When the geographic area covered is extensive and service issues complex, it can become relatively time-consuming and costly to carry out a reputable service inventory.

Service utilization   The study of service utilization patterns is also sometimes used for needs assessment purposes. It is an effort to combine client characteristics with service capacity information discussed above under the services inventory approach. In addition to documenting services used, the approach may include various identifying characteristics of clients, such as sociodemographic data, presenting problem, frequency of service received, outcome of service received, etc. This approach is also commonly called the *rates-under-treatment* (RUT) approach (Warheit, Bell, and Schwab, 1977).

Advantages to the service utilization approach for needs assessment can be found in the availability of data and relatively low cost of collecting and analyzing data. It can also lead to previously undisclosed insights for the needs assessor through greater familiarity with service programs and the characteristics of clients served. Also, it can serve an important function in increased communications between the human service agencies and providers in a community that often raise the general level of sensitivity to the needs of a community and, at the same time, foster greater integration of services possible (Warheit, Bell, and Schwab, 1977). The limitations of the service utilization, however, are several.

First is the problem of estimating need on the basis of those currently receiving services. Service utilization rates, for instance, describe the status quo. They may or may not be effective indicators of met need, depending on variables that can be difficult to identify immediately. Further, the patterns of current service utilization may offer a very weak generalization for expected use of a new service to respond to new or currently unmet needs. On an agency based level of data collection, even under the best of circumstances it can be a problem for an outsider to gain access to agency records. Unless a guarantee of complete anonymity and confidentially is possible, it can be expected that some data loss will result in this approach. Another major problem arises in the fact that there is little consistency in keeping of agency records and case records. Agency records are kept for the purposes of accountability and management control. Agency case records are kept for similar purposes, as well as for tracking progress of individual cases, not for potential use in need assessment. The point is that what is expected to be learned from agency service information can often fall short of expectations.

Service utilization can also be a useful approach to documenting program implementation, and a more detailed discussion on the technology of this approach is presented in Chapter Seven.

Statistical indicators The statistical indicators approach is based on quantitative measures of selected social characteristics of geographic areas and persons living within those geographical areas. It is an effort to infer need from the analysis of descriptive information thought to be closely associated (or correlated) with need. Commonly used as statistical indicators are a population's sociodemographic and socioeconomic characteristics, such as age, gender, race, education, employment/unemployment, income, family composition, etc. Other factors that can serve as indicators include physical characteristics, such as spatial arrangements of people and institutions, and of housing; natural barriers and divisions such as rivers and hills; and man-made divisions such as railroad tracks, highways, housing developments, etc. Especially popular for human services need assessment are the social behavior or social condition characteristics that can be obtained for a given population grouping. Some examples are mobility, marriage and divorce rates, crime rates, substance abuse, child abuse, teenage pregnancy, voting patterns, and church attendance.

Statistical indicators are aggregate measures, such as rates and averages, that characterize a given population. Statistical indicators are used to describe: (1) populations, for example, ethnicity, age, or place of residence, (2) government expenditures and other inputs, for example, spending on education or number of physicians, and (3) social welfare or quality of life measures, for example, crime rates and unemployment (McKillip, 1987, pp. 43–44). It should be remembered that statistical indicators are merely aggregate measures that serve to describe the collective of people and conditions within a given geographic area. Such measures, in and of themselves, do not serve to enumerate individual needs. The underlying assumption is that it is possible to make useful estimates of the needs and social well-being of those in given geographic areas by analyzing statistics on factors found to be highly correlated with persons in need (a population-at-risk) (Warheit, Bell, and Schwab, 1977).

A major source for statistical analysis data for the human service needs assessor is through the various levels of government, particularly the several departments of the federal government. Population characteristics, for instance, are available through the Bureau of Census, U.S. Department of Commerce. Census data are collected every ten years and updated periodically. The census data are available in tables and on computer tapes for states, counties, Standard Metropolitan Statistical Areas (SMSA's), census tracts, Minor Civil Divisions (MSD's), and special population groups, such as American Indian Tribes. A wide range of statistical indicators are available from other federal governmental agencies containing statistics on health, education, crime, commercial development, etc. In many cases these are statistical indicators on special topical areas. One such example of special interest to needs assessors in the human services is the Health Demographic Profile System (HDPS) (Goldsmith, Jackson, Doenhoefer, Johnson, Tweed, Barbano, and Warheit, 1984). HDPS includes such data as population characteristics, socioeconomic indicators, family structure, housing, community stability and disabled population. Each category of data includes indicators of high risk for physical and mental disorders by state, county, census tract, and minor civil division. Other levels of government routinely collect data with important implications for statistical indicators. State departments of education, public welfare, health, aging, and mental health are sources for information. At the community level, planning organizations and chambers of commerce are often good sources for data.

Through the analysis of statistical indicators, a target population, or *population-at-risk* is identified. A "population-at-risk is a qualitative idea, involving the establishment of observable sociodemographic, geographic, and other population categories, that in turn are related to defined problem categories" (Gates, 1980, p. 125). In other words, the analysis of statistical indicators involves an enumeration of people who fall within defined problem categories. Consider the situation involving the percentage of female-headed households found to be below the poverty threshold for a particular county *xx*. The two major variables here are female-headed households (a sociodemographic variable) and poverty threshold (a measure of a defined problem—poverty). When the frequency (numbers) of two or more such variables (events) are found to vary in roughly the same way, we can speak of a statistical relationship. Further, in this relationship, the idea of population-at-risk can be identified; from our example it may be determined that in *xx* county, female-headed householders are at-risk to experience the problem of poverty conditions if the percentage of such households below the poverty threshold is greater than for other households.

The example above describes the notion of risk with regard to the use of social indicators. The determination of risk through statistical indicators has been one of the most prevalent analytical approaches used with statistical indicators. Indicators are chosen by the needs assessor on the basis of their presumed ability to predict problems or service utilization by individuals. A particular problem can occur when multiple measures of risk are used, covering differing geographic areas, and using different metrics to enumerate statistical indicators. McKillip (1987, pp. 49–50) identifies four analytical techniques that can be applied for such issues in risk factor analysis: (1)standardizing data, (2) percentile ratings, (3) ranking, and (4) prevalence of risk.

Standardizing involves transforming observed data to a common base within a distribution. Data become interval measures by converting observed scores to standard, or (Z), scores. The Z *score* indicates how many standard deviations above or below the mean an observation falls in a distribution. Calculation of the Z score is carried out by finding the difference between the value of a particular observation X_i and the mean of the distribution of scores X, and then dividing this difference by the standard deviation:

$$Z = \frac{\text{observed score–minus–mean score for distribution}}{\text{standard deviation of observed scores}}$$

If the mean of an observed need variable is 10 and its standard deviation is 5, then a score of 15 would be one standard deviation unit above the mean (Z = +1), a score of 5 would be one standard deviation below the mean (Z = –1). The mean of Z scores is always 0, and the standard deviation is 1, creating a standardizing of data. By using this technique, a common measuring base is created to allow for comparison of scores from different distributions. For instance, an index of need by geographical area can then be created that combines the results of various statistical indicators, e.g., percent of adults living alone, ratio not in workforce/employed, percent of high school graduates, etc. Cagle (1984) demonstrates how this technique is used, along with a sophisticated normalizing procedure to create a mental health need indicator in New York state that aggregates data from some nine statistical indicators.

Percentile ratings can be at a level no more sophisticated than listings of the proportions of persons represented by a particular statistical indicator; e.g., 18 percent of adult males in the workforce unemployed. Through the use of percentile ratings, some limited comparisons can be made with different groups or geographical areas. Percentiles can also provide for the location of an observed score in a distribution, and usually expressed as percentile rankings.

The percentile rank of an observed score in a distribution is the sum of the percent of scores below it and one-half of the percent that the particular score comprises. Suppose county *xx* is one of ten counties in a state subregion and reveals a poverty index higher than exactly five other counties. In other words, 50 percent of the counties have poverty index lower than county *xx*, and four counties (40 percent) have a poverty index score higher than county *xx*. County *xx* comprises 10 percent of the scores in the distribution, one out of ten. To calculate the percentile rank of county *xx*, we then sum the percent of scores below the index score of county *xx* (50) and add one-half of the percent that the score of county *xx* comprises (5, one-half of 10). The result is a percentile rank for county *xx* poverty index score of 55 (50 + 5). Through the computation of percentile ranks, some comparisons can be made between scores in different distributions. In our hypothetical case, for example, it may be desirable to compare percentile rankings of counties in different subregions of a state.

The Mental Health Demographic Profile System (MDPH), developed by the National Institute of Mental Health, reveals percentile rankings for an array of statistical indicators. Goldsmith, Unger, Rosen, Shambaugh, and Windle (1975) demonstrate how percentile distributions are then to be broken into several levels with associated labels, as revealed in the following:

- Less than 10th percentile value . . . . Extremely low
- 10th–30th percentile value . . . . Low
- 30th–50th percentile value . . . . Low moderate
- 50th–70th percentile value . . . . High moderate
- 70th–90th percentile value . . . . High
- 90th percentile value or more . . . . Extremely high

When values for statistical indicators are given percentile ranks, a number of indicators can be summed, averaged, or weighted and averaged to produce composite need ranks for specified geographical areas (Cagle, 1984, p. 394). Further, rankings for need can be compared to rankings for such indices as service utilization, resources, etc. The resulting comparisons can be helpful to access discrepancies, establish priorities, and otherwise determine need by geographical area. Census maps of geographical areas can be used to enhance displays of percentile ranking data.

Ranking involves treating statistical indicators as nominal data and assigning a score to each geographical area or subarea on the basis of rank order for the statistical indicators involved. When ranking is undertaken for several statistical indicators, a sum of rankings by geographical area can be used to determine area(s) with greatest need evidenced.

Prevalence of risk involves simply the enumeration of persons at risk by statistical indicator in each geographical area or subarea. An example would be the number of teen pregnancies for a given geographical area. A comparison of geographical areas can be made on prevalence of risk indicated.

Numerous data analysis techniques have also been applied to address special areas of concern to the need assessor. The various report series on mental health statistics published by the Superintendent of Documents, U.S. Government Printing Office provide detailed information and reference sources.

Statistical indicators are widely used in needs assessment, and a number of advantages have been cited for their use. Warheit, Bell, and Schwab (1977) note that vast pools of data already exist in the public domain and can be economically tapped by the needs assessor. Advantages to using these data pools are the following: (1) only a limited amount of research training and experience are required to take advantage of statistical indicators; (2) differing sources of data for levels of differing geographical areas provide flexibility in use; and (3) the data can be of use in developing a foundation on which other needs assessment activities can be built and updated. However, statistical indicators are at best proxy measures that indirectly establish relationships between geographical area and individual characteristics. A central weakness is thusly related to concerns of validity. Warheit, Bell, and Schwab (1977, p. 38) cite the concerns of "ecological determinism," and "ecological correlations." *Ecological determinism* occurs through attributing to geographic areas under study the characteristics of social indicators being examined; *ecological correlation*, on the other hand, results from assuming that aggregate statistical measures for a geographic area really reflect the characteristics of individuals in those areas. Finally, statistical indicators in many ways are characterized as gross and insensitive measures of environmental and human conditions. "With few exceptions, given the current state of the art in social indicator theory and practice, it is probably best to consider them as just that: indicators of the possible existence of and interdependencies among problems, people, and needs" (Gates, 1980, p. 128).

Needs Assessment Survey

The needs assessment survey for program evaluation is a variant of the social survey in social research. It is a means to obtain information through direct responses from subjects selected on the basis of their knowledge about social conditions, or personal experiences relative to need. The survey may cover an entire population of a given geographic area, or a sample of subjects may be selected. This quantitative approach is perhaps the most commonly used information gathering source in needs assessment.

Three data gathering techniques are commonly employed in the design of needs assessment surveys: (1) personal or face-to-face interviews, (2) telephone interviews, and (3) mailed questionnaires. The choice of technique to employ is dependent on a number of methodological and practical considerations. Characteristics that are useful to consider as check points in planning the overall needs assessment survey and deciding on technique(s) to use are listed in the following:

1. *Sampling procedures*
2. *Length of the questionnaire or interview schedule*
3. *Format in which the questions can be asked, recorded, and coded*
4. *Amount of time required*
5. *Non return or refusal rates*

6. *Costs in time and dollars*
7. *Validity of the findings (Warheit, Bell, and Schwab, 1977, p. 43)*

It would be difficult to say which of these characteristics should be considered first, or even in what sequence they should be considered in designing the survey and choosing data gathering techniques. In all likelihood, reactions to each of these characteristics will play an important part in the decision-making process. We will briefly consider each of these characteristics in the discussion that follows.

Sampling procedures In needs assessment surveys sample design and procedures are important considerations both in terms of validity, and as a consideration in making a choice of data gathering technique(s). Sample design is concerned with the accuracy or congruence between the sample and the larger population of interest that the sample purports to represent. Systematic error is introduced when there is lack of congruence between the sample and the larger population. Sampling error is introduced through the uncertainties of selecting individuals as representatives of the larger population. "In contrast to systematic errors, which are extremely difficult to identify and evaluate, the effect of sampling errors upon the reliability of statistical inferences can be predicted and to a large extent controlled by the appropriate sample design" (Gates, 1980, p.129). Sample design options are discussed in detail elsewhere in this text. Our purpose here is to examine how choice of data gathering technique may be limited by sample design constraints.

In some cases the needs assessment survey can be appropriately undertaken through the use of purposive or non random sampling procedures. This would be particularly true when a well defined and available group of key informants, clients, or target population representatives will be involved as subjects. The key word in choice of data gathering technique is *availability* of subjects. To the extent that potential subjects cannot be located on the basis of physical location, mailing address, or telephone number, sampling constraints will be obvious and one or another data gathering technique deemed unacceptable (Frey, 1983).

When random sampling procedures are called for, as in a citizen survey, the potential for each of the data gathering techniques may reach acceptable levels by virtue of the sampling criterion. However, when the population group to be sampled includes what are determined to be substantial numbers of potential subjects who do not have a permanent address or telephone, the personal interview approach may be more appropriate. A particular criticism of the telephone interview technique in the past has been the difficulty associated with deriving a sampling frame or list due to unlisted numbers, new numbers, or recently changed numbers. Modern sampling approaches utilizing random digit dialing, by hand or computer assist, have substantially improved the applicability of the telephone interview technique (Lavrakas, 1987).

Length of questionnaire or interview schedule Length of questionnaire or interview schedule will, of course, depend greatly on the amount of information expected. However, a few suggestions can be made to guide the need assessor in survey instrument preparation. A rule-of-thumb is to include only items which have a direct bearing on the purpose of the survey. The tendency to include questions simply because they are interesting should be avoided, because:

> They tend to fragment the questionnaire/schedule so that it loses its structural integrity; the cost of gathering and analyzing the data is increased; and, by overburdening the respondent, the response rate is reduced, a combination which tends to reduce the validity of the findings (Warheit, Bell, and Schwab, 1977, p. 43).

Before finalizing the questionnaire/schedule, the needs assessor is advised to conduct a mock analysis of data to better judge data processing requirements that will be required later on.

Questionnaire/schedule format Questionnaire/schedule format will be guided by the nature of data to be collected and the population surveyed. Variation in format is particularly evident on the dimension of structure. Structured survey instruments feature fixed alternative type questions and are generally identified with quantitative program evaluation approaches, while unstructured survey instruments contain open-ended questions and are identified more closely with qualitative approaches. However, there is no rigid guideline forbidding the use of both open-ended and fixed-alternative type questions in either qualitative or quantitative approaches to needs assessment.

A survey instrument combining both structured and unstructured questions with a funnel schedule can be quite appropriate for needs assessment purposes. The funnel schedule is designed to start with an initial response to an open-ended question and funnel the initial response to a topical question or set of structured responses (Kerlinger, 1973). Used in this way, open-ended and structured questions offer the advantages of flexibility and in-depth inquiry on issues of special relevance to the respondent.

Structured survey instruments are designed to achieve uniformity among responses and simplify coding and analysis of responses. All questions are asked in a similar way, and survey subjects are requested to respond to predetermined alternatives for answers. The construction of structured survey questions is both skill and art. Variations in question format range from straightforward yes/no responses to complex rating and ranking schemes. Henderson, Morris, and Fitz-Gibbon (1987), Dillman (1978), and Babbie (1973) are useful resources on the design and construction of questions for structured social research instruments. Numerous survey instruments which have been developed for the purpose of an earlier needs assessment, or for other purposes, could be adapted for reuse. The reader is encouraged to check whether copyright requirements apply in such cases. Even though the structured survey instrument (mailed questionnaire or interview schedule) represents advantages in ease of administration, uniformity in coding, and amenability to statistical procedures, it is important that all parties to the needs assessment effort (interviewers, coders, data processors, and others involved) fully understand the instrument and be given opportunities to make suggestions while the survey instrument is being developed.

Amount of time required   Two dimensions of time requirements are identified here. First is the matter of the implementation time required to undertake the needs assessment survey. The second consideration is the amount of time spent eliciting responses from subjects.

Interview schedules for personal interviews can usually be structured for a longer time commitment of respondents than in the case of the mailed questionnaire or telephone survey. A mailed needs assessment questionnaire that takes longer than twenty minutes to complete will require significant commitment on the part of survey respondents. The amount of time to reasonably expect telephone survey participants to give also depends on such things as the convenience of the hour a call is made, interest in the issue, etc. In general, ten to fifteen minutes for a telephone survey call will probably approach the upper time limit. Many otherwise well-designed survey efforts have not produced the desired results simply because they expected too much of potential respondents. The amount of time required must be balanced carefully with informational needs; it reinforces the warning not to ask questions simply because they might elicit interesting responses. However, data needs (and the length of time they will take) can be an important consideration in which technique to use.

Non return or refusal rates   Non return or refusal rates represent the greatest fear of survey researchers. It is quite obvious that many factors play a part in return or participation rates. Some factors may be anticipated by the needs assessor and contingency plans made. Many such factors are difficult to foresee. Certainly it would be difficult to anticipate that a potential respondent might have received four or five mailed questionnaires in a week's time, a telephone survey subject may have just completed a lengthy survey interview a day or two before, or a prospective for a personal interview is on an extended vacation. That and many other situations happen, however, and are often out of control of the average needs assessor. Another major consideration is whether anonymity and confidentially can be assured and the means taken to do so. Still, there are many ways in which preventive planning can minimize low rate of return or participation. Probably the best advice to follow is the recommendation that, after preliminary planning is completed, a pre-test be conducted to serve as a trial run. This will allow for any changes that may be required, as well as insights into the reactions of respondents who are surveyed in the pre-test. Some practical suggestions to enhance return and participation rate are listed below:

1. Make the survey instrument attractive. At a minimum, show that you cared enough to ask understandable questions, and check grammar and spelling for written questions.

2. Offer an incentive for return/participation. It is becoming more common to offer small financial rewards for willingness to participate (a fresh dollar bill included with the mailed questionnaire, for instance). Quickness of response can accompany a monetary reward (first response receives $200 and fiftieth response receives $50, for example). Personal interviewees may be paid a token sum to participate. When dealing with key informants or social agency representatives, the offer to share survey results can instill a positive response for participation.

3. If at all possible, include a stamped or posted and preaddressed return envelope with mailed questionnaire.

4. Clearly identify a contact person and phone number on the survey instrument. Explain who that person is in the case of personal interview.

5. Plan on a follow-up reminder for those who have not responded to a mailed questionnaire. If the budget will allow, send along another stamped or posted and preaddressed return envelope.

6. Insure that interviewers are appropriately trained and appropriately courteous in arranging contact and during interviews. It is often critical when surveying client groups to arrange a letter of introduction or personal introduction of the survey interviewer prior to the survey interview.

7. Always end with a note of appreciation.

Even under the best of circumstances, a 100 percent response rate or rate of participation for interviewees is unlikely, except for small, specialized needs assessment efforts. What then is an acceptable response or participation rate? While no absolute guidelines exist on this issue, conventional wisdom holds that a response rate for a mailed questionnaire of 70 percent or greater is very good, 60 percent is good, and 50 percent is adequate for analysis and reporting (Babbie, 1986). A higher response rate would usually be expected for the telephone or personal interview, particularly when it is feasible to replace sample subjects who refuse to participate.

Costs in time and dollars The cost factor in time and dollars for the needs assessment survey is a variable that can often be greatly effected by seemingly small increments. Gates (1980) gives the example of a simple community survey instrument and related cost that is based on an adequate sample size to adequately cover respondent categories; the addition of only one more question with four categories of response in his example would quadruple the overall cost of the survey. Relative differences can be obtained depending on the choice of survey scope and design. Generally speaking, when compared in terms of costs in time and dollars, the personal interview technique rates most costly, while the telephone interview (local calling) tends to be the least expensive.

Validity of findings   Validity of survey findings is also heavily dependent on survey scope, design, and techniques used. Numerous factors can influence validity, however, and often these are not within the reach of control by the needs assessor. Some examples are negative attitudes toward the sponsoring agent for the survey, an unpredicted incident provoking strong feelings over a community issue, the competition of another survey being undertaken concurrently or in the recent past, or even unexpected environmental changes that dramatically reduce return rate.

To the extent that appropriate methods can be followed in the survey design and sampling procedures, and the needs assessor scopes out the many potential problems as above, there is still a good chance that a valid documentation of needs will result.

Needs assessors have found utility in combining the techniques discussed here for needs surveys along with other approaches to needs studies for practical application. Among recent reports of needs assessment surveys in the literature are the following examples. Rothman (1984) reports a survey of the needs of female patients in a Veterans Administration psychiatric hospital, employing a combination of a semistructured patient interview schedule, a demographic survey, and a clinical narrative completed by the interviewer. Both client and practitioner views on needs of the chronically mentally ill were tapped through key informant personal interviews reported by Lynch and Kruzich (1986). In a consumer-based mail survey, the needs for residential facilities for the mentally ill are reported by Randolph, Lindenberg, and Menn (1986).

Many advantages are attributed to the survey for needs assessment. When carried out under the requirements for sound social science research, the survey can be one of the most scientifically valid and reliable approaches for assessing needs. The survey can provide direct feedback and comparative data from key informants, clients, and target populations about specific issues raised in a needs study. The survey approach is also valued for flexibility in answering a wide variety of questions and as a means to expand the findings of other approaches into a useful system of research and planning (Warheit, Bell, and Schwab, 1977). Chief disadvantages to the needs assessment survey are time and expense factors, and problems which can result from low rate of return or participation.

Multiattribute Utility Analysis

Multiattribute utility analysis (MAUA) is an approach or model which has been adapted to simultaneously utilize the input of several sources of needs study data. The MAUA approach is derived from a decision theory technique used for program planning and allocation of resources among competing programs (Edwards, Guttentag, and Snapper, 1975). The purpose of the MAUA is to separate the elements of a complicated decision, evaluate each element separately within the context of overall goals, develop consensus on the criteria for judging desirability of competing programs, and finalize decisions on the basis of the criteria selected. As applied to needs assessment, this approach starts with the data input from several sources of needs studies; e.g., the findings or judgments made from a key informants structured group, social indicators, and a needs study survey. The summative judgments from each of the data input sources are disaggregated in a way that allows for partializing the original judgments, and involves decision makers in assigning discrete values to replace the summative inputs. The decision makers are also required to assign a weight to the influence of each data input source. The model then provides for mathematically integrating the discrete values of the decision makers into a new summative judgment that is influenced by the several sources of data input and the value judgments of the decision makers.

Central to the MAUA approach is the disaggregation of judgments, establishment of criteria for decision making, and synthesis through a summative or global judgment. A simplified version of the MAUA process is presented by Posavac and Carey (1985) as follows:

1. *Decide on the appropriate criteria on which to base a decision. These criteria are values that the decision makers wish to maximize through the program. These criteria will guide their choice among available programs.*
2. *Weight the criteria to reflect their subjective importance to the decision makers. This procedure determines the relative importance of the values of the decision makers.*
3. *Evaluate each possible program on the basis of each criterion. This step enables the decision makers to pinpoint the strengths and weaknesses of each alternative program.*
4. *Combine the evaluations made on the basis of individual criteria into an overall judgment. This step shows the overall desirability or utility of each program (p. 109).*

An illustrative example would be the consideration of several sources of need study data (criteria) conducted on the plight of the homeless in a given community. Table 4–2 gives an example of hypothetical findings from these several sources of need study data, with rows representing the choices or options in programming confronting decision makers. The columns represent data input sources in the model.

The resulting matrix in Table 4–2 can be helpful to decision makes, though it has the limitation of considering the length (or value) of each data

TABLE 4–2   •   *Observed Scores for Need Studies on Homeless*

	Data Sources		
Social Conditions/Needs	Client Survey*	Key Informants*	Forum*
Housing	2.14	3.91	4.86
Social Services	1.17	1.76	2.21
Medical Care	2.41	3.12	3.00
Food/Nutrition	3.43	3.25	2.73
Security/Protection	1.94	1.53	2.37
Job Training	1.46	3.52	3.14

*Average score ranging from 1 (not a problem) to 5 (a serious problem).

source equally. An attempt to overcome this problem is taken in MAUA when criteria are weighted to reflect their perceived importance. The decision on assigning weights to each criterion can be made by an individual decisionmaker, decision makers acting independently or by a group process. The results might be the following ordering of criteria:

Criterion	Rank or Weight	
Client Survey	1	50
Key Informant	2	37.5
Forum	3	12.5

The final steps in the completed MAUA model involve a rather detailed process of data manipulation which will not be described here. Readers wishing to apply the entire MAUA model are encouraged to consult McKillip (1987) for detailed instruction on the data analysis required. For purposes of illustrating the outcome of the MAUA model as applied to our hypothetical case example, the final matrix might look something like that presented in Table 4–3.

The resulting matrix in Table 4–3 takes into consideration the weighting of each criterion, importance attributed to each potential programming response, and presents a summative comparison for each program in a need index (N_i). If we were to follow a simple decision rule to maximize N_i, then in our example we should select the food/nutrition alternative for emphasis in dealing with the plight of homeless. It is important to point out, however, that many factors such as cost, feasibility, and social acceptability are typically not addressed directly or sufficiently in the MAUA model.

The advantages of the MAUA lie in the fact that it is a method to integrate the results of more than one need study data input source. It is a means to include quantitative data and qualitative judgments in one decision model

TABLE 4–3 • MAUA Utility Values, Weights, and Need Index for Needs Studies on Homeless

| | Data Sources | | | |
Social Conditions/Needs	Client Survey (50)	Key Informants (37.5)	Forum (12.5)	Need Index (N_i)
Housing	.27	.74	.99	54
Social Services	.02	.17	.29	11
Medical Care	.34	.53	.50	43
Food/Nutrition	.61	.57	.43	57
Security/Protection	.22	.11	.33	19
Job Training	.09	.64	.54	35

where the relative effects of each source of influence can be made explicit. MAUA is a prescriptive model of how decisions ought to be made, rather than of how they are made (McKillip, 1987). Some disadvantages of MAUA are the following. The model can be confusing, especially when data inputs do not meet the textbook examples for application. There is also a certain degree of razzle-dazzle to this approach which can be a source of suspicion for some constituents in the need assessment arena. MAUA appears to promise more than it really can deliver. The model does have the capacity to integrate relevant variables in order to enhance need assessment outcomes. However, like other rationally-based decision techniques it is important to remember that the model does not integrate all relevant variable in any needs situation. Finally, there is a dearth of literature to substantiate the successful application of MAUA in needs assessment.

Controversies About Needs Studies

The arena of needs assessment has not been without controversy. Issues of controversy lie in philosophical, theoretical, and technical areas. In fact it is hard to separate out the different levels of controversy. Our purpose here is not to attempt resolution to controversy, but instead to add perspective to concerns of human and social need.

In the beginning of this chapter we discussed some to the difficulties surrounding the definition of need and indicators of need, for the purpose of gaining perspective on conceptual clarity. Now we will examine need in a more philosophical dimension to hopefully gain perspective on the role of need in social welfare policy formulation and programming. One philosophical issue seems to pervade almost any consideration of need in our society.

The term *philosophical* is used here quite broadly to encompass arguments, both pro and con, in the search for rules to guide human relationships. Our concern then is with the concept of need as an anchoring point for social welfare obligation. The central issue can be summarized in the following question: What claims can be made of a society on the basis of need? Two opposing schools of thought define the range of responses to the question we have posed. On the one extreme, the collectivist response for needs (at least basic needs for the well-being of all citizens) can be equated with rights of entitlement. At the other extreme, entrepreneurialism recognizes needs more as economic demands to be fulfilled, and responds to the question involving reciprocity (benefits resulting from contributions). The point is that any discussion of needs, even their identification, will be caught up in the issue of how society expects needs to be met.

A test of how sensitive the above issue can be at times is demonstrated by the initial publication of *Common Human Needs* (Towle, 1987). This book was originally published as a pamphlet in 1945 by the Bureau of Public Assistance (a subunit of today's Department of Health and Human Services). Central themes of the book (pamphlet) were: recognition of the principle of public assistance services as a right, an argument that public assistance workers should have a solid understanding of the common human needs that govern behavior, and defining a role for government in meeting those needs. A dramatic wave of criticism from groups that were concerned that it would encourage a "socialized state" led the administration to withdraw the book and destroy the plates. The revised edition of the book is now published by the National Association of Social Workers.

The case of *Common Human Needs* is especially dramatic, and it serves to highlight the philosophical dilemma which confronts our society in regard to society's responsibility in meeting needs. However, a far more pragmatic process appears to be at work in sorting out the details of the dilemma with which we have been confronted. It is a process involving both collective strategies and entrepreneurialism in ways that often appear quite perplexing. Even the needs of the entrepreneur are made as claims for collective action (the needs of medical care givers in Medicare and Medicaid are illustrative). The way we have been dealing with this dilemma is captured in a quote from Morris (1986):

> . . . *American social programs evolved, especially since the 1930s, as a result of the continuous ad hoc interplay of varying interest groups each pressing claims about the wants and needs of the constituencies, which justify a federal role, at least in financing, to rectify special group inequity or distress (p. 17).*

We have identified this philosophical issue, as yet unresolved, and turn our attention now to methodological and technical issues of controversy that remain closely related to this philosophical dilemma.

The impetus for assessment of need can be traced to the anti-poverty programs of the 1960s. By the mid 1970s the idea of a front-end analysis of need in grant applications had gained popularity for most major federal social programs, and need assessment activities gained momentum at state and local levels. Kimmel (1977) notes that the reasons for requiring needs assessments for federal grants are probably as mixed and variable as the motives and interests of the individuals and groups who initiated, participated in, or promoted the requirements in the first place. One reason in particular, however, became the target for criticism and doubt. An over-arching theme of the times was a press for government to use rational, analytical approaches for greater cost effectiveness in resource allocations. Needs assessment could be, and was, promoted as supporting the cause for greater rationality in decision making for the allocation of resources in social programming.

At the center of the controversy is the claim that needs assessments have had little effect on decision making at federal or state levels. The report of an examination of the laws and regulations of Health, Education, and Welfare (now Health and Human Services) programs (Zangwill, 1977) found that needs assessment was most often intended as a means of resource allocation. But the requirements for grantees did not always provide clear direction and/or technical assistance to enable them to make the needs assessment a meaningful part of their program planning. A study of state Title XX programs (Benton, Field, and Millar, 1978) revealed that while nearly all the programs carried out some form of needs assessment, only in four states were the results used as principal determinants for social service priorities. However, the study also raised questions about whether everything that was called a needs assessment, in fact, represented a sound basis for policy making.

Facts and figures are not available to document the overall costs of needs assessments. However, as in other areas of program evaluation, a significant proportion of scarce resources can be diverted to needs assessment activities. Kimmel (1977, p. vii) points out that in the case of large state-wide surveys, for example, assessments can take up to years to complete and cost hundreds of thousands of dollars.

How much this situation has changed as a result of shifting to federal block grants for states' human services is not known. Although the specific programmatic requirements for needs assessments in categorical grants has changed, the role of needs assessment in state and local level resource allocation and planning activities appears to have been sustained.

Other concerns have been raised about the claims made for needs assessment results in resource allocation and program planning. Critics state that needs assessment technology is simply inadequate for its intended uses. Rapp (1982) presents a particularly harsh indictment of need assessment capabilities. He argues that the lack of correspondence between needs assessment and resource allocation may be attributed to three factors that emphasize technological and political limitations: (1) need is not a measurable concept, (2) needs assessment technology is weak, and (3) information from needs assessments does not recognize the nature of resource allocation decisions (p. 51). Supporting evidence for such criticism is found in the lack of a precise definition for the concept of need, weaknesses in need assessment methodologies, and a political system based more on interest group influence and consensus rather than analysis and data-guided choices.

The controversies in needs assessment are not likely to be resolved any time soon. And consideration of the controversial issues in needs assessment is important for several basic reasons: it helps to complete the broader contextual picture wherein needs assessment activities take place; it helps to focus our attention on the limitations of the technology involved; and it serves to identify areas for development and improvement. Needs assessment should not be touted as a cure-all for the human services. A proper perspective on the role of needs assessment sets the stage for future advancements. Such a perspective is put forth very succinctly in a statement outlining what is implied in needs assessment:

> *It suggests that planners (and, of necessity, the elected officials and appointed chief executives who direct and monitor the planners' activities) begin by asking: What is the problem? What are the facets and its causes? What are the characteristics of those who can be defined as having the problem? How many people are affected? Can they be located geographically? This approach presumes that needs can only be responded to through the management of resources, programs, and services if—and only if—such questions can be answered (Moroney, 1977, p. 128).*

To the extent that needs assessment can help accomplish what is implied above, it will have served an important role in the human services.

References

Advertising Research Foundation. (1985). *Focus groups: Issues and approaches*. New York, NY: Advertising Research Foundation.

American Psychiatric Association. (1988). *Diagnostic and statistical manual of mental disorders*. Washington, D.C.: Author.

Babbie, E. R. (1973). *Survey research methods*. Belmont, CA: Wadsworth.

Babbie, E. R. (1986). *The practice of social research*. Belmont, CA: Wadsworth.

Benton, B. B., Field, T., & Millar, R. (1978). *Social services: Federal legislation vs. state implementation*. Washington, D.C.: The Urban Institute.

Webster's New Collegiate Dictionary. (1975). Springfield, MA: G. and C. Merriam.

Bradshaw, J. (1977). The concept of social need. In N. Gilbert and H. Specht (Eds.), *Planning for social welfare: Issues, models, and tasks* (pp. 290–296). Englewood Cliffs, NJ: Prentice-Hall.

Cagle, L. T. (1984). Using social indicators to assess mental health needs: Lessons from a statewide study. *Evaluation Review, 8*, 389–412.

Connor, R. F., Jacobi, M., Altman, D. G., & Aslanian, C. B. (1985). Measuring need and demands in evaluation research: Results of a national survey of college and university administrators about desired evaluation services. *Evaluation Review, 9*, 717–734.

Delbecq, A. L., & Van de Ven, A. H. (1971). A group process model for problem identification. *Journal of Applied Behavioral Science, 7*, 466–492.

Delbecq, A. L., Van de Ven, A. H., & Gustafson, D. A. (1975). *Group techniques for program planning*. Glenview, IL: Scott Foresman.

Dillman, D. A. (1978). *Mail and telephone surveys: The total design method*. New York, NY: John Wiley.

Edwards, W., Guttentag, M., & Snapper, K. (1975). Effective evaluation: A decision-theoretic approach to evaluation research. In E. L. Struening and M. Guttentag (Eds.), *Handbook of evaluation research* (pp. 139–181). Beverly Hills, CA: Sage.

Frey, J. H. (1983). *Survey research by telephone*. Beverly Hills, CA: Sage.

Gates, B. L. (1980). *Social program administration: The implementation of social policy*. Englewood Cliffs, NJ: Prentice-Hall.

Goldsmith, H. F., Jackson, D. J., Doenhoefer, S., Johnson, W., Tweed, D. L., Stiles, D., Barbarno, J. D., & Warheit, G. J. (1984). *The health demographic profile system's inventory of small area social indicators*. 455–749/20133. Washington, D.C.: U.S. Government Printing Office.

Goldsmith, H. F., Unger, E. L., Rosen, B. M., Shambaugh, J. P., & Windle, C. D. (1975). *A typological approach to doing social area analysis*. ADM 76–262. Washington, D.C.: U.S. Government Printing Office.

Greenbaum, T. L. (1988). *The practical handbook and guide to focus group research*. Lexington, MA: D. C. Heath.

Helmer, O. (1976). *Gathering expert opinion*. Los Angeles, CA: Graduate College of Business Administration, University of Southern California.

Henerson, M. E., Morris, L. L., & Fitz-Gibbon, C. T. (1987). *How to measure attitudes*. Newbury Park, CA: Sage.

Jansson, B. S. (1984). *Theory and practice of social welfare policy: Analysis, processes, and current issues*. Belmont, CA: Wadsworth.

Kerlinger, F. N. (1973). *Foundations of Behavioral Research*. New York: Holt, Rinehart and Winston.

Kimmel, W. A. (1977). *Needs assessment: A critical perspective*. Washington, D.C.: U.S. Department of Health, Education, and Welfare.

Krueger, R. A. (1988). *Focus groups: A practical guide for allied research*. Newbury Park, CA: Sage.

Lavrakas, P. J. (1987). *Telephone survey methods: Sampling, selection, and supervision*. Newbury Park, CA: Sage.

Linstone, H. A., & Turoff, M. (Eds.). (1975). *The delphi method: Techniques and applications*. Reading, MA: Addison-Wesley.

Lynch, M. M., & Kruzich, J. M. (1986). Needs assessment of the chronically mentally ill: Practitioner and client perspectives. *Administration in Mental Health, 13*, 237–248.

Mayer, R. (1985). *Policy and program planning: A developmental perspective*. Englewood Cliffs, NJ: Prentice-Hall.

McKillip, J. (1987). *Need analysis: Tools for the human services and education*. Newbury Park, CA: Sage.

Moore, C. M. (1987). *Group techniques for idea building*. Newbury Park, CA: Sage.

Moroney, R. M. (1977). Needs assessment for human services. In W. F. Anderson, B. J. Frieden, and M. J. Murphy (Eds.), *Managing human services* (pp. 128–154). Washington, D.C.: International City Management Association.

Morris, R. (1986). *Rethinking social welfare: Why care for the stranger?* New York: Longman, Inc.

Posavac, E. J., & Carey, R. G. (1985). *Program evaluation methods and case studies.* Englewood Cliffs, NJ: Prentice-Hall.

Randolph, F. L., Lindenberg, R. E., & Menn, A. Z. (1986). Residential facilities for the mentally ill: Needs assessment and community planning. *Community Mental Health Journal, 22,* 77–89.

Rapp, C. (1982). Needs assessment—who needs it? *Journal of Social Welfare, 8,* 49–60.

Rossi, P. H., Freeman, H. E., & Wright, S. R. (1979). *Evaluation: A systematic approach.* Beverly Hills, CA: Sage.

Rothman, G. H. (1984). Needs of female patients in a veterans psychiatric hospital. *Social Work, 29,* 380–385.

Towle, C. (1987). *Common human needs.* Silver Spring, MD: National Association of Social Workers.

Ulschak, F. L., Nathanson, L., & Gillan, P. G. (1981). *Small group problem solving: An aid to organizational effectiveness.* Reading, MA: Addison-Wesley.

United Way of America. (1976). *UWASIS II: A taxonomy of social goals and human service programs.* Alexandria, VA.

VanGundy, A. B. (1988). *Techniques of structured problem solving.* New York: Van Nostrand Reinhold.

Warheit, G. J., Bell, R. A., & Schwab, J. J. (1977) *Needs assessment approaches: Concepts and methods.* Washington, D.C.: U.S. Government Printing Office.

Zangwill, B. A. (1977). *A compendium of laws and regulations requiring needs assessment.* Washington, D.C.: U.S. Department of Health, Education, and Welfare.

CHAPTER FIVE

Describing the Policy or Program Theory Base for Evaluation Purposes

Introduction

Before the evaluation of a social program or policy can go forward, the theory on which it is based must be made explicit. There are important reasons why this should be done; explaining why and how to do it will be the main subject of this chapter. First, let us try to be clear about what we mean by theory, for there are many ways to understand that idea. Notice that we are speaking of theory in only a very loose sense of the word—theory as a rough account of the logic of a social program or policy, "how it is supposed to work to effect the problem" (Bickman, 1987, p. 6). For our purposes it won't do to think of elegant theory, of tight deductive systems and precise definitions of major terms and operational models (for example). We simply have in mind the "real-life" form in which basic ideas shaping operating social programs and policies occur: that is, loosely associated sets of ideas setting out the cause-effect relationships which are the rationale for program or policy activities that are intended to solve a social problem (Scheirer, 1987). Sometimes they have a more systematic character, but not often.[1]

Although this is not the place to discuss its details, here is a simple example (in diagrammatic form) of a program theory, one taken from a currently operating social program. Figure 5-1 shows the theoretical underpinnings of a service program for the terminally ill. The program's services are based on the assumption that illness causes anger which causes suicide.

The Importance of Program Theory

Why bother with program theory at all? After all, it is common to hear that

FIGURE 5–1

Terminal illness

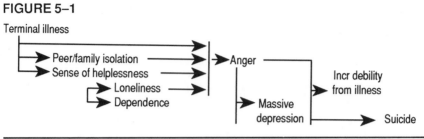

what counts is whether the program achieves its objectives. It turns out that there are good reasons why we ought not hold that opinion. However, one of them is not Chen and Rossi's (1983) reason—that it is somehow virtuous to be theoretical so that one might consider the evaluation enterprise to be social science (p. 339).[2] We will resist the temptation to argue at length some of the more arrogant aspects of Chen and Rossi's opinion in that regard.[3] Instead, let us go over the shortcomings of an anti-theoretical view precisely because it is so common and a source of so much mischief.

One of the main reasons program theory is essential to the evaluation enterprise is that the achievement of objectives is not actually, by itself, a sufficient reason to conclude that it was the program or any of its activities that is responsible for outcomes. Even an elegant research design with all its trappings (controls, random selection, and the like) does not allow an attribution of causality unless one can show that the program activities were actually set in place, so that it is plausible that they could have made an impact on the outcome. Now, in order to "set in place" a set of program activities, one must have some way to specify what they are. That is precisely what program theory makes possible. In fact, program theory is not more than a detailed account of the characteristics of independent variables, dependent variables, and the expected relationship between them. On the basis of those details, well-executed evaluation research monitors the program activities in order to see whether they actually have the characteristics they should (Scheirer, 1987). Or, at least, to see whether they are sufficiently standard so that it would be reasonable to suppose that desired outcomes could be expected (Conrad and Miller, 1987). Program theory is also an important management tool, a source of the performance standards that managers need in order to know what to require of themselves and their staff (Conrad and Miller, 1987).

Nor is that the only reason why program theory is essential to the evaluation of social programs and policies. It is essential in order to interpret evaluation findings. If, as is often the case, evaluation results show the program or policy to be a failure, there can be at least two general interpretations, as Carol Weiss showed us nearly two decades ago (Weiss, 1971). Most obvious, it can be a failure in implementation:

- It wasn't in operation long enough.
- It wasn't operating with sufficient intensity, at a high enough "level" of impact.
- The right activities weren't actually being performed (or in fact nothing was happening).

Or, if a person knows that the program was implemented accurately and with intensity, outcome data showing no effect can be interpreted as a failure of the whole theory on which the program is based. It is the most serious conclusion that can be drawn from evaluation data, and note that it can only be drawn after having satisfied the question about implementation. Our argument here is that program theory is an absolutely necessary condition for obtaining implementation data.

While those are the main reasons program theory is essential, there are other reasons that it can be helpful:

1. Program theory can assist in generalizing about where, or the conditions under which, program successes might be repeated.
2. Program theory can lead to the discovery of extra treatment and/or environmental factors which effect program outcomes or even negative side effects.
3. Construction or discussion of program theory has the potential to improve staff consensus on the goals and processes that are important in their program.

Good program theory, like any good theory, should set out the constraints and conditions under which its factors and their inter-relationships can be expected to work. After all we are not dealing with universal truth here, but with theory in the lower case, so to speak—theory which is strongly conditioned and local. Specification of those constraints and conditions can be used by those in authority over allocating funds to identify other localities and circumstances where they could reasonably expect additional program or program components to be successful (Bickman, 1987). Without being clear about those constraints and conditions, the process of deciding where next or how widely to diffuse a successful program innovation is likely to be over-stimulated and under-prepared: over-stimulated by the enthusiasm of success, under-prepared without a clear rationale by which to proceed.

Those constraints and conditions are useful in other ways. It is so easy for program designers (and implementers as well) to forget how virile are conditions in the empirical world in which social programs and policies are tested. When program theory sets out ideas about constraints and conditions, the ideas are potent reminders of the tenderness of our theories in the face of hard empirical reality. We have come to call those unpleasant realities *extra-treatment* factors. Tutoring programs for adult secondary or higher education are notorious examples of social programs vulnerable to extra-treatment factors. That is, no matter how clever the program or policy design and/or how devoted the staff who implements it, unless tutorees have an adequate income that provides housing, food, and shelter, the tutoring program cannot possibly achieve its educational objectives. Nor is this a peculiar example—on the primary school level, a similar rationale lies behind the school lunch and school breakfast programs. They were conceived as aids in overcoming an important extra-treatment factor within a theory about how to educate children living under poverty conditions. Program theory should be relied upon to identify what else is necessary to give the intervention program a reasonable chance for success. There is no counsel of perfection here, since it is important to use program theory to identify extra-treatment factors even though they aren't susceptible to control, to any important degree. The evaluation research enterprise that has taken the trouble to identify them has in its possession the tools to decide whether negative or "no-effect" evaluation data should be interpreted as a failure of the basic ideas behind the program, or as a failure of real-world conditions to provide the necessary context for success. It is an extremely important decision: the former interpretation would generate a recommendation to abolish the program entirely, the latter would generate a recommendation to try again and attempt to modify the locally negative conditions or locate the program in a more conducive environment. It is important to avoid throwing away (in error) good programs, policy, and intervention ideas when they have not succeeded for reasons that have little or nothing to do with their validity.

Although it is a strong requirement to meet, elegant program theory has another singular advantage: it should be able to see around corners even before they are turned, so to speak; i.e., it should deductively anticipate factors that might impede success or rise up as significant side effects even before the program is field tested. For example, one of the negative side effects of recruiting and training *indigenous workers* (staff people who had personally experienced the social problem toward which the social program is directed) was theoretically predictable. The objective of employing such staff members was to provide a communication bridge between the normative culture of the organization implementing the social program and the culture of its consumers, non-normative by definition. However, even the most simple theory of formal organizations will quickly lead to the conclusion that those embedded in an organization for very long will adopt its normative culture. Used as a theory base for a program design using indigenous workers, the predictable negative side effect of employing indigenous workers is that they will soon be socialized to the organization and thus alienated from the very group of consumers that they were hired to deal with. The conclusion is that there is a limited useful organizational life-span for indigenous workers and a continuous re-supply will have to be planned for. Program theory could have been important in anticipating that organizational need.

Finally, it can be useful to know that good program theory provides a powerful occasion for forging a strong consensus among those who have vital interests in the life of an organization. It is a common experience among those who conduct the evaluation of social program or policy systems to find that organizational actors are not clear about how they rationalize the connections between their objectives and the program activities and processes that it is their daily business to conduct—that is, their theory base (Bickman, 1987). When evaluation researchers use this as an occasion to help these groups conceptualize their work, not only does a workable program theory emerge, but, sometimes, a surprisingly strong group consensus about what they are doing and why they are doing it emerges. That is of great importance to organizations, for, on the basis of such consensus, work goes forward with greater efficiency, interactivity, morale, and personal effort. This is no great mystery: when people come to a common understanding of their enterprise, they develop a sense of shared ownership that is conducive to a broad sense of commitment and purpose. That is the stuff of which a devoted altruism is made. Organizations with a strong dose of that can hardly help be efficient at what they do.

Differentiating Program Theory from the Theory of a Social Problem

A social problem analysis ordinarily includes an analysis of its causation. Is that different from what we are here calling *program theory*, and, if so, how? The answer is yes, emphatically yes. In order to be clear about what is meant by the phrase *social problem theory* or *theory at a social problem level*, we need to give some attention to the idea of social problems.[4] Social problems are the very source, the substance, from which social programs and policy systems spring. Of course they are not the only source; the alternative is to think in terms of social needs. We believe that thinking of social needs is very different from thinking of social problems. Thinking of a social problem arises out of labeling some condition as undesirable—actually a somewhat negative approach which focuses on the question, "What's wrong?" On the other hand, thinking of a social need begins with identifying some conception of what is desirable for people; it focuses on the question, "What do we want for people, ourselves, and others?" We are inclined to believe that it is peculiarly North American to approach issues in terms of what is undesirable and therefore to be eliminated, rather than in terms of *human needs, what is to be supplied or insured*[5]. Europeans, for example, ordinarily conceptualize social policy issues along social need dimensions and are generally critical of the social problem focus.

Those who have evaluation research and social policy and program design responsibilities cannot afford to be ignorant of how the social problem of concern to the policy or program they are working on is (or was originally) conceptualized. The way the social problem is defined will determine some important, perhaps fundamental, expectations of it—by funders, top level decision-makers, the general public, etc. That in turn will create expectations of particular program/policy objectives, implementation processes, and, perhaps, the appropriate approach to its evaluation. Sometimes expectations arising out of the original social problem analysis create a burden for implemented program designs and policy systems. The reason is that to understand the origins, the antecedents, of a social problem is sometimes confused with also having a ready solution for it.

These contrasts are useful in making clear the social problem concept used here, but we also wish to take the occasion to observe some particular problems for social programs and policy systems that the social-problem-centered approach creates. First, it assumes that, if only society does away with all its problems, then somehow what the society wants for itself and its citizens will be present and available. A moment's thought shows that this does not follow logically; a metaphor will help—a gardener who systematically removes all the undesirable bugs and all the weeds (and anything else that is considered undesirable) from the garden certainly isn't guaranteed good vegetables. Any gardener will tell you that not all bugs are a problem, some are a help (ladybugs, for example); and it also takes the "right" kind of things to insure a crop. As helpful as it can be, the ordinary "problem" (solving) approach can only put things back to where they were in the first place. To notice it is to notice a key aspect to the social problem approach—it is inherently normative in the sense of its usefulness in restoring things to the status quo ante. To be sure, that has abundant merit under many circumstances. However, note that thinking in terms of a concrete problem suggests a very empirical and practical approach to social policy (Spector and Kitsuse, 1973).

A well-formed theory of a specific social problem is ordinarily embedded in a whole social problem analysis. And such an analysis includes, at least, a consideration of (a) how the problem is to be defined, how (b) causation and (c) ideology are to be understood. Perhaps the analysis might include an identification of assorted social costs and benefits, or its view on the primary gainers and losers (Chambers, 1986). Seldom do social program designers actually intend to attack the whole of a social problem, for the most part only a small part of it. And there is also the fact that causal analysis at the social problem level simply isn't concrete enough to yield a specification of program operations, ordinarily. The difference will be apparent if the reader will keep in mind that social problems are conceived on a much larger scale than social

FIGURE 5–2 • *Social Program Casual Analysis*

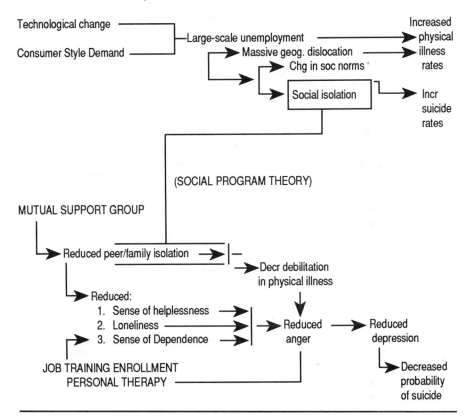

(SOCIAL PROBLEM CAUSAL ANALYSIS)

(SOCIAL PROGRAM THEORY)

programs. Consider for a moment some common social conditions defined as social problems: crime, drugs, illiteracy, etc. None of those conditions, when thought of as social problems, are dealt with by a single, monolithic social program or policy effort. In reviewing the best known social programs directed toward crime, the following might come to mind: *community corrections, scared straight, drug interdiction, methadone maintenance, witness protection, probation/parole/diversion*, etc. Note that none of those, however imaginatively construed, would be expected to deal with the whole of the social problem of crime—not even if we included all of the activities we ordinarily associate with a city police force.[6] Social problems have so many dimensions and subtypes that no one in recent memory has claimed to have ideas so powerful that they would address the whole of any of these social problems.[7]

Figure 5–2 is an attempt to illustrate the difference between theories about the cause of social problems and theories that guide actions at the program/intervention level. First, note that the upper right-hand part of the figure reveals that increased suicide and physical illness are the outcomes of concern to this social problem analysis. Then notice that, although the social problem analysis shows many antecedents for suicide, the program theory concentrates on only one—social isolation. Also note that terms in the social problem causal analysis refer only to large groups of people (thus rates), while the social program theory is clearly concerned only with individuals (thus all the terms are singular, though the theory could have small groups in mind).

Finally, notice that the program theory includes factors that never appear in the social problem causal analysis: e.g., *mutual support group, job training enrollment, personal therapy.* That is because the program intends to take actions of some kind that will change or remedy the consequences of the social problem—each factor named is believed to be able to do that. Social conditions, like many things, can arise from a number of causes (multiple-causation, some say). Fortunately for those of us who wish to remedy social problems' consequences, we are not limited to achieving that only by restoring the same causal factors to their original condition. Just because a social problem arose in one particular way, there is no reason to believe that it can't be reduced by another.

One reason this distinction between two kinds of theories is so apparent is that we are forcing the importance of considering broad social factors. Were we to adopt a reductionist position—that broad social factors were only the additive consequences of individual states of mind or small group interactions—we would not be so aware of two kinds of theory here. In fact, under those constraints, there would be only one sort of theory that had any fundamental importance. The "sociological bias" in the foregoing discussion should be clear, as it certainly should be kept in mind by those who might adopt our way of going at evaluation research.

It is fortunate that the consequences of social problems are commonly multi-causal, because, if we could deal with them only by restoring the "original causal factors" to their original condition, we would be faced with a hopeless task: they are quite frequently not within our control (or anyone else's control either, for that matter)—think of mass unemployment as an example. That is yet one more difference between social problem causal explanations and program theory. Because they are large scale, indeed global factors (oil prices, weather, food chains, etc.), they may be totally out of our control, while specific program or policy activities are small scale and, by definition, within our control—within what we believe at that moment to be in our capacity to manipulate.

However, beyond sheer scale, theory at the level of social programs can be directed toward only one end of the causal chain; at the level of program theory, the concern is very likely to be restricted to remediating the most immediate consequences, like those described above. How to get food to people who will starve tomorrow is, for example, an entirely remedial objective. A useful causal explanation reveals with clarity the specific transportation features a policy/program system has to have in order to deliver those foodstuffs to a specific group of people at a very specific time and location. Personal social service programs can be similarly characterized.

Consider for the moment that most causal explanations contain reference to both antecedents (*causal variables, independent variables*) and consequences (*outcomes, dependent variables*). The causal analysis of a social problem analysis is always concerned with both antecedents and consequences, while program theory may be concerned with only one or the other. Commonly, social problem analysis can speak about ultimate antecedents, such as genetic factors, now commonly thought to be at the root of psychosis. In that instance, we are left with goals that are primarily remedial—what we know how to do. And, what we do know how to do is often a matter of taking the worst edges off the consequences of a social problem, not antecedents (which can prevent it from happening in the first place) (Chambers, 1986). We might say that thinking about causality at the broad social problem level is relevant when we want to think about broad social change (Shadish, 1987).

The reader should be aware that there are a number of terms used to refer to what we are calling *social problem analysis*. Some use the phrase *program philosophy*. Usually they are referring to such things as beliefs, values, and goals and are interested in speaking about how they work to structure main features of a social program or policy system (like lines of authority and outcomes). Even though we have emphasized the causal aspects of social problem analysis in the discussion above, it is the case that, lying behind assertions about causality, are a whole host of fundamental values, beliefs, and purposes. Those are, in fact, part and parcel of a complete social problem analysis.

Making Program Theory Explicit

The ideas that lie behind beliefs in why a set of program activities should work are not always altogether explicit, even though most people believe that they are a potent influence. Social programs that rely on behavior modification are the leading exception. Beyond that, however, the evaluation practitioner will ordinarily find program theory to be a rather loosely conceived affair, sometimes not there at all.[8] Program theory is most explicit at the time the program is first implemented. That should be no surprise since there is almost always a demand to rationalize the need for it in negotiating its funding. Thus, a standard evaluation task is making implicit program theory explicit, or helping program and policy systems actually create it anew. There are three general approaches. The choice among them depends on the fundamental assumptions one brings to the program/policy evaluation enterprise and social theory plus the relationship between the two. We think of it in the following way. First, one might look at the problem as essentially ethnographic—the task then is to create a process and a context in which program/policy staff can give qualitative, meaningful answers to questions, revealing to the evaluator-cum-ethnographer (and perhaps, to some extent, to the staff members themselves) whatever operating program theory has been in effect. The venture here is essentially a search for meaning (McClintock, 1984). Second, one might use *conceptual heuristics,* a method of exploring ideas through metaphor and various devices that create an environment conducive to cognitive reflection (Wicker, 1985). Third, one might look upon the problem as essentially one of empirical sociological discovery. The task is then to contrive an empirical, probably quantitative, method. The implementers of the program/policy under study can report in a reasonably objective way the ideas that they believe drive their program, most likely through the use of a kind of survey method and statistical analysis of questionnaire responses (Conrad and Miller, 1987). In all these three approaches, the program staff members' ideas matter, and the evaluation practitioner's task is to facilitate the expression of those ideas. We reject the third approach, except for projects in which there are a large number of programs and the purpose is to characterize their similarities with regard to the program. Evaluation tasks that most practitioners are likely to encounter are not of that kind; rather, they concern single programs or those with a few separate sub-operations. It is our belief that to establish program theory among these relatively small operations via quantitative method is quantitative science misplaced. Its main descriptive purpose is to establish central tendency, i.e., commonalities. Where the task is to make program theory explicit for a single program (or a few such), it is better understood as characterizing uniqueness, quite the opposite of establishing commonality.

Endnotes

1. Lipsey found that two-thirds of the published evaluations he looked at could be described as non-theoretical or sub-theoretical (Lipsey, M., Scott, C., Dunkle, J., Pollard, J., and Stobart, G., 1987, p. 168).
2. In an article titled "Evaluating with Sense: A Theory Driven Approach," Chen and Rossi show a strong commitment here. Advocating clearheaded theory as a crucial element in evaluation research, they make clear that "the primary criterion for identifying theory in the sense used in this article is *consistency with social science knowledge and theory"* (italics ours) (Chen and Rossi, 1983, p. 339).
3. Chen and Rossi's arrogance is particularly unattractive because they apparently think that evaluators ought to be social scientists and, as such, concerned with

program theory, because administrators and practitioners aren't prepared to do so: "often enough policymakers and program designers are not social scientists and their theories (if any) are likely to be simply the current folklore of the upper-middle brow media." Of course the arrogance of that opinion is compounded by their own admission (a few sentences later) that it is an "embarrassment" to their point that "social science theory" is not well enough developed that appropriate frameworks and schema are easily available "off the shelf" (Chen and Rossi, 1983, p. 339).

4. Note that here we are not speaking of the sociology of social problems, that is, of the various methods by which one could study them.

5. Of course it is not, impossible for one to begin to think of what is needed out of an experience with the undesirable; but, even so, we insist that once one focuses on needs, the mind tends to turn to what we like to think of as positive issues—to what is, in the end, desirable, in contrast to which this particular concrete instance stands as opposite.

6. Notwithstanding this fact, social programs must retain a sense of relevance to the socially, local definitions of the social problem, lest their credibility suffer. This is a problem for social programs and policies, since they are called to conflicting expectations: the general expectation that social interventions will impact the total problem, while the organization and staff almost always know that their grasp is less than the reach of public expectations.

7. The outstanding exceptions are religious evangelists and some theologians; but, of course, it is their business to study and promote ultimate explanations.

8. Let's ignore the latter case since it is quite a different problem: in that case the evaluator must question whether there is a program at all, and thus whether there is anything tangible to evaluate. As we said earlier, while practitioners or staff members of an organization may be doing good things for their client-consumers even if they have no guiding theory, individually or collectively, there is nothing recognizable as a social program there—to be a social program or policy, there must be a demonstrable, stable pattern of activities.

References

Bickman, L. (Spring 1987). The functions of program theory. In L. Bickman (Ed.), *Using program theory in evaluation* (pp. 5–18). New Directions for Program Evaluation Series. San Francisco: Jossey-Bass.

Chambers, D. E. (1986). *Social policies and social programs.* New York: MacMillan.

Chen, H., & Rossi, P. H. (1983). Evaluating with sense: A theory driven approach. *Evaluation Review, 7*(3), 283–302.

Conrad, K., & Miller, T. (1987). Measuring and testing program philosophy. In L. Bickman (Ed.), *Using program theory in evaluation* (pp. 19–42). New Directions for Program Evaluation Series. San Francisco: Jossey-Bass.

Lipsey, M., Scott, C., Dunkle, J., Pollard, J., & Stobart, G. (1987). Evaluation: The state of the art and the sorry state of the science. In *Evaluation Studies Review Annual-1986.* Beverly Hills, CA: Sage.

McClintock, C. (1984). Toward a theory of formative program evaluation. In D. Deschler (Ed.), *Evaluation for program improvement.* San Francisco: Jossey-Bass.

Scheirer, M. (1987). Program theory and implementation theory: Implications for Evaluators. In L. Bickman (Ed.), *Using program theory in evaluation* (pp. 59–76). New Directions for Program Evaluation Series. San Francisco: Jossey-Bass.

Shadish, W. (1987). Program micro- and macrotheories: A guide for social change. In L. Bickman (Ed.), *Using program theory in evaluation* (pp. 93–108). New Directions for Program Evaluation Series. San Francisco: Jossey-Bass.

Spector, M., & Kitsuse, J. (1973). Social problems: A reformulation. *Social Problems, 20,* 145–159.

Weiss, C. (1971). *Evaluation research.* Boston: Allyn-Bacon.

Wicker, A. (1985). Getting out of our conceptual ruts: Strategies for expanding conceptual frameworks. *American Anthropologist, 40,* 1094–1103.

CHAPTER SIX

The Assessment of
Social Program Evaluability

Evaluability assessment (EA) is a means to determine: whether to conduct
a program evaluation; whether there are program changes needed before
conducting an evaluation; and which method or methods of program evaluation are most appropriate to judge program performance. An assessment of
evaluability also serves to assist policy makers and program administrators
in decision making, gauge the level of support to adequately carry out an
evaluation, and identify potential resource commitments required to complete the evaluation.

> *... EA answers the question, not whether a program can be evaluated (every program
> can be evaluated), but whether the program is ready to be managed to achieve desired
> performance and outcomes, what changes are needed to allow results-oriented manage-
> ment, and whether evaluation is likely to contribute to improved program performance
> (Strosberg and Wholey, 1983, p. 66).*

In chapter five we discussed the necessity of making explicit the "theory" on
which policy and programming are based. This chapter will begin with a brief
discussion on approaches which can be use to make theory and assumptions
about social programs explicit, and thereby, to test out the appropriateness of
program evaluation before it is undertaken.

The assessment of program evaluability involves a set of activities to
identify whether it is practical, technically feasible, or politically appropriate
to evaluate a program. Different terms have been used to identify the activities
associated with assessment of program evaluability: including *exploratory
evaluation, pre-evaluation, planning* or *pre-planning phase, program needs assessment,* and *pre-implementation.* Regardless of the terminology used, there appears to be a commonality in purpose and direction. The purpose of
evaluability assessment, according to Wholey (1979, p. xiii), is to: explore the
objectives, expectations, and information needs of program managers and
policy-makers; explore program reality; assess the likelihood that program
activities will achieve measurable progress toward program objectives; and

119

assess the extent to which evaluation information is likely to be used by program management.

EA involves a review of both subtle and salient factors that affect a program's evaluability. There are many reasons why a program or specific components of the program may not be amenable to traditional methods of program evaluation. Too often, problems which occur later on in program evaluation raise questions about the wisdom of carrying out a program evaluation in the first place. Four broad areas of concern that are identified in evaluability assessment are: (1) a determination of purpose(s) for program evaluation, (2) program reality, (3) technical feasibility, and (4) human and political feasibility. Although there is considerable overlap among these concern areas, it is useful to consider the dimensions of each concern in more detail.

The first area of concern addresses the matter of clarifying the intent of program evaluation, and expectations of results when the evaluation has been completed. Formal sources of information on purpose can often be found in Requests for Proposals (RFP's) that led to initiating the program and/or the call for evaluation, administrative charges, policy documents, and so forth. More in-depth information will probably require personal contact with persons who have declared an interest in, or have authorized a program evaluation. The second area of concern relates to how well the program to be evaluated is defined, specificity of goals and objectives, and whether the program can realistically be expected to achieve specified goals. A review of program documents and interviews with key program people are resources available to the program evaluator in addressing this general concern. The third area of concern above relates to whether methodology is available for the purpose of the evaluation, and any difficulties that may arise in selecting one method over another. Informational sources include the literature, experts in the field, and the data gathered from the program itself. The final concern is for all the relevant human and political factors that affect evaluability. Especially critical are the presence of any limitations and restrictions which might stand in the way (legal, political, ethical, and administrative). Informational sources for this area of concern are many, and include both formal and informal data gathered throughout the evaluability assessment process.

Evaluability assessment is undertaken to examine what can and cannot reasonably be subjected to the evaluation process. The aim of evaluability assessment is often less a matter of determining whether the program itself is evaluable, than it is to determine what aspects or components of a program may be successfully evaluated. Evaluability assessment starts with information gathering that can be used in analysis and, eventually, decision making about evaluability. Next we will consider the kinds of information needed in each of the four general areas of concern identified above.

Information Needs

Clarifying the Purpose of Program Evaluation

Information on purpose(s) of the program evaluation is especially important early on in the evaluability assessment. Until the intent and expectations of the program evaluation are known, it is difficult to specify parameters in the search for other data that may be relevant to evaluability assessment. A starting point is to examine the statements of purpose and information needs expressed by the party authorizing and/or funding the evaluation. It can logically be assumed that authorizers and funders play a significant role in determining the focus and nature of the evaluation. Usually, the authorizers and funders fulfill a policy making role; they also become the program administrators. When there is a clear distinction between policy makers and program administrators (as in legislative policy makers and state departmental administrators), then it is important to establish perceptions of purpose from each of these constituencies. Others who play important roles in the purposes of the evaluation are those persons and groups which also have some stake in the performance, outcome, or implications of the program evaluation. The term *stakeholders* is used in reference to the various parties who are involved in a program or directly affected by a program evaluation. As used in this context, the notion of stake may vary greatly among individuals and groups identified: the stake may be fiscal in nature, or encompass a host of other possibilities, including reputation, career aspirations, political influence, time, energy, efficiency, and so on (Guba and Lincoln, 1981). Key questions to be raised are: who are the stakeholders, what are the stakeholders' purposes of the program evaluation findings, and what kinds of information are needed by the intended users of the evaluation.

Program Reality Information

Basic information is required on the structure and function of the program to be evaluated. A starting point is the compilation of descriptive information. Descriptive information is needed on the program to be evaluated, the setting in which it exists, and the conditions under which both program use and evaluation take place (Guba and Lincoln, 1981). Essential data for a description of the program begins with the theory or philosophy of the program as discussed in chapter five. What is the program intended to achieve? What are the goals and objectives of the program? Key conditions of program design that can have a profound effect on the evaluability are:

- Program goals are knowable, i.e., there are goal statements that give evidence to a consensus of program efforts.
- Program objectives are well defined, i.e., there are clearly stated, measurable objectives that identify program performance indicators.
- Program goals and objectives are plausible, i.e., there is evidence that program activities achieve measurable progress toward fulfilling objectives and overall goals.

Descriptors on the parameters of the program provide information on the setting of the program. Is the program a unit of a larger organization structure, or a singular organizational unit itself? Does the organization have a narrowly defined mission, or is it multipurpose? Questions such as these about program structure and function are intended to establish a beginning framework for understanding the program in terms of it's overall mission and design.

Next are informational needs on program implementation. How is the program administered? Information is also needed on recipients or target groups for program services or interventions. Who does the program serve? The description of conditions under which program use and evaluation will take place includes information needs on service provision, service givers, and the transactions involved with program recipients. A more in-depth analysis of the program to be evaluated will be required to identify these factors of concern for practicality of program evaluation. Example questions are the following: What is the nature of the service or intervention, including timing? How is a unit of service designated? What are the qualifications of service givers? What is the entry behavior of program recipients in contrast to outcome behavior?

Information on Technical Feasibility

Information needed to determine the technical feasibility of conducting a program evaluation is closely linked with the purposes of the program evaluation discussed above. The purposes of evaluation establish methodological requirements and give initial indications for potential opportunities and limitations. It follows then that specific information is needed on: availability of methodology and technologies to achieve the given purpose(s) of the evaluation, access to appropriate data, and availability of data. Key questions are: Given the purposes of program evaluation, what are the methodological options for appropriate evaluation? What tasks are required in each option for evaluation design? Will needed data be available?

The needs for information to determine human and political feasibility of conducting a program evaluation are a little more open-ended. Data requirements can be difficult to specify until some parameters are in place concerning the other three concerns identified above. However, some of the more critical issues can be highlighted. First we will consider the issues of ethics and confidentiality.

Ethics   Ethical issues merit special consideration. As we have discussed in chapter two, a first matter of priority in program evaluation should be the safe-guarding of clients and organizational members who could suffer an adversity from the evaluation activities. The infamous Tuskegee syphilis experiment stands out as a reminder to carefully examine dangerous side effects that can be built in to a program evaluation design. Clients in a control group of that study were denied treatment and studied in comparison to clients who did receive medical treatment (Jones, 1982). More often our concerns will represent subtle questions about ethical practice. Is it appropriate to utilize one treatment or service strategy over another for purposes of evaluation? Are there ethical compromises in placing the importance of an evaluation above the best interests of clients? Closely related is the issue of confidentiality.

Confidentiality   A careful review should be made concerning matters of confidentiality, those potentially affected, and limitations imposed in safe-guarding unwarranted exposure of individuals. Confidentiality may be an issue for program clientele, program administrators, program personnel, and others associated with the program. Key questions which emerge are: Who could be adversely affected by the violation of confidentiality? How would they be affected? What compromises to the evaluation can be expected by confidentiality assurance?

Legality   The next critical issue which we will want to consider is the matter of legality. In many human service programs, eligible clients are entitled to services through statutory right. This can pose constraints for evaluation of alternative programs, or prohibit not serving control groups. Related to the above issue on confidentiality, are legal constraints on access to certain data without the written consent of involved persons covered by provisions of the Privacy Act of 1974 and/or other legal restrictions which might apply. Further is the issue of legal liability. The results of a program evaluation can have a profound effect on such matters as future funding and program resources, program continuation, professional careers, jobs for service givers and so on. To the extent that any of the program's stakeholders could be affected adversely by the evaluation, it is a good idea to review beforehand any potential questions of legal liability. Key questions for the evaluability assessment are: What are the legal constraints to program evaluation design and methodology which would alter clients' statutory rights? What are the legal limitations on data access, collection, and utilization? In what ways could the program evaluation result in legal liabilities?

Political economy Several issues are discussed next under the general rubric of political economy. First is the consideration of cost. Schmidt (1983) has identified major cost factors for conducting program evaluation in the following:

- Costs of collecting, storing, processing, and verifying the information for each event
- Rough system costs in terms of staff (internal) and dollars (contract costs)
- Cost burden on program operator staff (if they are required to supply data)

Opportunity costs should also be taken into consideration. By *opportunity costs*, we are referring to the costs of carrying out an evaluation when funds dedicated to this purpose could be used for another purpose. Can the program afford to carry out an evaluation at a particular point in time? What are the resource limits for carrying out a program evaluation versus resource expenditures for other program needs? These and related questions will usually require the input of program stakeholders in a decision making process.

Political constraints can be very influential in the evaluability of a given program. In fact, political influence can subvert plans for an evaluability assessment as discussed in this chapter. Examples are when a political timetable for program evaluation precludes anything more than a superficial EA; or methodological approaches such as control groups or random sampling requirements may be politically feasible but ethically unacceptable, or vice versa. Especially serious is the presence of political influence in determining beforehand what the results of the evaluation should show. Some examples are: approving for evaluation only aspects of the program which can be expected to "look good" under the microscope of evaluation, denying access to program data about which there is some degree of discomfort, and manipulating the evaluability assessment process in ways to either favor a particular approach to evaluation or discourage any initiative to carry out program evaluation. Although it would be difficult to offer specific advice for each and every political constraint that may come up, it is advised that the evaluability assessor check determine political influences and be prepared to respond appropriately when they are present.

Internal organizational politics At all levels of program operations, the request for information may be met with either acceptance or resistance. Choices of organizational response to evaluation information "are conditioned by the distributed beliefs of people about the effects of the action upon themselves, their peers, others in the organization, and others outside the organization" (Nay and Kay, 1982, p. 120). When higher-level members of the program exhibit resistance, special efforts may be required to establish administrative cooperation. Kay and Nay (1982) recommend overcoming administrators' resistance by involving them more in building the evaluation system and giving leadership prestige for their involvement.

The role of front line program personnel represents another important consideration for gathering of evaluability information. Staff to carry out the program evaluation may or may not be regular program personnel. The use of special investigators to carry out the program evaluation may be seen as an intrusion on program functioning, and beyond the control of program managers. Using regular program personnel may be interpreted as an intrusion on staff members' time, and met with considerable resistance if no release time is given from regular duties. Often overlooked are the demands that can be placed on support staff of a program during evaluation to access files, provide data, and explain program procedures. The point is, a program evaluation has the potential of disrupting the flow of service delivery in most programs and should be carefully evaluated in the evaluability assessment. Key questions are: How will the program evaluation affect the management control patterns in the program? How will service giving staff be affected by the evaluation? What demands will be placed on support staff of the program?

Methodology in Evaluability Assessment

Methodological approaches to evaluability assessment have not received the attention or refinement as has been the case for program evaluation itself. To a great extent methodology for evaluability assessment involves practical approaches, such as review of documents, interviews, and observation to assist in answering basic questions as identified in the preceding discussion. Helpful guidance is available, however, in the approaches that have been articulated in the program literature. We shall identify four major sub areas of evaluability assessment as (1) purpose assessment, (2) program assessment, (3)technical feasibility assessment, and (4) human and political feasibility assessment. Next we will discuss the specific techniques that can be utilized in these sub areas of assessment.

Assessment of Purpose

Assessment of purpose is undertaken to identify rationale for the program evaluation and the information needs of the stakeholders who commission and/or fund the program evaluation. The rationale or purpose of program evaluation, in turn, establishes the methodological requirements and provides a basis for examining the feasibility for the evaluation. A clarification of purpose(s), and mutual understanding of expectations between the parties involved, represent important beginning steps in a logical beginning for the evaluation process. Clues concerning the purpose of the evaluation can often be found in documents prepared by the party who commissioned the evaluation. When the evaluation is to be conducted in house, it may be necessary to supplement written documents with personal interviews about purpose and information needs. Increasingly, programs in the public sector are required to issue requests for proposals (RFP's) if the evaluation is to be done by an evaluator selected from outside the program. Private non profit sector programs may also use a competitive bid approach with an RFP to select outside evaluators. When the RFP is used, it will usually be a good beginning source for the stated purpose(s) of the program evaluation. Closely related are written materials and information provided during bidders meetings that may further elaborate on the purpose of the program evaluation.

A statement of understanding on the purpose for the evaluation, and points of agreement between the parties involved in the program evaluation, is recommended prior to the initiation of an EA. The terms of understanding about purpose(s) can be specified in the first draft of an evaluation contract. The evaluation contract may be a simple written letter of understanding, or an elaborate contractual document may be required which incorporates specific sets of topics decided upon following the evaluability assessment. In any event, even in initial stages of negotiation, the evaluation contract should be a source of reference on purpose and charges stated for the program evaluation.

It can be very difficult to meet the informational needs of all who might potentially benefit from evaluation findings. Specific needs of the primary user may be given a first priority or simply consideration among the range of potential users. The analysis of purpose for program evaluation remains a continuous process in the EA. While the above discussion makes the case for initial clarification of purpose(s) for evaluation, it should also be pointed out that the purpose may be modified as insights are developed through further assessment of program reality and program evaluation feasibility.

Program Assessment

Program assessment represents one of the central features, if not the core feature, in evaluability assessment. It serves to identify how well program components are defined and how clearly program goals are specified. Furthermore, an assessment of the program serves to validate accuracy of divergent perceptions about the program. "There is often a substantial discrepancy between the concept of a program as perceived by managers and policy-makers and the reality of that program as it exists in the field, as well as a hesitancy on the part of management to admit to the discrepancy" (Schmidt, Scanlon, and Bell, 1979, p. 7). The program assessment involves several informational sources for a thorough description of the program.

Four general methods are identified to gather information and carry out the program assessment: (1) reviewing program documentation, (2) describing the program, (3) modeling the program, and (4) conducting site visit(s) to confirm program description and better understand program operations, clientele, and effects that the program appears to produce. A somewhat different ordering of these general methods is taken in the procedures that provide detailed advice on program assessment. For the most part, however, each describes an iterative process with stages leading to the preparation of an end product. The end product is variously described as a "synthesis of information" (Wholey, 1979), "the evaluator's description" of the program (Schmidt, Scanlon, and Bell, 1979), or an "evaluable program model" (Rutman, 1980) that depicts the program components and goals/effects that give evidence of evaluability, or raise serious questions for the evaluator. A consideration of specific activities that make up program assessment methodology are taken up next.

Reviewing program documentation A review of program documents begins with the collection of available information that describes the program, its mandate to provide services or care, and other pertinent facts that may be useful to the assessment process. Examples of such documents are: formal mission statements, as in authorizing legislation, charter, constitution, or by-laws; grant proposals; funding requests; audit reports; program policy manuals and memoranda; brochures or bulletins which describe the program; legislative or administrative study reports; working papers; consultant reports; and previous program evaluation reports. The list of possible documents will, of course, vary form program to program. The important point is for the evaluator to develop as clear an understanding as possible about the mandate for the program, mission, and goals and commitments to program constituents. Information from the documents review provides leads for inquiry in later approaches to data gathering.

Once program documents have been collected, the next step is to organize pertinent information in a usable format. Rutman (1980) suggests a listing process to depict all the program components and goals/effects that have to do with activities directly related to the goals/effects of service or care delivery. He cautions that it is common to find goals stated in program documents that are in fact program components, and a distinction must be made between the program and its goals. For purposes of illustration, here is such a listing procedure for a hypothetical Women's Resource Center. Program components and goals/effects might include:

Program Components	*Goals/Effects*
Counseling services	Referral
Rape response team	Crisis intervention
Sexual assault	Improving coping skills
Prevention	Marital counseling
Shelter	Reduce trauma
	Increase community awareness
	Safe harbor

The next stage involves the preparation of a program description.

Describing the program   The program description for EA builds on information collected in program documentation and elaborates on the assumed cause and effect relationships occurring between program components and goals/effects identified as above. The essential elements required for a program description are presented in Table 6–1.

Information for program description comes from several sources, including program documents review as discussed above. Key informants may include program policy makers, management, program operators, as well as observations from the evaluator. However, at this stage of program assessment, information provided through interviews with policy makers and management tends to come front and center. Wholey (1979) advises that program management's objectives for the program will often be more process-oriented than those evident in legislation or as expressed by high level policy makers. He offers sample guides of questions from interviews in the field of health planning that can be useful in clarifying these differences, and, hopefully, provide a more accurate description of the program. The questions from his sample guide (Wholey, 1979) for interviewing policy makers are the following:

1. *In your judgment, what are the objectives of the program?*
2. *What would you consider acceptable measures/evidence of progress toward those objectives? [How would you know whether the program was accomplishing its objectives?]*
3. *What are the program priorities from your point of view? [How would you know if the program was a success? What information do you need on program areas that may be developing?]*
4. *What do you expect the program to accomplish in the next year? In the next five years?*
5. *What mechanisms exist [policies, guidelines, staff activities, etc.] to achieve those objectives?*
6. *Why will Event A lead to Event B? [Why do you think that program inputs or program activities will cause progress toward program objectives?]*
7. *What are the most serious difficulties facing the program in meeting its objectives?*
8. *Have you seen the program's present information system? Is it adequate for your needs?*
9. *How do you get the program performance information you need to do your job?*
10. *How satisfied are you with this information?*

TABLE 6–1 • Elements Needed in a Complete Program Description

Element of the Program Description	1. Event Sequence That Describes Program Behavior	2. Measures and Comparisons Describing Each Event	3. Expected Values for Each Event	4. Activities That Must Be in Place for Event to Occur	5. Information Systems Used to Provide Evidence of Event Occurring	6. Use of Evaluation Information
Information items that must be known for the program description to be well defined	1. Sequence begins with events over which management has direct control 2. Sequence includes all events that must occur for objectives to be achieved 3. Events include achievement of all objectives considered necessary to justify the program 4. Events include all positive and negative expected side effects	1. A set of measures and comparisons considered necessary and sufficient by owner to describe the event is identified 2. Measures and comparisons also describe the evidence acceptable to the owner demonstrating that the event occurred	1. The owner's* expected values for each event are identified 2. Time periods in which events should occur are given	1. The program activities that must be in place for each event to occur are identified 2. The characteristics of those activities necessary for expectations to be met are specified 3. The rationale or evidence indicating that the activity will achieve expected results is identified	1. The measurement systems that provide data on each event are identified 2. The measurement operation and instrument is described for each measure 3. Methods and mechanisms available to estimate and check for measurement and processing errors are identified 4. Costs of measurement systems are known	1. The users of evaluative information are identified for each event 2. Actions or processes for defining action to be taken on evaluative information are identified 3. How these actions are expected to affect the program or policies described

Source: Schmidt, R. E., Scanlon, J. W., and Bell, J. B. (1979) *Evaluability assessment: Making public programs work better.* Washington, D.C.: U.S. Government Printing Office, p. 10.

*"owner" refers to person or group from whom information is obtained, e.g., program manager.

11. *How do you use this information?*
12. *What would you like to learn from an evaluation of the program?*
    (p. 56)

According to Wholey, questions 2 and 3 can yield measures for assessing evaluability, and questions 5 and 6 yield intermediate objectives or causal assumptions linking events.

A set of ten questions guide the interview process for program management. The questions are the following:

1. *Could you describe your own Office or Division, its staffing, and its major activities?*
2. *How would you measure your progress in these activities? How can you tell what you are accomplishing?*
3. *From your perspective, what is the bureau [program unit] trying to accomplish and what resources does it have?*
4. *What accomplishments are likely in the next year or two?*
5. *Why would these activities produce those results?*
6. *What are your main problems?*
7. *How long will it take to solve those problems?*
8. *What kinds of information do you get on the bureau's [program unit's] performance?" What kinds of information do you need?*
9. *How would you/do you use this information?*
10. *What kinds of information do the Office of Management and Budget and Congress ask for? (Wholey, 1979, p. 55)*

Question 10 would, of course, pertain to a program assessment of a federal program. The phrases "Office of Management and Budget" and "Congress" could be replaced by budget office and legislature for assessment of state level programs, or board and funding sources for assessment of private sector programs.

It is noteworthy to observe that, contained in the question guide above, are questions which go beyond mere description of the program to address problem areas and information needs. This additional data input should prove useful later if it is determined that a program evaluation will take place.

The program description provided by management adds an additional ingredient to the evaluator's quest for clarity in program assessment. It serves also to engage management in the early stages of EA, and fosters the notion that it is a process to establish preconditions for program success.

Based on information derived from the sources identified above, the evaluator, working with program management, brings this stage of program assessment to a close by documenting the accuracy of the program description. "Working with the program manager, the evaluator assesses gaps or problems in management description and devises alternative descriptions or strategies for alleviating problems and producing—again, with the participation of management—an 'evaluable' program design" (Schmidt, Beyna, and Harr, 1982, p. 201). It is perhaps worth noting, however, that determination of an "evaluable" program design may be premature, before additional information is considered in the EA process.

Modeling the program Various terms are used to describe the modeling stage of program assessment. Regardless of terminology, the purpose of modeling is to visually present a description of apparent program activities and their objectives. Schmidt, Horst, Scanlon, and Wholey (1977) describe a rhetorical model which, for a publicly administered program, represents the program that has been defined by the manager and discussed in legislation. Schmidt, Scanlon, and Bell (1979) identify three models for program description: logic models, function models, and measurement models. The basic information elements of the three models are represented in Table 6–2.

Rutman (1980) suggests a flow model which incorporates many of the information elements of the models described above. A flow model can be prepared in a number of ways, most simply by noting goals/effects for each program component on an organization chart. Rutman (1980) suggests an approach which is based on experimentation with ways of entering program data. The suggested approach depicts program components on a horizontal

TABLE 6–2 • *Typical Sources of Information for Each Program Model Type*

Source of Description	Type of Information in the Description		
	Logic Models	*Function Models*	*Measurement Models*
Policymakers	Legislation Hearings Committee reports Interviews	Legislation Hearings Committee reports	Interviews
Management	Regulations Guidelines Interviews	Regulations Guidelines Work plans	Guidelines Data system manuals Evaluation designs Interviews
Operator	Interviews	Interviews Work plans	Interviews Files
Evaluator	Observation of program activity and flows	Observation of program activity and flows	Observation of program activity and flows

Source: Schmidt, R. E., Scanlon, J. W., and Bell, J. B. (1979). *Evaluability assessment: Making public programs work better.* Washington D.C.: U.S. Government Printing Office, 1979, p. 23.

FIGURE 6–1 • *Flow Model of Women's Resource Center (Rape Response Team Program Component)*

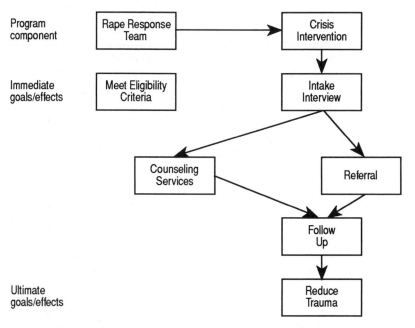

Source: Adapted from Rutman, L. (1980). *Planning useful evaluations: evaluability assessment*. Beverly Hills, CA: Sage, p. 94. Used by permission.

---

plane, with goals/effects placed vertically under the appropriate program components. An important consideration in this approach is an attempt to factor out hierarchical bias; the level at which a goal/effect appears in the flow model is not indicative of its importance, as might be assumed in an organization chart. Figure 6–1 provides an example of a flow chart model for our hypothetical Women's Resource Center. The program component chosen for illustrative purposes is the rape response program component, with its various services and goals. Flow linkages between program components and goals/effects may or may not be easy to infer from program documents. After preparing flow models for each program component, the evaluator then prepares a flow model for the entire program to help visually track what appear to be logical linkages between program components and goals/effects.

An alternative to a flow model prepared by the evaluator as described above is a request for program management to carry out the modeling procedure. In either case, the final stage of program assessment—site visitation—serves to confirm the accuracy of program modeling by checking into apparent linkages between program components and goals/effects.

Site visitation   Site visitation, or field study, represents efforts undertaken by the evaluator to observe first hand the work of the program. Site visitation involves direct contact with the program components giving care or service. There are, of course, limitations to this observation in terms of client confidentially and/or other sensitivities pertaining to the program's operations. Site visitation is basically an approach to gather further program information, especially for the issues of concern that have been identified in earlier stages of the program analysis. Usually, the activities undertaken in site visitation are purposefully time-limited and generally are carried out without adding substantially to the cost of program assessment. Far from being only a casual undertaking, the site visitation may nevertheless fall short of acceptable scientific standards (Rutman, 1984). The primary methods of data collection are observation and interviews with program personnel, clients, or others who can be expected to give informed responses to questions about program reality in the field. Particular advantages that can be gained from site visitation are: insights with regard to the processing of clients and special circumstances that arise in the field, a better understanding of the program's target population and how they are served, and identification of unstated program goals and unintended effects.

Procedures for interviewing relevant program personnel need not follow an established plan. However, it may be helpful to start by preparing a list of persons who are considered key actors in program implementation and can therefore be considered as key informants for program information. Particularly relevant are managers and supervisors who have specific responsibilities for day to day monitoring of program performance, front line workers, and possibly selected clients or former clients of the program. The main point in selection of persons to interview is that persons chosen have knowledge and understanding of the program and a willingness to cooperate in data collection at this stage of assessment. The interviews need not be overly structured, but as in any form of information gathering through the use of personal interviews, a schedule of questions is suggested.

Interview questions are posed to help guide the process of documenting the accuracy of program modeling, adding missing components/goals/effects, and securing additional information about how the program works. Basic questions to consider raising are suggested in the following:

1. *What are your objectives for the project or program?*
2. *What mechanisms exist [policies, staff activities, etc.] to achieve those objectives?*
3. *What evidence is necessary to see whether objectives are met? Is this evidence collected?*

4. *What happens if objectives are met? Not met?*
5. *How is the project related to local priorities?*
6. *What data or records are maintained?*
   Utilization, types of services, demographic characteristics
   Costs per unit of service,
   Other
7. *How often are these data collected?*
8. *What is the accuracy of these data?*
9. *How is this information used? Does anything change based on these data or records?*
10. *What major problems are you experiencing? (Wholey, 1979, p. 68)*

The degree to which a management-by-objectives posture is taken in the program may have a significant influence on clarity of information taken by questions as in the above list. Regardless, this information will be particularly important in considering feasibility of program evaluation taken up later in this chapter.

A further line of inquiry can be taken to distinguish between program inputs, outputs, and outcomes. The availability of outcome data will be critical in a program evaluation to determine the extent to which program goals/effects have been reached. The following additional questions may be raised with interviewees (especially program managers and supervisors) to confirm or reject the evaluators perceptions in this area. The questions are:

- What are the program outputs?
- How are program outputs measured?
- What are program outcomes?
- How are program outcomes measured?

It may be anticipated that answers to the interview questions will represent varying viewpoints. For instance, it may be quite revealing to examine outcome descriptions as stated by program personnel and former clientele. Difference in viewpoint does not mean, per se, that a program evaluation will be unfruitful. Nevertheless, it is important to determine at this stage of the program assessment whether potential problems for a program evaluation are revealed in clarity of program intent and consistency in approach. Descriptive information in the flow model, based on program documents and interviews with key program people, is given further scrutiny by examination of program reality through site visitation.

End product of program assessment   The final stage of the program assessment is the preparation of an end product based on an analysis of program assessment information. Schmidt, Scanlon, and Bell (1979) describe the analysis as using the descriptive framework prepared in program modeling as a guide for a checklist approach to develop an overall picture of program

TABLE 6–3 • *Checklist for Recording if a Program Description is Well-Defined*

Information Elements				
1. Event sequence	*Event 1*	*Event 2*	*Event 3*	*Event 4*
2. Event descriptions	Yes/No			
3. Measures and comparisons	Yes/No			
4. Expected values for each event	Yes/No			
5. Activities that must occur for event to take place				
6. Information system used to profide evidence				
7. Uses of evaluation information				

Source: Schmidt, R. E., Scanlon, J. W., and Bell, J. B. (1979) *Evaluability assessment: Making public programs work better.* Washington, D.C.: U.S. Government Printing Office, p. 34.

reality. Table 6–3 provides an example of information processing during the analysis process. Following analysis, the evaluator is in a position to describe program reality as he or she sees it, based on the input of others as described above, but reflecting the evaluator's perceptions of what actually appears to be occurring.

The end product is variously described in terms of a synthesized program model. Wholey (1979) describes the end product as an "equivalency model" that describes the operations of the program "in terms of feasible measures of project [program] inputs, activities, and outcomes, and indicates the extent to which data are obtainable on project [program] inputs, activities, and outcomes" (pp. 69–70). Rutman (1980) describes an "evaluable program model," which gives evidence whether: (1) program components are well defined and can be implemented in the prescribed manner, (2) goals/effects are clearly specified, and (3) plausible causal linkages exist for program components and goals/effects.

Feasibility Assessment

Feasibility assessment is concerned with whether the program reality presents indications of evaluable preconditions, appropriate evaluation research methods can be applied, and constraints or limitations can be overcome.

Program design and implementation In the above section of this chapter on program assessment, program reality was assessed in terms of clarity and consistency of identifiable goals/effects and structural components in program design. In Chapters Seven and Eight attention is directed to the matter of monitoring social program implementation. Here our attention is to an introductory examination of feasibility in achieving the purpose(s) of program evaluation, given the program reality identified. Rutman (1980) poses three general questions pertaining to this aspect of feasibility, which provide a useful guide to inquiry on program design and implementation. The questions and responses paraphrased from Rutman are as follows:

1. *Is the program designed so that the evaluation can attribute the findings to particular program components?*
Problems can be encountered when several program components are directed to a common goal, and the purpose of the evaluation is to test the effectiveness of particular components. It may be necessary to modify the original purpose of evaluation and/or utilize specialized statistical approaches to estimate program component impact.
2. *To what extent can the program be implemented in a prescribed manner?*
The concern addressed by this question is when the focus of evaluation is to determine effectiveness of a particular program approach, as in the case of a particular therapy. In order to test the program approach, assurance is necessary that the program can be implemented in the way it is planned and stays on that course until the evaluation is completed.
3. *To what extent can research requirements be incorporated by the program?*
The assessment of this concern requires the evaluator to examine the compatibility of applied research requirements, such as sampling, utilization of control groups, and data collection, with program service integrity (pp. 128–130).

Technical requirements Three major areas are suggested for review in the determination of technical requirements. First is the issue of information or program performance data available to successfully carry out the program evaluation research. The second area is the matter of research design and methodology appropriate to carry out the evaluation. Finally, the requirements for data analysis are the third area. Our aim here simply is to examine the line of inquiry required to determine technical feasibility as envisioned in the initial request for program evaluation. A more detailed line of questioning is provided in Chapters Seven and Eight.

Information requirements. A critical factor in program evaluability is whether information requirements can be sufficiently met to carry out the commonly accepted methods of evaluation research. This is a kind of chicken/egg question as to which comes first, since information needs depend on specific research design and methodology chosen or vice versa. Nevertheless, it behooves the evaluator to thoroughly examine several aspects of information availability as part of the feasibility assessment.

If the inquiry is focused on the potential use of a quantitative approach to evaluation using measures of program outcomes, the material in Chapters Nine and Ten should be addressed in terms of data requirements, reliability and validity to appropriately undertake an effective quantitative methodology for program evaluation. In cases where a qualitative approach is under consideration, the material in Chapter Thirteen should be addressed in terms of informational requirements for program evaluation.

It will be difficult, if not impossible, to estimate accurately at this stage all of the feasibility issues with regard to information needs for program evaluation. A beginning can be made, however, by posing a series of standard questions concerning information available and types and of volume required for alternative approaches to research design. The importance of being able to obtain information on which to base the program evaluation cannot be overemphasized.

Research design and methodology requirements. The feasibility of utilizing appropriate research design and methodology is intricately tied to informational needs discussed above. The standard feasibility questions for a quantitative approach to program evaluation would be addressed to issues of sampling procedures, need for use of control groups, and requirements for data analysis. In the case of a qualitative approach, questions would be directed to information access, intrusion into program processes, trained observers, etc.

Next we will briefly consider the need requirements for data analysis once an approximation can be made of program information needed, and the research design and methodology contemplated for the program evaluation.

Data analysis requirements. The final dimension considered in this phase of feasibility assessment relates to the requirements for data analysis. Advancements in recent years in both hardware and software for data analysis have been remarkable. However, it is important to consider beforehand the application of appropriate analytical techniques for the data to be collected. A common problem for the neophyte in social research is the collection of data in excess to the research questions being raised. The evaluator will do well to investigate the projected costs of data analysis in relation to expected benefits in study findings. A final point of advice is to seek out the advice and recommendations of experts on data analysis as part of the feasibility assessment; expertise in this area is usually readily found in the data processing department of major human service organizations and computer centers on college and university campuses.

The assessment of technical feasibility sets the stage for estimations of feasibility in terms of cost, as well as the important considerations of human and political feasibility for carrying out the program evaluation. Cost feasibility will be taken up next.

Cost feasibility Resources required to carry out a program evaluation are a major consideration in the determination of feasibility. Although it may be difficult to attach a value to anticipated costs, let alone anticipate in advance all of the cost factors involved, a beginning step is made in efforts to identify likely major resource requirements.

Schmidt, Scanlon, and Bell (1979) suggest a basic checklist procedure to examine financial feasibility on the basis of information needs and personnel costs. Their checklist includes estimating or calculating costs in the following major resource areas:

- *Costs of collecting, storing, processing, and verifying the information for each event.*
- *System costs in terms of staff (internal) and dollars (contract cost).*
- *Cost burden on program operator staff (if they are required to supply data) (p. 56).*

Cost feasibility, then, is determined when the costs fall within some determination of reasonable operating and evaluation budget.

Cost differentials can also be projected on the basis of research design and methodology. Wholey (1979) points out, for instance, that experiments and quasi-experiments tend to be more costly than performance monitoring. An experimental design for program evaluation research, if it is feasible on other grounds, may have the additional costs of obtaining data from control or comparison groups, sampling procedures, sophisticated data analysis techniques, etc.

Schmidt (1983) discusses the potential for applying cost analysis procedures during evaluability assessment to estimate costs for both EA and alternatives in later program evaluation. For the larger governmental programs from which his examples are drawn, program managers know aggregate costs for acquiring evaluation information. However, there is considerable opportunity to provide management with cost feasibility data on, say, the differential costs between use of personal face-to-face interviews and a mailed questionnaire. Ideas for cost considerations that could be applied in cost analysis for cost feasibility are covered in greater detail in Chapter Eleven of this text.

Human and Political Feasibility

A final area of concern for feasibility assessment is with the human and political factors. The ways in which human and political factors can influence the evaluability of social programs is more or less without limits. Nevertheless, questions can be asked to guide our assessment in this difficult area as well. The following are basic questions concerning human factors in evaluation:

- Can the program evaluation be adequately carried out as planned with due regard for maintenance of personal rights and integrity?
- Could any harm come to the program's clients and/or program personnel as a result of the evaluation process?
- Is it reasonable to expect the cooperation of clients and/or program personnel?

- In what ways will the evaluation be disfunctional to human performance?
- Who are the potential gainers and losers from the evaluation findings?

Political dynamics are a contextual reality of program evaluation. Weiss (1975) captures this perspective by noting that the policies and programs with which evaluation deals are themselves the creatures of political decisions; evaluation reports compete with other factors in the political decision making arena; and evaluation itself has a political stance and makes implicit statements about issues such as the problematic nature of some programs and unchallengeability of others. Political influence may be difficult to manage, but a starting point is to gain as much understanding as possible about how political factors might shape the evaluation. A sampling of basic questions concerning political factors in evaluation are the following:

- What kinds of political influence can be expected in the evaluation and from whom?
- What does the program have to gain or lose from the evaluation?
- What are the commitments to objectivity in evaluation methodology and report of findings?

The task for the evaluator is to make an effort to determine the extent of political imbalance that will be induced by the proposed evaluation. Given such knowledge, it is then necessary to assess, as far as possible, whether the information likely to be derived from the evaluation is sufficiently weighty to warrant the resulting political upset (Guba and Lincoln, 1981).

Evaluability Analysis and Decision Making

Each of the sub areas of assessment we have identified above yield both general and specific kinds of information. The next step is a thorough review of the information collected and the documentation of findings. One approach is to rate the various components of the evaluability information. For example, Table 6–4 depicts a procedure for rating methodological issues in the hypothetical Women's Resource Center we referred to earlier in Figure 6–1. The ratings in Table 6–4 help to present evaluability findings visually. Nominal rating of feasibility factors can also be carried out using a procedure similar to that presented in Table 6–4.

An evaluability assessment report is prepared to highlight the evaluability analysis, and to explore the major factors of cost, timing, political, and bureaucratic implications. The evaluability assessment report provides a basis for decision making on whether to proceed with an evaluation, how to

TABLE 6–4 • *Evaluability Ratings for Methodology—Women's Resource Center*

Program Components	Availability of Suitable Output Measures	Availability of Measures of Appropriate Environmental Variables	Availability of Appropriate Comparison Groups	Availability of Measures of Appropriate Input and Process Variables
Counseling Services	0	+	−	+
Rape Response Team	+	+	−	+
Sexual Assault Prevention	0	0	−	+
Shelter	+	+	0	+

Code: +: Existing methodology is sufficient and readily available for immediate application to evaluation.

0: Methodology is not advanced and application cannot be made with complete confidence. Development of methodology will be a critical part of the evaluation.

−: Methodology unavailable. Development of an applicable method appeared unlikely at this time.

Source: Adapted from Wholey, J. S., Scanlon, J. W., Duffy, H. G., Fukumoto, J. S., and Voght, L. M. (1975) *Federal evaluation policy: Analyzing the effects of public policy*. Washington, D.C.: The Urban Institute, p. 109. Used by permission.

proceed with the program evaluation when the decision is affirmative, and the preparation of the final draft of the evaluation contract.

The evaluability assessment culminates in a determination of program evaluability. No widely accepted standards now exist in the field to assist decision makers in deciding whether or not a particular program is evaluable. Examples do exist, however, to help summarize major factors of evaluability. A program may be determined evaluable, for instance, if it meets the criteria set out in Table 6–5.

Decision makers are still confronted with drawing conclusions from available evidence as to the degree criteria such as in Table 6–5 are met. When a degree of confidence can be expressed by the evaluator that evaluability criteria are met, an affirmative decision is indicated for proceeding with the evaluation as planned. The consideration of key evaluability factors will, of course, communicate the basis for any adjustments in the evaluation that may be indicated in a given social program. A more difficult situation confronts the evaluator and the party that has commissioned the evaluation when evaluability criteria are not met, or barely so. Several alternatives that may be considered are the following:

- Recommend not to carry out a program evaluation.
- Recommend program changes to enhance program evaluability.
- Recommend that a qualitative approach instead of a quantitative evaluation approach be utilized.
- Recommend selective program evaluation on program components with high evaluability.

An examination of these alternatives sheds light on the dynamics of each for the decision making process.

TABLE 6–5 • *What Programs Are Evaluable?*

A Program is Evaluable When it Has	Which (Who) Are (Is)	EA Process
Structure and operational relationships	Defined and in place	Equivalency functional model of the direct intervention is developed.
Agreed-upon key expectations	Plausible and attributable to the direct intervention	Testable expectations are located on functional model.
Agreed-upon potential measurements	Feasible to take	Measurement points and measurements are located on an equivalency functional model.
Defined, agreed-upon potential comparisons	Feasible to make	Structure of operation and nature of measurements are developed.
Users for the information to be purchased	Capable of acting or effectively recommending action	Action options are developed.
Value to the users of knowing various evaluation outcomes	Far in excess of the costs of conducting monitoring and evaluation	Sequential purchase is used to gain incremental insights into overall costs.
Links to the direct intervention through which action based upon monitoring or evaluation information will come	Described, plausible, and in existence	The oversight and those-in-charge structures are laid out in sufficient detail to permit confident action.

Source: Nay, J. N. and Kay, P. (1982). *Government oversight and evaluability assessment.* Lexington, MA: Heath and Company, p. 177. Used by permission.

Recommend Against Evaluation

Recommending against evaluation can be one of the most difficult of recommendations. At least a symbolic commitment to evaluation is initiated when the evaluator sets out to do the evaluability assessment. While the contractual agreement between evaluator and commissioning party for the evaluation can be clear on the matter that evaluability assessment may result in a recommendation against evaluation, the chances for such are relatively rare. Based on his many years with a national research and consulting firm, one expert finds it hard to imagine that a contractor who has gone to the expense of writing a proposal, winning it, building up a staff and committing management resources to undertake the evaluation will ever find that the program is not capable of being evaluated (Carter, 1982). Furthermore, we may reemphasize an earlier point that in one way or another probably any program is evaluable.

Recommend Program Changes

Recommending program changes to enhance program evaluability can be viewed as a by-product of EA, or even its main purpose. Nay and Kay (1982) note that when originally developed in the early 1970s, EA was perceived as a way of avoiding large, useless evaluation. Since that time, EA has been "more often used to test expectations against reality in government operations and to bring the expectations and reality of government into closer agreement, with or without the intention of eventually performing a large, formal evaluation" (Nay and Kay, 1982, p. 175).

Recommendations for program changes appear to have greater chance for success when a program is in the more formative stages of development. During early phases of program implementation an on-going relationship between evaluator and the program may develop, with an expanded role for evaluator more akin to program developer or consultant. In this role the evaluator serves the program, rather than simply judging it (Rutman, 1980). Built into EA is a "conscious attempt to establish consensus among program managers and policymakers on program design, on the measures to be used, on implementation and evaluation problems that limit program evaluability, and on actions to address the problems" (Schmidt, Beyna, and Harr, 1982, p. 204).

Recommend Qualitative Evaluation

Recommending a qualitative rather than quantitative approach to evaluation does not mean that qualitative research should only be considered a compromise to qualitative research when low evaluability is indicated. Palumbo and Nachmias (1983) argue that the dominant goal-directed paradigm for program evaluation sets forth preconditions for evaluability that can rarely be met for purely quantitative approaches because they do not sufficiently account for realities in organizational behavior and the ambiguity of organizational goals. They offer an alternative set of preconditions to test out evaluability; it is based on the philosophy that program decision makers act first, then analyze what they did. Their "reverse decision cycle" preconditions are as follows:

- Precondition 1: Some of the activities engaged in by program administrators lead to positive outcomes valued by some stakeholders.
- Precondition 2: The positive outcomes are related, even if only indirectly, to the formally stated goals of the agency [program].
- Precondition 3: The evaluation focuses mainly on positive outcomes.
- Precondition 4: Program managers trust the evaluators.
- Precondition 5: The evaluation may or may not be utilized, depending on the findings (p. 74).

A reconsideration of evaluability assessment findings along these lines may very well yield preconditions favorable to a naturalistic approach to program evaluation.

Recommend Partial Evaluation

Recommending selective program evaluation can usually be thought of as synonymous with a more limited program evaluation than originally proposed. Quite simply it involves using the results of the evaluability assessment in decision making about what to evaluate and what might be considered not evaluable. Wholey (1987) identifies lack of agreement on evaluation priorities and intended uses of evaluation as one of the major factors to inhibit the use of evaluation. He describes how an evaluability assessment of Tennessee's prenatal program helped decision makers to focus evaluation resources on intermediate outcome objectives that are subject to the influence of, but not completely under the control of, managers. While there is no suggestion that this program received low evaluability marks overall, it does provide documentation on the use of evaluability assessment to help policy makers and managers agree on key aspects of program theory to be tested in evaluation, outcomes to be monitored, and causal assumptions to test.

Controversies about EA

The development and utilization of EA is closely tied to large-scale programs in the federal bureaucracy. In fact, EA has achieved its widest application in one federal department, the Department of Health and Human Services (formerly the Department of Health, Education, and Welfare) (Strosberg and Wholey, 1982). Moreover, the interest in utilizing EA is often credited to a small group of influential evaluators, namely Joseph Wholey and his colleagues. It now appears that the use of EA has decreased significantly since Wholey's departure from that Department, and the spread of EA to other federal agencies has not occurred to any appreciable degree (Rog, 1985). How much utility, then, does EA offer smaller scale governmental or nongovernmental programs? While the EA approach certainly suggests itself for this range of social programs, the potential is largely untested at this time. Central to this controversy is the issue of plausibility and cost constraints that may be particularly crucial for smaller, low budgeted programs. These issues are taken up next.

The plausibility for program success has been raised as a controversy for EA by Schmidt, Beyna, and Harr (1982). They point out that while program managers and program researchers are both interested in minimizing information gaps and imperfections, the fact is that researchers often care more about the relative perfection of information than about the decision deadlines of managers. The evaluator can easily be caught in the middle between these opposing interests, and the controversy becomes most evident when the quest for "perfect information" appears to take precedent over practical decision making. "Often through examining a program design and collecting minimal information from the field, conclusions can be reached about the plausibility of success. . . . Why continue to collect information when you already have a believable [though imperfect] answer?" (Schmidt, Beyna, and Harr, 1982, p. 203). The dilemma is to determine how perfect the information needs to be for management decisions, and when the information search in EA has surpassed practical wisdom about plausibility for program success.

Rutman (1984) suggests that "collecting information about a program's activities and effects need not be expensive and time-consuming" (p. 35). Depending on perspective, however, the reports of cost for completed EA's raise an issue of resource utilization that may be controversial. According to Wholey (1979), EA uses three human resources: the time of evaluators, the time of intended users, and the time of field staff personnel. Calculations of actual costs for completed EA's differ somewhat, depending on whether the EA is contracted or conducted in-house. In either case, significant expenditures in time and resources may result. EA studies in the Department of Health and Human Services "typically cost from $50,000 to $120,000, and take between five and 10 months" (Strosberg and Wholey, 1983, p. 67). Schmidt, Beyna, and Harr (1982) report on an EA of the Community Mental Health Center program as costing approximately $78,000, excluding in-house staff effort, interview and review time of program management and policymakers, and other interviewees' time devoted to the project. While these costs may be relatively modest for large-scale programs at the national level, the costs for smaller, low budgeted programs, as mentioned above, may not be cost effective unless EA is conducted in-house (Rog, 1985).

The evaluability assessment approach described in this chapter represents an attempt to rationally determine the potential for achieving commonly accepted standards for program evaluation research. Realistically, the evaluability assessment model provides important referent points in a not so rational environment. The evaluator should bear in mind that decision making in the program evaluation arena will inevitably represent a mix of rational and extrarational responses to the evaluability assessment report. As a reminder to this, we have prepared a list of evaluation principles on which judgments of evaluability and assessment of data needs are viewed. The evaluation principles are offered to assist the evaluator in reviewing expectations and can be useful referent points for the decision making process. The evaluation principles are:

- Principle 1: The organizational influence of the evaluation process and/or product is a function of the organizational power of the stakeholders whose questions it answers.
- Principle 2: The ability of the product of a program evaluation to influence organizational decision making is a function of the clarity about what decisions need to be made and the options available during the planning of the evaluation process.
- Principle 3: All organizations have a limit on the extent to which they can tolerate program evaluation findings that will threaten their survival (or, more especially, the careers of the staff members who control the evaluation):
  Almost no organization has suicidal tendencies, even though they often do act in ways that damage their own self-interest.
  Every organization has "secrets" that it must keep and evaluation process or product can threaten their status.
- Principle 4: Almost all organizations can specify in advance what would be a useful product of an evaluation; and they should do so as part of the evaluability assessment.
- Principle 5: Outcome focused evaluations cannot be accomplished within an organization that cannot specify the objectives of its programs.
- Principle 6: All data (but especially program evaluation data) is very expensive. Data collection can almost never be successful if done by staff for whom it is an "add-on" to their regular duties, no matter how positively motivated they are or how great their stake in the product is.

Evaluability assessment and the resulting analysis of study results aim to improve the potential for subsequent program evaluation. Although this topic of program evaluation has not received the attention that has been devoted to other areas (i.e., methodology), there seems to be good reason to consider the importance of pre-planning for program evaluation. Documentation that is available from the field indicates that it has been effective in fostering needed changes in program design, improved program evaluation, and encouraging policy makers and program managers to act on the basis of evaluation findings.

References

Carter, L. F. (1982). The standards for program evaluation in the large for-profit social science research and evaluation companies. In P. H. Rossi (Ed.), *Standards for evaluation practice* (pp. 37–48). San Francisco, CA: Jossey-Bass.

Guba, E. G., & Lincoln, Y. S. (1981). *Effectiveness evaluation: Improving the usefulness of evaluation results through responsive and naturalistic approaches.* San Francisco, CA: Jossey-Bass.

Jones, J. H. (1982). *Bad blood: The Tuskegee syphilis experiment.* New York: The Free Press.

Nay, J. N., & Kay, P. (1982). *Government oversight and evaluability assessment.* Lexington, MA: Lexington Books.

Palumbo, D. J., & Nachmias, D. (1983). The preconditions for successful evaluation: Is there an ideal paradigm? *Policy Sciences, 16,* 67–79.

Rog, D. J. (1985) *A methodological analysis of evaluability assessment.* Unpublished doctoral dissertation, Vanderbilt University.

Rutman, L. (1980). *Planning useful evaluations: Evaluability assessment.* Beverly Hills, CA: Sage.

Rutman, L. (1984). *Evaluation research methods: A basic guide.* Beverly Hills, CA: Sage.

Schmidt, R. E. (1983). Evaluability assessment and cost analysis. In M. C. Alkin and L. C. Solmon (Eds.), *The costs of evaluation* (pp. 171–188). Beverly Hills, CA: Sage.

Schmidt, R. E., Beyna, L., & Harr, J. (1982). Evaluability assessment: Principles and practice. In G. J. Stahler and W. R. Tash (Eds.), *Innovative approaches to mental health evaluation* (pp. 195–219). New York: Academic Press.

Schmidt, R. E., Horst, P., Scanlon, J. W., & Wholey, J. S. (1977). *Serving the federal evaluation market: Strategic alternatives for managers and evaluators.* Washington, D.C.: The Urban Institute.

Schmidt, R. E., Scanlon, J. W., & Bell, J. B. (1979). *Evaluability assessment: Making public programs work better* (OS–76–130). PROJECT SHARE, Washington, D.C.: U.S. Government Printing Office.

Strosberg, M. A., and Wholey, J. S. (1982). Evaluability assessment: From theory to practice in the Department of Health and Human Services. *Public Administration Review, 43,* 66–71.

Weiss, C. H. (1975). Evaluation research in the political context. In E. L. Struening and M. Guttentag (Eds.), *Handbook of evaluation research* (pp. 2–26). Beverly Hills, CA: Sage.

Wholey, J. S. (1979). *Evaluation: Promise and performance.* Washington, D.C.: The Urban Institute.

Wholey, J. S. (1987). Evaluability assessment: Developing program theory. In L. Bickman (Ed.), *Using program theory in evaluation* (pp. 77–92). San Francisco, CA: Jossey-Bass.

Wholey, J. S., Scanlon, J. W., Duffy, H. G., Fukumoto, J. S., and Voght, L. M. (1975). *Federal evaluation policy: Evaluating the effects of public policy.* Washington, D.C.: The Urban Institute.

Monitoring Social Policy and Program Implementation, Part I

Program Participants' Characteristics, Utilization, Selection Bias, and Discontinuance/Drop-Out Rates

In the preceding two chapters we were concerned with making clear the theory which guides the social program we wish to evaluate,—purpose, and feasibility of program evaluation. In this chapter we will now be concerned with a determination of how well the theory the program says it will use to achieve its goals was actually implemented. We will call that *program monitoring* or *implementation monitoring*.

The Importance of Implementation Monitoring to Program Evaluation

There are important reasons why monitoring micro-implementation is a crucial step in evaluating social programs and policies. First, as we discussed in some detail in Chapter Six, unless we are quite sure that program activities were actually delivered—and delivered in the way they were designed (i.e., relevant to the program theory)—we cannot attribute desirable outcomes to the total program. As a part of an evaluation enterprise, an implementation monitoring scheme must give us a good picture of what program activities actually took place. Otherwise, we will be unable to usefully interpret evaluation findings; i.e., the program will not be able to claim credit for good results, nor will it be able to decide what part to repair or replace if the evaluation shows no results or negative results (Finney and Moos, 1985).

Second, the lack of program monitoring may go some way in explaining why so few interventions show positive, empirically demonstrable results when subjected to evaluation (recollect our earlier review of the long and serious debate that has arisen as a consequence of this vexing problem). It is perfectly possible, we believe, that social programs may fail empirical tests, not because their theory is bad, but because it is not well implemented, perhaps not implemented at all! The reader might want to think about the many ways that can happen. For example, there is the simple case in which a program design is implemented in madly different ways among practitioners. Under that circumstance a clear empirical test of its effectiveness is simply not possible, because the program evaluation procedures will not be observing the effectiveness of one program design and one program theory, rather the effectiveness of as many intervention designs (and perhaps theories) as there are practitioners and settings. The net positive effects of the theory based interventions may be severely diluted or, worse, obscured by the nil and negative results of others. The idea here is that, assuming there are a large number of practitioners, aggregate outcome data on a (more or less) random distribution of program activities will be most likely to score a net zero average effect! Think, too, of the simple case where there is, literally, nothing being done by a program staff. Or, the case where the program practitioners and / or administrators never had any intention to implement a program according to the intended design. In our experience, those cases are distressingly more frequent than one would hope.

The third reason why implementation monitoring is crucial is that program monitoring data are absolutely essential in order to have a current, up-to-date description of the social program. Surprisingly, a current, up-to-date program description is not easily obtained. Social programs are in constant change under the impact of their encounter with the complexities of real life (King, Morris, and Fitzgibbon, 1987). The magnitude and qualitative importance of such change varies, depending on the type of program under consideration; such change, however, is a particularly impressive characteristic of "soft" benefits and services—i.e., the personal social services (e.g., counseling, child care, protective services, rehabilitation). With regard to these programs, it is a mistake to believe that a crystal clear idea of the implemented program will emerge from descriptions of how it is understood at the command level of an organization (i.e., the highest or higher levels of organizational authority) (Palumbo and Harder, 1981). Policy and programs are designed at command levels (including legislative and judicial levels), but there they are on the order of intentions, not fact.

The classical opera of Dmitri Shostakovich, *Lieutenant Kiji*, is a hilarious celebration of this idea. A careless clerk misspells the name of a member of the Tsarist officer corps, writing *Kiji* by mistake—the Tsar was fascinated by a man with such an unusual name as *Kiji* and kept asking after him. Lower level bureaucrats responded by inventing continuing (interesting) episodes in Lt.

Kiji's career in order to keep the Tsar informed of his "progress." The whole plot turns on the ridiculous outcome of the idea that the Tsar could not possibly be wrong about anything, even so trivial a detail as the existence of an obscure Lieutenant in his vast army. Unfortunately, it is not a totally implausible story when applied to organizations, to which those who have long experience of them, public or private, will probably attest. Under the right (many) circumstances, subordinates tend not to dispute the beliefs of those in power over them. In order to keep that important idea clearly in mind, let us call it the *Lt. Kiji Error* when command level versions of how things really work on the operational level become implausible. The most important point for program evaluators is that:

1. At the micro-implementation level, those who actually make operating policy and who create program designs are those in face-to-face contact with clients and consumers (Berman, 1978; Hill and Bramley, 1986).
2. In order to accommodate local conditions, policy and program are "re-designed" or "re-negotiated" there, in the context of what Hjern and Porter (1980) call the "implementation structure." At this level, policy and program design must be conceived as "negotiated order," not fixed order.

There are yet other reasons to seriously consider the subject of implementation monitoring. Within an apparently benign exterior, implementation monitoring hides questions of elegant complexity. One of these arises out of the very issue discussed in the foregoing paragraph. Precisely because of the issues which we have just discussed—"extensiveness of local adaptations," "policy-as-negotiated-order," etc.—policy arising out of micro-implementation may not express the idea of public policy as the will of a people freely consenting to be governed. Palumbo, Maynard-Moody, and Wright (1984) have suggested that implementing policy is a continuation of the policy making process by other means. To say it another way, if in a democracy, public policy should be an expression of the will of the people (via the legislative or judicial act) and if it is inevitable that it is distorted by local adaptation and implementation negotiation, how can public programs of any kind be implemented so that the will of the people will not have been nullified? Even if we agree that local variation in implementation is adaptive and an absolute necessity, clearly there is a point at which a program implementation deviates so far from legislative intent (or judicial mandate) that it becomes not the will "of the people." Some might say that it is at that point that a democracy becomes not a democracy but some kind of bureaucratic anarchy, even when the implementer's motives are rational, and even when they conform to professional virtues and practice standards.

The literature of social work and public administration and policy tends to look at changes in local policy that are adaptive as basically positive. Certainly there is good reason to support the view that decisionmaking and implementation represents a kind of "muddling-through" process (Lindblom, 1959). However, despite our general agreement that muddling- through is not to be discredited as an administrative strategy, we think it is clear that it can disguise bad program implementation; there is no virtue in human organizations that muddle-through in ways that are always very dysfunctional and (literally) serve no ones' best interests (except, perhaps, those of the staff implementing the program). For example, local policy adaptations or the particular practices of individual practitioners may be so variable, so chaotic, that, even within a local operation, employees who work side-by-side do not appear to be involved in the same program or working toward the same purposes. When that occurs it is surely an instance of what some have called *policy drift:* cumulative changes under implementation conditions where stakeholders lose sight of the reasons for changes: confusion and conflict within the organization as stakeholders disagree over such things as priorities, objectives, performance standards, strategies, and the nature of the program itself (Kress, Koehler, and Springer, 1981).

We do not find it difficult to hold simultaneously for the conception of policy implementation as a creature of local adaptation and for the importance of implementing policy as an expression of conformity to political or judicial mandates—i.e., as an expression of the will of the people. Our opinion is also shared by others (see Sorg, 1981, p. 144). We conclude that a fourth reason to monitor implementation is to judge current program operations for evidence of policy drift of the kind that signals organizational chaos, or is beyond limits that are acceptable to main stakeholders in terms of their basic intentions or the democratic mandate. Compliance with mandated intentions is not a bad reason for monitoring, even in the face of the fact that actual implementation is often not a precise fit with mandated intentions. Clearly it should not be difficult to see the difference between implementation fairly characterized as adaptive local variation, and implementation for which there are no rational grounds. Nor should it be hard to see the difference between creative local adaptation and implementation that is continually disorganized and ineffective.

A fifth important reason to do implementation monitoring is that data from a good implementation monitoring system provides a *signal function* to external funding sources with respect to whether their funds are being used in a way they intended. Many public and private social programs are funded by a variety of external sources, and where that is the case, the program and its sponsoring agency are to some extent accountable to them.

A sixth reason implementation monitoring is so important is that it is a way to observe negative side effects of social programs and interventions. The scientific study of outcomes is tightly focused on specific factors—positive effects for the most part, those consciously built into the hypothesis of which every social program and intervention is a test. Scientific experiments are not usually designed to study side effects, so we should not be surprised that social programs designed as applied social science usually become aware of their unanticipated negative effects after the fact. That shouldn't have to be the case for social programs, really. It is only the most unusual social program in which there is not some political debate preceding its establishment, and therein is almost always contained the opponent's dire predictions of negative side effects. That should be a source for signal expectations. On the other hand, sometimes unanticipated side effects currently are judged to be negative simply because a social program was a good solution in one historical era but not in another.

Still, negative side effects are a common feature of all applied science. While science brings many blessings, surely we are all now quite aware that even the best science brings unanticipated negative side effects: chemical pesticides bring a wealth of food but also carcinogens; petroleum technology brings efficient mass transportation, but it has also added the word *oil-spills* to our common vocabulary. If we think seriously about exactly how experimental laboratory scientific findings are applied to real-life, it becomes immediately apparent that we apply them by recreating laboratory circumstances in real-life. And unless we can do so, it is unlikely that we can replicate the findings we think will be so useful.

Seldom is there any reason, strictly speaking, to believe that experimental findings in social science are replicable or generalizable except in the circumstances under which they were discovered. Thus, to reproduce findings in real-life, it is necessary to seriously interfere in real-life and impose those circumstances, constraining natural life so that those circumstances are duplicated. However, those social conditions in which findings are found to be valid may not be inhabitable by ordinary human beings over any extended period of time. And it is plausible, perhaps even likely, that this is the source of unexpected side effects in social programs. The easiest examples to give are those in which the laboratory conditions like states of mind involved acquiring a particular mental state; for example, a new way of perceiving their situation: if parents can view their home, or teachers can view their classroom, as behavior modification systems, (systems of rewards and punishments) contingencies can be implemented, and the undesirable behaviors modified. But whether people can maintain those states of mind long term and/or in the absence of a "coach," is always an issue, and thus an important aspect of the implementation question. Thought of in the way we have spoken about here, the implementation monitoring question is so important because the study of implementation is the study of humans actually living in an imagined world which first saw the light of day in the course of building a program or intervention theory (House, 1982).

Finally, an effective implementation monitoring system is strongly in middle management's self-interest, since it has the potential to identify indirect causes of weak implementation: e.g., deficits in fiscal support or personnel resources. For example, if program attendance is a problem, it may be due to the difficulties program participants have in obtaining transportation, not necessarily with poor program management or the inadequacies of the basic program theory or design. In a foster care program for extra-difficult children, high foster parent turnover rates (in fact, a chronic problem) may be due to a lack of crisis intervention resources or program components like foster parents' time-out from their high tension parenting responsibilities. Any of these problems above can easily be attributed to poor middle management if either foster parents, clients, or upper level management wish to find a scapegoat. The point being made here is that, assuming effective past and present management efforts, a middle manager with good monitoring data has the ability to demonstrate resource deficits. That ability will come in handy in constructing sound empirical arguments for additional resources for the program.

It is also an advantageous position because, indeed, organizations have their predatory moments. It is easy for command level administrators to charge inadequate middle management as a cause for lack of social program productivity—and the easiest defensive maneuver is usually irresistible to a threatened organizational commander. It is very difficult to pursue a charge of mismanagement against a well prepared middle level manager who has control of data that documents exactly how the program unit is operating, at what cost, what staff is responsible for what program elements, at what level of staff effort, and who has kept superiors informed of same. On that account, program monitoring can be middle management's secret weapon. If a good program monitoring system is in place, no one has a better data-based command of program operations. That situation is precisely why those who study organizations sometimes say that organizational executives and directorates are at the mercy of those who control day-to-day operations. The middle level managers of social programs must always have clients' needs as their first priority, but they will find it in both their own and their clients' self-interest to have at their command a good program monitoring system.

If we seem to place great emphasis on monitoring implementation, we assure the reader that it is not just our own peculiarity, but that the concern is widely shared in the program evaluation field. Two important examples from many are Gramlich and Koshel (1975) who found that performance contracting experiments failed to the extent they were not implemented (or implemented correctly) in the field and Levine (1972) who suggested that the main problem of the War on Poverty was the failure of programs to be implemented in the field.

Here is an example of the use of implementation monitoring. In evaluating a program delivering legal services to the indigent, some rural clients were provided with a part-time public defender who served all indigents, while others were assigned regular local practicing private attorneys by the local judges, who chose them from a list of attorneys who made themselves available and were paid a standard fee from local tax funds (Houlden and Balkin, 1985). An important evaluation question was whether, in fact, one was better than the other. Now we must be careful to notice that better legal services cannot be measured by looking at whether clients were or were not convicted or received sentences that were longer or shorter. Actually there are two reasons. First, the judgment of the outcome of a legal contest is almost always relative to the self-interest of the person making the judgment. From the point of view of the accused, not being convicted or obtaining a shorter sentence is always better, but most ordinary citizens (rightly or wrongly) would probably say just the opposite. Second, although there is no doubt that a good lawyer can make an important difference, the outcome for legal services can never be wholly determined by what a lawyer does. The issue for legal representation is not to produce a particular judicial verdict (innocence or guilt or a judgment of liability or no liability, for example), but to ensure that the client gets "justice," i.e., to ensure that even a client actually guilty of a crime doesn't get a more harsh punishment than what the law calls for. Thus, while attorneys can make a substantial difference, no experienced attorney ever promises a specific legal outcome; rather, she works to obtain only as much justice as the law demands. Evaluating legal services is therefore surprisingly different from evaluating other services, because one cannot focus on that judicial decision as an outcome, rather on how good were the services that were delivered. The evaluation we are discussing here measured "good" legal services by such things as whether the attorney convinced the judge to set an affordable bail bond amount (so the client could stay out of jail pending trial), the number of motions filed on the defendant's behalf, and how long it took (the number of days) from the first appearance in court to the time of disposition and sentencing. Those are measures of service, not outcome, because they don't concern the actual legal outcome, only professional practice efforts that were provided along the way.

Probably almost all of us would agree that these measures represent the pro-active kind of services we would want from an attorney: apart from whether our attorneys got from the judge what we thought was a fair sentence, we would want them to get us out of jail as quickly as possible, to file as many motions as might be necessary to assure that we got justice, and to settle the whole issue as quickly as possible. The monitoring of the way these programs of legal services were implemented showed clearly that, on two of the three measures, the part-time public defenders provided better quality services (Houlden and Balkin, 1985, p. 550).

The Status of Implementation Monitoring in Evaluation

Despite all the good reasons why monitoring should be done and the fact that the field has good ideas about how to do it effectively, implementation monitoring is not yet a standard feature of the social program and evaluation research enterprise. We think it is a shortcoming and emphasize it here hoping to contribute to overcoming that fault. In the personal social services it is only in the education and medical-care field that implementation monitoring is much used. Peer review and practice oversight systems now characteristic of hospital-based medical care and the various classroom observation systems, for example, have been developed as standard monitoring tools.

If it is so important and if the technology is available, why has the evaluation research field been so tardy in adopting implementation monitoring as a standard feature of its technology? The adoption of innovation always has its puzzling aspects, but it is to the point that the field is relatively young and subject to great pressure to serve the bidding of those who pay its bills. Thus, it has not built up the kind of social credibility that allows the traditional professions to take strong, righteous stands in favor of what they believe to be the best practice. Then it is true that monitoring implementation is a very expensive undertaking. To keep track of what human service practitioners actually do is both complicated to design and certainly a labor-intensive project (Hudson, 1983; Wimberley, 1989).

Finally, there is clear resistance on the part of human service agency practitioners and staff. Professionals and staff tend not to be persuaded by common arguments in favor of monitoring, probably for the same reasons that production line employees dislike constant monitoring of their work effort. Let us present here some uncommon arguments for it. Most professionals think of themselves as autonomous individuals, and monitoring their activities smacks of an invasion of their professional authority and autonomy. It is an invasion, of course, even though it proceeds out of the nature of their work with clients and the fact of an organizational work life. Indeed, we should pay close attention to the inherent contradiction between the concept *professional* and the concept *organization*. Important and non-debatable elements in these concepts are fundamentally opposed to each other. The traditional concept of an organization implies hierarchical authority, group responsibility, accountability to organizational superiors, division of labor, and all the rest. Notice that each of those aspects of organizations are at odds with basic concepts of what it means to be a professional practitioner: the right (authority) to take independent action, the responsibility of the individual practitioner for it, accountability to the standards of the profession, the difficulty professionals have in delegating responsibility, etc. We realize that organizations can be other than hierarchical, but it seems clear to us that this is only the beginning of our search toward a new, non-hierarchical conception of people working toward common ends. Since we cannot claim closure on this effort, we must take as given that professionals working in the context of an organization cede part of their authority to their organizational superiors—not all, but part. Clearly there is some point at which ceding professional authority becomes impossible for the professionals who will still call themselves professional practitioners. But professionals need to be quite clear about the reason why they are ceding authority, because some reasons are acceptable. The involvement of professionals in the implementation of a common program design does not necessarily constitute an unacceptable infringement on practitioners, since one supposes that before professionals agree to be a part of an organization, the programs in which they will work are clearly laid out. It is exactly at that point that professionals need to decide whether the program designs they will be working with are compatible with their judgment of the best interests of clients. Taking that judgment seriously, as a matter of vital professional responsibility, professionals are exercising their proper prerogatives. After all, any characterization of the concept of professional has, at bottom, the notion of service in the best interest of clientele. There is no inherent reason why professionals cannot circumscribe their actions on behalf of faithfulness to a particular program design in order to test out whether it actually works the way it is hoped—*IF* the design appears to be an improvement in services for clients. In fact, isn't that what the concept of the modern professional working with a scientific knowledge base implies that the practitioner should do? Isn't that what medical or dental practitioners do when they try out an untested drug or other clinical management approach? Indeed, they should do it for their clients, since it is clear that we have so little wisdom we can take for granted in the human services. Monitoring whether professionals actually do act consistently with the program design under consideration is only insuring an adequate test of its efficacy. We believe that active participation in that effort is always the discipline that characterizes the professional. Not only that. Social practitioners can so easily be characterized as dealing in "mystical," "black box" treatments. One way to deal with that characterization is to be committed to implementation monitoring and its establishment as a standard feature of good practice.

Some Important Distinctions and Some Basic Terminology for Monitoring

To help us talk easily about evaluating program implementation, let us set out some basic terminology. We will speak of *operationalizing* program theory as the process of program implementation. Setting out the program activities that constitute program implementation is an important step in the program evaluation process, and we will call that *program specification*. The program specification is important because it becomes the standard against which program activities are judged in the process of monitoring implementation. It provides the basis for a set of monitoring schedules that tell the evaluator what to look for in observing program activities. Making actual observations of the program in operation, using monitoring schedules based on program specifications, we will call *implementation monitoring.* We ought to note here, at the outset, that there are some aspects of implementation with which we will not be concerned. The customary distinction is between macro- and micro-implementation (Berman, 1978). An example of the study of macro-implementation is the study of how states vary over the nation in implementing large-scale (hence, *macro-*) federal incentives. An example of micro-implementation is studying the details of the small-scale operationalization of a particular program theory; the selection of particular local activities to express a particular program theory (Scheirer, 1987). We are concerned here only with micro-implementation.

Before we move on to speak about specific issues and methods of monitoring, let us take a moment to distinguish the common term *program auditing* from implementation monitoring. Audits are related to monitoring, but are not its equivalent; rather, they are just one small aspect of implementation monitoring. In this part of the book, where we are concerned with a quantitative approach to program evaluation, we will use the term *program audit* to refer to taking observations regarding program operations focused on only a small and particular aspect of a program: it may focus on general adherence to some particular administrative rule or regulation, for example, or on some other specific administrative question about a program or policy aspect. It consists of a careful, empirical description of selected program activities that are relevant to an administrative question and which routine organizational reports cannot answer. The question may concern adherence to particular organizational rules or practices, it may concern things like staff utilization (over/under staffing), the adequacy of facilities or future need for them, or even the rumor of internal conflicts within an organizational subpart. The questions that drive program audits are framed at the command level of an organization (and sometimes legislatures or the judiciary), and are answered by data from its operational level. (See Chelimskey, 1985, p. 64, for a different, more restrictive view of auditing.) Now, take careful note that in the context of some qualitative approaches to monitoring, program auditing has quite a different meaning; "constructivist" evaluation research has a procedure called an *audit* that is a type of validation for other data gathering procedures. For more on that, see Part Four of this book. Now let us turn to a consideration of the details of how to construct a social program implementation monitoring scheme.

Monitoring for Program Utilization, Selection Bias, and Program Discontinuance/Drop out

There are two main components in a system to monitor the implementation of a social program, and the purpose of the first is to obtain data by which to characterize program participants. These data are commonly expected from a program evaluation, since they are vital for administrators, program planners, and others who make decisions about funding—they are essential in making decisions about allocating organizational resources, e.g., in deciding to contract or eliminate unsuccessful programs or in deciding how and where to expand those which are successful. For example, since it is almost never the case that program groups are simple random samples of a larger population, expanding programs by generalizing a program design to other sites requires great care. It will be measurably assisted by data on program participants; with that in hand, an administrator hopes to find a location where a new program might draw participants with matching characteristics, or experiment with a program, initially small scale, where particular characteristics are markedly different. The assumption here, common though not uncontroversial, is that past empirical results will be likely to be repeated with similar persons and under similar conditions; thus it is crucial to find out what characterizes those persons and what those conditions are. It is our opinion that social interventions of the personal social service type are quite particular to such characteristics and environmental conditions. Thus, in addition to knowing whether a social program is successful, we must always want to know with whom and under what conditions.

Monitoring for Selection Bias

We could assume that the program participants are simply a representative sample of the whole group (population) who have the targeted social problem. However, there are some important reasons why that is often not very useful:

1. Not everyone subject to the targeted social problem chooses to participate in the program (a utilization issue, here under-utilization).
2. Not all of those who do participate in the program actually have the targeted social problem (another utilization issue, here off-targetting, perhaps over-utilization).
3. The group that does participate may not be at all representative of those who have the targeted social problem (a selection bias issue).
4. Some participants drop out from the program before the service or intervention is completely delivered (discontinuance).

Notice that if a group (of program participants) is biased in any of these ways, it is not a random sample of those with the social problem of concern. It may be a problem, because the biasing characteristics can interact with program services or interventions in mischievous ways: for example, for either noble or ignoble reasons, a group of unemployed, selected for training to new skills with the objective of helping them to be employed, may have been selected such that it includes only those with the best past employment record or educational history (*creamed* is the term usually used here).[1] Or the reverse might be true: for whatever reasons, the group may have been selected such that only those with the poorest employment and educational records were included. In either case, a judgment of program effectiveness would have serious shortcomings in the absence of monitoring data on program participant characteristics. The reader might contemplate what a waste of scarce program funds it would be to generalize this program design, not realizing that it was only shown to be successful with the unemployed who have the best employment and educational history. Or, on the contrary, what a waste it would be to discard a potentially useful program design simply because it didn't work on the worst-case group of unemployed.

We are not implying here that selection bias is always a negative attribute of a program participant group; rather, that ignorance of program group characteristics makes it difficult to get the best use out of program evaluation findings, even if they are quite positive. Actually, there are some occasions when good forward planning would encourage specifying a program group that has a serious degree of selection bias: for example, when a new program theory or program design is undergoing its first field test. If it is possible to be reasonably sure of the characteristics of those who would be most likely to benefit from the program, it is a good strategy to do the initial field test on a group that has those characteristics. The logic is that it is a good test because it will generate a clear decision about the worth of the theory or the design: if it won't be beneficial with this group, it is unlikely to be beneficial for anyone.

One of the most difficult problems in constructing procedures to monitor for selection bias is choosing the factors on which to take observations. Certainly they are not usually obvious, nor are they always straightforward demographic factors—age, sex, ethnicity. If that is true, then how are program evaluators to make this choice? It is an extremely important choice, because selection bias goes undetected if the choice of monitoring factors is incorrect. The choice has to be made at the beginning of the evaluation, since, after data is gathered there is neither time, money, nor opportunity to make further observations. Thus, it is a mistake that is not easy to remedy. Those who carry evaluation responsibilities are more often than not in the unenviable position of having to choose potentially biasing factors without much guidance. That comes about, in part, because our program and intervention theories (and social theory in general, for that matter) are usually not good enough, usually insufficiently complex, to give our evaluation enterprise much direction in these matters. Good scientific theory should (but doesn't) contain scope specifications (Willer and Anderson, 1981) which identify these kinds of crucial factors, since it is precisely the function of good theory to do that. Since we cannot hope for much improvement in these problems in the near future, we must contrive some substitutes.

It is our experience that the best recourse is to elaborate the program theory speculatively, using practitioners, staff, and clients most close to the program and the phenomenon with that it deals. The process is one of identifying factors which they expect to be important in determining positive program outcomes for clients. Those factors are then included in the monitoring scheme and become those on which observations are taken in order to make judgments about selection bias. Ordinarily we find practitioners, staff, and clients willing and eager to contribute to an evaluation project in this way, often taking their own personal time to discuss these issues. To engage program staff and others in such a discussion, we have found that simply setting out the problem and asking for help with it is sufficient. An obvious alternative is to use empirical studies found in the social science and program evaluation literature on the social problem, but we are usually disappointed there. We must take care, however, not to expect too much, for, after all, program theories, designs, and target groups are quite particular, and conclusions from studies in the professional or academic literature may have to be elaborated and otherwise re-tailored to cover the same ground and be otherwise relevant.

Evaluators should avoid the tendency to consider only personal characteristics (or personal attitudes, beliefs, personal experience) to be useful data in observing for selection bias. We believe that, while they may be important, their utility is over-rated here. They are widely used probably not because people always and seriously believe them to be sole determinants, but because the data seems so easy to gather! On the contrary, we caution evaluators to pay close attention to characteristics of the social milieu and physical environment, for it may well be that they are more crucial to our concerns here than personal or even the simple demographic characteristics. Notice that in the employment training example above, simple demographic characteristics like age, sex, education, income, etc. would have been interesting but would not have captured the creaming features of the program group. To get at that requires some theoretical thinking about what factors might interact with skill training to produce the best and worst outcomes. Once that approach is taken, common sense will lead a person to factors more detailed than simple demography, i.e., length of time previous jobs were held and level of skill they required would capture the creaming of interest here. Thus, those with responsibility for designing program evaluations should avoid the *demographic fallacy*: i.e., assuming that common descriptive demographics (age, sex, race, income, etc.) are always and everywhere important factors. There are no data we know of to suggest that, although the temptation to routinely collect such data is strong. Perhaps out of a habit of mind, when one omits the collection of these simple data, it feels like one is committing some terrible transgression of the traditions of social research. At the least we would suggest maintaining modest expectations of the utility of simple demographics.

Finally, let us look at an example of a problem and a solution in choosing factors by which to judge selection bias. Consider a new social program in a general medical hospital, one that desires to evaluate its services, and whose main objectives are directed toward reducing the rising number of acute care admissions of the chronically ill and disabled for what are readily preventable problems. A further objective of this program was to delay or eliminate involuntary nursing home admissions, since it was the obvious but least desirable solution.[2] A typical example of the clientele of this program are elderly persons with an arthritic condition which significantly impairs mobility and who have difficulty in caring for themselves at home for reasons which are, ordinarily, relatively easily remediable: medication lapses, medication errors, malnutrition, anxiety, or neglect of household cleanliness (which may or may not represent a health hazard). The typical solution is to ensure that such persons have a meal-delivery service and housekeeping aides. Most human service practitioners will recollect their experiences with unnecessary general hospital admissions as a result of the consequences of these preventable conditions.

The program staff had good reason to believe that their program was generally successful, but one of their important evaluation questions was the issue of selection bias. How typical of the person-in-need were their program participants? In trying to think about monitoring their client population for that purpose, here is how they reasoned. First, those who are most likely to be in the program are those who are referred by others, and, in fact, those "others" often need only organize their effort a little to solve the problem. In contrast, those who have the most need of services are those who have no (or almost no) "others," i.e., those without close relatives, who are old enough so that their close friends have (mostly) passed away, or are themselves frail elderly who live quite socially isolated lives. Consider also that people with these characteristics sometimes refuse to accept services from strangers. Think for example of the isolated, older person with no immediate family who not only does not maintain good self-care but is also mildly paranoid about strangers—not an unusual feature of a person who lives alone and grows uncomfortable with strangers. Of course, anyone who provides housekeeping help or meal-delivery is a stranger, by definition, to such a person. Then, it is also true that social isolates are most likely to be referred to social services at the moment of a crisis, a difficult circumstance under which to deliver services, but also a moment when an otherwise uninterested client may be the most amenable to help. Not only that, such clients are the most likely of all to drop out, their own independence, assertiveness, and suspiciousness leading them naturally in that direction.

From these conclusions, based as they are on the experience and collective wisdom of practitioners working in this program, a set of monitoring factors can be constructed. They will constitute dimensions along which this program staff thinks it will be fruitful to characterize their program participants:

1. The identity of people who make face-to-face or phone contact with the participant
2. The basis for the relationship, the frequency and duration of contact
3. The history of the acquaintance, identity of the person who made the referral, and basis for the relationship
4. Whether there is a present state of crisis or emergency
5. Assertiveness and independence of action
6. Suspiciousness
7. Level of independent functioning (estimate of frailty)

Notice that a factor like chronological age might well be irrelevant here. Wouldn't most readers agree that a factor like "level of independent functioning" is more critical for program planning, for which chronological age is not only not a good proxy but might actually be misleading?

Monitoring to Determine the Extent of Program Utilization

Monitoring for the purpose of estimating program utilization is another important and useful aspect of a program evaluation. The main concern here is to estimate the proportion of the total population in need actually served by the program. This has been a mainline concern for income maintenance and other "hard benefit" programs for years, where the surprise has been that take-up rates for cash benefits (or benefits that are freely substitutable for cash), are often surprisingly low.[3] It is also an important and unattended issue with regard to personal social services: think of the concern of public school systems for attendance and of the medical field for the medically underserved whose numbers, these days, have been growing way out of proportion to the general population increase. However, the readers of this text are more likely to be concerned with a different kind of service delivery—personal social services—and much smaller scale operations. It is clear that such programs have quite different problems concerning program utilization. Utilization must be thought of in a somewhat different way because, for example, the services of these programs are often not voluntary but imposed upon clients; many such programs either have no ambition to serve total populations or could not do so even if they wished because of funding or staff capacities or because they are newly designed demonstration programs, clearly experimental in nature and intended to function on a small scale.

The usual procedure for estimating program utilization is simply to locate or construct estimates of the total number (*population*) who have the

problematic condition or circumstance, and determine the proportion between that number and the number of actual program participants. That turns
out not to be so simple with regard to many, if not most, of the problematic
conditions with which personal social services are concerned. Think for a
moment about the difficulties in accurately estimating the total number of
battered wives and women or sexually abused children in any given geographic area of this country. No doubt the number is large compared to what
was generally believed to be the case twenty years ago, but estimating exactly
how many for the purpose of estimating program utilization is difficult
because of the negative social stigma associated with the social problems
served by personal social service programs. Whenever an attempt is made to
count such facts, all the problems of asking people to reveal socially negative
details are set in motion. We think no one doing social program evaluation
should be sanguine about the difficulties in making social problem population
estimates nor over-confident about their accuracy. That said, it is still possible
to construct crude minimum estimates from various sources.

Rate of service utilization (or rates-under-treatment "RUT") can be used
to garner information on program implementation. By utilization rate, we are
referring to the proportion of a given population using the service. The basic
formula for rate is given as follows:

A rate is a fraction, with a numerator (the top) and a denominator (the bottom). The
numerator comes from agency records and the denominator from the target population
description. The numerator is the number of people served or number of services provided;
the denominator is the number eligible in the population (McKillip, 1987, p. 58).

For purposes of communication and understanding, rates are presented with
a base in multiples of 10, i.e., 5 out of 10 is 50 percent and 20 out of 100 is 20
percent and so on. Now let us assume that the numerator for a country-wide
meals on wheels program serves on the average 430 persons a month, while
the eligible population is 8,200 persons. The calculation is 430 divided by 8,200
for a result of 5 percent. Since we are dealing with numbers in the thousands
(remember that there are 8,200 eligible for the service), it makes good sense to
use a base of 1,000. Therefore, we would express the rate of service utilization
in our example as 52 out of 1,000. The calculation is determined simply by:

430 divided by 8,200 = .052 times 1,000 = 52

When service utilization rates are used to compare one service program to
another or many, or to some norm or standard, ratios or percentages of unmet
need can be estimated.

Rates of service utilization have been used fairly extensively of broad
based planning and needs determination within a large geographical area;
state-wide planning, regional planning, and even on a national basis. In this
regard, examples are prevalent from the fields of health and mental health.

When considerations of service utilization take on a more localized specter, the data collected will more likely be agency based.

Once it has been determined what the informational needs are, it should be possible to determine the specific data to be collected. Typically the kinds of data collected are the following:

1. *The sociodemographic characteristics of the clients, e.g., age, race, sex, ethnicity, education, place of residence*
2. *The presenting problem or problems*
3. *The characteristics of care/services provided*
4. *The frequency and duration of the care/treatment process*
5. *The sources of referral*
6. *Where possible, the outcomes of treatment or services provided (Warheit, Bell, and Schwab, 1977, p. 27)*

A worksheet for data collection purposes can be designed to fit the specific data that will be collected. It is recommended that consideration be given at this point to a coding procedure that will lend itself to data storage, retrieval, and analysis through computer entry. The software packages SPSS and SAS are now readily available for use with personal computers, and provide very flexible formatting for data collection of this nature.

An important note of concern should be taken and plan of approach developed before the data collection begins. Anonymity and confidentially in data collection of service users is often a major obstacle to access of agency records and other indicators of client utilization. While there are no pat responses to this concern, every effort should be made to guard the safety of clients involved. At a minimum, it should be possible to collect sufficient information without the use of names or other means of personal identification.

As we discussed in Chapter Four on needs assessment, there are relevant data in the archives of various public bureaus in addition to the U.S. Census and private national survey and opinion research organizations. An example of the former is the massive longitudinal study of the disabled conducted by the National Institute of Health involving very large national samples and by now accumulating many volumes of findings (*The Survey of the Disabled*, 1976). It contains a great variety of findings on the disabled, and even though some of it is dated, they are obtainable nowhere else; projections can be derived. Another example is the Survey of Income Program Participants (SIPP) data base which contains Census Bureau survey data on recipients of all kinds of public benefits. There are other such social-problem-relevant national surveys among government documents, and a search through the government document indices will locate them handily. Some examples from the archives of private research organizations are the archives of the Institute for Social Research at the University of Michigan, or of the National Opinion Research Center (NORC). The former contains data from the valuable longitudinal survey of income and expenditures of a national sample of persons with less than poverty level incomes. NORC archives have survey data available to the public covering many years, and even though it was related to all sorts of consumer topics and generated for commercial reasons, it often has data of social problem relevance. Upon request NORC will provide descriptions, costs (sometimes free), and methods of working in this archive.

Even though estimates of need and incidence/prevalence are often crude when constructed from some of these sources, they can be useful. For example, where the social problem is one of social control by law enforcement officers, it is likely that the number of those who are reported by law enforcement is a reasonably accurate reflection of the size of the group whose behavior society wishes to change. And, while those with program evaluation responsibilities should be clear that this number is quite different from the sum of all those who are committing the problematic deviancies (and quite full of bias—e.g., the high visibility of the poor and the greater acceptability of white collar crime), it is quite relevant to the amount of financing society is likely to give to fund the intervention!

Consider also the advantages and difficulties within another example: a proposal to use data from the U.S. Census Bureau on age, literacy, and recent immigration in order to make a crude estimate of the population in need for a city-wide (SMSA) adult literacy program. Indeed, there are problems with this data: data on age almost always has a certain inaccuracy built into it because, in this youth oriented culture, citizens are either reluctant to say how old they are or fear that giving accurate age data to the government may raise questions if they have at other times given inaccurate data, etc.; data which reveals low levels of literacy or illiteracy is socially stigmatizing. However, notice that these kinds of errors are unlikely to affect new immigrants, for example; so, for some groups, the three in combination could be useful in constructing a minimum estimate of the population of new adult immigrants who need to learn English as a second language in a given geographic area. And finally, consider a proposal to use the number of persons served by (receiving cash or medical benefits) the SSI-disabled (mentally ill) program to estimate the population in need of a program of case-management services for the chronically mentally ill in a given geographic area. It would, indeed, have (at least) these problems: not all the chronically mentally ill do in fact receive the SSI benefits they are entitled to; not all such mentally ill beneficiaries are in need of case-management services (monitoring medication, giving impetus to their efforts to seek social contacts, employment, education, and the rest), since it may in fact be supplied by families; not all the chronically mentally ill can benefit from such services. Still, the SSI-mentally ill population is a basis for a crude estimate, and if a program that had maximum utilization achieved coverage of an important percent of this group, most people in the field would probably count it an achievement.

Data from those already using personal social services of some kind can sometimes be used to make minimum estimates of the incidence or prevalence of a social problem. They are, of course, notoriously biased with respect to selection; for example, those utilizing services have somehow overcome all the barriers to access that are common to many social and human services (race, transportation, spendable income, child care, etc.). The U.S. Census Bureau has many demographic estimates and various (long) data series on descriptive social variables available in its standard collections and over long periods of time (age, race, sex, school attainment, literacy, poverty, immigration, for example) and the Department of Justice maintains data on various aspects of crime and delinquency. They present serious difficulties for our purposes here. Among only the most obvious are the following: (1) the fact that these simple variables are often not those that are relevant to describing the social problem of interest, (2) the possibility that the way the official Department defines them is not consistent or congruent with the definition used by the intervention or program theory, and (3) the fact that while data on crime and delinquency can sometimes be useful for estimating changes in incidence over time, crime reporting in general is conceded to be fraught with problems regarding selective law enforcement. On that account, for example, minorities always show up as more frequent perpetrators, and the socially prominent, better educated, and salaried white collars the less frequent perpetrators.

It pays to be alert to the fact that population in need estimates can be used for a variety of purposes, and those purposes shape the way such estimates are constructed. For example, while we have focused on population in need—that is, the total numbers of people who actually have a given problem, circumstance, or condition—there are occasions when that is not the pertinent number, but the number who could *potentially* develop the problem: the population at risk. The occasion for this is when social programs or interventions intend to be preventive rather than remedial or rehabilitative. If the program wishes to prevent problems from appearing in the first place, rather than remediating the negative effects of problems after they appear, the size of the target is the number of people who *could* develop it, or the number who *have a high probability of developing it*. A moment's thought will reveal how different that can be from the population in need idea. For example, at any given time or place, the number of people who could develop chronic anxiety, who could abuse their children or their wives or housemates, or who could enter a nursing home is very different from the number who actually are subject to those conditions or doing those things. Estimating populations at risk is even more risky and difficult, as should be obvious from the above examples. Of course, those numbers can also be estimated from the sources discussed above. The point emphasized here is that the program evaluator needs to be clear that preventive and rehabilitative-remedial programs require different population concepts in order to construct program utilization estimates.

There is another pair of concepts that is sometimes useful in estimating target populations: incidence and prevalence. *Prevalence* is based on the total number of persons who have a problematic condition or circumstance in some given place, during some given time period. *Incidence* is a different idea, since it is based on the total number of new cases of the problem or conditions. In short, prevalence refers to all the people already afflicted, while incidence refers to those who have been newly afflicted. Sometimes it is useful to use one, sometimes the other. Preventive programs are most interested in incidence because a reduction in new cases is an immediate measure of both their immediate task and whether a program is having an impact. Note that even a program producing good results has to wait a long time in order to effect a large backlog of cases, that is, to effect a *prevalence estimate* (total number of cases). However, remedial or rehabilitive or long term care programs are most interested in prevalence because it tells them the outside parameters of their task at a given moment. A change in prevalence indicates whether it is getting bigger or smaller, and thus gives clues to the adequacy of present provisions to deal with the problem.

Consider, as an example, common programs like those which seek to prevent child abuse through early identification of families with high potential for abuse, by early identification among those taking newborns home from the hospital. Keeping in mind that incidence rates concern only new cases, such a program will naturally be interested in watching incidence rates; if such a program intends to provide universal coverage and is successful at all, it should rather quickly effect incidence rates, since it makes direct contact with all families who could potentially be new cases. The program can affect the total number of physical abusers in their area (and thus prevalence rates) only over *very* long term, since it makes no contact at all with families who are already abusers (we leave aside for the moment the issue of those who are repeated abusers). Nonetheless, prevalence is important for social programs with objectives concerning remediation: presumably food programs for the aging, such as meals-on-wheels, would be interested in the reduction in the prevalence of malnutrition among the housebound population over 70, for example.

Since AIDS is a prominent and contemporary social problem, let us consider how the incidence/prevalence concepts play out there. Note that, at the present moment, there is neither cure nor prevention for AIDS (other than avoidance of carriers). On that account the main interest must lie in planning facilities or personnel for the care of those seriously afflicted. The key concept, given the present state of knowledge, is prevalence, since it will quantify the large backlog of existing cases. If, in the future, enough science is developed to produce some technique for the primary prevention of AIDS and the large backlog of those seriously afflicted with AIDS is no longer present, the main interest will change so that it lies in knowing immediately whether the preventive strategy or technology is continuing to work (keep in mind that, as with influenza or syphilis, pharmacological technology is not always enduring). The key concept under those circumstances will be incidence, since it will provide that signal by quantifying changes in the rate of new cases.

There is yet another task assisted by data received from monitoring the characteristics of program participants: understanding program dropouts, sometimes called *program discontinuers*. Attending to program dropouts is important in several ways, most obviously because a high proportion of program participants not completing the program signals a great inefficiency: expenditures on program dropouts are almost surely a total waste from the point of view of what social benefits a program can claim to be responsible for producing. Most important, they are probably a waste from the point of view of the availability of benefits in short supply for people who badly need them. Here is the way we reason about that. In these days, when the public purse is so strained for social welfare purposes, most programs are likely to be based on a minimalist intervention theory (program elements derived from the theory and included in the program activities constitute only the least and most necessary exposure it takes to produce the desired outcome). Any program element that isn't thought of as necessary is probably not included. Thus, it seems reasonable to conclude that exposure to less than the total program is likely to omit exposure to key factors, and, assuming that the intervention is worthwhile, it is thus incapable of producing the desired outcomes. Finally note that dropouts cannot contribute to the accounting of a program's net gain for participants (even if they did benefit from the program!) because, ordinarily, dropouts cannot be located in order to give data about post program accomplishments.

It is important for those involved in evaluating social programs always to calculate drop-out rates in order to avoid a surprisingly common mistake: that of calculating the benefits produced by a social intervention on the basis of the number of people who *enter* a program, rather than on the number of those who complete it. The former is misleading. Moreover, it is a particularly costly mistake, because, given dropouts, it will inevitably reduce both the estimate of average benefit and of net program gain. As a first order consequence it will then lower its cost-benefit ratio to participants and ultimately the judgment of the worth of the program. While a very good program could overcome that, no social program manager or practitioner would be pleased about that. Surely good results from social interventions in general and personal social services in particular are hard enough to achieve without making it harder on ourselves. While drop-out rates should always be a feature of a good comprehensive evaluation in personal social service programs, the intervention theory and the program operation itself should only have to be held accountable for results on those who complete the full program cycle.

Drop-out or discontinuance rates are easy enough to calculate, for they are simply the proportion of program participants who complete the full program relative to the number who begin. But while the calculation of the proportion is simple enough, deciding who is or is not a program participant and how much of the program has to be completed in order for them to count as a *completer* is sometimes not so easy. This should be obvious, thinking only of a good many programs in which people inquire, are referred for services, only give names and demographics, or officially register or even show up at the first session or appointment, but never continue beyond that: parenting classes, various kinds of mutual support groups for those whose lives are deeply involved in a particular kind of social problem, and recreation programs of various sorts are familiar examples. The problem is to decide whether any of these steps count as program entry and whether, therefore, such a person should be included in an estimate of program dropout. The trick is to make some decisions about how much of the program has to be completed in order for the participant to be counted as program completion, i.e., how many sessions, how long a time, etc. While most personal social service programs are minimal these days, still programs do sometimes have certain kinds of activities deemed to be desirable but not essential. In such cases no one would wish to count as a dropout a participant who had completed all but some non-essential aspect of the program.

Drop-out or discontinuance rates can also perform another service: they can provide crucial feedback on service delivery. Obviously, if drop-out rates are sufficiently high, it raises serious questions about service delivery: i.e., the acceptability of a particular kind of service by the people to be served, perhaps about its applicability, the environment in which it is delivered, or about the personnel who do the face-to-face work with program participants. If a program diverts people away, it surely cannot be very effective, at the best, selectively effective. The critical reader will notice that high drop-out rates can significantly affect selection bias. Even if people who enter the program are a random sample of those who are subject to a particular social problem, unless those who drop out are a random sample of those who enter, the program group will be seriously biased along selection lines. Only if the program keeps careful track of those who drop out or discontinue can it make a judgment of that.

One interesting example of this is Ewalt's (1981) work on discontinuers in an outpatient mental health program. She found that this program served people who were, at the moment of the request for service, in a state of serious crisis. While the initial finding was a very high drop-out rate, it was in the context of an intervention theory that directed program activities toward long-term emotional support. In fact, she found that program participants dropped out after the crisis subsided. That is a drop-out problem if one conceives of the objectives of service as long-term emotional support, but not if the program conception is focused on helping people survive short-term crises. This example illustrates how conceptually dependent the idea of drop-out or program discontinuance is on the underlying program theory. Thus, it supports the advice above, suggesting that the key decision about monitoring dropout is where program entrance begins and where program completion ends. Paradoxically, perhaps, reflection on discomforting drop-out rates may reveal mistakes in service delivery or program theory.

Nor is Ewalt's finding an isolated example. Consider the experience of adoption programs in the 1970s: that minority applicants commonly had a high drop-out or discontinuance rate (aside from the fact that their application rates under-represented their population numbers.) For a time, that data was generally (and mistakenly) interpreted to mean that formal, legal adoption was simply not acceptable to minority applicants, especially those other than middle class applicants. However, when adoption agencies were staffed with minority personnel and used recruitment devices based on an understanding of how the needs of these children were communicated in black and minority communities, minority application rates increased, the drop-out problem was markedly reduced, and the problem of placing minority infants in adoption in many, though not all, localities was no longer substantial.[4]

Summary

This chapter has argued for and, we believe, demonstrated the crucial, albeit neglected, status of monitoring the grass-roots, day-to-day implementation of social programs. Even though our review of the evaluation literature points to its absence, we concluded that monitoring is crucial because of its importance in:

- Attributing outcomes to program effort
- Obtaining an up-to-date program description
- Identifying "policy drift" and deviation from program theory, goals and objectives;
- Providing a signal function to external funding sources
- Observing negative side effects of social interventions
- Serving in the interest of the defense of middle management roles

The main body of the chapter considered problems and methods in monitoring for program participant characteristics, program utilization, selection bias, and program discontinuance or dropout. Choosing factors by which to monitor for selection bias is a particularly difficult problem for which particular examples were examined and suggestions offered. Solutions for the problems in monitoring program utilization and estimating populations in need were examined, and the importance of the concepts of prevalence and incidence were discussed. The chapter closed with some attention to the importance of constructing drop-out or discontinuance rates and various problems associated with it: deciding how much program exposure determines when a person becomes a program participant and/or a program completer, for example.

The chapter that follows will discuss other aspects of monitoring the implementation of social programs, in particular, the monitoring of program activities that are part of designed interventions.

Endnotes

1. The term *creaming* refers to the fact that fresh milk, direct from the cow and left in a container, will separate, and the best part—the cream—will rise to the top, where it can be skimmed off. Thus, creaming means to take the best of the lot.

2. This example was part of a term paper written for one of the authors by Monica Flask, a graduate student at the University of Kansas in 1989, and we wish to thank her for supplying it.

3. *Take-up rates* refer to the proportion of program eligibles that receive program benefits. While the AFDC program has had 90 percent take-up rates for a decade now, the Food Stamps program has always had take-up rates of around 50 percent, and the energy assistance and SSI programs only slightly more (Menefee, Edwards and Schreiber, 1981; Congressional Budget Office, 1985).

4. Clearly there were other events contributing to this change, although we think that they are not as important. For example, the number of non-minority children was dropping, and the placement of minority children with non-minority adoptive parents was increasing. The rise of substantial objection to this form of adoption on the part of minority communities was influential in curtailing, though not eliminating, its use—in general, a good outcome we believe. The numbers of such placements were never large, relative to either the total number of adoptions or the number of adoptions of overseas children.

References

Berman, P. (1978). The study of macro- and micro-implementation. *Public Policy, 26,* 157–184.

Chelimsky, E. (1985). Comparing and contrasting auditing and evaluation: Some notes on their relationship. *Evaluation Review, 9*(4), 483–505.

Congressional Budget Office. (November 1988). *The food stamps program: Eligibility and participation rates.*

Ewalt, P. L., and Honeyfield, R. M. (1981). Needs of persons in long term care. *Social Casework, 26* (3), 222–236.

Finney, J., & Moos, R. (1985). Environmental assessment and evaluation research. *Evaluation and Program Planning, 7,* 146–151.

Gramlich, E, & Koshel, P. (Summer 1975). "Is real-world experimentation possible?" *Policy Analysis, 1,* 511–530.

Hill, M., & Bramley, G. (1986). Analysing social policy. Oxford: Basil Blackwell.

Hjern, B., & Porter, D. (1980). Implementation structure: A new unit of administrative analysis. Conference paper, Institute for Advanced Studies, Vienna, Austria. Unpublished Monograph. International Institute of Management, Berlin.

Houlden, P., & Balkin, S. (1985). Performance evaluation for systems of assigned service providers. *Evaluation Review, 9*(5), 547–593.

House, E. (1982). Scientific and humanistic evaluations. In E. House, S. Mathison, J. Pearsol and H. Preskill (Eds.), *Evaluation Studies Review Annual, 7* (pp. 15–26). Beverly Hills, CA: Sage.

Hudson, J. (1983). Measuring the costs and benefits of QA. *Quality Review Bulletin, 9*(6), 164–166.

King, J., Morris, L. L., & Fitzgibbon, C. T. (1987). *How to assess program implementation.* Beverly Hills, CA: Sage.

Kress, G., Koehler, G., & Springer, F. (1981). Policy drift: An evaluation of the California Business Enterprise Program. In D. Palumbo and M. Harder (Eds.), *Implementing public policy* (pp. 19–28). Lexington, MA: Lexington Books, D.C. Heath and Company.

Levine, R. (1972). *Public planning: Failure and redirections.* New York: Basic Books.

Lindblom, C. (1959). The science of muddling through. *Public Administration Review 19,* 79–88.

Menefee, J., Edwards, B., & Scheiber, S. (1981). Analysis of non-participation in the SSI program. *Social Security Bulletin,44*(3), 3–21.

McKillip, J. (1987). *Need analysis: Tools for the human services and education.* Newbury Park, CA: Sage.

Palumbo, D., & Harder, M. (1981). *Implementing public policy.* Lexington, MA: Lexington Books, D.C. Heath and Company.

Palumbo, D., Maynard-Moody, S., & Wright, P. (1984). Measuring degrees of successful implementation. *Evaluation Review, 8* (1), 45–74.

Scheirer, M. (1987). Program theory and implementation theory: Implications for evaluators. *Using program theory in evaluation.* New Directions for Program Evaluation Series, No. 33. San Francisco: Jossey-Bass.

Sorg, J. (1981). Pursuing policy optimization by evaluating implementation: Notes on the state of the art. In D. Palumbo & M. Harder, *Implementing public policy* (pp. 144–146). Lexington, MA: Lexington Books, D.C. Heath and Company.

Warheit, G. J., Bell, R. A., & Schwab, J. J. (1977). *Needs assessment approaches: Concepts and methods.* Washington, D.C.: U.S. Government Printing Office.

Willer, D., & Anderson, B. (1981). *Networks, exchange and coercion.* New York: Elsevier North Holland.

Wimberley, E. (1989, March). *How much quality assurance can a social work department afford?.* Paper presented at the meeting of the Council On Social Work Education, Chicago, Ill.

CHAPTER EIGHT

Monitoring Social Policy and Program Implementation, Part II

Program Activities

Introduction

After a brief review of the importance of monitoring program implementation from a quantitative perspective, the three common types of implementation errors will be presented so as to provide a backdrop for the discussion of methodology which follows. There, we will be concerned with describing the use of program theory in constructing program specifications, issues in pre-selecting program activities for monitoring, reliability, validity, pre-tests of monitoring procedures, attending to organizational and staff acceptability, costs, and deriving performance standards for program implementation.

In the immediately preceding chapters recall we discussed the monitoring of program participant characteristics. Although those are very important, the actual heart of implementation monitoring lies in a preoccupation with observing actual program activities. While that can be a difficult task, advance planning can make actual monitoring operations surprisingly simple. So, in order to help readers do good advance planning, let us briefly review what it is that shapes its essential character.

First, as we keep reminding readers, basic assumptions are always determining: thus, what one believes about the nature of the human condition determines what one believes about helping people with problems, and what one believes about implementing programs of help determines what one believes about how implementation monitoring should be done. That being the case, it should be obvious that there may be many different kinds of implementation monitoring. Here we will speak from the point of view of standard (quantitative) empirical social science, leaving to a later section of the book a discussion of monitoring from a qualitative point of view.[1] Before we become more explicit about this heavily quantitative view of implementation and monitoring, we will argue that, even apart from considerations of ideology or paradigmatic choices, there are some good reasons for *not* choosing a quantitative approach to implementation monitoring. We believe that a qualitative rather than a quantitative approach may be a good choice under certain circumstances; for example, when:

1. A program theory can't be made explicit, elaborated, or standardized for some reason.
2. The social program is thoroughly atheoretical.
3. The program is one where practitioners operate with theoretical inconsistency or with an extreme eclecticism.
4. Staff practitioners work out of consistent theoretical frameworks, but among program staff there are many different theoretical commitments.

The use of a qualitative approach under these circumstances will usually make all this explicit. The problem for an organization operating in these conditions is to find some ground on which to congeal or standardize its program operations. If a program cannot do that, there is not one program; rather, there are as many programs as there are practitioners.

Now, from the quantitative point of view, what should we expect from our monitoring scheme? First, we will want it to assure us that program activities are "up and running" in a dependable way—recall that, absent that, we will be unable to write an evaluation report that attributes results to program effort. Second, we will want it to give us an up-to-date description of actual program operations so that funders, command level decision-makers, and (perhaps) legislators can decide whether it suits their purposes (and, perhaps, to provide some protection for middle-managers should they come against some of the more outrageous slings and arrows of organizational fate). Finally, if there are unanticipated negative side effects of a social program, we will want the monitoring scheme to reveal it. Now let us turn to a discussion of how to construct a monitoring scheme that will accomplish those tasks.

Three Implementation Errors

In monitoring implementation, evaluation practitioners should keep in mind that there are three common implementation errors that a monitoring scheme should always be able to pick up. (Let us speak of program activities as *treatments* here since we are dealing primarily with evaluating personal social service programs.) The first error is when no (or insufficient) treatment or intervention is being provided by the program. The second is when the program is providing the wrong treatment, and the third is when the program is providing unsystematized or inconsistent treatment or interventions. Let us discuss each one and think about some examples.

First consider wrong implementation. While it may not seem that a well intentioned treatment could ever be wrong in any sense, indeed it can be if we assume that social programs ought to be both intentional and prescriptive. An intervention based on a scientific way of going about things will always assume that. And, here at least, so do we. But the reader should note that it is not uncontroversial. In a quantitative, empirical social science approach to knowledge, an a-priori hypothesis is formed to guide practice behavior(s), and its source may be either a general guiding idea out of past experience or perhaps a theory. In the human service and social work literature, this idea is referred to in phrases such as "every program [or practitioner act] is a hypothesis" (Logan and Chambers, 1987). Hence, monitoring implementation is essential in following the central (scientific) paradigm. It is contradictory to the nature of science to cast, in some loose way, just any old effort against the world and then look for results, attributing everything observed to that cast. Science is about strongly controlling environments[2]—laboratory conditions are the metaphor here—and so a "scientific" approach to social programs must be committed to certain controls over program effort and practitioner acts. (And, of course, that is what the qualitative paradigm is so critical of.)

If the reader followed the above argument, it should be clear that, like any good scientific experiment, a social program design can only implement one theory at a time, for, if it implements more than one, to which theory can the program attribute results? Thus, if it implements a theory other than the one it intends to implement, it is making the *wrong-treatment error*. That is not to say that it is invariably a mistake (with respect to helping people), although it certainly may be that. Here is an example of this implementation error. Consider a social program for children, whose goal is to achieve *permanent* kinship bonds for them. If such a program uses foster parents from their customary operations and provides only the ordinary program of temporary foster care, they will use foster parents who never intended to give a permanent home to children. This program must show activities which could be expected to result in permanent kinship bonds; for example, a selection or screening device or a special retraining program for those who have been foster parents in the system, etc. Since the ordinary foster family care program is commonly associated with children moving nearly annually from one foster home to the next, using the usual type of foster parents is an implementation error because these operations cannot meet any ordinary definition of *permanent kinship bonds*. It is not an imaginary example, unfortunately. But, note, the error here does not necessarily imply that such foster parents are always doing bad parenting, just not the type of parenting the program theory prescribes. (An example of program theory exercising its prescriptive nature, notice.)

Here is another example, one which displays a different aspect of the wrong treatment implementation error. Consider a program design now commonly called *case-management* applied in relation to the social problems of the chronically mentally ill (CMI) and one which has the reduction of alienation and maximum social functioning as goals. Put as concisely as possible, its theory explains that alienation results from lack of integration with the community, that social functioning is impaired because the chronically mentally ill person doesn't have adequate survival resources, the psycho-pharmacological medications aren't doing what they should, and because alienation (lack of community integration) places barriers between the person and the needed resources, including medical assistance. Further, the theory asserts that tailoring particular social interventions to the peculiarities and needs of particular CMI persons (individualizing) is necessarily instrumental in reducing these barriers. Now, suppose a program that sets up six program activities at a psychiatric unit of the local general hospital (e.g., a talk therapy group, a job seeking training group, a medication review schedule, a recreation program, etc.) and requires the attendance of all program participants as a condition of eligibility for any of the program benefits or services is making an implementation error. In the first place, requiring all program participants to receive all program features offends the commitment of the program theory to individualization. The theory implies "client centered programs, not service centered programs . . . " (Rose, 1988). In the second place, situating services in segregated settings like psychiatric units in general hospitals, places where ordinary community members never go, offends the commitment of the theory to community integration. Any of the above list of services can be situated within paths commonly traveled by ordinary citizens: public schools, physicians' offices, public recreation centers, public health clinics, county court houses, etc.[3] To say that a general medical hospital psychiatric unit is socially segregated is only to imply one of its characteristics, not that it is unnecessary or inevitably non-useful, only that this feature is contradictory to this particular program theory and these particular (non-acute stage) clients.

This example is usefully interesting, because it suggests applying program theory in some mechanical way in imitation of a production line, an analogy that requires the assumption that program participants are homogenous materials (like clay) to be shaped (like pots) by the will of the program machinery. Programs based on those kinds of assumptions almost always entail an implementation error. Or consider this analogy: While it requires an elegant chemistry to transform petroleum from a well in the ground into a plastic, it doesn't mean that there can't be several sets of machinery that will produce the same product, even though it looks and acts very differently. Good program theory is prepared to cope with human variation and unique qualities in both implementers and program participants because it has an abstract quality (by definition); it must be sufficiently abstract to accomplish that, but, at the same time, it must be sufficiently clear and particular so that not every set of practitioner and program actions are admissible. If one cannot distinguish the difference between program activities that fit the theory and those that don't, the theory isn't likely to be powerful enough to do much good for program participants. The ability to design a study of implementation to make such distinctions is a reasonably good test of that quality of a program theory.

The concepts of program theory and program implementation never imply that everyone involved in implementing the program elements must be doing exactly the same things. The distinction between equivalence and identity is important here—doing absolutely identical things is not necessary; although it is necessary that they are at least conceptually equivalent with respect to the definitions of program elements ultimately based on the program theory. It is the task of a good implementation monitoring scheme to be able to capture this kind of implementation equivalence. Of that, more later.

A good implementation monitoring scheme should also pick up another common implementation error we earlier called *insufficient treatment* or *insufficient intervention*. This implementation error is the instance in which the practitioner or human service worker does some, but not a sufficient number, of the required program activities for them to be expected to have the desired result. Insufficient treatment or insufficient intervention is wrong because there isn't enough of it. There are several possible ways in which there "isn't enough." The most simple case is when the program elements do not express the logically necessary theoretical variables or factors. There are some painfully obvious instances; take, for example, some of the common "case review" program efforts in the child welfare field of the 1970s. Many states have legally mandated, regularly scheduled court-hearings, appearance at which is required of all major actors in the care of a child outside the home of its own kin, usually in the custody of the state. Case review programs were created as a response to a general concern arising in the 1970s that children in temporary foster care were *"drifting"*: placed in foster family or group homes and unattended to thereafter, so that those with professional or legal responsibility were ignorant of their present situations (and futures) and so that they were often moved from one set of parents to the next at frequent (perhaps 18 month) intervals with no real effort to return the child home or to place the child in adoption (Fanshel, 1978). Contributing to that picture was a very large increase in the rate at which children were entering the foster care system, along with significant fiscal shortfalls for payments for foster care, an increase in payment rate for some children, and a decrease in personnel needed to staff this system. As a program design, case review was a mechanism which came out of a theory intended to provide an increase in funding for foster care personnel, reduced entry of children into foster care, and an increase in the decision-maker information level. Long-term effects were expected: longer term foster placements (at least) and increased reunions of children with consanguineal kin. Case review systems have come under criticism when they go no further than the increasing information level (Magura, 1984), and for good reason, since it is an excellent example of insufficient implementation of the program theory. Obviously, information level increases alone cannot provide the necessary financing, adequately staff the program, nor recruit specialized foster parents for children with increasingly difficult problems.

The *no-treatment* implementation error must find both weak evidence of program activities and/or activities which do not bear upon the social problem of concern. In our experience the no- treatment implementation error is rare, but that should be no surprise, considering for a moment how difficult it is to do nothing. It is characteristic of human beings to do things, for, without cynicism, we can say that it is only the most daring of well practiced mystics and saints who can tolerate doing nothing at all. Thus, the judgment of no implementation does not usually refer to a program staff that is doing nothing at all; rather, it refers to a staff doing work that has almost no recognizable relationship to an explanation of the social problem of concern. Consider the example of a program dealing with juvenile delinquents, one of the many during the 1970s directed toward the prevention of negative social labels on children who "penetrate" deeply into the criminal justice system. Without analyzing the merits of these ideas, we simply observe that the basic idea was standard sociology at that time: i.e., encarcerating first offenders for significant periods of time may simply teach them how to be better criminals and may establish a negative reputation that becomes a self-fulfilling prophecy when access is denied to important social opportunities in the process of completing their education and obtaining employment. Program activities that would fit with such a theory are fairly straightforward: diverting first offenders out of the justice system and attempting to reduce apprehensions and eliminate official charges for first and trivial juvenile incidents, at least. Other program activities are necessary: reinforcing a positive social label on each child, increasing the access of clients to significant, socially positive opportunities in school and to initial employment.

Thus, what is the evaluator to conclude if one conceives of these program activities as a good theory-fit and if the monitoring data show neither contact with judges nor law enforcement officers and a pattern of inadequate contact with children (an initial contact with a child, one contact eight weeks later, and then no contact subsequently)?[4] In fact, it is difficult to think of any theory that this program might possibly be implementing. If program staff cannot show other activities and/or cannot account for how they relate to the social problem, we would conclude that no treatment or intervention is being done here. We take the position, not controversial we think, that human service practitioners ought to be able to make a rational account for their actions and one that is plainly related to the social problem at hand. Complexity is not the criterion here, for simple explanations have the virtue of scientific parsimony. However much doing good in general may be prized, and however much it may count as a down payment on an unearthly paradise to come, it can't count as program implementation.

Finally there is the implementation error we call *unstandardized treatment*. A social program is a calculated design to solve or remediate a social problem by means of an organizational effort. It might be a one-person organization, but most typically we are speaking of several, perhaps hundreds of, persons who are employed or who volunteer to engage in this effort. One of the tasks of evaluation research is to generate findings that bear upon the application of program efforts. In order to do that evaluation, data regarding the collective outcomes of the efforts of hundreds of people must be based on some assurance that these people were doing equivalent things. If they weren't, the evaluation report cannot speak of program outcomes as if they were, in fact, collective outcomes. Organizational non-conformists may be doing valuable things, perhaps even more valuable than their colleagues, but there is a point at which activities outside those parameters accumulate to destroy the ability to attribute outcomes to program efforts. That is the instance we wish to call unstandardized treatment, an implementation error that any good implementation monitoring scheme must be capable of picking up. Personal social service programs and human service practitioners in general do not have an easy time implementing social interventions in ways that are equivalent to their professional and organizational colleagues. School counseling programs dealing with school dropouts come to mind as interesting examples. Often we find that some counselors do a type of interpersonal counseling, some do environmental manipulation with either parents, teachers, or the school system, or all three, some do vocational counseling, etc. Now all may be effective in themselves or effective with regard to a particular child or school, but they cannot be considered to be equivalent intervention strategies. Notice that, in order to evaluate such a program, one would have to design a separate evaluation for each practitioner, since there are as many programs as there are practitioners! In fact, it stands outside the boundaries of what we want to consider a social program to be: that is, a *group* of people working to achieve *a particular social policy* for an *identified segment of society* through a *shared explanation* and *common means or mechanism* (key concepts italicized). Clearly, we would never say that single practitioner-programs are not an effective way to serve particular individuals (for some social problems, it may be quite sensible), just that it is a different sort of enterprise from social programs in which it is a conceptual and fiscal mistake to use a standard program evaluation approach to judge their nature or effectiveness. To do so would be impossibly expensive and would require the use of implausible assumptions about its nature. Note that one way to evaluate the practice of single individuals pursuing social objectives is called *single subject design,* but, reasonably enough, it runs on quite different tracks than what we are speaking of here. We will consider it in greater detail in Chapter Ten.

Constructing Program Specifications

If one of our main objectives in doing program implementation is to detect the presence of the three major implementation errors, we must have a criterion for adequate implementation. We propose this one: in order to consider a program to be adequately implemented, it must expose its participants—at both the required level of impact and in the required sequence (if any)—to the influence of all of the factors believed necessary to achieve its objectives. When this criterion is concretized with regard to some specific program, we will call it the *program specification*. Creating it is a process of identifing the crucial variables (factors) that must be implemented, using the program theory as the authoritative source. This task should not be difficult, but it will be if the program theory is not sufficiently explicit—sometimes it is necessary to return to the program theory and further specify it. Devising a program specification is simple where the program theory is minimal, the variables are not very abstract, and all the variables (factors) are considered necessary for adequate implementation. In that case there is no decision to be made among the variables.

But often a program theory is sufficiently imaginative so that it carries "excess baggage," i.e., contains factors that are interesting but not essential to the logic of the construction. We are fortunate when the theory sets out the relative importance of variables (factors) in the program theory, because the program specification can then be structured using that information to sort out those which are most important. Note however that eventually we must consider practicalities, because at a later point, when we use the program specification for its practical advantages—as a basis for constructing a scheme to monitor (take observations of) program activities—we cannot ignore the fact that evaluation expenses cannot exceed the funds available. And, because funds are always in short supply, it is seldom that any evaluation enterprise monitors all the variables in a program specification, even all those thought to be important for one reason or another. Keeping all those things in mind, let us look at an example of a program specification task, one which is straightforward, although not a simple case. Figure 8-1 is an example (in diagram form) of the program theory for a social service program concerned with the primary prevention of child abuse.[5]

The first task here is to locate the factors the program theory considers to be the ultimate explanatory variables. Recollect that we spoke of them earlier as antecedents. Given the diagrammatic form here, it is not difficult to locate them—simply follow the arrows backwards to their most ultimate source: here, these antecedent variables are external stress and interactional conflict among adults. It is here that this program theory, like all theories, chooses to "stop explaining."[6]

FIGURE 8–1 • *Program Theory*
(Child Abuse Prevention)

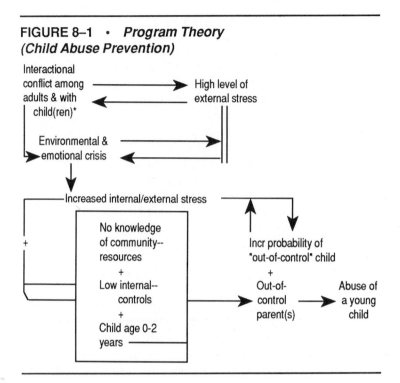

There are other arbitrary cognitive choices being exercised here; for example, this program will choose to focus its efforts on decreasing external stressors and interfamilial interactional conflict (variables with an *). Notice that other choices could have been made; for example, the program could have focused on reducing internal stressors or increasing the low internal controls of parents. That, the observant reader may have already concluded, might lead to one of the implementation errors previously discussed—insufficient implementation. Indeed, it will be considered an error if the program doesn't meet its objectives. We conclude that the program stands ready to take that risk since it is assuming (at least) the following: that the two variables it is attending to are those which are the most determinant, and that the internal stressor factor is a second order consequence which can be left unattended to as long as those of the first order are dealt with. Clearly, these assumptions may or may not be correct, but of course it is precisely the task of an evaluation to test that out. One way to accomplish that is by including a method of observing (monitoring) omitted variables to do that. Thus, our first task in constructing a program specification is to list all the variables indicated by the theory as being of sufficient importance to monitor. And, not only do we include all the variables judged to be of premier importance, but we may also include some on which the program wishes to take observations in order to double check themselves on their operating assumptions.

Notice also that this program will not focus on (the variable called) *the young child* in Figure 8-1. It is not that the program isn't concerned with the welfare of young children; clearly they are the ultimate object of its attention. It is rather that the program strongly assumes that benefits for children (not suffering the consequences of abuse) will come about as consequences of changes in the factors it will attempt to influence. Of course that kind of assumption would seem to be in the nature of all primary prevention programs. The observant reader will recollect from our earlier discussion our point that one never discovers "ultimate" causes, so that is not the issue here; Rather that, in implementing social programs, some selection must always be made in choosing the causal variables, addressed, and of course that implies assumptions about what one expects as consequences.

To summarize: the program specification identifies all the variables for which a method of observation must be constructed in order to judge proper program implementation. In the context of program specification, each of those variables (or sets thereof) are called the *program elements,* and, in order to be complete, each must include a description of a set of program activities that must be put into place in order to operationalize the program element. Thus, a program element consists of one or more theoretical variables plus program activities operationalizing it (them). A program specification will name all the variables of importance but may not include a complete description of all program elements, since almost no monitoring scheme includes only a selection of them.

Now let us work out a program specification, using the program theory above. This program chooses to try to influence the antecedent called *high level of external stress,* which it defines as a continuing event that actually deprives the family (person) of basic material or social needs or statuses (self-defined), or anxiety about that future possibility. The program will attempt to reduce this deprivation by (1) identifying external stressors and applying basic remedies that the program believes are effective and it is prepared to apply: here (for example) (a) inadequate or low income, (b) unemployment/underemployment, (c) housing or profound medical problems among family members. It will also attempt to reduce (2) interactional conflict among adults and between adults and children by specific measures. For simplicity, however, let us restrict this example of program specification to only the external stress variable.

Table 8-1 is an outline diagram of a program specification. Notice also that we will want to specify the different kinds of external stressors and interactional conflicts to which the program will pay special attention, for there is no program that could deal with them all. When we do that kind of specification, we are determining the *program range.* Thus we would say that (for the external stressor variable) the program range here will be: inadequate or low income, unemployment/underemployment, housing or profound medical problems among family members. Of vital concern here is to observe that, as the range of the program enlarges, the complexity of the program specification (and ultimately its monitoring scheme) also enlarges. A complete program specification must include a specification of everything that is in the program range. Because here we are only interested in illustrating program specification and don't need to demonstrate a complete one, let us focus on only the housing subelement. The program sets out to reduce the housing stressor by a program which, if effective, results in the participant obtaining housing. The program specification sets out all the activities believed to be necessary to accomplish that.

It is nearly always true that a program activity-set of any kind must make certain assumptions. They are obvious here: i.e., the participant must have sufficient income available for minimum cost housing, and actual housing must be available. Income may be a problem, but is distinguishably different

TABLE 8–1 • *Program Specification: External Stressors*

Program Element: external stressors

Program Range (i.e., of external stressors):
inadequate or low income, unemployment/underemployment, housing or profound medical problems among family members

Program Activity(s):

a. (re: reducing the housing stressor)
—required assumptions: adequate income for minimum cost housing, housing stock is actually available

1. Assessing housing need
2. Assessing program participants' level of information about housing resources in the community
   a. types (commercial sector units/public housing units
   b. locations and location implications (areas, transportation available, schools, and shopping)
   c. cost (monthly/weekly rents, utility turn-ons, deposits)
   d. conditions (leases, care standards, times, deposit refunds, restrictions on children or pets)
3. Supplying participant the lacking information
4. Assessing participants' presentation of image
5. Teaching participant how to maximize image
   a. presenting the concept: verbalizing the idea, participant gives examples of how it applies
   b. modeling the concept with surrogates: participant group creates examples, performing all the relevant roles
   c. modeling the concept in the field: participants, in pairs, watch the "coach-expert" apply for actual housing
   d. feedback on image presentation when participant peers accompany each other when applying for housing

---

from the housing problem; nor is there any point in attending to housing unless this assumption is tenable. The point here is that a monitoring scheme must make provision for observing whether those assumptions are tenable for clients. If it doesn't, program efforts will surely be taking responsibility for more than they should, and they may be judged to be either a failure or cost-ineffective, not because the program efforts were unsound, but because the economy could not supply the necessary external conditions. If the monitoring scheme ignores this possibility, a good program intervention may be discarded in error.

Now, the next move is to make explicit the minimum set of program acts or activities necessary for achieving the objectives. This program design assumes that in order for a person to be successful in obtaining housing, they must have some minimum level of information about available housing stock: what types, where it is located, the important consequences of its location (e.g., access to transportation for work); costs (e.g., rents and deposits); and conditions of lease contracts (e.g., standards of care, deposit refunds). In Table 8-1 these have been entered into the program specification as information the program must be sure the participant has or which it must supply (teach) to them. Notice that we have added certain subelements to the lists (e.g., "restrictions on children or pets") so that what we have are all the subelements this program considers essential. Now let us suppose that the program also assumes that in order to be successful in obtaining housing a person must present a positive social image, based on the theory that more than money enters into a rental property owner or manager's decision to lease. Thus, where obtaining housing is an issue, this program must equip (teach) the participant to present a positive image for that specific purpose. Notice in the program specification we have entered elements which might be required to accomplish that (e.g., modeling, coaching, etc.).

Let us do a specification for one other program variable just to be sure that the points above are sufficiently illustrated. This time let us suppose that this same program chooses to focus on the variable in the program theory called an *out of control child* (see Figure 8-1). It defines this variable as a child who displays behaviors that, either because of the long time span over which they occur or because of their particularities, produce extreme stress for a parent. Note that here the basis for this variable is not determined by some (developmental) norm for children, but by the particularities of a child's parents; here, what is an out-of-control child for one parent is not presumed to be so for another. While this is a tad unusual, it could be justified on the basis of concern for avoiding serious injury to the child. All that aside, there are any number of strategies a program might pursue to deal with this problem, but this program opts to install a parental behavior that will remove the child from the occasion for expression of parental violence, continuing in its devotion to minimal intrusiveness and behavioral focus. This option is commonly known as the *time-out*. A place is chosen where the child can be removed to when the parents' tolerance is exceeded (and/or there is fear that the child's behavior will provoke a physical attack or other negative approach by the parent, another motive for choosing this strategy). Other recourses must first be tried and fail: direct command and/or diversion to alternate activity. The child is required to remain there for a short period of time, the time varying with the child's age. The underlying idea is that during this time the child will regain its composure and be amenable to less intrusive interventions like direct commands or diversions. In the program specification that follows (Table 8-2), actions consistent with these ideas are embedded along with others, so that, taken together, they constitute all that should be required to produce the program objectives pertaining to this particular factor.

Notice that many things have been added to the program specification that didn't appear in the first description (Figure 8-1), often restrictions on such things as when the time-out is legitimate and certain limitations on it. Those limitations have been established in response to findings of certain negative side effects, so they are quite important. The point here is that time-out is a very specific technique, and when program participants don't use it in this way, they cannot count as cases of implementation success.

Earlier we spoke of the definition of what constitutes an adequate implementation and said that it must expose its participants—at both the

---

TABLE 8–2 • *Program Specification II*

Program Element #2

Theory Element:
  out-of-control child

Program Range:
  child of "educable" intelligence, with physical mobility, absent psychotic episodes, age 2–8 years

Program Activities (for time-out as a disciplinary strategy)
  Necessary program activities:
  (Parent taught to understand the . . .)

1. Definition of the *time-out* and objectives thereof
2. Conditions prior to application
   a. unsuccessful in direct command and directing child to alternative activity
   b. child's clear understanding of the act or situation which made the time-out necessary
   c. available and satisfactory place for the child to serve the time-out (well lighted and within the hearing parent or caretaker, a place neither familiar or frightening to the child)
3. Negative conditions for application (no more than thre time-outs or 60 minutes total time-outs per day per child)
4. Child must serve the time alone (e.g., not when in same room as a sleeping caretaker); no sibling or other visitors during time-out

---

required level of impact and in the required sequence (if any)—to the influence of all of the factors believed necessary to achieve its objectives. Now, in some ideal world, any program theory ought to be very clear about the "level of impact" it takes to produce the desired results (say, metaphorically, the "strength of the dose"). Almost no program theory does that, and we believe that it is because of the "primitive" nature of most social theory. However, we call it to the reader's attention because, perhaps, social and program theory will get there someday and because program evaluators should recognize the sign of a strong set of ideas when they present themselves. There are a few weak examples, but we shouldn't fool ourselves: most social programs and social practitioners work from the principle of continuing an intervention until it shows evidence of success. Indeed, there are both practical and theoretical reasons to think that this principle may have problems (what if an intervention produces gains only over the long term), but we advise that it should be honored in the breach. At the moment we cannot supply anything better.

The criterion for adequate implementation has another aspect—if the program theory implied sequences (order of presentation) among the theoretical variables, the program specification should reflect that, since it should be a feature on which the monitoring scheme should take observations. The program theory above provides an example of that: clearly, obtaining housing implies that the first step is to secure the income required for making the initial housing contract and for its continuing support. The theory (as presented above) doesn't explicitly say that, but then program theory presentations don't always say everything they could, so program evaluators should expect to have to ferret out common sense assumptions like this. To make this program feature clear, the program specification should construct and present a *client pathway*, a set of one-word or one-phrase descriptions of the order in which *program elements* must occur. The one-word/phrase descriptions may not be named identically with the program elements since they may include more than one program element. Figure 8-2 is a simple example of a client pathway for the program we have been discussing here. (Recall that the objective here is to reduce the incidence of the physical abuse of young children.) Notice that it does not elaborate on the program elements; it only sets out their order.

Observing Implementation

Introduction

Having set out the program specification, the program evaluator is in a position to construct a *monitoring scheme*: a set of instructions for making

---

FIGURE 8–2   •   *Program Theory (Child Abuse Prevention)*

Recruitment Contact
+
Enrollment Meeting
+
Pre-Birth Home Visits
+
Hospital Visits
+
Home Visits: every 3 weeks in newborn's 1st year
+
Home Visits: every 4 weeks age 1–2
+
Baby's 2nd Birthday: (program termination) party

---

systematic observations of program activities for the purpose of judging the adequacy of program implementation. Even though we may have already sorted through the variables for those that are in some sense essential, we are usually faced with another selection task—squaring the need to take monitoring observations with the size of the available evaluation budget. Thinking about and contriving observational methods for monitoring implementation has all the difficulties ordinarily associated with measurements in social action in natural settings,[7] so we will review some but not all of those standard measurement issues. The more technical aspects we will save until the later chapter on measurement, where we will cast the discussion in terms equally applicable to the measurement of both inputs and outcomes, that is, of both monitoring and program effectiveness.

Choosing an Observational Strategy

In order to make it easier to speak of the various strategies available for obtaining the observations that go into monitoring implementation, let us speak of three issues in particular and the seven common alternative observational strategies associated with them:

1. Who does the observing (self-report vs independent observers)
2. Where and when the observations are taken (on-site vs after-the-fact judgments)
3. The form in which the question is put to observers of the action (structured vs open-ended vs narrative interrogatives)

In selecting who does the observing, the evaluator must pay close attention to the *reactivity* of those who are being observed and the many other sources of bias, both deliberate and unintentional. There are many reasons why people are reactive, but one of them is a very good reason indeed: if the program evaluation project is of any importance at all, readers should remember that the person being observed is bound to have a stake in its outcome. On that account it is too much to expect that they (or us, were we in a similar situation) will not be tempted to shade observations in favor of their own self-interest, wherever that is possible. Then, there is the undeniable fact that monitoring involves closely observing people doing their jobs, and few people are comfortable with that, since it is such an unusual feature of our work settings. That means the observations must be as unobtrusive as possible and that their relationship to data reporters' self-interest must be as obscure as possible. Indeed those prescriptions may well be counsels of perfection, for some data is nearly impossible to disguise. Hence, that sort of situation would be the strongest possible argument against a self-report strategy.

One of the alternatives is to have someone else take the observations, a person hired to do that—or perhaps a co-worker in some situations. However, there are some who believe that the presence of a person solely in the role of an observer inevitably changes a natural setting, and, of course, they have the Heisenberg Principle as a prestigious authority for their opinion.[8] The argument is particularly persuasive, certainly not hard to imagine, when applied to human beings interacting in organizations. One solution to that is to use program participants as observers of services and benefit delivery. It is our experience that they are, on the whole, rather good observers of the delivery of social services or benefits. They are not alien to the context; rather, they are part of its natural composition, always a positive feature of an observational strategy. They also have an investment in the thing being observed (it isn't entirely removed from their lives) and are often not people who are used to being asked to take an important role in these kinds of operations. While that feature calls for the need for some training and instruction, its positive feature is that it can motivate the observer to be meticulous in following directions and persevering until its completion. Using benefit and service recipients as observers goes some way toward reducing biases of this kind, we believe. Of course, that is not to say that program participants are always the best choice or entirely without self-interest of their own which might give them a motive for obfuscating data. Where their reports on services given can be linked to their identity (and in our experience we have found that most program participants can readily isolate those occasions), the program evaluator must assume that observations will be tempered by that fact—certainly it will deflate negative reports, though there may be less reason to think that it will inflate positive reports.

Endnotes

1. If the reader wishes to be reminded about the nature of these divergent assumptions, they may wish to return to the first chapter, where they are discussed under the heading of qualitative and quantitative types of program evaluation.

2. Where it is possible, controlling environmental conditions for experimental purposes is always the ideal in science. Of course, astronomy and geology are examples of how interesting and useful science is conducted even where controlling laboratory conditions or environments in a closed experiment are not possible. We don't think these are contrary examples; rather, that it isn't too much to say that scientists would probably insist on moving the sun and the stars in the interest of science (i.e., controlling them for experimental purposes) if it were at all possible.

3. This example was kindly supplied to Donald Chambers by Walter Kisthardt, a doctoral student at the University of Kansas in 1989.

4. Exactly how much contact is "enough contact" has to be determined by the program theory.

5. Portions of this example were kindly supplied to Donald Chambers by Anne Gaffney, a graduate student at the University of Kansas in 1989.

6. All theories have just such a point. It may be puzzling because it seems clear that, in this example, theorists worth their salt could easily have gone on to explain why there was "interactional conflict among adults" or why there was a "high level of external stress," certainly why parents lack problem solving skills. There is always a quality of arbitrariness about where to stop explaining, at least according to those who study the subject of theory construction. Thus, it is no good asking for the reason for stopping—there isn't one, for we are at the level of arbitrary assumptions.

7. By natural settings we mean nothing more than environments in which people have placed themselves (or are placed by others) for reasons other than research objectives.

8. Heisenberg was a German physicist, a contemporary of Einstein, whose name is attached to an idea about how some orders of observations must always include the effect of the observing instrument (originally, with regard to a problem in observing and counting subatomic particles in collision with each other).

References

Fanshel, D. (1978). *Children in foster care*. New York: Columbia University Press.

Logan, S., & Chambers, D. E. (1987). Considerations for starting where the client is. *Arete*, 12(2), 1-12.

Magura, S. (1984). Clients as evaluators in child protective services. *Child Welfare*, 62(2), 99-112.

Rose, S. (August 1988). Presentation at a meeting of Regional Mental Health Directors, New York State (unpublished).

CHAPTER NINE

Measurement Strategies in Program Evaluation*

Program evaluation, like other branches of research, involves comparison. Comparison, in turn, requires measurement. How shall we decide what to measure, and how? A diversity of measurement tools are available to the program evaluator. This chapter begins with an overview of reliability and validity and then discusses measurement decisions in the evaluative context. A multiple measurement strategy, using tools with complementary strengths and weaknesses, is advocated as the most effective approach. Measurement methods that have been found particularly useful in the human services are discussed. They include: standardized instruments, evaluator-developed measures, global assessments, client satisfaction measures, hard data, and Goal Attainment Scaling.

Distinguishing Between Reliability and Validity

Reliability of measures has to do with the repeatability and consistency of measurements. Do repeated measurements at different times, with different forms or with different observers, yield consistent results? If so, the measure is reliable. Validity of measures is concerned with whether an instrument measures what it is intended to measure. Suppose that an instrument purports to measure self-esteem. How would one establish that the instrument actually measured self-esteem rather than some tangential concept such as physical attractiveness or, perhaps, conceit? Similarly, how might one establish that subjects did not simply give socially desirable responses? When an instrument is shown to measure what it intended, the instrument is valid.

Not all reliable measures are valid measures. Nunnally (1978) illustrates how the concept of reliability would apply if we attempted to measure

*This chapter is written by James A. Rosenthal and Kenneth R. Wedel.

189

intelligence by conducting two rock-throwing contests. If how far children throw in the first contest predicts well how far they throw in the second—that is, if results are repeatable—then rock throwing is a reliable measure of intelligence. But clearly rock throwing is not a valid measure of intelligence.

Reliability has a narrow meaning in the social sciences. In everyday conversation, something that is reliable is dependable, even good; in social science parlance, reliability conveys only consistency. A measure may be consistently good or consistently bad. The rock-throwing contest referred to above yields consistently bad (invalid) measurements of intelligence. Nevertheless, measurements were consistent and therefore reliable.

Most situations in which reliable measures lack validity are more subtle than our illustration. Suppose that an instrument purporting to measure delinquent behavior is administered on two different occasions and that consistent results are obtained, i.e., respondents who admit to high levels of delinquency on the first administration do so again on the second. Similarly, those who report low levels initially do so again in subsequent testing. The instrument is reliable. Yet, perhaps many respondents lied on both tests. While reliable, the instrument is not valid.

Problems with reliability are problems with random errors. Nunnally (1978) presents an example of a nearsighted chemist who, because of blurred vision, sometimes reads a thermometer too high and sometimes reads it too low. There is no systematic bias in the measurements—the errors follow a random pattern. When random errors are held to a minimum, reliability is high.

Problems with validity deal with systematic errors. In the delinquency example above, reported delinquency is lower than actual delinquency. The errors in measurement systematically bias responses. The errors are akin to a thermometer that consistently reads five degrees too low: temperature is measured consistently, but readings are systematically biased relative to the actual temperature. Such a thermometer is reliable but not valid.

Assessing reliability is straightforward and statistical—we simply take two measurements and compare scores; if scores are similar, the measuring instrument is reliable. Assessing validity is inherently complex and requires non-statistical decision making. Experts agree about reliability but disagree about validity. For instance, most experts agree that intelligence tests are reliable, as scores from tests taken at different times are reasonably consistent. The controversy in intelligence testing involves validity. Do intelligence tests actually measure intelligence or instead some tangential concept, perhaps "middle-class school smarts"? There is no clear-cut statistical procedure for addressing this question. Issues of validity invite debate and are never fully resolved.

Reliability: The Consistency of Measurements

Methods for Assessing Reliability

Procedures for assessing reliability differ somewhat according to the type of measurement. Often the task is to determine the reliability of multiple-item "paper and pencil" scales. These scales may measure single or multiple concept(s). Measures may be of attitudes (self-esteem, for example) or knowledge based (knowledge of the facts of reproduction among participants in a sex education program, for example).

Four approaches can be used to assess the reliability of multiple-item scales: (1) test-retest reliability, (2) multiple forms reliability, (3) split-halves methods, and (4) internal consistency. *Test-retest reliability,* the method presented in examples so far, is established by administering the same instrument at two different times and comparing results. To assess *multiple forms reliability,* two alternative but equivalent forms of the same instrument are administered and the consistency of results across forms is assessed. The *split-half method* divides an instrument into two parts, usually odd and even items, and assesses the consistency between scores on each half. The logic behind the split-half method is that if both halves of the test measure the same concept, then scores on the halves should be similar.

Internal consistency approaches assess how well responses to individual items agree with one another. Nunnally (1978) defines internal consistency as the average correlation between items. A hypothetical self-esteem scale can be used to describe the internal consistency approach. If this scale possesses internal consistency, those conveying good self-esteem in their response to a given item will tend also to convey good self-esteem in responses to other items. Similarly, those conveying bad self-esteem on the given item will tend to convey the same on other items. Hence, if those who respond affirmatively on the item "I do good work" also respond affirmatively on other items ("I respect myself," "My opinion is valued," etc.), this demonstrates internal consistency. Where responses to individual items follow the pattern just described, the items are positively correlated with one another, and the scale, therefore, possesses internal consistency. A scale in which items do not show a pattern of positive inter-correlations lacks internal consistency.

Using one of the above approaches, the researcher determines the *reliability coefficient* for the instrument in question. A reliability coefficient is the correlation of scores obtained on one administration or form with scores obtained on a second administration or form. The reliability coefficient may vary from 0.00 to 1.00. Hence, if the test-retest reliability of an instrument is 0.85, scores on a first administration correlate at 0.85 with scores on a second administration. An alternate forms reliability of 0.70 conveys that the correlation between scores on different forms was 0.70. A reliability coefficient of 0.80 is sometimes regarded as the minimum acceptable level of reliability (Monette, Sullivan, and DeJong, 1986).

A statistical adjustment is ordinarily used in calculating split-half reliability. The first step is to determine the correlation between halves. This yields a reliability coefficient for the two halves. Yet the interest is not in the reliability of the halves, but instead in that of the whole. The Spearman-Brown formula is used to adjust the reliability coefficient so that it pertains to the whole test (Nunnally, 1978). This results in a moderate increase in reliability.

The most common reliability coefficient based on the internal consistency approach is *Cronbach's alpha* (or alpha or coefficient alpha). The average correlation of items is important in calculating alpha but is not identical to it. Alpha is a function of two factors: (1) the average correlation and (2) the number of items. Increases in either (or both) of these factors raise the value of alpha.

The items comprising an instrument may be viewed as a random sample of items from a universe of possible items. Alpha may be interpreted as the predicted correlation with another instrument of the same length also composed of a random sample of items from the same universe (Nunnally, 1978). In this sense, alpha is similar to multiple forms reliability and to the split-half reliability coefficient following the Spearman-Brown adjustment. Although it is beyond the scope of this chapter, the notion of internal consistency is indeed important in understanding all of the different approaches we have discussed.

Reliability of Judgments and Observations

The reliability of judgments is typically assessed in a different way than the reliability of paper and pencil tests. Typically the reliability of judgments is established by determining the level of agreement between independent judges or observers. Establishing that independent persons concur is important whenever subjective judgments are required. Depending on the specific circumstances, different terms describe this process. The terms *inter-observer reliability, inter-judge reliability, inter-rater reliability,* and *inter-coder reliability* are all in common usage (Polster and Collins, 1988). The key to good inter-judge reliability is the establishment of clear unambiguous rules for judges to use in decision making.

The reliability of judgments can and should be established in a variety of situations. For instance, two observers might each count the number of times a student behaves aggressively, as defined by some rating scheme. The more similar the counts, the higher the reliability. Similarly, therapists' statements could be coded into several categories—say, interpretive, reflective, supportive, advice-giving—by two observers. Agreement in categorizations would reflect high reliability. Perhaps an administrator is required to determine the percentage of ineligible clients served according to a fairly complex set of criteria. Two independent judges could review cases. High levels of agreement would convey high inter-judge reliability.

Inter-judge (or inter-observer or inter-rater) reliability is sometimes defined as the percentage of agreements. For instance, in the previous example, reliability could be defined as the percentage of times that the two judges agreed on their assessments of eligibility. While it is appropriate to present the percentage of agreements, this percentage can be artificially high because of agreements due to chance or "luck". The *kappa statistic* statistically adjusts for chance agreements and is a particularly useful measure of inter-judge reliability (Siegel and Castellan, 1988).

The Importance of Reliability

When subjective phenomena are measured, there is the potential for measurement error, and thus the reliability of measurements is an issue. Some measurements are assumed to be 100 percent reliable and without measurement error. For instance, if birth weight was measured, reliability would not be formally assessed; accuracy would simply be assumed because we generally assume that weight scales are used properly.

High reliability is essential in evaluation or practice situations where decisions pertain to individuals, but, it is only desirable when decisions pertain to large groups. Consider, for instance, a second-grader who is tested for possible transfer to a special education classroom. Given that results will significantly affect the child's future, only modest measurement error—random or systematic—should be tolerated. It is critical that the results reflect the child's true abilities. Similarly, high reliability is crucial in drug testing, as false accusations could have marked consequences. In this situation reliability might be defined as the consistency of results in tests by two independent labs.

On the other hand, in studies with large samples, random error is ordinarily a lesser concern. Suppose that self-esteem is over-reported by some (random measurement error in a positive direction) and under-reported by others (random measurement error in a negative direction). Over a large sample of, say, 100 respondents, these random errors tend to cancel out, and the mean level of self-esteem is largely unaffected. This being the case, and given that no systematic bias is introduced by random error, productive analysis of results can be carried out.

This does not mean obviously that one should strive for low reliability. As a general rule, the less the measurement error, the better. Also, one loses some of the advantage of the law of large numbers when data are disaggregated and subgroups are examined. In studies where decisions pertain to large samples, reliability coefficients below 0.80 are acceptable; the criteria of 0.60

is a more pragmatic minimum level. Where important decisions for individuals are made, 0.90 is the more pragmatic minimum.

As stated previously, the reliability coefficient of a multiple-item instrument is determined by the average correlation of items and by the number of items. Hence, the longer the test, the more reliable the test. College entrance examinations, for instance, are highly reliable in part because they are long. Similarly, some psychiatric instruments (for example, the MMPI) are very long and very reliable.

Many social science instruments were designed primarily for use with individuals and are thus longer than they need to be for effective use with moderate or large samples. The modest gains in precision must be weighed against the frustration and/or tedium which may be introduced. This frustration, in turn, may lead to invalid responses or, perhaps, reduce response rates to a mailed questionnaire. Particularly when attitudes are measured, look for, or develop, short crisp instruments of perhaps five to twenty-five items.

Given adequate sample size, responses to single questions may yield useful reliable data. The authors know of an instance where the exact same question was repeated inadvertently in a long attitudinal instrument. The correlation between responses—in effect, the test-retest reliability—was 0.60, demonstrating sufficient reliability for productive analysis.

Validity: Measuring What Is Intended

Definitions

Validity concerns whether an instrument measures what is intended. The three major types of validity are: (1) content validity, (2) criterion validity, and (3) construct validity.

Content validity   Content validity assesses whether important aspects or dimensions of a concept are covered. For instance, an instrument purporting to measure social relationships would be judged deficient in content validity if almost all questions pertained to relationships at work and very few concerned other relationships such as those with friends and family.

Criterion validity   Criterion validity assesses whether an instrument yields results that are consistent with a well established external criterion. For instance, police logs of arrests could be regarded as a criterion of delinquent behavior. The self-reports of youth on a delinquency inventory could be compared with the police logs. If youth with police records reported higher levels of delinquent behavior on the inventory than those without records, the criterion validity of the delinquency scale would be demonstrated. If this pattern was not observed, one would be suspicious about the inventory and perhaps wonder whether respondents had answered honestly. Clearly the validity of measurements would be suspect.

A second example may prove useful. One might develop a brief scale pertaining to the perceived helpfulness of agency services. A good criterion for assessing validity might be the referring of friends for services. If the scale indeed measures perceived helpfulness, we would expect those who score high to refer their friends more often than those who score low. If this pattern was observed, criterion validity would be supported.

Construct validity   Construct validity is complex and subsumes the other types of validity. In particular, criterion validity can be viewed as a particular type of construct validity.

Construct validity evaluates the pattern of relationships between scores on an instrument and other variables. If this pattern matches expectations, the instrument possesses construct validity. Suppose that a scale of "emotional stability" is developed. One might assess whether persons who score high on this measure are also rated as stable by mental health experts. Similarly, one might assess whether those in a "normal" population scored higher on stability than those in a clinical population. Finally, scores might be compared with scores on a closely related trait, say, self-esteem, as measured by an established instrument. A good match between observed results and expectations would support the construct validity of the newly developed measure. On the other hand, if expected relationships are not evident, content validity is suspect.

The list of relationships which might be studied is, for most concepts, quite large, if not unending. In theory, the assessment of construct validity is never-ending. Each new piece of data can be viewed in terms of how it enhances or detracts from construct validity. From a pragmatic perspective, if three or four expected relationships are demonstrated, this is sufficient to establish construct validity.

To be still more pragmatic, rigorous establishment of validity is most common for educational and psychological instruments that will be used again and again in testing situations with individuals. Even though one strives to use valid measurements, small and moderate size program evaluation efforts may require the use of instruments where validity has not been thoroughly tested. Similarly, when the evaluator develops measures for the study, rigorous testing of validity is often not feasible.

Factors Influencing Validity

Response sets   Response sets are tendencies of respondents to respond to attitudinal instruments in ways which are unrelated to the concept being addressed. Response sets are personal response tendencies that individuals take with them into the measurement situation. These tendencies are influenced by the testing situation and other factors. The task of the evaluator is to arrange the testing situation so that response sets are minimized.

The most ubiquitous and problematic response set is the *social desirability response set*, the tendency for persons to respond in socially desirable ways. Hence, respondents to a self-esteem inventory give socially appropriate, rather than honest, responses. Other response sets include the *acquiescence response set* (the tendency to agree—"yea-sayers" versus "nay-sayers") and the *error of central tendency*, the tendency to choose the middle or "noncommittal" response (Bostick and Kyte, 1988). While not formally a response set, respondents may lie, particularly when they perceive they have something to gain or lose.

The program evaluator can minimize the influence of the social desirability response set. Some respondents, unfamiliar with attitudinal scales, confuse them with academic tests and search for the "right" or socially desirable response. A brief statement encouraging honest responding and conveying that there are no right or wrong answers discourages socially desirable responding. Providing adequate anonymity or confidentiality encourages honest reflection and response.

Specificity and anchoring   Validity is enhanced by specificity and behavioral description. For instance, when response categories are *anchored* with detailed description, responses are less subjective and more consistent from person to person. Anchored response categories are presented in Figure 9–1, which is taken from an instrument for assessing the functioning of families receiving child welfare services. The anchoring approach defines and clarifies the meaning of the different response categories.

Generalized non-specific items are an invitation to subjective responding and to response sets. Using the self-esteem example, the items "I feel happy," "I have a good sense of myself," and "I am glad to be me" are all quite generalized. Some items such as these can be valuable. Yet, items such as "I feel good about my personal appearance," "I take pride in my work," and "Others value my opinions" direct the respondent to more specific aspects of self-esteem and, while still subjective, will yield more valid results.

The measurement context   How an instrument is administered affects responses. For instance, social desirability is less of a concern in mailed questionnaires than in in-person interviews. In general, the evaluator's task is to present a neutral objective atmosphere, emphasizing confidentiality.

Covert aspects of the study environment may communicate that the "correct" response is a positive one. For instance, if clients fill out an outcome instrument in the presence of a therapist who has worked with them, they may feel an obligation to respond positively. If clients fill out an instrument in a

FIGURE 9–1 • *Parental Consistency of Discipline*

1. *High consistency*

Parent/guardian always follows through on promised rewards and punishments with children: rarely will contradict herself or himself; children know what to expect; punishments fit behavior.

2. *Marginal consistency, but open to improvement*

Parent/guardian does not always follow through on sanctions. Sometimes will contradict herself or himself, but makes corrective efforts when inconsistencies are brought to attention.

Consistency is understood and valued, but parent/guardian sometimes forgets, acts impulsively, etc.

3. *Marginal consistency, but not open to improvement*

Same as description for (2) above, except that children do not always know what to expect and parent/guardian seems indifferent to this.

Parent/guardian does not seem to value consistency, or perhaps doesn't understand it.

4. *Low consistency*

Parent/guardian often reacts indiscriminately or inconsistently to children's behavior; punishments often do not fit behavior.

Parent/guardian may be hostile when problems are brought to attention.

May believe he or she is being consistent, according to own logic; may claim his or her behavior benefits children (e.g., helps them cope in the "real world").

U Unknown—insufficient information

Z Not applicable

Source: Magura, S., and Moses, B. S. (1986). *Outcome measures for child welfare services: Theory and applications.* Washington, D.C.: Child Welfare League of America, p. 135. Used by permission.

group setting, they may be hesitant to respond negatively because of concern that their responses will be seen by others. Where the clout of the law is involved, in child protection situations for instance, clients may fear that negative responses will jeopardize their future.

In the first author's initial experience as a program evaluator, a group of delinquent youth preparing for a wilderness skills program filled out three standardized instruments, including a self-esteem inventory. Most of the "correct" steps were followed. Confidentiality was assured. Youth sat far apart as they filled out the instruments so they could not see each other's answers. On calculating self-esteem scores, the author was greeted with surprising results. The mean level of self-esteem was far above the norm. In fact, only two youth among twelve admitted to any problems with self-esteem. As measured by the test, the others had "perfect" self-esteem.

The wilderness counselors were faced with the impossible task of building self-esteem in a group with no problems in this area. Why were self-esteem scores artificially high? In the eyes of the youth, the author may have looked like a counselor. He may have been too "chummy" with the counseling staff, some of whom were personal friends. The author's non-verbal communications and actions were contradictory to formal statements of confidentiality. The youth may have felt that their responses would be shared with counselors even though it had been stated otherwise.

Clients may perceive that they are better simply because they have had treatment. Their reasoning may go something like this: "Treatment is designed to make folks better. I had treatment. I am better. I will respond as such." Placebos are used to counter such thinking. In drug studies, the experimental group receives the actual drug while the control group receives a placebo, often a "sugar pill" which looks like the real drug. Neither group knows which pill they are receiving.

In mental health, counseling, and educational studies, *attention placebos* are sometimes used. The experimental group gets the real treatment, while the control group gets all the "trimmings" of treatment (the attention placebo)—attention, contact with concerned persons, perhaps a group experience, or a lecture on the topic in question. The attention placebo subjects are, theoretically, unaware that they are not receiving the real treatment.

Blinding minimizes the potential for biased judgments. In a *single-blind study*, subjects are unaware of the type of treatment they are receiving. In the *double-blind study*, subjects and observers (raters) are both unaware.

When some aspect of a study or measure (perhaps the knowledge that one is in a study) causes a respondent to behave differently than she would in everyday life, the study or measure is said to be *reactive*. Hence, in a new program engendering enthusiasm and increased morale, the increased spirit of staff could influence the client judgments. When the program evaluated represents a pronounced change from usual procedures, findings may not generalize outside of the new and possibly artificial environment. Webb and colleagues (1981) have written extensively on non-reactive measures and methods.

Reliability versus Validity

Reliability and validity are closely linked: "Reliability is a necessary but not sufficient condition for validity" (Nunnally, 1978, p. 214). Yet reliability and validity may be in tension.

Content validity, for instance, is increased at the expense of internal consistency. The best way to insure high reliability (other than to use long measures) is to ask similar questions over and over. It is self-evident that responses will be consistent and the measure reliable. On the other hand, incorporating varied questions about diverse aspects of the concept in question—at the heart of building content validity—will encourage diverse responses and modestly reduce reliability. We think it good advice to let reliability suffer some in the interest of content validity.

A sometimes unasked question is whether what is measured is what is most important; there is no term in the literature to address this concept, so we'll term it *relevance validity*. Suppose that an evaluator seeks to measure the social functioning of mental health patients following treatment. Social functioning involves a myriad of interwoven concepts. Issues such as adjustment and performance in home, work, and leisure, and relationships with others might be considered.

How would one measure this abstract, multi-faceted concept (these being characteristics shared by many other social science concepts)? One "solution" is not to attempt to do so, and instead use only objective measures, that is, measures of directly observable events. One might measure, for instance, how many hours clients worked (as indicated by work records) and the number of rehospitalizations. Such measures render questions of reliability meaningless. Assuming the accuracy of records, these measures are 100 percent reliable. The measures serve as indicators of social functioning; those with good social functioning will tend to work and not require hospitalization.

Yet, there are important aspects of social functioning that can not be conveniently assessed by objective measures. These more subjective aspects—things such relationships with others, satisfaction with work, participation in social activities—were, in essence, "forgotten" in the interest of obtaining highly reliable, objective measures. When important human factors relevant to programmatic goals are not addressed in an evaluation, the relevance validity of measures is weak and conclusions will be subject to criticism by practitioners and clients alike.

Think for example of a child welfare agency which seeks to decrease the number of children placed in out-of-home settings. This number can be measured with 100 percent reliability. An equally important but not easy to measure issue concerns the impact of remaining in less than desirable homes on the children's well-being. This cannot be addressed by simply counting heads. A combination of measures often provides a balanced view of program outcome. For instance, the data on the numbers in out-of-home placement could be combined with attitudinal data assessing the social functioning of children and families.

Multiple Measures

Understanding of events is enriched through the use of multiple measures, each with its particular strengths and weaknesses. The *multiple measures* strategy is rooted in the logic of *triangulation:* "The goal of triangulating methods is to strengthen the validity of the overall findings through congruence and/or complementarity of the results from each method" (Greene and McClintock, 1985, p. 524). The reader will note that triangulation as just defined concerns the use of multiple research methods, i.e., integrating, for instance, survey, experimental, and field research methods into a single study. Yet, the same logic applies to the use of multiple measures. Some examples may demonstrate how a multiple measures approach enhances validity.

A multiple measures strategy was used to evaluate an intensive family treatment program designed to prevent out-of-home placement for children and adolescents (Rosenthal and Glass, 1990). The number of children requiring placement was reduced and cost savings accrued. The school attendance and grades of children receiving family services were modestly better than those of children in placement. Delinquency rates of family services and placement children were very nearly equivalent. Hence, by objective hard data criteria, the program was successful. Telephone follow-up interviewing, however, revealed that parents receiving family treatment services rated the services as somewhat less helpful than did parents of children who had been placed. Also, family services parents tended to report less change in problem areas. The telephone follow-up provided a broader view of the program's outcomes than would otherwise have been available.

In 1972, youth correctional services were rapidly deinstitutionalized in Massachusetts. Recidivism rates were compared for samples of children who received services prior to and following deinstitutionalization (Coates, Miller, and Ohlin, 1978). These rates were slightly higher for the deinstitutionalization group, suggesting that the new services may not have been more effective than those that they replaced. A survey was administered to deinstitutionalization youth who rated their living environments (cottages, group homes, etc.) on various characteristics. Environments which were rated high on client concern, honesty, and involvement in the local community discharged children who were less likely to recidivate. If only recidivism rates had been analyzed, the deinstitutionalization effort would have appeared unsuccessful. In contrast, the second measurement strategy, the survey, identified program characteristics which were associated with success.

Finally, the validity of self-reports in alcohol research has been seriously questioned. The emerging consensus is that multiple measures are needed: "serious analysts of this issue agree that several measures of drinking behavior must be utilized in alcoholism treatment studies to obtain a valid picture of treatment effectiveness" (Fuller, 1988, p. 186). New measures of drinking which are being considered include improved blood tests that could measure drinking over extended time periods and a patch applied to the skin that could collect sweat, which in turn could be analyzed for alcohol content.

As demonstrated in the above examples, the multiple measures/triangulation strategy often introduces complexity—perhaps at considerable financial cost. At a minimum, the use of multiple measures provides a balanced broad perspective regarding program outcome.

Sometimes triangulation clarifies matters. This occurs when diverse measurement strategies yield similar findings. Where two measures yield similar findings, the validity of each measure is cross-validated, and the evaluator gains confidence that findings do not reflect the biases or idiosyncrasies of a particular measure.

The possibilities for effective triangulation of measures are limited only by the creativity of the evaluator and the available resources. Examples of complimentary measures include:

1. Perceptions of client and of therapist
2. Self-reports (client) and reports of a *key informant* (a key informant is someone else with knowledge of the information queried for, perhaps with a less biased perspective than the client)
3. Perceptions of child and parent
4. Hard (objective) data and soft (subjective/attitudinal) data
5. Reactive and less reactive measures (subjective data is often reactive; hard data is often non-reactive)
6. Administrator, staff, client, and community perspectives (groups with different stakes in the evaluation, the stakeholders)
7. Measurements at different points in time, for instance, at program completion and at six months and one year post-completion
8. Knowledge-based and attitudinal measurements (e.g., measure both knowledge of biological facts and attitudes about sexual behavior following completion of a sexual education program)

Measurement Tools

Next we consider the tools of measurement, appropriate to differing types of data.

Hard data measurements Hard data is directly observable, contains no random measurement error, and is objective rather than subjective by nature. These measurements often involve the counting of entities, the specification of percentages, and the like. Some examples pertinent to program evaluation include: the attendance of students as measured by official records, the birth weights of babies of mothers who had participated in a nutritional program, the percentage of patients who are readmitted to a psychiatric program, and the percentage of couples who stay together for at least one year following marital counseling.

Hard data measurements are easy to implement. These data enhance the credibility of the evaluative effort and may be particularly important to selected audiences. For instance, most legislators would be more interested in finding out whether delinquent youth who have received a given service stay out of trouble as indicated by police records and less concerned with attitudinal measurements. Carter (1987) provides examples of hard data outcome measures utilized by the state of Texas in the evaluation of child protective services. These include:

> [the] percentage of abuse/neglect cases reinvestigated and reopened . . . [the] percentage of children whose permanency plan is achieved . . . [the] percentage of families who had all their children returned to the home following removal . . . [and the] . . . percentage of non-reunited families in which parental rights were terminated by the courts (p. 76).

Hard data can be effectively combined with a variety of soft measurement tools in a multiple measurement strategy.

Hard data measures can serve effectively as indicators of abstract concepts. For instance, indicators of school performance might include grades, attendance, suspensions, dropout, and the number of extra-curricular activities. The development of objective indicators of subjective phenomena is one of the fundamental aspect of social science measurement. Sometimes it is difficult to identify hard data measures that are central to the program's goals. For instance, an irrelevant hard data indicator might be the number of books read in the past six months as a measure of "general well-being."

Global assessments Global assessments are single questions that focus directly on key issues. For instance, one probe might be: "Think about the most important problem facing you when you began services. What progress, if any, has been made towards solving this problem?" The ability of global assessment to hone in on key issues from the client's perspective is a key advantage. This is counterbalanced by weak reliability, susceptibility to response sets (particularly social desirability), and high reactivity.

Social desirability can be countered by introducing a response choice that unequivocally conveys a positive attitude. For instance, a global assessment might request participants in a training workshop on, say, resolving conflicts among employees, to evaluate the workshop as excellent, good, fair, or poor. These response choices are fairly standard ones. The introduction of the additional response choice "outstanding, exceeded all expectations" would serve to identify participants for whom the workshop was an exceptional learning experience.

Standardized instruments Existing measures are available for a multitude of attitudinal and cognitive concepts. Many instruments are copyrighted and are available only through publishers specializing in standardized testing. Other tests are in the public domain and may be used without the author's permission. Measures that are standardized come with instructions and a technical manual, and have undergone testing for reliability and validity

(Henerson, Morris, and Fitz-Gibbon, 1987). Many standardized tests have norms that enable comparisons with national reference groups. Figure 9–2 presents a standardized instrument for measuring self-esteem.

The Mental Measurements Yearbooks (Mitchell, 1985; Mitchell, Conoley and Kramer, 1988), published periodically by the Buros Institute, review the reliability and validity of thousands of tests. This series of publications is perhaps regarded as the "Bible" of tests and measurements. The location of appropriate standardized instruments is often time-consuming. With improvements in computer technology, this task should become less difficult (Corcoran, 1988); for instance, computerized data bases of measures should become increasingly available.

While most instruments are designed for the client, others are intended for the caseworker, therapist, teacher, or observer. Instruments addressing the ecology of living institutions (see Moos, 1986), child behavior (see Miller, 1981; Achenbach and Edelbrock, 1983), child welfare needs (see Magura and Moses, 1986; Magura, Moses, and Jones, 1987), family functioning (see Moos, 1986; Moos and Moos, 1987; Olson, McCubbin, Barnes, Larsen, Muxen, and Wilson, 1985; Weiss and Jacobs, 1988) and client functioning (see Corcoran and Fisher, 1987), and social attitudes (see Miller, 1977; Robinson and Shaver, 1973) are available. *Measures for Clinical Practice: A Sourcebook* (Corcoran and Fisher, 1987) is an excellent guide for the practitioner. Corcoran (1988) lists selected books published since 1970 that pertain to measuring instruments as well as the major publishers of measuring instruments.

Many standardized tests were designed for making assessments at the level of the individual. As such they may be quite long. Put simply, some standardized tests possess more reliability than is needed in many evaluation efforts. As discussed earlier, long length may decrease response rates and introduce boredom, frustration, and response sets. The established reliability and validity of these measures is their major advantage.

Developing Questions and Measures

Many possess a seemingly innate impulse to locate a standardized test prior to thinking about what is being evaluated. This is, in part, because standardized tests add credibility and legitimacy to an evaluation. The average administrator perhaps reasons: "After all, since only statisticians and research professors understand the reliability/validity jargon, the standardized test is the safe choice."

The problem with instinctively reaching for a standardized instrument is that thinking is precluded. Rather than asking first: "What are the important evaluative issues?" and then choosing appropriate measures, such a response lets the available outcome measures define the evaluation's purpose. With careful work, good brief instruments can often be developed that

FIGURE 9–2 · *Index of Self-Esteem (ISE)*

NAME _____   Today's Date _____

This questionnaire is designed to measure how you see yourself. It is not a test, so there are not right or wrong answers. Please answer each item as carefully and accurately as you can by placing a number by each one as follows:

1. Rarely or none of the time
2. A little of the time
3. Some of the time
4. A good part of the time
5. Most or all of the time

Please begin.

1. I feel that people would not like me if they really knew me well. _____
2. I feel that others get along much better than I do. _____
3. I feel that I am a beautiful person. _____
4. When I am with other people I feel they are glad I am with them. _____
5. I feel that people really like to talk with me. _____
6. I feel that I am a very competent person. _____
7. I think I make a good impression on others. _____
8. I feel that I need more self-confidence. _____
9. When I am with strangers I am very nervous. _____
10. I think that I am a dull person. _____
11. I feel ugly. _____
12. I feel that others have more fun than I do. _____
13. I feel that I bore people. _____
14. I think my friends find me interesting. _____
15. I think I have a good sense of humor. _____
16. I feel very self-conscious when I am with strangers. _____
17. I feel that if I could be more like other people I would have it made. _____
18. I feel that people have a good time when they are with me. _____
19. I feel like a wallflower when I go out. _____
20. I feel I get pushed around more than others. _____
21. I think I am a likeable person. _____
22. I feel that people really like me very much. _____
23. I feel that I am a likeable person. _____
24. I am afraid I will appear foolish to others. _____
25. My friends think very highly of me. _____

Copyright The Dorsey Press, 1982 3, 4, 5, 6, 7, 14, 15, 18, 21, 22, 23, 25

Source: Hudson, W. W. (1982). *The clinical measurement package: A field manual.* Homewood IL: The Dorsey Press, p. 9. Used by permission.

meet evaluation needs more directly. The reliability and validity of the developed instrument can sometimes be established in data analysis.

Items should be clear, crisp, at low reading level, and short. Avoid negatives and double-negatives, as well as double-barreled questions (Was the program helpful and did you accomplish what you intended?). If possible, items should serve as indicators of the concept.

Figure 9–3 presents examples of different formats for structuring questions, including Likert scales, which measure the extent of agreement with an issue, and semantic differential items in which respondents choose between two extremes. Anchoring and specific behavioral description are useful with all of these formats.

Open-ended questions complement the traditional *closed-ended questions* that comprise most questionnaires. They provide an opportunity to express ideas and feelings and, as they may elicit unexpected findings, are particularly useful in new areas of inquiry. Open-ended questions can elicit rich vivid responses which increase understanding in ways that checks in boxes can not. In a study of special needs adoption, the first author asked: "Please COMMENT on anything you wish. What advice would you offer to persons

---

FIGURE 9–3 • *Examples of Different Scaling Formats*

A. Questions in Likert format

   1. This out-of home placement was helpful to my child.

strongly agree	agree	undecided	disagree	strongly disagree

   2. The counseling staff was courteous to me.

strongly agree	agree	undecided	disagree	strongly disagree

B. Assessments on a five-point scale

   Please rate the following . . .

	Low				High
1. The courtesy of staff	[1]	[2]	[3]	[4]	[5]
2. The progress on treatment goals	[1]	[2]	[3]	[4]	[5]
3. The overall helpfulness of service	[1]	[2]	[3]	[4]	[5]

C. Semantic differential format (evaluations of a workshop)

very poor	___ ___ ___ ___ ___ ___ ___	superior
boring	___ ___ ___ ___ ___ ___ ___	riveting
useless	___ ___ ___ ___ ___ ___ ___	essential

D. Semantic differential concept with increased description and anchoring

boring	interesting	very interesting	riveting
___	___ ___	___ ___	___

thinking about adopting older or special needs children?" A sample response provides insight into the dynamics of special needs adoption: "In spite of what idealistic social workers tell you, these children never catch up or overcome the years of neglect and abuse. Daniel to this day is terrified to stay alone . . . and his school work reflects the deprivation of those early years."

Responses to open-ended questions have a real-world ring. One may learn more from finding out that a given special needs adoptee "broke several windows, mauled the cat, and set small fires" than from learning a percentile rank on a behavior sub-scale.

Utilization-focused questions are an important tool in the evaluation of workshops and training sessions. Suppose one evaluates a workshop which provides training to child care workers in the handling of crisis situations. Six months after the workshop, a questionnaire could probe whether the skills/concepts taught have been used in day-to-day work. Where they have been used, the questionnaire should probe for specific examples.

Observational methods The advantage of direct observational methods is that data are taken directly from the real-world setting. Very detailed coding schemes may be worked out to record, for instance, interactions in a classroom or therapy setting. On the other hand, more flexible, less structured observational systems may also be used. These systems may be more likely to elucidate unexpected behaviors or issues. Less structured observation is particularly useful when observers are experts in the field of inquiry (Henerson, Morris, and Fitz-Gibbon, 1987). Observations may be for extended periods of time, for instance, a full day at a day treatment program, or quite brief, perhaps several randomly selected five-minute segments of a counseling session.

Goal Attainment Scaling Many evaluative methods are not sensitive to the treatment objectives of the individual client. Goal Attainment Scaling (GAS) provides a method for quantifying progress on individualized client treatment goals (Kiresuk and Sherman, 1968; Choate, Smith, Cardillo, and Thompson, 1981).

In GAS, client and counselor identify problem areas. The relative importance of each area is identified and numerical weightings of importance are assigned. In addition to the identification and weighting of problem areas, up to five levels of outcome, from most to least favorable, are established for each area. For each outcome level, a behavioral indicator is established. At the conclusion of treatment, or at strategic points in treatment, client progress is assessed. The higher the performance in a particular area, the higher the points earned. Points earned in each area are adjusted to reflect importance and added together to generate a total score. Figure 9–4 presents a modified goal attainment scale.

One disadvantage of GAS is that different counselors may tend to direct clients towards different kinds of goals, or may have different perceptions of

FIGURE 9–4 • *A Modified Goal Attainment Guide for a Hypothetical Client in Inpatient Mental Health Treatment*

Monthly Goals and Assigned Weights

Treatment outcome and value	Percentage of possible ward points earned (20)	Visits with family (15)	Score on Index of Self-esteem (15)	Group therapy sessions (10)
Most unfavorable thought likely (-2)	49 or below	none	60 or above	miss two or more
Less than expected (-1)	50 to 64	at hospital only	53 to 59	miss one
Expected level (0)	65 to 79	day visit	46 to 52	attend all
More than expected (+1)	80 to 94	one overnight	39 to 45	average one comment
Best anticipated (+2)	95 or above	two overnight	38 or below	average two comments

favorable versus unfavorable outcomes. As such, differences in outcome scores may reflect these differences, rather than actual differences in progress. To mitigate this problem, Goal Attainment Scales could be developed before clients are assigned to different counselors or programs. Differences in outcomes then would be less likely to reflect idiosyncratic aspects of the goal formulation process.

While good reliability has been demonstrated for GAS, correlations of GAS scores with other measures of client change tended to be low. Hence, validity is questionable (Calsyn and Davidson, 1978). The major advantage of GAS, the specification of goals sensitive to individual client needs, can be a disadvantage in program evaluation. An evaluator might, for instance, compare mean pre- and post-treatment scores for agency clients. A higher mean on the post-test would demonstrate good progress on goals. Yet, because goals are individualized, the evaluator may not know the general kinds of problems on which this progress was made. The utilization of GAS in conjunction with other measurement tools, for instance, standardized tests, would mitigate this problem and is an attractive evaluation strategy (Calsyn and Davidson, 1978).

Client satisfaction measures Measures of client satisfaction with services can be an important asset in evaluation. Client satisfaction is often viewed as a multi-dimensional construct (Poertner and Wintersteen, 1988). Among the different aspects of satisfaction tapped by existing measures are "satisfaction with the agency and its services . . . staff helpfulness and understanding . . . goal attainment . . . staff-client cooperation . . . [and] agency or administrative amenities" (Poertner and Wintersteen, 1988, p. 7). The full-scale reliabilities of six client satisfaction scales reviewed by Poertner and Wintersteen were 0.83 or higher, excellent for attitudinal scales.

Client satisfaction is positively correlated with mental health treatment outcome (Attkisson and Zwick, 1983), but at least somewhat distinct from problem severity (Damkot, Pandiani, and Gordon, 1983) and goal attainment (Fiester, 1979). The assessment of client satisfaction can provide needed impetus towards shaping services to more effectively serve client needs. Most of the developed client satisfaction measures attempt to provide a general perspective on satisfaction, an overview. Yet, the enterprising evaluator or administrator could easily develop questions focusing on different aspects of agency services. One might probe satisfaction with, for instance, parking facilities, the waiting area, the comfort of the counseling rooms, the courtesy of staff, the times available for appointments, and so on.

Existing records Existing records are a rich and often neglected data source. Evaluations based on existing records might include content analyses of case records or in-depth analyses of data available from a large computerized data base. Existing records are non-reactive, a distinct advantage. On the negative side, existing records often do not address key issues and may be incomplete or inaccurate. Changes in record keeping procedures can be mistaken for program effects; for instance, a change in district attorney policies affected juvenile records and introduced bias in a recent delinquency study (Rosenthal and Glass, 1984). Finally, records may be corrupted by program demands: "[Boy] Scout leaders . . . inflate their membership lists to satisfy the expectations of their national headquarters" (Cochran, 1978).

Conclusion

Data gathered in diverse ways enrich the evaluative effort. The recommendation to use multiple measures is entirely in accord with the maxim, "Don't put all your eggs in one basket."

The prospective evaluator should use, rather than be used by, social science measurement tools. Some standardized measurement tools may evidence excellent properties of reliability and validity as described in testing manuals, but not be effective in a specific evaluative context. On the other hand, brief scales developed "in-house" may elucidate critical information. The evaluator should strive for specificity and clear description to enhance the validity of measurements. This is particularly the case when subjective phenomena are measured.

The counsel has been for appropriate confidentiality and a neutral "scientific" climate. For instance, we cautioned that filling out an instrument in the presence of a therapist could bias responses. Some drawbacks may result from an overly strict attention to such "scientific" concerns. In particular, the opportunity is lost to integrate evaluation and practice. Increasingly scholars and practitioners are advocating for this integration (Ho, 1976; Hudson, 1982; Barlow, Hayes and Nelson, 1984; Bloom and Fisher, 1982). Concerns for objectivity and detachment then should be balanced against the sometimes more compelling argument that evaluation and practice should go together.

In summary, the use of multiple measures, an orientation towards detail and specificity, careful attention to issues of validity, and a willingness to ask important questions are at the root of effective measurement.

References

Achenbach, T. M., & Edelbrock, C. (1983). *Manual for the child behavior checklist and revised child behavior profile*. Burlington, VT: University of Vermont, Department of Psychiatry.

Attkisson, C. C., & Zwick, R. (1983). The client satisfaction questionnaire: Psychometric properties and correlations with service utilization and psychotherapy outcome. *Evaluation and Program Planning, 5*, 233–237.

Barlow, D. H., Hayes, S. C., & Nelson, R. O. (1984). *The scientist practitioner: Research and accountability in clinical and educational settings*. New York: Pergamon Press.

Bloom, M., & Fischer, J. (1982). *Evaluating practice: Guidelines for the accountable professional*. Englewood Cliffs, NJ: Prentice-Hall.

Bostwick, G. J., Jr., & Kyte, N. S. (1988). In R. M. Grinnell, Jr. (Ed.), *Social work research and evaluation* (3rd ed.). Itasca, IL: F. E. Peacock.

Calsyn, R. J., & Davidson, W. S. (1978) Do we really want a program evaluation strategy based solely on individualized goals: A critique of goal attainment scaling. In *Evaluation Studies Review Annual*, 701–713.

Carter, R. K. (1987). Measuring client outcomes: The experience of the states. *Administration in Social Work, 11*(3/4), 73–88.

Choate, R., Smith, A., Cardillo, J. E., & Thompson, L. (1981). Training in the use of goal attainment scaling. *Community Mental Health Journal, 17*(2), 171–184.

Coates, R. B., Miller, A. D., & Ohlin, L. E. (1978). *Diversity in a youth correctional system: Handling delinquents in Massachusetts*. Cambridge, MA: Ballinger.

Cochran, N. (1978). Grandma Moses and the 'corruption' of data. *Evaluation Quarterly, 2*(3), 363–373.

Corcoran, K. J. (1988). Selecting a measuring instrument. In R. M. Grinnell, Jr. (Ed.), *Social work research and evaluation* (3rd ed.). Itasca, IL: F. E. Peacock, pages 137–155.

Corcoran, K., & Fischer, J. (1987). *Measures for clinical practice: A sourcebook*. New York: The Free Press.

Damkot, D. K., Pandiani, J. A., & Gordon, L. R. (1983). Development, implementation, and findings of a continuing client satisfaction survey. *Community Mental Health Journal*, 265–278.

Fiester, A. R. (1979). Goal attainment and satisfaction scores for CMHC clients. *American Journal of Community Psychology*, 7(2), 181–188.

Fuller, R. K. (1988). Can treatment outcome research rely on alcoholics' self-reports? *Alcohol Health & Research World*, 12(3), 180–186.

Greene, J., & McClintock, C. (1985). Triangulation in evaluation: Design and analysis issues. *Evaluation Review*, 9(5), 523–545.

Henerson, M. E., Morris, L. L., & Fitz-Gibbon, C. T. (1987). *How to measure attitudes*. Newbury Park, CA: Sage.

Ho, M. K. (1976). Evaluation: A means of treatment. *Social Work*, 21(1), 24–27.

Hudson, W. W. (1982). *The clinical measurement package: A field manual*. Homewood, IL: The Dorsey Press.

Kiresuk, T. J., & Sherman, R. E. (1968). Goal attainment scaling: A general method for evaluating comprehensive community mental health programs. *Community Mental Health Journal*, 4(6), 443–453.

Magura, S., Moses, B. S., & Jones, M. A. (1987). *Assessing risk and measuring change in families: The family risk scales*. Washington, D.C.: Child Welfare League of America.

Magura, S., & Moses, B. S. (1986). *Outcome measures for child welfare services: Theory and applications*. Washington, D.C.: Child Welfare League of America.

Mitchell, J. V., (Ed.) (1985). *The ninth mental measurements yearbook*. Lincoln, NE: The University of Nebraska.

Mitchell, J. V., Conoley, J. C. & Kramer, J. J. (1988) *The supplement to the ninth mental measurements yearbook*. Lincoln, NE: The University of Nebraska.

Miller, D. C. (1977). *Handbook of research design and social measurement* (3rd ed.). New York: David McKay.

Miller, L. C. (1981). *Louisville behavior checklist manual*. Los Angeles, CA: Western Psychological Services.

Monette, D. R., Sullivan, T., & DeJong, C. R. (1986). *Applied social research*. New York: Holt, Rinehart and Winston.

Moos, R. H. (1986). *The social climate scales: A user's guide*. Palo Alto, CA: Consulting Psychologists Press.

Moos, R. H., & Moos, B. S. (1987). *Family environment scale manual* (2nd ed.). Palo Alto, CA: Consulting Psychologists Press.

Nunnally, J. C. (1978). *Psychometric theory* (2nd ed.). New York: McGraw-Hill.

Olson, D. H., McCubbin, H. I., Barnes, H., Larsen, A., Muxen, M., & Wilson, M. (1985). *Family inventories: Inventories used in a national survey of families*.

Poertner, J., & Wintersteen, R. (1988). Measurement of client satisfaction with social work services. Unpublished paper, School of Social Welfare, University of Kansas.

Polster, R. A., & Collins, D. (1988). Measuring variables by direct observations. In R. M. Grinnel, Jr. (Ed.), *Social work research and evaluation* (3rd ed.). Itasca, IL: F. E. Peacock.

Robinson, J. P., & Shaver, P. R. (1973). *Measures of social psychological attitudes* (revised ed.). Survey Research Center, Institute for Social Research.

Rosenthal, J. A., & Glass, G. V. (1984). Comparative impacts of alternatives to adolescent placement. *Journal of Social Service Research*. 13, 19–38.

Siegel, S., & Castellan, R. J. Jr. (1988). *Nonparametric statistics for the behavioral sciences.* New York: McGraw-Hill.

Webb, E. J., Campbell, D. T., Schwartz, R. D., Sechrest, L., & Grove, J. B. (1981). *Nonreactive measures in the social sciences.* (2nd ed.). Boston: Houghton Mifflin.

Weiss, H. B., & Jacobs, F. H. (Eds.). (1988). *Evaluating family programs.* New York: Aldine de Gruyter.

CHAPTER TEN

Designing Research for Evaluating Outcomes

Introduction

Necessary Preliminaries to the Design of Research Evaluating of Program Outcomes

The reader should recall an argument from the initial chapter of this book: There is a logical order in which an evaluation should proceed. In fact, the order in which this book is organized reflects that idea: Studies of client need come first, followed by clarification of goals and objectives, implementation monitoring of program designs, etc. The ordering is because all these are necessary to interpret outcome data about the relationship between program interventions and how things turned out for clients, consumers, or service delivery organizations. Later readers will see how complicated and expensive are outcome evaluations. No one would wish to waste the time and expense of such an effort before establishing the preconditions for its success. Our point is not more than what common sense would indicate: it is folly to try to evaluate outcomes of a program that no beneficiary needs, for which it is impossible to develop measurements, because no one knows what the program goals and objectives are, or when no one can be sure the program activities ever occurred, were inconsistently applied, or were mysterious. No outcome evaluation effort should proceed, nor can it possibly succeed or even justify itself, without these prior tasks completed.

Finally, we want to make a special note that even though we are asking readers to take great care with outcome studies, we do not mean to over-emphasize their importance. While outcome studies are worthwhile, they are not necessarily the most worthwhile. Need studies, implementation studies, and studies of consumer response are not merely instrumental to outcome studies, they generate important insights and have purposes all their own.

Establishing the empirical questions for study and exactly what kind of data will be useful First, it is crucial that there be clarity on which specific questions the evaluation should attempt to answer. Consider that social programs usually have multiple objectives and that reasonable people can almost always disagree on which are primary or should be attended to first.

Notice here our implication that specific evaluation questions are intimately related to program objectives, not goals. Program goals are almost never the subject of a program evaluation precisely because it is in their nature to be quite abstract. Program objectives are only one concrete rendering of the program goals (Chambers, 1986). Like any abstraction, they are only one of the many possible ways in which they could be operationalized. Think for a moment of the abstract concept *music* and then of the innumerable ways in which it can be concretized: jazz, classical, rock, punk, folk, etc. Thus, it would not do to concentrate an evaluation on program goals since that could set the enterprise way off the mark—the program needs to be evaluated against the specific objectives into which form it has chosen to render its goals.

Second, even though they are more concrete than goals, program objectives still do not always translate directly into evaluation questions—that is, into the direct hypothetical statements that are necessary in order to bring actual data to bear on the issue. Like goals, even the most concrete objectives still admit of alternative data points by which they could be measured or observed. Taking only an obvious example, consider a program for the homeless, one with a straightforward objective such as "providing shelter to persons who lack it." Now, just for the moment, let us suppose that there is substantive agreement on what constitutes shelter and on how to identify those who lack it. Here is a list illustrating the abundance of data points which might be used to evaluate what this program did in relation to what it set out to do:

1. The number of different people who received shelter care
2. The length of time people in need received shelter
3. The number of people who received shelter during periods when the night temperature was below freezing
4. The proportion of people in the community in need of shelter who received it from the program
5. The reduction of admissions to hospital emergency rooms for exposure or frost bite
6. Reduction in the number of people in a given area of the city who can be observed sleeping "in the rough" (i.e., not inside a building)

Some might say that these are all measurement issues. Indeed there are measurement problems to contend with, but to leave it at that obscures important issues, issues that are not so much technical as conceptual. We advise restricting the term *measurement issues* to those which can be resolved on technical grounds (i.e., reliability of measurement, scaling, instrumentation, choice of observational strategy, etc.). At bottom, choice between the alternatives suggested above cannot be made on technical grounds alone, but instead on the fit between the terms in which social program objectives are expressed and the terms of the above evaluation questions. We believe that the fit can be judged only by those with personal and professional interests in the program. And the evaluator must seek clarity from the major stakeholders in the program: those who control the program or are subject to its effects (i.e., those who control its funding, administration, implementation, and consumers or beneficiaries; of course, the evaluator herself is clearly a stakeholder, but not commonly the important actor). The point here is that there is an important difference between these interests and their hopes for what the program will produce. It is our view that the evaluator must search out those stakeholders and work to achieve a clarity (if not a consensus) on what kind of data will be meaningful. It is not always easy to obtain those agreements, so the task may take organizational and group process skill of the first order.

Establishing budget constraints Another preliminary to an outcome evaluation is obtaining a firm idea of the budget constraints that will apply to the evaluation effort. Our experience suggests that any discussion of alternative ways to design evaluation research must be framed by budget constraints. There is great variability in the ways in which evaluation research can be designed; hence there is great variability in the costs of such an effort. No organization has an unlimited budget for evaluation and there is little point in long discussions of alternative types of outcome data or complex comparison groups when some types will always exceed budget constraints.

Establishing decision points—how much outcome is significant, how much difference is a difference that makes a difference Finally, and perhaps most important, our experience leads us to believe that prior to the evaluation effort, a consensus must be established within the stakeholding groups on not only what types of outcomes count as important, but how much outcome is significant, useful, and/or justifiable in order to judge the program to be a success. Why is this issue so important? Shouldn't evaluations simply be looking to see whether, in aggregate, the program made some difference? And, for that matter, why isn't the traditional concept of statistical significance ("the 5 percent level of confidence" criterion, for example) a good standard here? The simple answer is that, for most social programs, such standards are not useful. Simple statistical significance is, nothing more than a measure of the probability that findings are due to chance, and the plain fact is that non-chance findings are not necessarily important (Schneider and Darcy, 1984). Think, for example, of the fact that a laboratory test will almost always show some intestinal bacteria (coliform, for example) to be present in even the best run, modern, good quality municipal water system. The point is that even though the presence of these malicious, distressful bacteria is not a chance event at all but clearly indicates some source of contamination, it is only when their quantity reaches a certain level that it is of any practical importance. The statistically significant presence of bacteria here is ordinarily trivial since the bacteriological fact is that they are present (in a non-chance way) almost always and everywhere. In summary, all that statistical significance (at traditional levels) will tell us is that we can rule out chance as an explanation for a finding. Statistical significance doesn't automatically tell us the importance or the magnitude of the effect. And, it is the magnitude of effect attributable to the influence of a social program that consumers of program evaluation findings are ordinarily interested in—how many fewer abused children are now seen in hospital emergency rooms, how many fewer foster home placements were made, how much more earnings did adolescent single parent mothers make? Further, statistical significance is poor as a single criterion because it is a function of many factors other than actual strength of impact. A finding of statistical significance can be altered, sometimes rather arbitrarily, simply by number of cases used in the analysis, their variability, and the complexity of the analysis (the number of variables and subvariables). Finally, Schneider and Darcy (1984) make the point that if evaluators recommend using traditional statistical significance levels as decision points, they effectively rule out the important normative philosophical and political judgments that (we believe) should control decisions about the amount of impact a policy or program should have in order to be supported further by public monies.

There are those who advocate that if significance levels are used at all, they should be set with a view toward the consequences of making a mistake— where lives and livelihoods are at stake as a result of the findings, significance levels for ruling out chance findings should be set quite stringently, say at the .001 level or higher (Rudner, 1966). Where no serious negative consequences are at stake and the greatest error is to overlook a positive finding, the significance level should be set so that there is little likelihood of doing that, say at the .10 or .20 level. We believe that that is very often the case for social programs and personal social services, thought not always, of course. In actual experience, in neither case does the more or less traditional .05 level seem to offer any advantage.

But, even with that caveat, this discussion of the inadequacy of using standard statistical confidence levels still doesn't yield the full answer to the question about what criteria should be used in evaluation research. Granted that we should deal in magnitudes, we are still left with the issue of how much is enough—and a knotty issue it surely is. One approach is to think carefully about the users, the consumers of the evaluation product and what use they will make of the findings. There are, of course, purely personal commitments to a program effort, but aside from that, every stakeholder has a somewhat different audience to whom they are accountable in some way. Think of these audiences as representing certain pressures to which various stakeholders are subject. For example, administrators will commonly be accountable to funders (legislators, boards of directors, etc.), and their vital question may well be how much outcome will they need to justify to them the expenditure of the time and resources of their organization on this program. It is also the nature of those who hold administrative positions to be commonly concerned for efficiency of operations—how much does it cost in personnel and facilities to produce this much outcome? One of the decisions administrators have to make concerns whether this outcome is worth the scarce personnel, facilities, or time they must allocate to it, relative to the other choices open to them. Then note that legislators can usually be depended upon to be concerned about accountability to their own political constituency: how much difference will it take to deal comfortably with the questions voters raise about their support of this program effort? Finally, professionally credentialed practitioner-staff members will have their own versions of what counts as outcome and how much is important. It is their calling to be more worried than other stakeholders about how much side effect is produced by the program intervention, since they will generally have a greater knowledge and consciousness of that issue. We believe that professionals working in social programs have an ethical obligation to positive outcomes for clients, over and above such issues as political constraints, of program supporters' personal agendas, or or even for the survival of the organization. (This argument is discussed in some detail in Chapter Two.) The important amount of outcome to any of these stakeholders is not just a significant difference or just any amount of difference, but an amount that will be important (and quite particular) to the time and space of their own local social, political, professional, or organizational situation.

The reader should take special note that for stakeholders themselves, this question is neither easy nor always straightforward to answer. They will have to think carefully and will often resort to the educated guess on the matter. It is in the nature of this issue that it be resolved by calculating subjective probabilities with all their contingencies and uncertainties. Still, these hazards are no reason to decrease the importance of obtaining these kinds of judgments. Without them even the most elegant measurements and research designs will simply not be interpretable: without them no one can say whether an increase of 10 or a decrease of 5 points on some scale measuring self concept or the incidence of child abuse or teenage pregnancy is or is not important.

The reader should be alert to how important it is to establish these kinds of interpretive standards *before* the data comes in. Theoretically, it should not matter whether a standard was constructed before or after the data is collected, but the great temptation, when one already knows the results, is to construct a standard that is shaded toward validating cherished preconceptions or self-interest. It is so rewarding to validate preconceptions, and it is so clear that *invalidating* them requires great moral courage. If a person is favorably disposed toward a program idea (or those who run the program) and already knows that the evaluation data has shown that it has achieved a 20 percent improvement over a no-treatment group, isn't it extraordinarily easy to set a standard that will confirm what one already thought, i.e., to set it at less than 20 percent? Why not 25 percent? Few people will set a performance standard that puts them in the wrong. A serious evaluation will insist on setting standards for interpreting outcome data in advance, very early in the evaluation process, certainly before outcome data is in hand.

Drawing Conclusions About "Causal Relationships" in Evaluating Program Outcomes

Designing research is the focus of this chapter, and its basic concern is how to construct comparisons in order to draw conclusions about outcomes. Without doubt, drawing conclusions about program outcomes always involves, at some level, attributing causality to program efforts. However, we will avoid the use of the term *cause* because there is a great and unresolved contention about whether it is even possible to make such statements validly. Thus, we will speak only of the association of outcomes with program efforts and never of program efforts as directly causing outcomes, although we will assume that such associations are the signature of some underlying causal relationship. Surely, it is a crude way of thinking, because we know (just as every undergraduate social science student knows—or should know) that this viewpoint flies directly in the face of the doctrine that "correlation is not causation." The rationale for this doctrine is simple enough: to notice that two things seem to regularly occur together (and/or one after the other) does not necessarily allow a person to say that one causes the other. If a famous basketball coach rants and raves at players and referees, and even if after those behaviors occur, the team totally dominates their opponents, is it a sufficient reason to think that the one caused the other? Surely not. Think about how hard it is to connect those rantings and ravings with the improved performance of the team: teams with ranting/raving coaches lose games, coaches who rant and rave don't always win games. And, for all we know, might not the team do even better without all the ranting and raving? Most athletes would tell you that things like athlete conditioning, player skill and will, team cohesiveness, and the like are what makes the difference. The way we propose to think about the relationship between program outcomes and program efforts or interventions—taking associations for indicators of causal factors—is crude because it can lead to embarrassing errors. For example, if you didn't understand that an automobile ran on gasoline, you wouldn't know that the gas gauge on a car was connected to the gas tank. Thus, when the car stopped running every time the gas gauge showed empty, you might actually try to find some way to fix the gas gauge itself—perhaps you might even do something silly like take the gauge apart and manually raise the needle to the full mark. Of course it seems silly to those who know, but it might not seem silly to someone ignorant of the workings of an automobile engine.

We are embarrassed to report that for many areas in the study of social program and policy efforts, this might be a good analogy to our present level of skill and understanding about the human condition. However, if we wish to affect human affairs at all (and that is the ultimate justification for evaluation research), we have no choice other than to regard persistent associations between antecedents and consequences as the tracks left by some kind of causal relationship. On that account we will be totally unembarrassed in recommending this view to our readers. We will advise them to use those tracks as a basis for intervention in human affairs, even though we are clear about the problems involved. How marvelous it would be to have an alternative approach to causality, and we applaud the efforts of those who are attempting to work that out. However, the rather simple fact is that, in the meantime, we must get on with practical affairs, and, in our opinion, the only basis on which the empirical evaluation of social programs and policies can be approached is to adopt the viewpoint we are advocating.[1] Thus, we will ignore the whole complicated debate about the hazards of attributing causality, pending auspicious future developments. Of course, we are not alone in taking this position, for it is a common assumption of any empirical science that "the past can be expected to repeat itself in the future." Mark (1986) calls it the "similarity principle" (p. 12). Donald Campbell (1986) says "all treatments . . . are [to be] regarded as imperfect proxy variables for latent causes and effects." (p. 73). Finally, it should be observed that the way we propose to view causality is the way most ordinary people look at it when they conduct their everyday affairs. That is not an argument for its inherent validity, but one that suggests its utility in presenting evaluation findings to people in power over funding and the initiation of social programs. We believe that, indeed, such folks most often use ordinary approaches to thinking about causal relations (and, of course, are commonly puzzled by all its pitfalls) (Cordray, 1986).

So, let us take Donald Campbell's advice seriously and regard program efforts and data on program outcomes as "imperfect proxy variables for causes and effects," and on those wheels move toward specific issues in drawing valid conclusions about how a social program performs. Interpreting outcome data in terms of whether it made a difference to those who were exposed to its influence seems like such a simple idea, and, at one level, it is. However, when thought about for very long or at any depth, it turns out to be more than a little complicated, often by things a person doesn't think of in the course of everyday life. But before we tackle those problems, let us first clarify several points that can be confusing if we don't get them straight at the outset.

Types of Validity

Readers should be clear by now that there are a number of different types of validity. In this chapter we are concerned only with the validity of findings, that is, with making correct statements about program outcomes. It is the task of program evaluation to be able to say with confidence that associated with program x is (or is not) positive outcome y; for example, to say, "associated with attending parenting program x is (or is not) an increase in score on test y of good parenting." Assuming that there is something real about the concept *good parenting*, and assuming that the good parenting test validly measures it, then we would like to be able to say that attending parenting program x will (or will not) predictably increase scores on measures of good parenting. The validity with which we are concerned here is the validity of that statement. We will not be concerned with the validity of the measure good parenting (or its reliability either) or of the concept *good parenting* itself, though we certainly should have been concerned about both of them earlier. Traditionally this kind of validity is called *internal validity* (by Stanley and Campbell and others before them), where the contrast was to another term —*external validity* (Campbell and Stanley, 1966, p. 12). Internal validity was intended to refer to the validity of findings with respect to the numerous factors that could contaminate clean findings within (i.e., internal to or "inside") the original research environment. External validity, on the other hand, was intended to refer to the ability to validly generalize findings "outside" (in the sense of "beyond") the original research context. We prefer the term *validity of findings* because the internal/external validity contrast has come upon hard times lately. On the one hand it has become clear that external validity is of considerably less relevance to social program evaluation than we thought at one time, and, on the other hand, it has become increasingly difficult to draw the distinction between external and internal validity cleanly. Later we will speak in some detail about these difficulties.[2]

The type of validity discussed above is different from our earlier concerns with other types of validity—for example, the validity of measures, as in content validity. There the concern was for the validity of, say, question-items about self concept, observations of the aggressive behavior of a sixth-grader, or ten units on a scale of good parenting performance, etc.)—and whether those ways of measuring the concepts were actually related to the terms in which the concept was defined. The validity of findings that is of concern here is also different from our earlier concern for the validity of constructs, where the issue was whether an abstraction (a construct) should be considered a figment in the mind of the theorist or researcher, rather than as something which actually exists in the real world—for example, whether the whole idea of emotional abuse or, say, stress is real in some way.

Well, the reader might ask, why should there be a big problem about making statements about the validity of findings; in fact, aren't people heard to make those kinds of statements every day? The big problem is this: in order to make the statement in a valid way, we must show that there is not a single other factor except the program (or intervention or treatment) which could plausibly account for the change in the outcome measure. That is, indeed, a tall order because there are so many other factors that could have caused the change, and it becomes very difficult to rule them out. Basically, that is what the validity of findings comes down to: to what extent have other factors been ruled out as plausible explanations for a research finding. What we will now wish to turn to are the various issues in, and methods of, ruling out factors as rival explanations for, or contaminants of, research findings.

Methods and Issues in Protecting the Validity of Findings

Introduction

Let us begin with an example: say, a small group of practitioners implementing a small local program. The objective of this program is to help the frail elderly over 75 remain in their own homes and out of nursing homes by improving their physical well-being and social interaction.[3] These practitioners wish to discover in a way more systematic than their own casual, on-the-scene personal judgment, whether they were having the desired effect. In their first attempt to estimate the effect they were having, they did what most people might do—simply measured the number of frail elderly who had been exposed to their program for a period of time, and then three months later observed how many were still in their own homes and not in nursing homes. They then translated this into a proportion and concluded that "60 percent of the frail elderly we have worked with have remained in their own homes." The statement is not incorrect, factually it is quite true. However, it could be taken to mean that the fact is attributable to the effort of the program, although the statement doesn't literally say so. Nor is there much doubt that that is actually what the program staff wanted to say: "Due to the effects of our program, 60 percent of the people we work with remain out of nursing homes." That is the issue which concerns our task here: is it valid to say that this outcome is due to the program effort? Let us picture the scenario in the following way, using the capital letter O for the observation we have made of the effect and the letter X for the program activities. Let us attach a subscript p to the X to stand for the program of our exemplary practitioners. And, we'll put the symbol Xp in front of the O to signify that it came first in time. We can now diagram the situation in the standard way:

$X_p O$

Once diagrammed and conceived of in this formal way, we can call this a diagram of a research design. Now in order to examine the validity of a finding taken from a research design like this one, our task is to answer the following question: What are all the other factors other than the effect of the program that might explain the observed outcome ("rival conjectures," or "contaminating variables," as some have called them)?

Actually this program staff got some (uninvited) help with that task. When they made this claim public, they found themselves in the letters-to-the-editor column, where the children of these frail elderly went to some length to point out (indignantly) that actually they would have placed their aged aunt (mother, cousin, etc.) in a nursing home, but the fact was that there were no nursing home beds available in their community! We will call that *the history effect*. Also, the publicity around this claim brought further calls disputing it—for example, the one from the local visiting nurse program whose staff is involved with a large proportion of these frail elderly and who always thought their program effort legitimately accounted for 60 percent of the frail elderly remaining out of nursing homes. We will also call that an effect of history. Our group of practitioners were further demoralized when an antiquarian statistician reminded them that forty years ago, before there were any such social programs, she was chairperson of the visitation-of-the-sick committee in her church and happened to keep track of the proportion of her church congregation who went into nursing homes at various ages. She is interested in this issue because, as chance would have it, most of the participants in this program group were recruited out of her particular congregation! It turns out, she says, that after people in that generation in her congregation pass age 75, about 60 percent do not enter nursing homes. So, is it possible, asks this not-very-frail-minded curmudgeon, that the same effect might have occurred whether or not your program was functioning?

And, all those uninvited critiques were basically good questions! In sum, the reader should conclude that this particular design is quite weak. One reason is because it must attribute all that is observed to the program. Unfortunately, program participants are also exposed to all the forces of contemporary and passing history, in addition to the program effort, and so it becomes difficult, usually impossible, when using this particular design, to disentangle the effects of current history from the intended effects of the program. That is why this "contaminating factor" is called *the effect of history:* i.e., the possibility that outcome findings might be plausibly explained by a factor (or event) which occurred alongside the program effort and to which the program participants are exposed. Notice that it is only in some "total institutions" that history as a contaminant to social program evaluation research might be thought of as unimportant—prisons, some institutions for the severely mentally ill, or the developmentally disabled, some military establishments, or boarding schools for children. Thus, unless program participants are caged in a closed, hermetically sealed environment, it is nearly impossible to prevent that kind of factor from being an influence and entangling ("contaminating") the influence of the program with the influence of the historical effect, i.e., the effect of not having nursing home beds available, or the presence of a visiting nurse program supporting the frail elderly in remaining in their own homes. So, there is little in this design that either persuades or obliges us to believe that the program effort (the "intervention," the "treatment") was necessarily responsible for the outcome observed. Note, however, that none of these arguments have actually refuted the statement about findings— they have only rendered it less plausible because they have cited "rival explanations."

So the next question to be faced by our practitioner group is how they can design an evaluation which will avoid the embarrassing questions raised by folks like their visiting nurse colleagues and the curmudgeon statistician. Here is a partial solution: Locate another group of the frail elderly who are similar to the program participants, and were exposed to the visiting nurses program but not exposed to our practitioners' program. The idea is to compare the difference between groups with regard to the rates of remaining out of nursing homes (and at home). Whatever differences arise between the groups will be attributed to the effect of the program. Even though there are some problems with this comparison, it is clearly an improvement over the first design. Let us symbolize the visiting nurse program by X_{vn}. Here is its diagram:

(Visiting nurse program + practitioners' program) $X_{vn}\ X_p\ O$
(Visiting nurse program only) $X_{vn}\ \ \ \ O$

Since the first group is the one exposed to the practitioners' program, an X_p symbol appears on their line, and since they are also exposed to the visiting nurse program an X_{vn} symbol is used. The O following it (on the same line) stands for observation of whether their client group stayed in their own home or entered nursing homes. The comparison group has an X_{vn} on their line (but not an X_p), because they were exposed only to the visiting nurse program. This is an improvement over the first design because it rules out (in a manner of speaking) important pieces of the effect of history. Furthermore, it does it in a way that neither violates the humanity of the clients nor places the whole evaluation research effort in an entirely artificial laboratory context. The design achieves the ability to rule out many history effects by *exposing both groups* to whatever history is occurring. Thus, to the extent that groups were relatively similar, we can presume that both groups will equally absorb and/or be equally affected by exposure to the visiting nurse program (the history factor); thus any differences in the number who entered nursing homes cannot be due to that history factor. The history effect cancels itself out if it occurs in both groups—just as x's cancel each other out if they appear on both sides of the equations you recall from elementary algebra.[4]

In part, the objection of the curmudgeon statistician is also dealt with, because, if there is a difference between the groups on the rate of nursing home placement and it favors the program group, it doesn't really matter what the rate of nursing home placement was forty years ago—by having two program groups we have a relevant (and contemporary) comparison to substitute for the one the statistician proposed. No doubt there will be some elderly, perhaps many, in the comparison group who will remain in their own homes too, but the relevant piece of data is the *difference* between the proportions in the two groups. But wait just a moment, says the curmudgeon statistician over the phone speaking to one of the practitioners who was explaining this newfound elegance, that still isn't sufficient to answer my question about the validity of your findings: how can you be sure that *either* program did better than forty years ago? And, indeed, she has a point: perhaps neither program is really contributing anything by their presence (although the issue may only be of historical interest).

In order to deal with that we will need to add yet another group—this time one that isn't exposed to either program, a no-program group. That way we will have a (more or less) unbiased baseline, an estimate of how things might be if there weren't any program at all. So, with these three groups, we can observe how many frail elderly enter nursing homes from a no-program group, how many enter from the visiting nurses program only, and how many enter from the group that experienced both programs. In that way we can see how much effect each program has uniquely (and rule out the effects of history on both as well). As before, we will distinguish the two programs by subscripts, the practitioners' program group by X_p and the visiting nurses program group by X_{vn}. The new design diagram would look like this:

Practitioners' program group	X_{vn}	X_p	O
Visiting nurse program group	X_{vn}		O
No-program group			O

When presented with this design, the practitioner program staff became incensed. If the visiting nurse program was going to have to risk an evaluation that could show that they weren't effective, the least that could be done is that the practitioner program might have to endure the same risk! Therefore, they wanted a group who was exposed only to their program *without also* being exposed to the practitioner program. That way, the independent contribution of the visiting nurse program could show up. "Fair is fair," they said. And so it was done, and here is what that design looked like:

Practitioners' program group	X_{vn}	X_p	O
Practitioners' program only group		X_p	O
Visiting nurse program group		X_{vn}	O
No-program group			O

Notice that in the discussion above, we have not emphasized designs that are standard or exemplary, like the basic controlled experiment, the case-study, or the "Solomon four-group design" (Cook and Campbell, 1976). Rather, we have tried to illustrate how a research design develops out of arguments about the validity of findings, out of a concern for creating unambiguous findings. It is always the validity of findings that research design is striving for. Our literary device used to present this principle—an argument between service providers—is only that and nothing more, but, by its use, we want to urge readers that they need to closely examine each proposed research design for evaluating a social program through exactly this kind of argument. It is this kind of argument that program evaluators should have among themselves, even with themselves. We will avoid presenting a standard typology of research designs for program evaluations because it is our experience that those standard types are infrequently used—they are almost inevitably modified by local conditions or concerns. Even more important, we must avoid giving readers the impression that evaluation designs should be forced into one or the other of those illustrative types. The principle here is the following:

Choices in regard to how research designs are constructed (i.e., the number of control or contrast groups, whether pretest, post test, or both kinds of measures are used) should not be based on their conformity to abstract types of designs but on the particularities of the individual evaluation context.

We will call it the *Particularity Principle,* and it will stand for the fact that, in actual practice, it isn't often that a standard type of research design is used. Rather, the features of a research design are selected expressly to create findings that are "clean" in quite particular ways. All contaminated findings are not equal—some are almost always deemed to be worse than others. The concern should focus on how to deal with particular variables that are inherently problematic in the nature of the client/consumer/beneficiary group, the social problem or benefit or intervention involved, or the social context in which the research is to take place.

As an example, take the standard experimental design which requires features such as the following: pretest and post tests, random selection/assignment, and a control group that isn't exposed to the program. Now consider the problems of duplicating those design features in the following program whose objectives are socializing severely emotionally disturbed children—helping them acquire less destructive ways to cope with their own aggression, perform routine household duties, take some responsibility for taking medication, etc. It is not in the nature of this program to deliver its services within a single time frame. Rather, this program is carefully designed to help children work on one task at a time and, having completed that, to go on to another. In fact, the program staff would like the evaluation to help them satisfy their curiosity about whether the sequence in which different coping behaviors are acquired makes a difference in acquiring the whole package— for example, does a child learn to sit still better while practicing reading/writing after or before learning the performance of some routine household tasks? (Recollect that in an earlier chapter we spoke at some length about how essential it is to incorporate into the evaluation enterprise some of the agendas of the program staff). In order to accommodate the nature of the program design and the agendas of the program staff, we must deviate from the traditional true experimental design. Recollect that the true experiment is most often diagrammed in the following way (the R stands for random assignment from the waiting list into that particular group):

R O X O (Experimental group)
R O O (Control or no-treatment group)

First, in order to accommodate our research design to treatments that are not unitary, but broken into many parts, we have to symbolize our design like this (the subscripts $a, b, c,$ and n differentiate between successive treatments and measures):

R OX_aO OX_bO OX_cO .... OX_nO (Experimental group)
R O_a O_b O_c .... O_n (No-treatment group)

The reader can see in these diagrams how this research design differs from the traditional true experimental design. It is important to distinguish program packages from each other—in this case because the staff will learn something important about their achievement with regard to each of them separately. Note however that the above design doesn't yield information to the staff on their question about the sequencing of teaching different tasks. What we must do to accommodate that agenda is construct several experimental groups, varying the sequence of tasks in each:

R OX_aO OX_bO OX_cO .... OX_nO (Experimental group #1)
R OX_bO OX_aO OX_cO .... OX_nO (Experimental group #2)
R OX_cO OX_bO OX_aO .... OX_nO (Experimental group #3)
R O_a O_b O_c .... O_n (No-treatment group)

While this doesn't account for all the ways sequences could be varied, it is illustrative, and, following our earlier principle about particularities, we would advise choosing sequences on the basis of those which might be thought most likely to make a difference.[5]

The opportunity to do random assignment to experimental groups in this program evaluation is made possible because, having a reputation in the community for its success, the program has a waiting list. Thus, it is possible to select a program group from this list (that is, randomly assign therefrom) and avoid ethical problems as well as community criticism. (Random assignment is symbolized by *R*.) The reason is that random assignment from a waiting list is arguably a more fair way to gain access to a program than the old "first-come, first-served" principle.[6]

Why constitute the groups by a random procedure? The short answer is because it is the best hope for creating groups that are homogenous. And what virtue is there in group homogeneity? It lies in the fact that, in comparing outcome results for non-homogenous groups, there is the possibility that outcomes are associated with some factor on which the groups differed (rather than being associated with program effort). Traditionally this is called *the selection effect,* or *selection bias.* It is easiest to understand by reference to the kind of scientific experiment in biological science in which the idea originated—an agricultural scientist trying to contrast the effects of fertilizers upon corn production. Many different plots of ground were staked out, and some were assigned to the fertilized group and some to the non-fertilized group. Unless one could be absolutely certain that the sets of plots were homogenous in terms of fertilized and non-fertilized corn, it would be difficult to attribute differences in corn production to the fertilizer—it may have been due to differences in the ground itself. The solution was to randomly assign the plots among the two groups. Social science adapted this idea to its own purposes. Note that random assignment doesn't guarantee that the groups will be homogenous (that is, that they will in aggregate have the same mean and variance on most factors), but the procedure can be constructed so that its probability is very high indeed.

Random assignment can be a simple procedure. When you wish to randomly select from a small waiting list, you can obtain a table of random numbers, select (arbitrarily) a page and a place (a number) to begin, and run down the list of numbers choosing every successive number that appears that is less than the maximum number on your waiting list. You will stop when there is sufficient to fill the quota for your no-treatment group. Or, alternatively, simply have a personal computer generate a sufficient set of random numbers of the required number of digits. Almost all spreadsheet programs have that capability these days.

It is important to design program evaluations using random assignment where the design calls for group comparisons. Consider again the practitioner program for assisting the frail elderly to remain in their own homes that proposed using group comparisons—a no-treatment group, a visiting nurse group, and a group exposed to the practitioners' program. In order to draw clean conclusions from these comparisons, we must take every precaution to try to insure that these groups are homogenous in ways that we think might make a difference to their outcome. For example, if people are selected from the waiting list for this program on the basis of some staff-practitioner expectation that they have greater potential for making use of it (and assuming the practitioners' predictions are correct), it will leave the waiting list full of those who are unlikely to benefit from the program. Thus, any no-treatment comparison group selected from the waiting list will (systematically) perform less well than those in the program group. This is a selection bias, here a bias in favor of showing the program group's performance to be better than its comparison. The bias is, of course, an artifact and doesn't show the effectiveness of the program at all, for it is the fact of pre-existing group differences that creates the superior effectiveness, not the real attributes of the program. Of course, selection biases can work in the other direction—against the demonstration of effectiveness of a program—as well.

Random assignment to groups has a long history, and it teaches important lessons about its application. While it is extraordinarily simple in theory, in practice there are many ways in which it can be difficult to implement successfully. Negative attitudes toward it on the part of personnel who carry it out are one obstacle. In one carefully constructed random assignment procedure in a mental hospital, the clerical staff of an admission office responsible for the random assignment procedure thought that some mental patients were indeed too dangerous to be sent back to their home communities (even though the professional staff approved of the random assignment procedure and even though there was a procedure for eliminating very dangerous patients from the assignment process). They acted on their convictions by simply casting out certain patients from the random assignment pool! (Test and Burke, 1985). Program evaluators must constantly monitor random assignment processes unless the monitoring is totally under the control of someone committed to its importance in the evaluation (Bickman, 1985). There are other obstacles to adequate implementation of random assignment to groups. Clearly a random assignment process assures that some people in need of the program services won't get them. Sometimes agencies who serve as referral sources refuse to do so any longer once they become aware of that fact, indeed for understandable reasons. That can be handled easily—simply guarantee services to a set proportion of an agency's referrals and randomly choose that number from among the total referred from that agency (Bickman, 1985). That implies constraints on the number of other persons chosen from other referral agencies of course. Because persons in need don't get treatment, there are ethical issues with regard to random assignment. The reader should refer to Chapter Two on ethics and professional standards for more material on that topic.

Finally, notice that we are here speaking of random assignment to groups, not random selection from a target population. Random assignment intends to increase the confidence one has in the validity of findings of a local experiment—here, the validity of statements about the relationships between factors as they arise out of the contrasts between program and alternative program or no-program outcomes (internal validity). Notice that the intention of a random selection procedure is quite different: to increase one's confidence in generalizing findings across times, places, and target groups (external validity). We won't talk much about that in this book, and a few pages later we will discuss the reasons why.

Further Complications in Protecting the Validity of Findings

Other types of designs are necessary to cope with all the real-world difficulties involved in fielding experiments there. Let us look at a specific example: constructing a design to evaluate a program for teenage runaways, a program whose key element is its short-term, time-limited nature. The basic program idea is to serve as a first response to a child's runaway on the occasion of the police picking them up on the street. It is a solution to the problem of the police who don't want to put runaways in jail (when and if that is the only reason for their apprehension) and is intended to be a first order solution to whatever social or familial problems created a runaway. The program targets first-time runaways, rather than those with an established pattern or more entrenched problems—for example, severe physical or sexual abuse, sexual exploitation, severe mental illness, or family violence. The needs of these children are dealt with in other, rather straightforward, ways by law enforcement officers. The basic premises of this program design are (1) to return the child to the family as quickly as possible, always within a few days, and (2) to provide a time-out period for the family during which the program provides temporary, but short-term, shelter for the adolescent, and in which they have a setting in which they must communicate with each other (with the assistance of the program staff) and must focus on basic problems, but don't have to face each other twenty-four hours a day. The specific intermediate objectives of the program are to increase communication and positive attitudes among family members and the self-concept and optimism about their future with regard to the runaway, while the ultimate objective is to decrease runaway incidents by family members.[7]

The features of a traditional true experimental design—random assignment/selection, a no-treatment group, and pretest/post test measures—are simply not feasible here. The problems of composing a no-treatment or alternative treatment group are imposing. Think how silly it would be to propose inducing teenagers to run away from home so they can serve as a control group. The social experiment this program represents can only be done with naturally occurring subjects. Another alternative is to withhold treatment from a randomly selected sub-group, but note that it would require a jail stay for those teenagers selected, and that would provoke much negative response from the police and district attorney, to whose problem the runaway program is a solution—perhaps charges of being unethical as well. Both of these endanger the survival of the program, in particular because, in this instance, the support of the police and the district attorney was vital to its initiation and funding by the local county commissioners and the United Way. Nor, in this community, is there even an alternative program to which this program could be contrasted. On these accounts this program effort simply cannot accommodate a design that involves a control group. Nor should it apologize—it only illustrates how different field research in naturally occurring settings is from research in laboratory settings where the social context is so tractable.

We can, however, provide a substitute by simply using each child as their own control, that is, we will contrast each child to themselves over a substantial period of time. Thus, during the child's first encounter with the shelter, observations will be made of the four intermediate outcome variables of importance (see above: family communication, self-concept, etc.). During the week at the shelter, observations will be taken at midweek and upon completing the program, just prior to leaving the shelter. Then, the key observations will be taken at intervals during the year following the program (observations of subsequent runaways). We might diagram this as follows:

$$01 \qquad X_1\, X_2\; X_3 \quad 02 \quad X_4\, X_5\, X_6\; X_7 \quad 03 \qquad 04 \qquad 05 \qquad 06 \qquad 07$$

| | | | | | | (3mo) | (6mo) | (9mo) | (12mo) |

(Pre-program)   (.... During program ....)   (..... Post program .....)
measures   measures   measures

If program participants show increases in self-concept, personal optimism, and family communication patterns, as well as no runaways, the program will be evaluated as successful. The first four changes are evaluated by showing differences between pre-program (01) and during program measures (02 to 03) or during program and post program measures (04 to 06). This kind of design has been called time-series because of its sequential series of program features and measures of effect across time (and it has also been called *quasi-experimental*). Notice the importance of the pre-program measures in drawing conclusions about program effectiveness. Those pre-program measures are called *baseline measures* because they serve as a basis for determining whether change has occurred.

Now let us examine the validity of findings from these kinds of contrasts. The issue here is whether those changes can be attributed to the program. First note that without a control or contrast group offering no treatment or some alternative treatment, this design cannot rule out the effect of history as a way of accounting for the findings, because we have no way to challenge the objection that the observed changes might have happened even without the program. It is a serious matter, particularly for programs whose participants are exposed to many influences simultaneously. Especially where these programs deal with adolescents, they must compete with the powerful influence of peer groups whose everyday wisdom is urged on by the adolescent's need to express conformity in every possible way. But notice that with regard to our program example above, the program is delivered in the context of a total institution, that is, the adolescent program participant and his/her peer group is totally immersed in the program so that the opportunity to contradict the viewpoint and ideology of the program is minimized. In addition, the program is quite short term.[8]

But notice that what we said immediately above referred only to immediate outcomes. In fact, there is a way in which the effects of history is a major issue for our program example—that is, in terms of its long-term objectives. Once the program participants return to their own families they will be exposed to an open environment, including peer groups and all the interactional pressures of living in the family that may have produced their original runaway. One of the important questions for this program is not only whether the program can produce outcomes while the children are out of the home, but whether there are long-term outcomes that are stable and continuous after its clients return to their families—after all, of what possible use are even huge improvements while in the program at the shelter, if those improvements vanish once the children return home? So we see that even for fairly simple and straightforward program designs there are a number of ranges of outcomes. One principle is that program impacts must be, shall we say, robust in the face of ordinary, expectable realities. In this regard, the effect of history is a problem for the validity of findings for this particular program design. It can also be a problem for this particular program in other ways. For example, the reader ought to keep in mind that this program, like many, has multiple objectives: changing the interpersonal attributes of children, the interactional attributes of families, preventing further runaways, *and* (lurking not far in the background) offering an alternative to jailing adolescent runaways.

It is perfectly possible that the main program objective might be to simply serve as an alternative to jailing runaways, and if it were successful in doing that, its funders might well still consider the effort a success. The necessary data points are simple—count the reduction in the number of jailed runaways over a given time period. Although it is aside from the issue of contaminants, let us note here that social control objectives are common in many social programs, even though good professional practitioners are called to do more than that. Note that the validity of this finding might well be jeopardized by an effect of some particular history. For example, in one community we know a particularly spectacular and serious crime was committed by a runaway just preceding the period of evaluating a runaway shelter program. The law enforcement system abruptly changed their minds on runaways, subsequently believing that they represent a potent threat to the safety of the community. Thus, they thought they ought to take less risk with runaways and responded to their new perceptions (a new political reality) by increasing the jailing of runaways. Thus, the historical facts had nothing at all to do with the effectiveness of the program but, clearly, effected the outcome measures.

Note that we would be seriously misled here if we considered the validity of findings guided only by a very general principle that the effects of history are always a contaminant for time-series designs. While that principle is true in some instances (see examples above), it is also not true in others (again, see examples above). Certainly it is not true unconditionally. This example, like others before it, suggests that we are best advised to think of challenges to the validity of findings using what we earlier called the particularity principle: the validity of findings is specific to the uniquenesses of program designs, program target groups, and social contexts. The same applies to other common threats to the validity of findings, for example, maturation. It is, in fact, a common problem in designing for social program evaluation, but here, because of the short-term nature of the program design, it is not likely to be of much consequence. The idea of maturation as a serious problem for the validity of findings concerns, in general, those instances in which program participants change in regularly expected ways, over the course of a program cycle. When that happens it is sometimes impossible to untangle the effects of the maturational changes from the effects of the program. Thus, one might mistake one for the other, and the validity of findings becomes suspect. The best examples are the effects of physical developmental sequences. Think, for example, how difficult it would be to interpret the findings on program outcomes where the objective was to decrease the gender stereotypes of pre-adolescent children. If the program cycle extends across the time when children are sexually maturing, it will be difficult to untangle the effects of the program from the effects of maturation, which brings along with it a whole new viewpoint on the opposite sex. But note that the social program for runaways we are now considering restricts itself to post-pubescent adolescents so that this particular maturational issue is not relevant.

Paired Treatment - Withdrawal Designs

There is a way of constructing an evaluation design that represents some advance in increasing our certainty about the validity of our conclusions about findings. Its use is somewhat limited in social programs, but it is a powerful design and thus worth speaking about nonetheless. Its virtue is that it shores up confidence in findings from this design by a series of *paired withdrawals* and *reinstatements* (*reversals*, some term them) of the intervention (treatment) (Bloom and Fischer, 1982). For example, consider the instance of a successful use of a schedule of rewards and punishments to reinforce desirable behaviors. We may have some discomfort about the finding: was it really the reinforcement schedule that was actually responsible for the behavior change, or was it some current unknown (indeed unknowable) piece of current history? (e.g., like the serendipitous inclusion of the child in an ultra conforming peer group to which she has been long dying to be admitted). One way, however, to decrease doubt is to withdraw the reinforcement schedule during the program and see whether the desirable behaviors continue. If they don't continue, then we reinstitute the schedule once again. If they reappear, we have demonstrated that our reinforcement schedule indeed controls the behaviors, rather than some historical event outside the control of the program. Now, that withdrawal/reinstitution procedure doesn't completely rule out the effects of history, but it is clear that it considerably enhances the confidence of most people in the association between the program effort and the outcome.

Evaluation designs based on withdrawing treatments have sharp limitations in evaluating social programs. The alert reader will recognize that they cannot be used when the targeted behaviors or conditions are indubitably harmful to others or even potentially so. Nor can they be used when their effect is to reinstitute a seriously painful condition or one that is socially deleterious. Social programs are not alone in that problem—physicians and hospitals cannot always withdraw pharmaceuticals or other treatments willy-nilly just to see if the disease or the pain reappears. Further complicating the use of withdrawal designs is the fact that some changes that can be worked in human beings become enmeshed in attitudes and viewpoints in such a way that they cannot be reversed—"you can't go home again" is a practical wisdom. Think of an attempt to withdraw a program and reinstitute a negative self-concept. It is most unlikely, especially over a short term, simply because (most personal therapists would tell you) a renewed and positive self-concept tends to be self-fulfilling and thus creates a tendency to rise simply on the surge effect of its own change. Even more unlikely to succeed is an effort to reverse the learning of factual information or even alternative frames of reference ("unlearning"—perhaps the intervention equivalent of trying not to think of a white bear). And, if the reader doesn't believe that is a difficult piece of unlearning, try it. Finally, the practitioner and the program must be honest with program participants; how would one explain to clients that something is going to be withdrawn that was successfully provided by the program and produced a positive change? The reader may wish to consult Bloom and Fischer's (1982) suggestions about that matter, although we don't find them convincing (p. 313).

There are other challenges to the validity of findings. It is interesting that social facts can often be increased as a function of how much attention is drawn to them, rather than at some true rate. An example is where child abuse reports increase with the attention given to the topic in the mass media, or where increased attention is created by widely publicized or shocking instances in a particular community. It is a problem when child abuse and neglect reports are spuriously inflated during the evaluation of a program whose objective is to decrease child abuse and neglect incidence, and when change in official reports is used as a proxy for true rates. That change may have nothing to do with either program effects or with the true rate; rather it is a function of a change in the alertness of the general public to child abuse and neglect, thus increasing their propensity to report it. For that reason it can invalidate (contaminate) statements about the outcomes of child abuse and neglect social programs. Sometimes this is called an *instrumentation error*, signifying that the instrument used to make observations of program outcomes (perceptions of citizens who report child abuse) has become destabilized and issues unreliable reports (Cook and Campbell, 1976). Of course, we cannot say that these changes represent necessarily invalid reports. For all we know, they may be more valid than the old reports! But that is unimportant with respect to its effect on the validity of findings about the outcomes of the program. The paradoxical thing is that, even if the program is mildly successful in reducing the incidence of child abuse and neglect, the instrumentation unreliability may suggest an increase in incidence and suggest that the program is associated with increases rather than decreases in child abuse! While it doesn't seem likely to affect the validity of the findings on the program we are using as an example here, it is probably important to keep the possibility in mind in other evaluation enterprises. Jeanne Marsh's (1980) interesting example of the instrumentation effect concerns the effects of biased instrumentation in the investigations of sexual assault: they were conducted by those who were systematically disposed to doubt the credibility of victims. The validity problem it created was to artificially inflate the arrest rate for sexual assault as compared with other crimes. The bias produced more thorough investigations compared with other crimes, thus stronger requests for arrest warrants, which resulted in a spuriously higher arrest rate for sexual assault.

In the end it is never possible to completely settle concerns about every factor that could contaminate the validity of our findings, or stand as a rival conjecture in explaining them. Thus, the selection of variables to be either concerned about or ignored must be, to some extent, based on the subjective or political priorities of stakeholders. Choices can arise out of such things as budget constraints—every contrast group, pretest, or post test costs money and requires such things as negotiations between the stakeholding parties. Only in the rarified air of a laboratory setting can a research design be pursued to ultimate perfection and, even then, the conclusive or ultimate experiment that settles large and important questions is rare indeed, even in the physical sciences. So, those with program evaluation responsibilities should get over being embarrassed by findings that are not completely clean—excepting of course the ignoble case where simple possibilities for cleaner less contaminated findings were not taken advantage of.

Generalizing Findings Across Places, Times, and People: External Validity

Thus far in this chapter we have been concerned with a particular kind of validity, what is commonly called *internal validity*, that is, the validity of conclusions drawn from comparisons within an experiment (or in our case, a social program evaluation design). We have used the phrase *the validity of findings* rather than *internal validity* because we will not want to contrast it with *external validity*. In the sense we will use it, external validity concerns generalizing findings across places, times, and people, yea even organizational contexts. In fact, we will not give the issue of generalizing findings much room in this book. We are persuaded by our experience of the practical conditions under which most evaluations of social programs occur that it is not usually fruitful to make statements about whether findings can be generalized across places, times, target groups, and organizational settings. It is often misleading or, at worst, likely to be dead wrong. But note that we are speaking here to human service practitioners and middle managers and about the particular kind of social programs they are most likely to encounter—personal social services. These are most often delivered by individuals to individuals or small groups and in close encounters: runaway or abused spouse shelters, substance abuse treatment programs, to children in foster care, or to foster parents or negotiators among spousal pairs who are trying to make arrangements with regard to child custody or child support. The mechanism through which those treatments or interventions are delivered is the human person, the social services deliverers themselves. The medium in which that mechanism operates is the social interaction between that person and the program participant or group thereof. The portability of such interventions depends not only on the replication of the basic ideas/models/theories behind the intervention, but also the replication of the medium (the social interaction) and the mechanism (the person) through which all of it flows. That scenario is not likely to be analogous to the various models in which generalizability are usually discussed: restricted closely controlled, even laboratory, settings, simple relationships, and concrete outcomes. To anticipate somewhat, we will end by concluding that, for our purposes, concern about generalizability across places, times, and people is of low priority. Here are some additional reasons.

At one level, the concepts of internal and external validity are quite related to each other. The matter is easy to put: one way to improve internal validity is by decreasing the variability in factors in the natural setting of the research—in doing that, one increases the confidence with which the findings can be asserted but must inevitably decrease the ability to generalize to other natural settings. Thus, for example, a researcher or program evaluator might well increase the validity of findings by designing an evaluation so that the program or intervention takes place in social settings that are deliberatedly contrived to be as exactly the same as is humanly possible to make them—say, an AIDS education program which is organized so that it will be offered to only Asian ethnic boys 17 years old at 10:45 in the morning and presented by the same educator eight times in successive weeks. Now, adopting those constraints will allow the evaluation to sort students into several more or less homogenous groups (homogenous on at least these factors), so that one group can be exposed to the program and the other group not exposed to it. If it is found that the group who experienced the program knows more about AIDS, then the internal validity of this conclusion is increased, because the finding can be asserted without worrying whether the results were due to the way the educator presented the program or the time of day when they received it. Reducing variability in natural settings clearly increases internal validity, because variability in teacher presentation and time of day were equalized across both groups. On the other hand, notice that this gain in internal validity was purchased, in part, at the price of a decrease in external validity, for in this scenario one must now have less confidence in generalizing these findings across classroom settings—a classroom in the real world has different teachers, scheduled times available for AIDS presentations, and classroom ethnic composition. That is the problematic and vexing trade-off between internal and external validity.

We would advise our readers that they opt first for increasing the validity of findings (internal validity), increasing the certainty or the confidence one has that a relationship between program and outcome is truly present, and let the generalizability issue take the lower priority. Trading off confidence in findings is no bargain when, in any event, generalizability must be re-established for particular sites, times, and target groups, one at a time. The viewpoint we are arguing for is that every extrapolation of the kind of human service technology of concern here is, in fact, a new experiment. Nor are we peculiar in having these opinions, for authorities in the field argue along somewhat similar lines. We find some support from Cook and Campbell (1976), for example, long-time leaders in the whole debate about quasi-experiments in field research:

> *Our experience in generalizing social science findings shows that higher order interactions abound, precluding unqualified generalization of our principles not only from one lab to another but especially from lab to field applications. . . .*
> *In program evaluation I recommend formal abandonment of the goal of nationally representative sample selection (pp. 73–75).*

Recently Campbell (1986, p. 69) proposed a relabeling of validity concepts for applied research and the use of a new term—*local molar causal validity.* One implication of that new terminology is that, in applied or field research at least, causal relations are indeed peculiar to context in applied research. We think that the straightforward implication is that external validity is a question that must always be tested in each new applied context.

Endnotes

1. Note that we emphasize that we are speaking here of quantitative evaluations. As readers will learn in Part Four, there is a type of evaluation that goes a long way toward resolving this knotty issue—constructivist evaluation. There is an argument that it does not suffice for all purposes, particularly those in which the audience for the evaluation believes that there is nothing other than hard data that qualifies as a useful product of the evaluation enterprise.

2. Recently, Campbell has proposed to solve these problems by use of the term *local molar causal validity*. We don't share that opinion but believe that the program evaluation field and its practitioners need, rather than more terminology, to learn to keep firmly in mind (a) a healthy skepticism about any claim for the generalizability of findings regarding social programs, and (b) that generalizations about the human condition are peculiar to contexts (culture, time, place, person, and social group) so that the only truly satisfactory basis for generalizability is continual replication—site by site, client group by client group, etc. See Campbell, D. (1986) Relabeling internal and external validity for applied social scientists in W. Trochim (Ed.). *Advances in quasi-experimental design and analysis*, San Francisco: Jossey-Bass.

3. We are indebted to Yvonne Konderski, M.S.W., for this program example.

4. When you have the same x or y on both sides of the equals sign, they cancel each other out. In the equation $a + x = b + x$, the x's on each side of the equals sign cancel each other out. So, you eliminate them from the equation as unimportant.

5. Readers might notice that some kind of ideal design could be constructed by figuring out all the logically possible sequences. We think that is a violation of two evaluation principles: the first is that all evaluations are conducted with a finite budget; the second is that it is a violation of the particularity principle that would lead a person to expect that some sequences are of particular importance in the minds of those who staff the program.

6. If readers are curious about why it is more fair, think for a moment about all the reasons why people show up first on a waiting list. Among only the most obvious are access to information about the availability of the program, access to competent information about its competence, access to transportation, time available to make waiting list arrangements, and sufficient income to meet the expected fee (later data showed that there was a widely held expectation that the program charged a fee—even though that was not the fact). None of those are arguably just reasons to be given priority for receipt of a desirable public service. Upon close examination, almost no application of the "first come-first served" principle turns out to most people a sense of ordinary fairness. (See Boruch, R., & Wothke, W. (1985), Seven kinds of randomization plans for designing field experiments, in R. Boruch and W. Wothke (eds.), *Randomization and field experiments*, New Directions For Program Evaluation Series (#28). San Francisco: Jossey-Bass, pp. 95-114.

7. We are indebted to Gigi Moyers, M.S.W., for this program example.

8. The reader ought to notice here the issue of brainwashing and the moral and ethical issues entailed in programs in closed institutions, and refer to the chapter on ethics earlier in this book. Thus, the validity of immediate outcomes of the program being contaminated by contemporary history is probably not the major issue for this program example that it would be in a program in the context of a program entirely open to external, non-program influences.

References

Bickman, L. (1985). Improving established statewide programs: A component theory of evaluation. *Evaluation Review, 9*(2), 189–208.

Bloom, M., & Fischer, J. (1982). *Evaluating practice: Guidelines for the accountable professional.* Englewood Cliffs, NJ: Prentice-Hall.

Campbell, D. T. (1986). Relabeling internal and external validity for applied social scientists. In W. Trochim (Ed.), *Advances in quasi-experimental design and analysis* (p. 73). San Francisco: Jossey-Bass.

Campbell, D., & Stanley, J. (1966). *Experimental and quasi-experimental designs for research* (p. 12). Chicago: Rand-McNally.

Chambers, D. E. (1986). *Social programs and social policies.* New York: Macmillan.

Cook, T. D., & Campbell, D. T. (1976). *Quasi-experimentation: Design and analysis issues for field settings.* Chicago, IL: Rand-McNally.

Cordray, D. (1986). Quasi-experimental analysis: A mix of methods and judgment. In W. Trochim (Ed.). *Advances in quasi-experimental design and analysis* (pp. 9-23). San Francisco: Jossey-Bass.

Mark, M. (1986). Validity typologies and the logic and practice of quasi-experimentation. In W. Trochim (Ed.), Advances in quasi-experimental design and analysis (pp. 0-23). San Francisco: Jossey-Bass.

Marsh, J. (1980). Combining time series with interviews in evaluating the effects of a sexual assault law. In R. Connor (Ed.), *Methodological advances in evaluation research* (pp. 93- 108). Beverly Hills, CA: Sage.

Rudner, R. (1966). *Philosophy of social science.* New York: Prentice-Hall Co.

Schneider, A., & Darcy, R. (1984 August). Policy implications of using significance tests in evaluation research. *Evaluation Review, 8*(4), 573-582.

Test, M., & Burke, S. (1985). Random assignment of chronically mentally ill persons to hospital or to community treatment. In R. Boruch and W. Wothke (Eds.), *Randomization and field experimentation* (pp. 39-54). New Directions for Program Evaluation Series, #28. San Francisco: Jossey-Bass.

CHAPTER ELEVEN

Cost-Effectiveness and Cost-Benefit Studies

In this chapter, we set out to describe the basic concepts of cost-effectiveness and cost-benefit studies and their applicability for program evaluation. Both of these terms belong to a family of techniques which are used in the human services to predict and formally evaluate efficiency and the effectiveness of different options open to policy makers and administrators for social programming.[1] The aim is to introduce the reader to these techniques and explain generally how they work, with references made to the more technical literature dealing with this subject matter. A detailed example reported in the literature is provided for each of these techniques. The chapter concludes with a discussion of the controversies that are identified with these approaches to policy analysis and program evaluation.

Cost-effectiveness and cost-benefit studies share a common purpose as techniques to examine relationships and tradeoffs among various components of value in social programming, alternative strategies to achieve goals, and monetary costs associated with each alternative. Beyond this general commonality of purpose, important distinctions are noted in the definitions that follow.

Definition of Terms

Cost-Effectiveness Defined

Cost-effectiveness analysis attempts to evaluate program alternatives according to summarized costs for each alternative and effects for each alternative to produce desired results. While a monetary value is placed on the cost side of the equation, no attempt is make to place a dollar value on the effectiveness side of the equation. Program goals are assumed given and beneficial, and the focus is on the most efficient means of attaining them. "It is assumed that (1) only program alternatives with similar or identical goals can be compared and (2) a common measure of effectiveness can be used to assess them" (Levin, 1983, p. 18). Examples of effectiveness measures include such things as service utilization rates, service delivery options, and program dropouts. A particular advantage for cost-effectiveness studies in the human services is its wide range of applicability when program results are difficult to estimate in monetary value.

Cost-Benefit Defined

Cost-benefit analysis carries the evaluation a step further in attempting to evaluate program alternatives for both monetary costs and monetary effects involved in producing desired results. Program alternatives are examined in terms of the ratio of costs to benefits, e.g., the degree to which benefits exceed costs in the equation. Since cost-benefit analysis assesses all alternatives in terms of the monetary values of costs and benefits, it allows decision makers to (1) compare all the desired effects (benefits) with related sacrifices (costs) to judge whether it is better implement or not to implement a program, (2) determine which alternatives are best (have the lowest cost-benefit ratios), and (3) decide what collection of programs or projects constitute the best expenditure within a set, overall budget limit (Thompson, 1980). From a narrower perspective, cost-benefit analysis is a technique to evaluate how successful a particular program is or could be on the basis of economic efficiency and effectiveness.

Rudimentary Concepts in Cost-Effectiveness and Cost-Benefit Studies

Several concepts present common concerns for both cost-effectiveness and cost-benefit analysis. Key concepts are discussed here under the following broad areas: (1) determination of costs, (2) the valuing of costs, and (3) estimating costs per unit of service. First we will consider the identification and specification of costs.

Determination of Costs

At first glance it may appear that the determination of costs for either cost-effectiveness or cost-benefit analysis should be a fairly straightforward and simple matter to determine. The agency or program budget and accounting system should display costs in monetary terms of dollars, leaving little doubt about program expenditures. Unfortunately, traditional social program budgetary and accounting systems usually do not contain all of the cost information required to adequately apply the analytical techniques we are discussing. A comprehensive approach to measurement of social program costs is recommended by Knapp (1991), and it requires some thoughtful preparatory work. Initial illustrative considerations which go beyond what would ordinarily be contained in an agency budget are the following:

- *Do clients receive more than one service, and from more than one agency?*
- *Does the program use volunteers or unpaid professional interns?*
- *Does the program depend on donated in-kind resources such as building space or equipment?*
- *Is the program budget skewed for a given time period because of unusual expenses or savings such as capital improvement or staff turnover?*
- *Are any research (or program evaluation) costs involved which should be considered?*

The above line of questioning suggests that, budgetary information alone is normally insufficient to provide more than a crude estimation of program cost. While supplementation with cost expenditure data can be helpful, a more systematic approach to cost calculation is usually required. An application of program budgeting logic offers assistance in cost determination.

While program budgeting information and program expenditure data may not be available for a given program in a form that allows one to reasonably estimate program costs, the logic of this approach may be applied. Levin (1975) suggests an "ingredients method" to determine costs of an intervention and how the cost burden is distributed among the sponsoring agency, funding sources, donors, and clients. The ingredients method is a several step process involving the following:

- Identify the intervention, e.g., parenting education.
- Identify the ingredients that are used in the intervention, e.g., share of program costs to attribute to the intervention.
- Specify the ingredients, e.g., personnel, facilities, equipment and materials, other program inputs, and client inputs.

General considerations in identifying and listing ingredients in the Levin (1983) method are: (1) specification in sufficient detail that their value can be ascertained in subsequent stages of analysis, (2) consistency in categories of ingredients, and (3) the degree of specificity and accuracy in listing ingredients should depend upon their overall contribution to the total cost of the intervention (p. 56). Assuming that either program budgeting and expenditure data or the logic of program budgeting in an ingredients method is applicable, a reasonable estimation of program cost should be possible. If not, a serious question should be raised whether cost-effectiveness analysis can actually be carried out. Next we consider the issue of valuing costs once they have been identified and specified.

Valuing Costs

Costs in the calculation of cost-effectiveness and cost-benefit are typically measured in increments of monetary currency—dollars. As we have noted in the discussion above, a first concern is to identify and appropriately determine the dollars which will be, or have been, utilized by a particular program. In turn, these identified dollars provide a measure of cost attributable to program activities leading to identifiable results/effects. Even though we are able to measure cost in dollars at this stage of preparation for analysis, additional concerns are focused on a determinant of how much value to place on monetary currency (dollars) as a cost. Monetary currency is a medium of exchange and also a valuable commodity in our society; the dual utility is reflected in the common saying, "It takes money to make money." Several conceptual and analytical approaches have been developed to help in establishing some precision in valuing monetary costs. First we will discuss the concept of opportunity costs.

Opportunity costs Opportunity costs imply that limited resources restrict the number of options that can be pursued for a given goal. When one option is chosen over others, cost of the choice would include the worth of foregone options. A simple example would be when a social agency forgoes the delivery of services to send a staff member to a skills development workshop. Assuming direct costs of tuition and expenses such as travel to send the worker to the workshop, an additional cost would be the value of lost services for the time period involved. In human service programming it may be difficult to identify all foregone options, and even when alternative options are distinguishable, estimates of opportunity costs often require assumptions before cost measures can be projected. "Opportunity cost is a decision making rather than an accounting concept" (Stokey and Zeckhauser, 1978, p. 152). However, when the concept can be applied, it adds a dimension to the true value of costs involved. Whether directly identifiable costs or opportunity costs are being considered, the approach to pricing costs represents another important consideration.

Pricing costs The two principal methods for pricing costs are market pricing, and shadow pricing when conditions of the normal market place are absent.

Market pricing of costs involves the use of market information on the price and quantity of a good or service. In economic terms, under conditions of a perfect market place, the price (value) would be established by the equilibrium between supply and demand. Price, or value, then is what a rational person would be willing to pay for a product or service. Obvious advantages of market pricing for cost analysis in the human services are that a wide range of ingredients are normally covered, including readily available pricing for personnel, facilities, equipment, travel, training, and so on; and competitive market prices may be easily applied to identifiable program ingredients. In some cases, however, market prices are unavailable or do not accurately reflect social value. An alternative approach to valuing costs may be appropriate. *Shadow pricing* is the term used for valuing cost when market prices are unavailable or inappropriate. A shadow price is a substitute value used in place of a market price. Situations which give rise to the use of shadow pricing are: (1) the case of imperfect market conditions such as few buyers or sellers and (2) when no financial transaction takes place in the exchange of goods or services. An example of the first situation would be in placing a value on the cost for services of a uniquely skilled professional. Shadow pricing in the second situation above would be to place a value on the services of an unsalaried practicum student assigned to the program. Assumptions made and procedures used in deriving shadow prices should always be clearly stated by the evaluator.

Bias in market prices gives rise to conditions that may call for the use of shadow pricing techniques. When the price of a good or service changes dramatically without a corresponding change in the quantity available, the change in *consumer's surplus* can be used to place a value on cost. The consumer's surplus is the excess amount of utility that can be obtained because the price of the good or service is less than what the consumer would be willing to pay to buy the quantity desired (Sylvia, Meier, and Gunn, 1985). Other biased market conditions that can affect the price of goods or services are when prices are set too low (as in the case of government subsidies), or deviations from normal price/quantity ratios in the form of taxation, regulation, and price controls.

In the absence of market prices, shadow prices may be applied to situations involving *externalities* or the use of public goods. Externalities, or spillover effects, are unintended program outcomes (as in the case of air or water pollution) that may be represented as costs. Public goods and services may be characterized in the following ways:

- *The use of a public good by one or more individuals does not affect its availability to others.*
- *Public goods are in theory nonexclusive in that, once the public good is provided, citizens are not selectively excluded.*
- *Public goods will not be provided by individuals if it is left strictly up to them, even though such goods provide a net benefit to society as a whole (Sylvia, Meier, and Gunn, 1985, pp. 59–60).*

Shadow pricing for externalities and use of public goods is often a difficult task to carry out objectively. However, the evaluator should be aware of such costs, and efforts should be made to estimate their effects when ignoring them would present serious limitations to cost-effectiveness and cost-benefit studies.

Finally, we consider the situation in which a variety of cost estimates arise when there is no previous experience on what a particular input may cost. An example might be a program in a rural area that requires the expertise of a highly trained practitioner in a profession where shortages exist. In order to attract the professional needed, it may be necessary to make unusual concessions, find employment for a spouse, provide housing, and so on. Because of uncertainty in the cost factor involved, a range of cost estimates can be considered through an approach called *sensitivity analysis*. Sensitivity analysis is carried out as part of the cost-effectiveness and/or cost-benefit analysis described later, but the basic ideas of the approach are introduced here under the treatment of cost issues.

Sensitivity Analysis

Nagel (1985) defines sensitivity analysis in general terms as "changing the goals, alternatives, and/or relations between goals and alternatives to see how the changes affect which alternative is best or how scarce resources should be allocated to the alternatives" (p. 772). It involves estimating costs under different assumptions to see how the overall cost figures change. Details on the method for carrying out sensitivity analysis in cost-effectiveness studies can be found in Levin (1983). Reference to the application of sensitivity analysis associated with a cost-benefit study example is cited later in this chapter.

In cost-benefit studies the approach taken with sensitivity analysis is to vary the value of one effect (i.e., productivity in work days) until the net benefits are equal to zero. A productivity rate below the breakeven rate as determined by sensitivity analysis would result in positive net benefits for the program. As in cost-effectiveness studies, sensitivity analysis provides an insightful look at how crucial various assumptions are to the overall outcome of cost-benefit analysis. Next we will take up the matter of composite cost through an examination of unit costing measures.

Cost Per Unit of Service

Cost per unit of service (*CPU*) is a summary measure of program efficiency or productivity. It is the comparison of a standardized measure of cost with a standardized measure of service. *CPU* is one of the most commonly used indicators of financial status and is of particular use to administrators and evaluators because it relates costs to program activities. A number of basic issues must be addressed, however, in order to arrive at standardized measures of cost and service activity that may be applied in cost-effectiveness and cost-benefit analyses. Zelman (1987) refers to these issues as problem areas occurring at three stages of the data collection/reporting process: (1) definition, (2) collection, and (3) processing problems.

Definitional problems require that agreement be reached on exactly what elements constitute the components of cost on the one hand, and service on the other. Optional ways to conceptualize cost, for example, are discussed above. Further practical issues must be addressed in choosing among options in defining cost for program resources used. Costs incurred are typically classified as: (1) direct costs or expenditures made by the program responsible for the service, as in salaries to service workers, equipment, supplies, and so on; and (2) indirect costs, as in costs for program supervision and administration, training, maintenance, and the like. Units of service in the human services are usually of four types:

1. *The time unit, i.e., one hour of homemaker service, one day of day care for children*
2. *The episode/activity unit, i.e., one counseling session, one arrangement, one contact*
3. *The material unit, i.e., one meal, one contraceptive device*
4. *The outcome unit, i.e., one (1) placement, one (1) substitute home found (Bowers and Bowers, 1976, p. 9)*

CPU is thus illustrated in a rudimentary way by the rule and example for room and board for group home care in Figure 11–1.

Additional issues surface when we consider the possibility of factors that may influence variations in program costs. For instance, the total expense or cost for a program will usually vary with the volume of activities carried out. A useful classification scheme to identity the influence of cost variations is presented by Sorensen and Phipps (1975). The classification of costs includes

---

FIGURE 11–1 • *Cost of a Unit of Service*

Rule

$$\text{Unit cost} = \frac{\text{Total cost of service}}{\text{Number of units of service provided}}$$

Example

$$\text{Unit cost of room and board} = \frac{\text{Cost of room and board}}{\text{Number of days of care provided}}$$

$$\$33.50 = \frac{\$335{,}000}{10{,}000}$$

Source: Richardson, D. A. (1981). *Rate setting in the human services: A guide for administrators* (OS–76–130). PROJECT SHARE, Washington, D.C.: U.S. Government Printing Office, p. 31.

[*Note:* The calculation of a unit cost depends upon prior collection by the agency of statistical data on service utilization, in addition to the cost data obtained from traditional accounting records.]

TABLE 11–1 • *Outpatient Type of Expense and Two Different Volumes of Visits*

Type of Expense	Number of Outpatient Visits			
	5,000		6,000	
	Total expense	Per visit expense	Total expense	Per visit expense
Fixed	$25,000	$5.00	$25,000	$4.17
Variable	5,000	1.00	6,000	1.00
Step-variable	2,500	.50	2,700	.45
	$32,500	$6.50	$33,700	$5.62

Source: Sorensen, J., and Phipps, D. W. (1975). *Cost-finding and rate-setting for community mental health centers,* ((ADM) 76–291). Washington, D.C.: U.S. Government Printing Office, p. 17.

(1) variable expenses, (2) step-variable expenses, and (3) fixed expenses. Within this classification scheme, *variable expenses* are treated as costs which are expected to fluctuate directly with some measure of activity, such as clientele seen, patients boarded, and so on. Examples of such variable expenses could be specialized equipment requirements, clerical support services, hours of program operation, or food consumption requirements. Some expenses may be considered as *step-variable* when the variation is over a wide range but not in direct proportion with measures of program activities. Professional labor costs could serve as an example. There is usually some practical limit of workload before a professional staff position would be added or deleted from a program. Finally in this classification scheme are the *fixed expenses,* those which remain constant in total amount regardless of the level or fluctuation in volume of program activity. Examples could be found in salaries of administrators, rent costs, and depreciation of equipment. An illustration of how this expense classification scheme may be applied for outpatient mental health service expenses is projected in Table 11–1.

While it is not the intent in this chapter to consider all of the possibilities for cost variation, an additional illustration should help acquaint the reader with the issue identified. The discussion which follows concerns so-called artifactual differences in costs that appear depending on the accounting procedure used (Zelman, Stone, and Davenport, 1982). In Table 11–2, for example, a cash basis of accounting or cash flow (Row 8), yields a considerably different cost factor on an annual basis than does the accrual basis of cost accounting (Row 9). The implications which arise from the choice of accounting method concern how to best represent costs over time, and total amount of cost that will eventually be recognized. No easy answer can be given for

TABLE 11–2 • Effects of Using Cash Flows Versus Resource Flows as the Basis for Calculating Costs and Unit Cost on a Hypothetical Example of Purchasing Two Vans for $20,000 Each

	1985	1986	1987	1988	1989	Total
1. Total purchase price: $40,000						
2. Down payment	$ 1,000					$ 1,000
3. Principal payment	$ 1,000	$ 3,000	$ 5,000	$10,000	$20,000	$39,000
4. Depreciation	$ 8,000	$ 8,000	$ 8,000	$ 8,000	$ 8,000	$40,000
5. Other (operating costs, salaries)	$ 2,000	$ 2,000	$ 2,000	$ 2,000	$ 2,000	$10,000
Amount Reported as Cost:						
6. Cash flow (cash) basis	$ 4,000	$ 5,000	$ 7,000	$12,000	$22,000	$50,000
7. Resource flow (accrual) basis	$10,000	$10,000	$10,000	$10,000	$10,000	$50,000
Amount Reported as Cost Per Unit: (assuming 10,000 units/year)						
8. Cash flow (cash) basis	$0.40	$0.50	$0.70	$1.20	$2.20	
9. Resource flow (accrual) basis	$1.00	$1.00	$1.00	$1.00	$1.00	

Source: Zelman, W. N. (1987). Cost per unit of service, *Evaluation and Program Planning*, 10, p. 203. Used by permission.

Note: For illustrative purposes, straight line depreciation has been assumed and no reimbursement or tax effects have been included.

this problem, but it does appear that the accrual accounting method is more accurate for judging the true efficiency of an organization over time (Zelman, 1987).

Another definitional problem concerns variations that result in choice of service units. Displayed in Table 11–3 is an illustration of how options for unit of service can differ on the basis of choice between service provider or clients receiving the service, and criteria for choosing an option. The hypothetical situation in Table 11–3, developed by Zelman (1987), involves the delivery of one hour of outpatient mental health service by a team consisting of a psychologist and a social worker to a family of three. Service boundaries are usually defined in terms of time and/or activity. The expenditure of time combined with activity is commonly used in the human services to distinguish unit of service, i.e., hours, days, weeks, or months of service. In the example depicted in Table 11–3, service boundary is based on the time involved (in hours) in providing or receiving the service, and the criteria list the implications of each alternative in time specification. Depending on the criteria chosen in the example, unit of service could vary from one to six hours. The appropriate unit of service to choose depends on the criteria to satisfy, and that, in turn, can vary according to program circumstance. It is important to remember, however, that consistency be followed for use of unit cost comparisons in cost-effectiveness and cost-benefit studies.

Once definitions of cost and service unit have been determined, the next stages are routinized data collection and processing. Data collection for *CPU* requires systematic reporting procedures to document both costs and services provided, consistent with agreed upon definitions as discussed above. Accuracy in reporting (especially in terms of service units) depends in large measure on the motivation of practitioners and others who routinely report their service activities. Incentives for cooperation of persons who report data to the information system may be enhanced by involving them in both the design of the information system and control functions to ensure accuracy of information reported (McCleod, Dieter, Suver, and Zelman, 1984).

The data processing or transformation stage presents an additional set of options. A choice of approach is required on how the cost data and service data are combined to determine *CPU*. In the example from Figure 11–1, a fairly simple and straightforward approach to calculation of *CPU* is presented. While the equation in Figure 11–1 serves to acquaint the reader with the basic approach commonly used by smaller programs in the human services, Zelman (1987) identifies four major issues which have emerged for data transformation in large complex delivery systems such as community mental health centers: "[1] the type or method of allocation to be used, [2] the nature and number of cost centers, [3] the way in which they are sequenced in cost-finding (allocation) methods, [and 4] the nature and appropriateness of the basis upon which costs are allocated" (p. 205). Each of these issues poses choices for cost-accounting procedures which are quite technical in nature. For further

TABLE 11–3 • Alternative Ways of Reporting the Number of Units of an Outpatient Service Delivered by a Team Consisting of a Social Worker and a Psychologist to a Family of Three with Implications of Each Method in Regard to 7 Criteria

| | Providers | | | | Clients | | | |
	(A) Elapsed Time: One Gets Full Credit	(B) Elapsed Time: Each Gets Partial Credit	(C) Elapsed Time: Each Gets Full Credit	(D) Time Spent per Client: Each Gets Full Credit	(E) Elapsed Time: One Gets Full Credit	(F) Elapsed Time: Each Gets Partial Credit	(G) Elapsed Time: Each Gets Full Credit	(H) Time Spent Face to Face Each Gets Full Credit
Service provider:								
Psychologist 1	1 or	1/2	1	3				
Psychologist 2	1	1/2	1	3				
Service Recipient:								
Mother					1 or	1/3	1	2
Father					1 or	1/3	1	2
Child					1	1/3	1	2
Units reported:	1 hr.	1 hr.	2 hrs.	6 hrs.	1 hr.	1 hr.	3 hrs.	6 hrs.
Criteria:								
Accurately reflects Total staff time spent	too low	too low	yes	too high	too low	too low	too low	too low

Unit of Service is Recorded from the Point of View of:

Full credit: Each staff for time spent	one yes, other low	too low for both	yes	too high	n/a	n/a	n/a	n/a
Full credit: Each staff for time with each client	too low	too low	too low	yes	n/a	n/a	n/a	n/a
Accurately reflects Total client time spent	too low	too low	too low	too high	too low	too low	yes	too high
Accurately reflects elapsed time by clients	yes	yes	too high	too high	yes	yes	too high	too high
Accurately reflects the Total amount of hours of service received by each participant	too low	too low	too low	yes	yes			
Reimbursement	depends on reimb. conditions	depends on reimb. conditions	depends on reimb. conditions	depends on reimb. conditions	depends on reimb. conditions	depends on reimb. conditions	depends on reimb. conditions	depends on reimb. conditions

Source: Zelman, W. N. (1987) Cost per unit of service, *Evaluation and Program Planning*, 10, p. 204. Used by permission.

elaboration the reader is referred to Sorensen and Phipps (1975); the National Institute of Mental Heath, Division of Biometry Methodology Reports series; and the Department of Health and Human Services (formerly Department of Health, Education and Welfare) PROJECT SHARE collection in U.S. Government Documents.

From the discussion above we may conclude that we are dealing as much with art as with science, when it comes to cost finding for cost-effectiveness and cost-benefit studies. This pronouncement appears equally or even more valid when we consider the outcome or effectiveness side of the ledger. Nevertheless, progress continues in this area of evaluation, and amid the discussions of conceptual and methodological design, reports of application offer encouragement. First we will turn our attention to the application of cost-effectiveness analysis.

Applying Cost-Effectiveness Analysis

In order to assess cost-effectiveness for a given program, it is necessary to begin with a clear conception of the costs associated with program options or alternatives and the goal to be achieved by the program. The discussion above explains how dollar values can be assigned to the costs (program resource expenditures), including costs which are more or less hidden to the casual observer. No less important is a clear conception of the goal to be achieved and the program options or alternatives which may be considered. Consider, for example, a community based service program for the treatment of alcohol abuse with the goal of alleviating chemical dependency. Among the strategies to reach the program goal are two alternatives which have come into common use: partial hospitalization with outpatient treatment, and inpatient hospitalization treatment. Each program alternative has the same overall program goal, and a determination may be made of costs associated with each alternative. The purpose of the cost-effectiveness analysis is to determine which program alternative (or combination of alternatives) will result in the greatest effectiveness for the program. An example from the professional literature will serve to illustrate how the analysis is actually carried.

An Example of Cost-Effectiveness Analysis

Our example is a study reported by McCrady, Longabaugh, Fink, Stout, Beattie, and Ruggieri-Authelet (1986). They performed a cost-effectiveness analysis of alcoholism treatment in partial hospital versus inpatient settings after brief inpatient treatment. The analysis involved data on program alternatives for the twelve-month follow-up results on 115 subjects who participated in the two program alternatives. The subjects were patients in a private, nonprofit psychiatric hospital and were randomly assigned on a 2:1 basis to either Partial Hospital Treatment (PHT) or Extended Inpatient Treatment (EIP). Subjects in the PHT group totaled 78, and there were 37 in the EIP group. A structured treatment program for each group included teaching patients and families behavioral skills to maintain abstinence and provided educational materials and an introduction to Alcoholics Anonymous.

Determination of cost and effectiveness measures are described by the study authors (1986) as follows:

> *Baseline data were collected in face-to-face interviews with patients and telephone interviews with one person designated by the subject (a spouse, relative, roommate, or close friend) who could serve as a collateral data source. Telephone follow-up interviews were done monthly with patients and bimonthly with collaterals. Outcomes were evaluated by measuring drinking quantity, frequency and problem consequences, occupational functioning, and physical health (p. 709).*

Treatment cost estimates were derived from several sources. Direct costs of initial treatment were extracted from hospital bills. Indirect costs of treatment included income lost for time missed from work and child care costs during hospitalization. Income loss was calculated by multiplying daily income by working days hospitalized. Child care costs were estimated for subjects who were homemakers, unemployed, or disabled who had children under 10 living at home (n=10). Child care costs were estimated at $1.50 per hour, based on 8 hours per day for PHT subjects and 9.5 hours per day for EIP subjects.

Subsequent treatment costs included direct and indirect costs for readmissions to the same or other treatment facilities and costs for outpatient treatment. Because cost data were not directly available for outpatient treatment, average treatment costs were estimated at $35 per visit. Costs of hospitalizations at other facilities were not available and therefore were estimated at the same daily rate as the primary treatment facility ($183 per day).[2] The cost estimates did not include volunteer resources used during treatment, or legal or additional medical costs incurred during treatment of follow-up, as these data were not available.

Total treatment costs were calculated by summing the direct and indirect costs of the initial treatment, the direct and indirect costs of any subsequent hospitalizations, and the direct costs of outpatient treatment.

The measures for program alternative effectiveness are reported by the study authors in Table 11–4. Both groups showed significant improvement in drinking behavior over their baseline levels, although collateral reports were not as positive as subjects' self reports. The groups did not differ on drinking outcomes. Note that standardized measures, the Quantity-Frequency Index (QFI) and Residential Status and Stability Index (RSSI), were utilized along with other attributes of successful life functioning to measure program effectiveness through patient behavior. Based on the outcomes presented, the

TABLE 11–4   •   *Twelve-Month Drinking and Life Task Outcomes*

Measure	PHT (n = 78)		EIP (n = 37)	
	Baseline	12 month	Baseline	12 month
QFT*				
M	8.74	0.48	6.44	1.24
SD	8.73	1.04	5.41	3.07
Proportion abstinent days				
Client report				
M	0.24	0.85	0.26	0.82
SD	0.26	0.22	0.31	0.28
Collateral report				
M	0.23	0.68	0.32	0.71
SD	0.29	0.29	0.37	0.32
Continuously abstinent	NA	27.7%	NA	32.4%
0–3 drinking days per month	NA	32.1%	NA	40.5%
Rehospitalizations				
Client report	NA	34.6%	NA	27.0%
Collateral report	NA	32.1%	NA	24.3%
Days rehospitalized				
M	NA	9.62	NA	10.92
SD		5.52		7.73
Employed full-time*	67.9%	62.7%	67.6%	70.6%
Full-time role	75.6%	71.6%	81.1%	82.4%
Work missed due to drinking	51.3%	25.6%	56.8%	18.9%
Job losses due to drinking	6.4%	10.3%	2.7%	16.2%
On disability	6.4%	9.0%	5.4%	2.9%
Arrested	6.4%	5.1%†	13.5%	8.1%
RSSI				
M	0.92	0.69	0.88	0.68
SD	0.23	0.29	0.23	0.24

Source: McCrady, B., Longabaugh, R., Fink, E., Stout, R., Beatte, M., and Ruggieri-Authelet, A. (1986). Cost effectiveness of alcoholism treatment in partial hospital versus inpatient settings after brief inpatient treatment: 12-month outcomes, *Journal of Consulting and Clinical Psychology*, 54, p. 710. Used by permission.
Note. PHT = partial hospital treatment; EIP = extended inpatient treatment; QFI = Quantity-Frequency Index; RSSI = Residential Status and Stability Index.
*n = 67 for PHT; n = 34 for EIP because of missing data.   †Includes one jailed subject who is excluded from other analyses.

authors concluded that positive clinical outcomes were observed with no differences between the two program alternatives.

Cost measures for the program alternatives are presented by the study authors in Table 11–5. Program alternatives were compared on total costs associated with initial treatment, continued treatment, and rehospitalizations.

Total costs were regarded by the study authors as high, but significantly lower for the Partial Hospitalization Treatment program alternative.

The analysis concluded with cost-effectiveness estimates as presented in Table 11–6. Unit costs of improvement were defined by the study authors as difference between baseline and follow-up abstinent days divided by total treatment costs, yielding an estimate of how many abstinent days were obtained per $100 of treatment costs. To determine how much it cost to produce one continuously abstinent subject, total treatment costs were divided by the number of abstinent subjects. Similar calculations were carried out for infrequent drinkers. As seen in Table 11–6, cost-effectiveness measures for each comparison favored the Partial Hospitalization Treatment program alternative.

TABLE 11–5 • _Treatment Costs ($)_

	PHT (n = 78)		EIP (n = 37)	
Treatment costs per patient	_M_	_SD_	_M_	_SD_
Initial hospitalization				
Room and board	1,022.73	433.12	3,099.27	866.74
Ancillary charges	295.44	298.41	266.32	177.71
Day treatment program	1,482.24	585.09	1,042.43	388.80
Work missed	351.78	423.49	403.11	390.39
Child care	12.76	61.95	40.05	112.75
Total inpatient costs	3,164.95		4,851.18	
Outpatient treatment	687.88	605.82	627.16	602.18
Rehospitalizations				
Inpatient*	486.93	1,037.36	688.66	1,514.43
Day treatment program	104.74	341.87	95.00	343.26
Other facilities†	383.30	1,122.60	84.27	336.53
Work missed‡	107.47	299.23	75.69	272.36
Child care	2.01	13.73	10.60	42.79
Total rehospitalization cost	1,084.45		954.22	
Total treatment costs	4,983.04	2,195.58	6,432.56	2,697.90

Source: McCrady, B., Longabaugh, R., Fink, E., Stout, R., Beatte, M., and Ruggieri-Authelet, A. (1986). Cost effectiveness of alcoholism treatment in partial hospital versus inpatient settings after brief inpatient treatment: 12-month outcomes, _Journal of Consulting and Clinical Psychology, 54_, p. 711. Used by permission.

Note. PHT = partial hospital treatment; EIP = extended inpatient treatment.

*_n_ = 22 for PHT and 11 for EIP.   †_n_ = 14 for PHT and 3 for EIP.

‡_n_ = 76 for PHT on this variable because of missing data.

Table 11–6　•　*Cost-Effectiveness Estimates*

Measure	*PHT**	*EIP* [†]
Abstinent days/$100 treatment costs[‡]		
M	5.4	4.2
SD	3.0	3.3
Changes in QFI/$100 treatment costs[§]		
M	0.2	0.1
SD	0.2	0.1
Total treatment costs/abstinent subject	$18,935	$21,637
Total treatment cost/abstinent or moderate drinking subject	$9,966	$13,222

Source: McCrady, B., Longabaugh, R., Fink, E., Stout, R., Beatte, M., and Ruggieri-Authelet, A. (1986). Cost effectiveness of alcoholism treatment in partial hospital versus inpatient settings after brief inpatient treatment: 12-month outcomes, *Journal of Consulting and Clinical Psychology*, 54, p. 712. Used by permission.
Note. PHT = partial hospital treatment; EIP = extended inpatient treatment.
*n = 78.　[†]*n* = 34.　[‡]*Number of abstinent days over baseline*
[§]Ounces reduction in alcohol consumed.

It is interesting to note that in their concluding calculations in Table 11–6, the study authors came close to performing a cost-benefit analysis. However, abstinence from alcohol usage (and moderate drinking) remained the program goal rather than purported benefits to be derived from abstinence. Further, as we will see later in the section on cost-benefit analyses, a more in-depth treatment of costs and outcomes is required to arrive at cost-benefit results.

In discussion on the findings of the cost-effectiveness evaluation, the study authors are careful to point out the limitations to their study and parameters used in cost calculation. They believe that their analysis captures the bulk of costs of treatment for the patient population under study, and offer the following account of cost-finding data:

> The cost analyses included direct costs of initial treatment, outpatient treatment, and rehospitalizations, as well as estimated costs for time lost from work and child care. These latter figures were estimates and based on 1979–80 figures, but as they were small relative to the costs of hospitalization, different estimates would not have altered the outcomes substantially. Our cost estimates did not include more indirect costs of alcoholism, such as lost productivity, costs of motor vehicle accidents, involvement in the criminal justice system, use of social welfare programs, or costs of fire or public safety personnel attributable to subjects who continued to drink (Saxe, Doughtery, Esty, and Fine, 1983). These latter costs, although socially significant, are difficult to estimate and most appropriate for large sample analyses because of their low rate of occurrence. Our data, albeit incomplete, suggest that social costs did not differ between the groups (McCrady, Longabaugh, Fink, Stout, Beattie, and Ruggieri-Authelet, 1986, p.711).

The example of cost-effectiveness analysis given here reveals the potential of this method for program evaluation. While not all human service programs offer as clear cut program alternatives as in the example presented, readers are encouraged to consider applicability to programs with which they are familiar. Next we will consider the application of cost-benefit analysis, with special emphasis on the human services.

Applying Cost-Benefit Analysis

In cost-benefit analysis, the same considerations are given to treatment of program costs as above, in the case of cost-effectiveness analysis. The treatment of benefits, however, goes beyond the measures of effectiveness (or goal attainment) to consider also the value of the measures of effectiveness (benefits). Before cost-benefit analysis can be applied, even further consideration is required for both the cost and benefit sides of the equation. Social programming is viewed as investment, with alternative program options judged against the criterion of "profitability" (Gates, 1980). As in the business world, the assumption is that social programming will generate a stream of costs and benefits (in dollar values), and future program costs and benefits are adjusted to their value in the present. Dollar values for both costs and benefits are therefore discounted to "present value" in final output of the benefit/cost ratio. First we will take up the matter of program benefits and the problems in assigning dollar values to identified benefits.

Identifying and Valuing Program Benefits

Counting program benefits involves deciding what to include and what to exclude. Having decided what to properly include as benefits, the next concern is placing a value on identified benefits. As in the case of program costs discussed earlier in this chapter, market price provides a convenient resolve to valuation of benefits as well as costs when the basic assumptions of the market place are extant. Similarly, when market price is unavailable or deemed to be biased, an attempt is made to estimate value of benefits through imputed or shadow prices.

Klarman (1974) provides a useful breakdown of program benefits for health services that appears to have wider applicability for the human services. The three categorical areas include: (1) direct benefits, (2) indirect benefits, and (3) intangible benefits. Our discussion will begin with some of the salient issues involved in the determination of direct benefits for cost-benefit analysis.

"Consumers' values," or "willingness to pay" for a good or service provided by a proposed action, is central to the economic model of market place transactions. The ideal transactional exchange in the market place for receipt of direct benefits is captured in the following: When commodities or services are exchanged in perfectly competitive markets, the market price measures the willingness to pay for the last unit consumed. The area under a demand curve represents the total willingness of a consumer to pay (with given income) for all that is purchased. Thus, for commodities or services which are exchanged on such markets, benefit measurement is reasonably straightforward (Smith, 1986, p. 16). Unfortunately, this tidy economic model of the market place is rarely sufficient to determine direct benefits and their values in health or human services. Not the least of concerns with the simplified economic model above are distinctions between willingness to pay and ability to pay. Klarman (1974) offers a definition of direct benefits as "that portion of averted costs currently borne which are associated with spending for health [human] services. . . [with benefits representing] potential tangible savings in health [human services] resources" (p. 331). A problem occurs, as in the case of costs discussed earlier, in that benefits (as costs averted) are often tied in to total costs of the provider program, and means are taken to factor out just which amount of benefit accrues to the service or services under analysis. Another complication noted by Klarman (1974) is the simultaneous presence of two or more diseases [human service problems]; the presence of problem B when intervention is carried out for problem A serves to raise or lower the costs of intervention and therefore the corresponding benefits (p. 331). Another problem occurs in the tendency to take direct benefits from a single-year estimate of costs; single-year estimates reflect the prevalence of a disease [human service problem], not the incidence. Finally is the problem that transportation expenses for medical care [human services] as a resource cost are often disregarded.

Indirect benefits include such things as aversion of earnings loss due to debility, value of housewives' services, and opportunities for employment, including the effects of the economy for this variable. Klarman (1974) notes that such indirect benefits may or may not be appropriately identified and considered in analysis. For instance, what is often not taken into account is the tendency that persons rehabilitated after serious illness or injury find fewer job opportunities than persons who have remained healthy and on the job. Finally, calculations of indirect benefits should be based on more than implicit assumption of life expectancies for cohorts of potential survivors.

Intangible benefits would include adverting current costs of illness or human problems such as pain, discomfort, grief and so on experienced by the individual and significant others. Klarman (1974) points out that such benefits accrue partly to the individuals directly affected, their friends, relatives, and society at large, to the extent that we take pleasure in the happiness of others. "Looming even larger is the averted premature loss of human life" (p. 334). These intangible benefits can be extremely important and very difficult to give an assigned value. However, considerable attention has been given to estimating the economic value of human life for application in cost-benefit analysis. Two approaches have emerged in treating the economic value of life: the human capital approach and the willingness to pay approach. The human capital approach to life value is based primarily on a measure of future production potential, while the willingness to pay approach is based on values placed on avoiding risks to life (or on the individuals' willingness to accept compensation) for small changes in their probability of survival. For a discussion on the state of the art concerning value of life estimates, the reader is referred to Rhodes (1980) and Landefeld and Sesken (1982) for estimates based on the human capital approach.

Consideration must be given also to the matter of externalities, identified briefly above in the discussion on shadow pricing. Cost-benefit analysis measures the benefits and costs generated by any action in terms of the effects on each decision making unit. However, in the case of most social program actions, individuals other than direct participants will feel the impact in one way or another. "Hence, in measuring costs and benefits, the analyst must not be satisfied to enumerate solely the outcomes for direct participants . . . Victims or beneficiaries of externalities must have their net spillover impacts added up as well" (Rothenberg, 1975, p. 70). These so-called spillover effects (externalities) may be positive or negative. In this section, we have been considering benefits both tangible and intangible. It is the intent here to call attention to externalities which have occurred and which, by their effect, should be considered in the cost stream. A hypothetical example would be in the case of a neighborhood where initiating a methadone treatment facility resulted in decreased real estate values. It would be quite important, of course, to verify that this effect had indeed taken place, especially since there would likely be high emotional feeling involved on the part of neighborhood residents. Valuing externalities involves first their identification, and then application of pricing techniques as described above in this chapter.

Discounting to Present Value

Program benefits and costs usually begin in the present and continue to points in the future. Current estimates of benefits therefore require value adjustments (discounting) for the dollar flows of costs and benefits to a single point in time, expressed as the present value of costs and benefits. Discounting is based on the same logic as investing, and in fact works the investment theme backwards. For example, $100 invested today at 10 percent yield would result in $110 a year from now; $100 expected a year from now, but discounted at 10 percent, would represent a present value of $90. The general formula for calculating present value of costs and benefits is:

Present value (PV) = *Dollar amount of future cost or*
$$\frac{Benefit\ (FV)}{(1 + d)^t}$$

where d is the discount rate and t is the number of years in the future. In the case of $100 in benefits expected a year from now at 10 percent discount, the present value would be determined as follows:

$$PV = \frac{100}{(1 + .10)^1}$$
$$= \$90.90$$

The value of the discount rate can have a significant effect on the estimation of benefits to accrue for a given program. Projected over time, even a 1 or 2 percent variation in discount rate can mean a great difference in expected program benefits. Setting the appropriate discount rate can be problematic. For most human service programs the appropriate discount rate is equated with the *social discount rate,* the rate at which society will trade off present costs and benefits for future costs and benefits. Economists and policy makers have proposed a variety of indicators to derive social discount rate, though no single indicator has received prominence. Examples which have been used as indicators for social discount rate include government borrowing rate, corporate discount rates, and market investment rates as in the case of government bonds and private sector interest rates. In the application of cost-benefit analysis, the discount rate is often simply presented as an organization's estimated opportunity cost of resources, with a high and low rate presented (10 percent and 5 percent respectively). It is also important to note that present value analysis does not explicitly attempt to adjust for trends of inflation or deflation. When consideration of inflationary projections are made in the case of future estimated benefits, indices such as the Consumer Price Index may be applied.

Comparing Costs and Benefits

When the appropriate program costs and benefits have been identified and present value analyses calculated, a comparison of costs and benefits is in order. A program is allocatively efficient if it returns benefits over costs incurred in producing the benefits. Alternative criteria which are typically used to determine whether to accept or reject a program on this basis are: (1) net present value of benefits, (2) internal rate of return, and (3) benefit/cost ratio.

Net present value　Net Present Value (NPV) is often used and considered by some as the most generally useful criterion for cost-benefit analysis (Anderson and Settle, 1977). NPV is derived by comparing present value of benefits with present value of costs to yield a monetary measure of program value for the time frame considered. When benefits have been previously discounted, NPV is determined by subtracting discounted costs from present value of program benefits. A more involved formula for calculating NPV including time and discount rate is:

$$\frac{B_t-C_t}{(1+d)^t} \quad \cdots \quad \frac{+B_n-C_n}{1+d)^n}$$

where B_t is the dollar value of benefits at time t, C_t is the dollar value of cost at time t, d is the discount rate, and n is the number of years for the program. For example, a program that yields net benefits of $500 for year 1, $1,000 for year 2, and at a 10 percent discount rate, would receive an overall NPV of $1368:

$$
\begin{aligned}
NPV &= \frac{500}{(1+.10)_1} + \frac{1,000}{(1+.10)_2} \\
&= 454 + 909 \\
&= 1368
\end{aligned}
$$

The multi-year variable for cost-benefit analysis has particular applicability for projects such as construction of a reservoir or other public works projects. In the human services, a more limited time frame for program activities (often a year) is used in cost-benefit analysis. Two other criteria which have use in displaying the results of cost-benefit studies are internal rate of return and benefit-cost ratio (B/C).

Internal rate of return Internal Rate of Return (IRR) is determined by increasing the discount rate until costs and benefits are equal. The amount of discount rate required to equalize costs and benefits specifies the percentage of return for resource investment and determines the IRR; i.e., if a discount rate of 20 percent achieves equal costs and benefits, the IRR is determined to be 20 percent. Generally speaking, a program that is unable to achieve an IRR at less than lending rates of interest would not be deemed very successful. While the IRR has been a popularly used criterion in the past, concern over limitations in this approach have curtailed its present use. For one thing, the IRR "is difficult to derive and can be ambiguous" (Anderson and Settle, 1977, p. 97). In addition, critics have pointed out that the IRR approach is not as appropriate as the NPV when discount rate is subject to change, when costs are spread throughout the life of a program, or when budget constraints are experienced (Sylvia, Meier, and Gunn, 1985).

Benefit/cost ratio Benefit/Cost (B/C) Ratio is determined by dividing the total discounted benefits by the total discounted costs. For example, if total discounted benefits are calculated at $1,000 and total discounted costs are $500, the resulting B/C ratio is expressed as 2 for the program involved. As in the case of the IRR, B/C ratio as a criterion for determining program allocative efficiency has decreased in popularity. The B/C ratio is easier to calculate than the IRR, but appears most useful in situations where the amount of money to be invested in a project or group of projects is limited (Sylvia, Meir & Gunn, 1985).

An Example of Cost-Benefit Analysis

In order to illustrate the various steps involved in cost-benefit analysis, we will examine the approach taken by Weiss, Jurs, Lesage, and Iverson (1984) as applied to a smoking cessation program. The authors report a follow-up study of one program which began several years ago, and on the basis of information derived from the survey, they have developed a simulation of cost-benefit analyses for other similar programs. The comparison of costs and benefits was done from the perspective of the employer of the participants who took part in the smoking cessation program. Therefore, benefits to the firm were used as criteria for comparison with program costs, instead of focusing on benefits to the participants themselves. Obviously, benefits would accrue to successful program participants as examined by life improvement measures. However, as in the case of many cost-benefit studies, external criteria for valuing benefits are chosen for the sake of objectivity, difficulties in dealing with the uncertainty of effects such as prevention of disease, and availability of standardized monetary measures.

The parent organization for the smoking cessation program is the Health Aware program at the Toledo, Ohio, Hospital. Health Aware was begun in 1979 as a health promotion and information program for the employees of the hospital, and was subsequently offered to the entire community. The overall goals of Health Aware are to: (1) inform people about ways in which they can improve their health, (2) motivate people to want to develop health practices, and (3) help people learn the necessary skills to adopt and maintain healthful practices and lifestyles. The smoking cessation portion of the program involved meetings twice a week for one and a half hours over a four-week period. The goals of the smoking cessation program included teaching participants: (1) to become more aware of the reasons they smoke, (2) behavior modification techniques to assist them in smoking cessation, and (3) techniques to help maintain the non-smoking behavior.

Program participants in the smoking cessation program were quite diverse on the basis of age and number of cigarettes they had been smoking before entering the program (median of one pack per day). Sixty-two percent of the participants were female. One-third of the participants had ceased smoking. The survey was performed using follow-up data on the 70 persons who had completed the program at least six months earlier. A total of 33 responses were usable out of the 38 return responses. Information collected through the follow-up survey formed the basis for a simulation model to derive costs and benefits of similar programs.

Costs and benefits of a smoking cessation program were based on measures of:

- The savings to a firm in reduced costs of fire, life, health, and workman's compensation insurance
- The savings in excess absenteeism and disability to the firm due to cigarette smoking

Values for costs and benefits were determined by assessing reductions in insurance, absenteeism, and debility for representative participants, and through a simulation for males and females aged 25, 35, 45, and 55 years.

Insurance savings to a firm as a benefit from smoking cessation were calculated by first using estimates available in the literature for health care costs attributable to smoking. The estimates of $196 (in 1979 dollars) formed the basis of a projection of insurance saving benefits to the year 1990 in constant 1979 dollars. A linear regression model was then used to forecast the health component of the Consumer Price Index to derive at the deflated 1979 figure for health insurance savings as shown in Table 11–7.

The authors were presented with additional problems in the estimation of benefits due to savings in life, fire, and workman's compensation insurance. Their discussion of the problem and approach taken is described in the following:

> *Lack of usable data on the extra costs of life, fire, and workman's compensation insurance due to smoking allows the possibility of only crude estimates based on national averages. Kristein has estimated the costs as follows in 1979 dollars: fire insurance—$10; life insurance—$20–30; and workman's compensation—$40 (Kristein, 1980) (Weiss, Jurs, Lesage, and Iverson, 1985, p. 341).*

A sensitivity analysis was conducted using different discount rates, and present values of costs and benefits were calculated using 5 percent and 10 percent discount rates, as shown in Table 11–7.

Data on estimates of work life by age and sex were then introduced in the analysis to determine the net present value of insurance savings discounted at 5 percent and 10 percent, as shown in Table 11–8.

Savings in absenteeism costs were based on survey data from studies conducted in 1974 by the U.S. Department of Health, Education and Welfare (1979) and in 1970 by Wilson (1973) on work loss days for smokers and nonsmokers, and based on national average wage rates from the census data. The estimated benefits to a firm from reduced absenteeism associated with

TABLE 11–7 • Insurance Savings 1979–1990

Annual Discounted Savings:*
(1979 dollars)†

	Health Insurance		Total Insurance	
Year	i = 5%	i = 10%	i = 5%	i = 10%
1979	192	192	262	162
1980	182	174	249	238
1981	175	158	239	217
1982	168	144	229	196
1983	160	131	218	178
1984	154	119	209	162
1985	148	108	200	134
1986	141	98	191	122
1987	134	89	182	111
1988	129	81	174	101
1989	123	74	166	91
1990	118	67	159	83

Source: Weiss, J., Jurs, S., Lesage, J. P., and Iverson, D. C. (1985). A cost-benefit analysis of a smoking cessation program, *Evaluation and Program Planning*, 7, p. 341. Used by permission.
*Total insurance = health + fire + life + unemployment compensation insurance.
†The real increase in health care costs was projected with the following formula:

$$\frac{CPI^H}{CPI} = .875 + .016 \text{ time} - .002 \text{ (time trend)}^2$$
$$\quad\quad (.58) \quad (4.89) \quad (-1.41)$$

R^2 = .92, *t* values in parenthesis
CPI = Consumer Price Index.

smoking cessation is presented in Table 11–9. According to the authors, Table 11–9 allows the reader to analyze the sensitivity of the benefits to assumptions with respect to the age and sex of the target population, the rate of discount chosen, the survey used, and the number of cigarettes smoked.

> For example, based on the 1974 survey the present value of potential benefits for smoking cessation ranges from $45 for a 55-year old male to $2,090 for a 25-year-old male at a 5 percent discount and $37 to $1,377 for the same age and sex comparison at a 10 percent discount rate. A second example is the negative benefits or costs for males aged 45 and 55 who smoke 15 to 25 cigarettes per day (Weiss, Jurs, Lesage and Iverson, 1985, p. 342–343).

The authors attribute the strikingly smaller figures for women to their lower wages and the higher likelihood of leaving the work force.

TABLE 11–8 • *Simulated Insurance Saving by Age and Sex*

Category by Age and Sex	Work Life Expectancy	Health Insurance Discounted at		Total Insurance Discounted at	
		5%	10%	5%	10%
Male					
25	33	$3,072	$1,837	$4,193	$2,507
35	25	2,706	1,743	3,693	2,378
45	16	2,081	1,502	2,840	2,049
55	8	1,241	1,024	1,693	1,398
Female					
25	23	$2,590	$1,706	$3,534	$2,327
35	17	2,165	1,540	2,954	2,102
45	11	1,595	1,247	2,176	1,702
55	5	831	728	1,134	993

Source: Weiss, J., Jurs, S., Lesage, J. P., and Iverson, D. C. (1985). A cost-benefit analysis of a smoking cessation program, *Evaluation and Program Planning*, 7, p. 341. Used by permission.

Debility savings to the firm were based on estimates of extra cost of debility due to smoking as: (1) a measure of illness on the job attributable to smoking, and (2) a measure of the resulting productivity lost. The approach taken by the authors is described as follows.

> *As a lower bound proxy for on-the-job illness, we subtract work-loss days from five times restricted activity days [RADs] due to respiratory illness. Using Boden's [1976] estimate of 40 percent, we then attributed this portion of the extra debility days to smoking related illness [columns 1 to 5 in Table 11–10].*
>
> *Information on the loss of productivity due to debility is inadequate at best. Nevertheless, Mushkin [1979] has found a consistent pattern of 25 percent to 30 percent loss of productivity due to illness on the job in various studies ranging over time and place. We have applied 25 percent to our measure of on-the-job illness days to arrive at a measure of productivity loss due to smoking related debility shown in Table [11–10], column 6. The final step is to apply wage rates to arrive at a dollar magnitude.*
>
> *Calculations of debility savings by age and sex are shown in Table [11–8]. The discounted present value of the benefits to the firm of reduced debility for a worker who quits smoking ranges from $231 for a 55-year-old female at a 10 percent discount rate to $1,497 for a 35-year-old male at 5 percent (Weiss, Jurs, Lesage, and Iverson, 1985, p.343).*

The authors' concluding steps in the cost-benefit analysis were to produce a simulated estimate of opportunity costs and net present value of benefits for a hypothetical firm similar to the Toledo Hospital Smoking Cessation Clinic. The analyses are based on an assumption of a firm purchasing the smoking cessation program for twenty participants at $30 per participant or $600 total for the service. An additional added cost was computed on the basis of prevailing wages for loss to the firm of twelve hours off the job by

TABLE 11-9 • Benefits from Reduced Absenteeism* 1970 and 1974 Health Interview Surveys

Category by Age and Sex	1974 Survey: All Smokers Discount Rate		1970 Survey: All Smokers Discount Rate		Smoked 1-14 cigs Discount Rate		Smoked 15-25 cigs Discount Rate		Smoked 25+ cigs Discount Rate	
	5%	10%	5%	10%	5%	10%	5%	10%	5%	10%
Male										
25	$2,090	$1,377	$2,324	$1,559	$2,525	$1,295	$1,630	$1,179	$3,037	$1,784
35	1,547	1,226	2,143	1,452	2,946	1,723	903	878	2,886	1,914
45	84	61	1,291	938	3,163	2,297	-813	-591	1,948	1,414
55	45	37	724	598	1,771	1,462	-452	-373	1,092	902
Female										
25	$ 414	$ 215	$ 955	$ 894	$ 820	$ 542	$1,162	$ 761	$ 711	$ 453
35	366	256	818	579	621	482	1,002	707	726	485
45	290	227	612	492	448	350	787	1,094	812	635
55	147	128	316	277	225	197	394	345	411	360

Source: Weiss, J., Jurs, S., Lesage, J. P., and Iverson, D. C. (1985). A cost-benefit analysis of a smoking cessation program, *Evaluation and Program Planning*, 7, p. 342. Used by permission.

*In 1979 dollars.

TABLE 11–10 • *Productivity Loss Due to Smoking Related Debility*

Category (1)	RADs Due to Respiratory Illness (2)	Work Loss Days (3)	Debility Day Estimate 5 x (2) – (3) (4)	Debility Day Attributed to Smoking 40% of (4) (5)	Productivity Loss in Days 25% of (5) (6)
Male (age in years)					
17–44	2.9	1.3	13.2	5.3	1.3
45+	3.1	1.1	14.4	5.8	1.5
Female (age in years)					
17–44	4.3	1.8	19.7	7.9	2.0
45+	4.3	1.6	19.9	8.0	2.0

Source: Weiss, J., Jurs, S., Lesage, J. P., and Iverson, D. C. (1985). A cost-benefit analysis of a smoking cessation program, *Evaluation and Program Planning, 7*, p. 343. Used by permission.

each participant to attend the program. The total opportunity costs to a firm under the assumptions given are presented in Table 11–12.

Finally, the authors provide a simulation of total benefits to a firm purchasing the smoking cessation program. The simulation utilized the two sets of health survey data referred to above (the 1970 survey and the 1974 survey) and the same assumptions of twenty participants as in the determination of opportunity costs. The resulting calculations for present values of the program benefits appear in Table 11–13. In a discussion of these results,

TABLE 11–11 • *Benefits from Reduced Debility*

Category by Age and Sex	Loss in Days	Wage (dollars)	First Year Loss (dollars)	Discounted Present Value 5% (dollars)	10% (dollars)
Male					
25	1.3	$59.16	$ 76.91	$1,074	$883
35	1.3	77.68	100.98	1,497	952
45	1.5	76.54	114.81	1,215	883
55	1.5	70.21	105.32	679	560
Female					
25	2.0	$30.45	$ 60.90	$ 830	$545
35	2.0	30.82	61.64	697	499
45	2.0	31.54	63.08	542	437
55	2.0	30.48	60.96	264	231

Source: Weiss, J., Jurs, S., Lesage, J. P., and Iverson, D. C. (1985). A cost-benefit analysis of a smoking cessation program, *Evaluation and Program Planning, 7*, p. 344. Used by permission.

TABLE 11–12 • *Opportunity Cost of a Smoking Cessation Clinic*

Category by Age and Sex	Hourly Wage x 12 (dollars)	Direct Cost of Program (dollars)	Total Cost of Program (dollars)	Total Cost Program x 20 (dollars)
Male				
25	$ 88.74	$30	$118.74	$2,347.80
35	116.52	30	146.52	2,930.40
45	114.81	30	144.81	2,896.20
55	105.32	30	135.32	2,706.40
Female				
25	$ 45.68	$30	$ 75.68	$1,513.60
35	46.23	30	76.23	1,524.60
45	47.31	30	77.31	1,546.20
55	45.72	30	75.72	1,504.00

Source: Weiss, J., Jurs, S., Lesage, J. P., and Iverson, D. C. (1985). A cost-benefit analysis of a smoking cessation program, *Evaluation and Program Planning*, 7, p. 344. Used by permission.

the authors demonstrate the net present values of benefits with two extreme examples from their simulation. The two extremes represent the range from lower bound to upper bound in benefits over costs for the authors' data.

> *The lower bound is found by using the 1974 survey with a 10 percent discount rate, assuming that twenty women aged 55 years participated in the clinic and, using a conservative estimate of smoking cessation research, four quit smoking. With a 10 percent discount rate, the present value of the benefits of $5,408 minus costs of $3,904 equals a net present value of $2,702. Even if the benefits are cut in half, the program more than pays for itself. The upper bound is found by using males aged 25 at a 5 percent discount rate and the 1970 survey. The present value of the benefits equals four times $7,591, or $30,364, the costs equal $2,375, and the net present value of the program equals $27,989* (Weiss, Jurs, Lesage, and Iverson, 1985, pp. 344–345).

The example of cost-benefit analysis on a simulated smoking cessation program affords the reader an opportunity to observe the utilization of multiple sources of information on which to base calculations, assumptions which are required to perform the calculations, and sensitivity testing of the assumptions required.

Controversies in Cost-Effectiveness and Cost-Benefit Analysis

Cost-effectiveness and cost-benefit studies have been used most extensively in policy development stages to assist in decision making for selecting one program over others, or a set of program components or over others, and to

TABLE 11–13 • Simulation of the Present Value of Benefits by Age, Sex, and Survey for 1970 and 1974 Data

	Male (Age in Years)				Female (Age in Years)			
	25	35	45	55	25	35	45	55
1970 Survey **Discount Rate = 5%**								
Insurance	$4,193	$3,693	$2,840	$1,693	$3,534	$2,954	$2,176	$1,134
Absenteeism	2,324	2,143	1,291	724	955	818	612	316
Debility	1,074	1,497	1,215	679	830	697	542	264
Total Benefits	$7,591	$7,333	$5,346	$3,096	$5,319	$4,469	$3,485	$1,714
1970 Survey **Discount Rate = 10%**								
Insurance	$2,507	$2,378	$2,049	$1,398	$2,327	$2,102	$1,702	$ 993
Absenteeism	1,559	1,452	938	598	894	579	492	277
Debility	883	952	883	560	545	499	499	231
Total Benefits	$4,949	$4,782	$3,870	$2,556	$3,766	$3,180	$2,631	$1,501
1974 Survey **Discount Rate = 5%**								
Insurance	$4,193	$3,693	$2,640	$1,693	$3,534	$2,954	$2,176	$1,134
Absenteeism	2,090	1,547	84	45	414	366	290	147
Debility	1,074	1,497	1,215	679	830	697	542	264
Total Benefits	$7,357	$6,737	$4,139	$2,417	$4,778	$4,017	$3,008	$1,545
1974 Survey **Discount Rate = 10%**								
Insurance	$2,507	$2,378	$2,049	$1,398	$2,327	$2,102	$1,702	$ 993
Absenteeism	1,377	1,226	61	37	215	256	227	128
Debility	883	952	883	560	545	499	499	231
Total Benefits	$4,767	$4,556	$2,993	$1,995	$3,087	$2,857	$2,366	$1,352

Source: Weiss, J., Jurs, S., Lesage, J. P., and Iverson, D. C. (1985). A cost-benefit analysis of a smoking cessation program, *Evaluation and Program Planning*, 7, p. 345. Used by permission.

make budgetary choices. Application of these techniques during or after program implementation can serve to guide decision making in efforts to improve program effectiveness. However, as noted by Levin (1987), cost-effectiveness and cost-benefit studies have not yet been used extensively for program evaluation, even though they have a good potential for this purpose. Critics have raised concerns over a number of methodological issues with regard to such problems as securing adequate amounts of usable information, valuing unique assets such as human life, and the potential of manipulating outcomes to reflect predetermined agendas. It might also be said that the numeral technology involved often gives an impression of precision in measuring cost and program worth which is not yet possible. Indeed, the data included in analyses involve a good deal of what many may consider "guesstimates" rather than absolute measures of factors involved. And as we have observed in the examples presented above in this chapter, various measures of cost or benefit fluctuate considerably depending on differing survey data as input and rate of discount applied. These more or less technical and methodological limitations not withstanding, perhaps the greatest controversies surrounding cost-effectiveness and cost-benefit applications have been more philosophical and political in nature.

An overview of the more systematic attacks aimed at the underlying economic philosophy of cost-benefit analysis is discussed by Pearce and Nash (1981). From an economic viewpoint they address both the so-called liberal attack and the radical attack on the structure of cost-benefit analysis. Major points of their overview are as follows. The liberal school of thought (liberal in the traditional sense, but conservative by today's terminology) endorses the preservation of "negative freedoms"—the right not to be coerced into doing something against one's will. "The argument then proceeds that the underlying value judgments of cost-benefit analysis are at variance with this fundamental principle of liberalism. If liberalism is appealing, then cost-benefit analysis cannot be embraced; and vice versa" (Pearce and Nash, 1981, p. 12). The radical critique of cost-benefit analysis represents an attack on two fronts: (1) an opposition to cost-benefit analysis because the method is based on neoclassical welfare economics and (2) the belief that cost-benefit analysis ignores income distribution, or worse, that it assumes prevailing conditions as optimal. For further elaboration on these economic arguments, the reader is encouraged to follow-up on the reference herein cited.

Cost-effectiveness and cost-benefit studies have typically been undertaken with the specific purpose of studying policy alternatives to make political decisions. However, critics claim that because these methodologies are often at least indirectly put forward to replace the inefficiencies of political processes, critical societal principles such as equity, conflicting values, and personal choice are ignored. The argument follows that decision makers are encouraged to put too much weight on quantitative information, and, in fact, the technically-oriented analysts really become the decision makers. The counter argument is that rather than systems analysts placing valuations for costs and benefits, it should be carried out by the political decision makers themselves. The result would be to maintain the traditional process of political decision making, with systems analysts, with their tools of cost-effectiveness and cost-benefit analysis, serving in a consultant role.

The problem of dealing with externalities, or spillover effects, in cost-benefit analysis represents a special problem issue. Mishan (1988) likens the issue to the classic recipe for making horse and rabbit stew on a fifty-fifty basis, one horse to one rabbit. The rabbit represents the scientific calculus of costs and benefits in goal achievement, and the horse represents the externalities, or spillover effects. "No matter how carefully the scientific rabbit is chosen, the flavour of the resulting stew is sure to be swamped by the horseflesh" (Mishan, 1988, p. 154). The argument goes that in too few cases of cost-benefit analysis the matter of externalities has been given little more than a footnote. In social programming it is also often difficult to arrive at a consensus on the desirability/undesirability of these spillover effects. An example can be found in the case of experiments undertaken by the U.S. Office of Economic Opportunity (OEO) to test income-guarantee programs. One unexpected effect was an increased divorce rate for families participating in the experimental groups (Hannan and Groenvald, 1978). Does the increase in divorce represent an undesired effect, indicating that guaranteed-income programs cause family breakdown, or a desirable effect, indicating that an increase in financial security fosters decision choices to terminate dysfunctional marital relationships? Lacking complete understanding of externalities which result from social programs, and capabilities to calculate spillover effects, the evaluator is challenged to make clear the limits of study results obtained.

From a practical standpoint, the program evaluator should be aware of the controversies surrounding cost-effectiveness and cost-benefit analysis. Neither of these techniques for program evaluation rests on a cut-and-dried formula. Rather, they are tools for identifying and making explicit the assumptions and information by which to evaluate whether a given human service program has realized a standard of effectiveness and efficiency. To successfully carry out cost-effectiveness and cost-benefit studies, the role of program evaluator in the human services, the human services practitioner will do well to know when these techniques are useful in program evaluation, pitfalls and constraints in application, and how to interpret results to relevant decision makers.

Endnotes

1. Related terms which are sometimes used interchangeably in the literature are *cost-effectiveness, cost-benefit* (or *benefit-cost*), *cost-utility* and *cost-feasibility analysis.* For a discussion on the similarities and differences among these cost-analysis techniques, the reader is referred to Levin (1975; 1983).

2. Sensitivity analyses were carried out using different estimates for several variables (e.g., child care costs, outpatient treatment costs). The analyses revealed that the results were not substantially affected by these different estimates because the costs of the initial hospitalization so completely dominate the other costs (McCrady, Longabaugh, Fink, Stout, Beattie, and Ruggieri-Authelet, 1986, p. 709).

References

Anderson, L. G., & Settle, R. F. (1977). *Benefit-cost analysis: A practical guide.* Lexington, MA: Lexington Books.

Bowers, G. E., & Bowers, M. R. (1976). *The elusive unit of service* (OS–76–130). PROJECT SHARE, Washington, DC: U.S. Government Printing Office.

Gates, B. L. (1980). *Social program administration: The implementation of social policy.* Englewood Cliffs, NJ: Prentice-Hall.

Hannan, M. T., & Groenvald, L. (1978). *The Seattle-Denver income maintenance experiment, midexperiment results and a generalization to the national population.* Stanford, CA: Stanford Research and Mathematics Policy Research.

Klarman, H. E. (1974). Application of cost-benefit analysis to the health services and the special case of technologic innovation. *International Journal of Health Services, 4*, 325–352.

Knapp, M. (1991). Cost. *Administration in Social Work, 15*, 45–63.

Kristein, M. M. (1980). How much can business expect to earn from smoking cessation? Paper presented at Ohio Department of Health Conference on Smoking and the Workplace, Columbus, OH.

Landefeld, J. S., & Seskin, E. P. (1982). The economic value of life: Linking theory to practice. *American Journal of Public Health, 72*, 555–566.

Levin, H. M. (1975). Cost-effectiveness analysis in evaluation research. In M. Guttentag and E. L. Struening (Eds.), *Handbook of evaluation research* (pp. 89–122). Beverly Hills, CA: Sage.

Levin, H. M. (1983). *Cost-effectiveness: A primer.* Beverly Hills, CA: Sage.

Levin, H. M. (1987). Cost-benefit and cost-effectiveness analysis. In D. S. Cordray, H. S. Bloom and R. J. Light (Eds.), *Evaluation practice in review* (pp. 83–99). San Francisco, CA: Jossey-Bass.

McCrady, B., Longabaugh, R., Fink, E., Stout, R., Beattie, M., & Ruggieri-Authelet, A. (1986). Cost effectiveness of alcoholism treatment in partial hospital versus inpatient settings after brief inpatient treatment: 12-month outcomes. *Journal of Consulting and Clinical Psychology, 54*, 708–713. Copyright 1986 by the American Psychological Association, Inc.

McLeod, K., Dieter, F. A., Suver, J. D., & Zelman, W. N. (1984). Approaching cost reduction through responsibility centers. *Healthcare Financial Management, 39*, 20–25.

Mishan, E. J. (1988). *Cost-benefit analysis: An informal introduction.* Boston, MA: Unwin Hyman.

Mushkin, S. J. (1979). *Biomedical research: Costs and benefits.* Boston, MA: Ballinger.

Nagel, S. S. (1985). New varieties of sensitivity analysis. *Evaluation Review, 9*, 772–779.

Pearce, D. W., & Nash, C. A. (1981). *The social appraisal of projects: A text in cost-benefit analysis.* New York: John Wiley.

Rhoads, S. E. (Ed.). (1980). *Valuing life: Public policy dilemmas.* Boulder, CO: Westview.

Richardson, D. A. (1981). *Rate setting in the human services: A guide for administrators* (OS–76–130). PROJECT SHARE, Washington, DC: U.S. Government Printing Office.

Rothenberg, J. (1975). Cost-benefit analysis: A methodological exposition. In M. Guttentag and E. L. Struening (Eds.), *Handbook of evaluation research* (pp. 55–88). Beverly Hills, CA: Sage.

Saxe, L., Dougherty, D., Esty, K., & Fine, M. (1983). *The effectiveness and costs of alcoholism treatment* (OTA–HCS–22). Washington, DC: U.S. Government Printing Office.

Smith, V. K. (1986). A conceptual overview of the foundations of benefit-cost analysis. In J. D. Bentkover, V. T. Covello, and J. Mumpower (Eds.), *Benefits assessment: The state of the art* (pp. 13–34). Boston, MA: D. Reidel.

Sorensen, J. E., & Phipps, D. W. (1975). *Cost-finding and rate-setting for community mental health centers* ((ADM) 76–291). Washington, DC: U.S. Government Printing Office.

Stokey, E., & Zeckhauser, R. (1978). *A primer for policy analysis.* New York: W. W. Norton.

Sylvia, R. D., Meier, K. J., & Gunn, E. M. (1985). *Program evaluation for the public manager.* Monterey, CA: Brooks/Cole.

Thompson, M. S. (1980). *Benefit-cost analysis for program evaluation.* Beverly Hills, CA: Sage.

U.S. Department of Health, Education and Welfare. (1979). *Smoking and health: A report of the surgeon general* (DHHS Publication No. PHS 79–50066). Washington, DC: U.S. Government Printing Office.

Weiss, S. J., Jurs, S., Lesage, J. P., & Iverson, D. C. (1985). A cost-benefit analysis of a smoking cessation program. *Evaluation and Program Planning, 7,* 337–346.

Wilson, R. W. (1973). Cigarette smoking, disability days and respiratory conditioning. *Journal of Occupational Medicine, 15,* 236–239.

Zelman, W. N. (1987). Cost per unit of service. *Evaluation and Program Planning, 10,* 201–207.

Zelman, W. N., Stone, A. V. W., & Davenport, B. A. (1982). Factors contributing to artifactual differences in reported mental health costs. *Administration in Mental Health, 10,* 40–52.

CHAPTER TWELVE

A Critique of the Quantitative Approach to Program Evaluation

A Brief History of Evaluation from a Non-Quantitative Perspective

The idea of evaluation is not new. The emperor of China was using formal tests of efficiency as early as 2200 B.C. But evaluation as it is today can be said to be less than 100 years old (see Guba and Lincoln, 1983; Madaus, Scriven, and Stufflebeam, 1983). During that time, as reality, needs, and tools evolved, evaluation, too, evolved. In order to sense the breadth and scope of the current critique of the quantitative approach to program evaluation and to understand the basis of the various alternatives gaining currency today, it may be helpful to briefly review the history of the major schools of thought and the main concepts involved in evaluation work during the last century.

For evaluation, the time prior to the 1900s, as in much of social services, can be called the *Age of Reform*.[1] Evaluation (or at the time, measurement) efforts were focused on understanding differences observed in measures of human attributes. During that period, the United States was facing the beginnings of industrialization and, with it, the great social needs of immigrants. For the first time, methods of science were adopted in the study of social phenomena. With the development of achievement tests by such researchers as Joseph M. Rice and Alfred Binet in the very early 1900s, the Age of Reform was replaced by the *Age of Efficiency and Testing*. Hard measurement data was becoming legitimated in the fledgling social sciences such as social work, psychology, and education.

It was during this period that the goals of scientific management were brought from the business/industrial environment into social and educational bureaucracies such as social welfare agencies and local classrooms. Previously, the focus had been on explicating individual differences, with little acknowledgment of the relationship of evaluation to social or school programming. Now, with the time and motion studies and other experiments that guided industrial development, the classroom program, not just the individual student, became the major focus of evaluation activity aimed at school improvement.

This environment greatly shaped the *Tylerian Age* in evaluation, from approximately 1930 through 1945. Due to Ralph W. Tyler's influence, curriculum evaluation became the emphasis. It was Tyler who first asserted that curriculum needed to be established around defined objectives in order to serve as a program guide and as the basis of a systematic study of the educational program. Tyler was the first to separate the concepts of *measurement* and *evaluation*. Instead of simply viewing students in relation to test norms, evaluation expanded to become a mechanism of program improvement. The idea of explicating what a program was attempting to accomplish and using those objectives for curricular feedback and modification permeated evaluation and is still present today. As we will see, this expected link between evaluation and program objectives serves as a basis for some of the criticism leveled against an essentially a priori evaluation process.

Nonetheless, 1946 through 1957 saw Tyler's influence expand in the *Age of Innocence*. This was the time that, in retrospect, was filled with the innocent belief that the problems of shaping successful programs were solved. Locally based evaluation was combined with standardized testing. It was felt that the process and the product of a program could now be assessed and managed. A good deal of satisfaction and faith in the evaluation enterprise existed. Throughout this time, it was felt that social programs were being managed and improved through evaluation (see Back, 1956; Birdwhistell, 1952; Festinger and Katz, 1953; Jahoda, Deutsch and Cook, 1951a & 1951b; Merwin, 1969).

However, on October 4, 1957, when the U.S.S.R. launched the Sputnik space rocket, the shock in the U.S. quickly turned into calls for action that required that millions of federal dollars be poured into various social systems in order to improve our national and world status. All this investment of resources meant that the results should be evaluated (Rossi and Wright, 1986). It was an *Age of Expansion,* and, from approximately 1958 through 1972, evaluation and evaluators began to be perceived professionally and with great expectations. In addition, the first serious dissatisfactions with the evaluation process and product also began.

The Great Society programs of the mid-1960s were a part of this period, and, in their company, evaluation research came into prominence as an applied social scientific activity. The belief among policy makers and administrators was that evaluations could be conducted systematically using social scientific research methods and could produce results of more use and validity than previous approaches (Campbell and Stanley, 1966; Campbell, 1969). Conceptual work on evaluation research design and the development of large scale field experiments fueled high expectations for evaluation results.

But it was also during this time that managers began complaining that evaluation was not serving them well. Efforts had become so complex that evaluations could only be carried out by the technically sophisticated. Agencies were being forced to choose between hiring a practitioner to deliver the services for which they were being paid, or to hire an evaluator of the services for which they were being paid, because it was becoming clear to managers that one professional staff person could not do both. Further, real ethical and legal limitations prevented the development of the types of controlled experiments in evaluation that seemed to be the expected norm. And finally, the evaluations, as now prescribed, were too time- and resource-consuming to be tolerated in the policy and administration environments.

As we will see later, there were other substantive criticisms. These attitudes and experiences in combination with real constraints in U.S. economics and the later, Reagan inspired, massive reductions in funding of social programs have set the stage for the current *Age of Professionalization,* from about 1973 to the present (Rossi and Wright, 1986). Retrenchment, controversy, and the needs of basic survival have provided impetus for expanded communication and for an examination of the diversity in methodological and ideological perspectives. The boom in evaluation ended in about 1981 with the drastic reduction in the amount of federal money available for evaluation research. But conceptual work continues. Evaluation researchers continue to struggle with the limitations of field experiments and other efforts at controlled scientific inquiry in the evaluation of social programs.

Experience during expansion, and the reactions to controversies surrounding some of the large-scale experimental and quasi-experimental evaluation designs, have helped to shape the evaluation field as it exists today. Evaluation no longer has an expected model nor a singular body of procedures. One taxonomy which includes major proponents of each model gives just a glimpse of the variation. According to House (1983), evaluation includes the following major models: systems analysis (Rivlin); behavioral objectives (Tyler, Popham); decision making (Stufflebeam, Alkin); goal free (Scriven); art criticism (Eisner, Kelly); accreditation (professional associations); adversary (Owens, Levine, Wolf); and transaction (Stake, Smith, MacDonald, Parlett-Hamilton).

There can be objectives-based, question-oriented evaluations, accountability, experimental research, testing, or management information studies. Or one can encounter values-oriented approaches that involve accreditation/certification studies, policy studies, and decision-oriented, consumer-oriented, client-centered, or connoisseur-based studies (Stufflebeam and Webster, 1983). All this variation has emerged in an effort to respond to the many problems of both experimental and quasi-experimental approaches to evaluation research. And all this variation leads to ambiguity about evaluation itself—what is it, which is best, and what should standards for good evaluation be?

A critical reappraisal of the dominant experimental paradigm has also evolved. From this historical perspective, and with a view of diversity that may, admittedly, verge on what the reader may understand as polarization, we will now look more closely at several major aspects of this reappraisal of the traditional scientific methodological underpinnings of evaluation practice that have been presented in some of the earlier sections of this text.

The First Critique: The Quantitative Approach Hasn't "Worked"

Dissatisfaction with field experiments and other evaluations using quantitative research methods comes from many directions and takes many forms. With the large-scale expansion of evaluation research, it was discovered that it is extremely difficult to design programs that produce noticeable effects in any desired direction.[2] Some of this disappointment can be attributed to overly optimistic expectations on the part of program planners and framers, but recognition must also be given to the difficulty of implementing a program as planned. Problems and funding sources just do not respond as straightforwardly as needed for controlled evaluations. Thus, evaluation using only a priori objectives as the ultimate measure of program success often leads to minimal effects. Much sentiment supports a closer examination of this quantitative approach. Program administrators, practitioners, and even clients reject the notion of no definitive results. The estimation of net effects as the major effectiveness measure appears to overlook important aspects of the evolving nature of most programs.

Unfortunately, even when effects were found, there was suspicion that these effects were simply artifacts of evaluation design and method taken for true program effects. At times, the evaluation process, with all the monitoring tools necessary for evaluating results, was seen to impede effective practice. This concern was especially prevalent when the results were seen as not helpful because the results lacked relevance to the tasks at hand, or when results were presented using aggregate data that were insensitive to important program or client differences. For example, state-wide average results did not necessarily speak to local realities.

Particularly disturbing, especially when results were less than expected, were suggestions that evaluations limited analysis to indirect rather than direct measures of success, such as increased self-esteem being measured by length of time on a new job. What was important was not being measured directly due to a lack of ability to operationalize the phenomena or measure it once it had been operationalized. It was apparent that, inherent in using either experimental or quasi-experimental designs, is the difficulty of selecting satisfactory criteria for success. In addition to operationalization and measurement issues, much of the difficulty exists because the program situation is essentially uncontrolled. Agencies cannot control for natural or personal disasters that might befall clients before or during services. In addition, treatments, no matter how detailed, are not standardized, but change dependent upon the practitioner and the client system involved.

Another criticism was that experimental designs are limited in the information they can produce. Experimental designs tend not to look at details of treatment, at new conceptualizations, alternative models of evaluation, or evaluation goals. Instead they tend to look at the presence or absence of intended outcomes. In rare instances, examination of inputs, implementation, and delivery of services may occur but with little attention to unintended outcomes.

In short, negative findings and no-effect results have been disheartening. Evaluators, program administrators and others were frustrated by the difficulty in designing programs that produce noticeable effects in any desired direction, particularly when other non-quantitative information suggested program merit. Unfortunately, the overall practical yield of the quantitative approach has done little to improve social service theory or practice, particularly in the arena of personal social services.[3]

With this then, not surprisingly, is another common problem. When the quantitative approach does produce findings of effects, these findings are seldom used. Increased efforts to implement evaluation processes and to learn from evaluation results did not succeed in setting social problems right. In fact, it seems that quantitative rigor did not help much. This is largely because the lack of clarity of social innovations cannot be usefully dealt with by typical approaches to evaluation. Evaluation is a rational approach that may just tend to confuse administrators and policy makers dealing with essentially irrational problems and environments. No matter what prior evaluation results reveal, clarification of objectives that can logically lead to goals to be implemented by precise action on the part of practitioners in a particular setting with particular clients cannot be easily articulated and are even more difficult to measure. It is felt by many that the process and the product of quantitative evaluation are not suited to the imprecision of most social innovations, and, in fact, rational strategies often create more problems than they solve.

Much has been written about the underutilization of evaluation research results by policy makers (see Cronbach and Associates, 1980; Madaus, Scriven, and Stufflebeam, 1983; Rossi and Wright, 1986; Weiss, 1977). Evaluation and policy analysis have not had great impact on governmental decisions. It is no wonder, when evaluators rarely come out with strong recommendations and often report that a given service has no measurable effect on clients. Interpretation of evaluations based on statistical significance tend to mitigate against strong recommendations when the evaluator lacks strong evidence of results. When old and new programs are compared, small, if any, differences in outcomes rarely have the statistical clout to change program proponents into skeptics or visa versa. When all things are considered equally, major statistical differences in favor of innovation seem to be required to provide impetus for changing the status quo. The information has not been produced to aid in real-world decision making that might require major change.

From another perspective, evaluative information has seemed to lack political punch. An excellent study, no matter how well designed, that produces little by way of results just does not have the power to sweep political sentiment and power aside. Evaluation results have to be not just statistically significant, but very strong and nearly unambiguous to succeed politically, especially if they express conclusions about which the contemporary political scene is hostile or ambivalent. Lacking this, proponents will find reason to suspect negative results based on the measurement of wrong outcomes or inattention to important details, just as opponents will find reasons to suspect positive outcomes. Quantitative evaluation has not had the capacity to recognize and respond to conflict over program development.

Some would argue that evaluation will not become influential until studies are carried out properly. In other words, only when the quantitative craft has developed sufficiently to guard against alternative explanations of results will evaluations have more impact. This is really the argument of Part Three of this text. From that perspective, when evaluations can avoid the pitfalls of question definition, threats to validity, implementation, instrumentation, analysis, timing, and communication, then evaluations can be a basis for decision making. From this point of view, until then, the impact of evaluation will probably be less than substantial because the results do not tell decision makers what they need to know. As we will see in the next section, there is an even more radical and less hopeful position regarding quantitative evaluation.

At this stage it is sufficient to note that the myriad of complaints about quantitative evaluation tend also to be contradictory. One person complains that evaluations take too long to come up with findings; another complains that studies are conducted too hastily. One critic says that personal and institutional values intrude in the findings; another objects that evaluators concentrate on the facts to the exclusion of values. Is the problem with the evaluation sponsors who tie evaluators' hands so that appropriate judgment cannot be exercised? Or is the error in the failure of policy makers to define just what they want to know from the evaluation? The questions and recriminations continue . . . .

The Second Critique: The Quantitative Approach Can't Work Because its Premises are Wrong

We have shown that quantitative evaluation may be justly criticized by its lack of accomplishments, but some would say no degree of technical adjustments, no increase in training, no modification of expectations can improve it. At issue are the very intellectual roots of the traditional evaluation enterprise. Some critics, recognizing some of the specific criticisms discussed here, go beyond the instrumental to reject traditional scientific positivist assumptions underlying the dominant experimental approach. For them, the quantitative approach to evaluation cannot be expected to work because its basic premises are wrong.

This argument is really an argument about ways of knowing and about beliefs regarding reality. It could be said that this argument is of a paradigmatic type because, at issue, are the general organizing principles governing perceptions, such as beliefs, values, and techniques used to describe what exists, where to look, and what researchers can expect to discover (Ritzer, 1980). The debate involves epistemological questions, i.e., questions about how we know what we know; for example: Is reality external to the individual or is it the product of the individual's consciousness? These are questions about the ground on which knowledge can be obtained: is knowledge hard, real, capable of being transmitted in tangible form? Or is it softer, subjective, spiritual, of a unique and personal nature that can only be acquired or personally experienced? What about human nature? Do humans relate to the environment in a mechanistic, deterministic way? Or are humans creative, with free will creating their environment? (see, for example, Bloom, 1978; Fischer and Hudson, 1983; Haworth, 1984; Morgan, 1983; Reason and Rowan, 1981; Rosen, 1978; Schwartz and Ogilvy, 1979; Tripodi and Epstein, 1978).

At issue in this argument is whether laws of nature are absolute, clear, regular, final, or unchanging, or whether they are relative, changing with whatever paradigm is in use. Is the problem whether we are willing to measure a continually changing environment? Or is the problem whether laws of nature are related to or shaped by the activity of the scientist's looking? Do the questions shape the results and therefore the reality? The answers to these questions can tell us whether the quantitative approach can work, because the answers will settle whether the premises underpinning quantitative evaluation are right or wrong.

To better understand the basis of this second critique, it would be well to explore some assumptions underpinning the positivist perspective of traditional scientific inquiry and compare those with the assumptions of an alternative perspective, known as constructivism.[4] Each paradigmatic perspective has a different view of reality, of ways of knowing, of the goals of research, and of appropriate methodology. The two paradigms under discussion are contrasted in Table 12–1. The next section will detail the positions of both perspectives, underscoring their fundamental differences. These differences will be reviewed with an eye toward the development of an alternative approach to program evaluation based on the alternative constructivist perspective that will be covered in the next chapter. For its proponents, in contrast

TABLE 12-1 • Contrasting Conventional and Alternative Positions*

Assumptions About	Positivist Paradigm	Constructivist Paradigm
Ontology: the nature of reality	Single, tangible, fragmentable, convergent	Multiple, constructed, holistic, divergent
Purpose: generalization	Context and time-free generalizations; nomothetic statements focus on similarities	Context and time-bound working hypotheses; idiographic statements; focus on differences and similarities
Explanation: causality	Real causes, temporally precedent or simultaneous	Interactive mutual shaping
Objectivity: the inquirer-object relationship	Independent	Interrelated
Axiology: the role of values	Value-free	Value-bound

This table heavily borrows from a similar table in Lincoln, Y., & Guba, E. (1985) *Naturalistic Inquiry*. Beverly Hills, CA: Sage, p. 37. Reprinted by permission of Sage Publications, Inc.

to traditional quantitative evaluation, the alternative constructivist approach offers much by way of potential for meaningful, useful evaluation results.

Arguments Regarding the Nature of Reality

The positivist/quantitative position is that there is a single, tangible reality out there, independent of any observer and operating in a lawlike fashion. It is fragmentable into independent variables and processes, any of which can be studied independently of the others. From this position the goal of social inquiry is to find the regularities and relationships, converging on reality until, finally, it can be predicted and controlled. This is possible because, in principle, it is always possible to discover the causes of social phenomena. Every action can be explained as the result (effect) of a cause that precedes the effect temporally (or is simultaneous with it). In fact, the ultimate test of the success of a science (and of scientific evaluation) is the ability to predict and control using knowledge of those causes.

It is from this ability to predict and control scientifically determined regularities that the main purpose of scientific inquiry is derived. The aim of inquiry is to develop a lawlike body of knowledge. This knowledge can be encapsulated into lawlike generalizations. From this perspective, these generalizations are truth statements independent of both time and context. These truths will hold anywhere and at any time.

The alternative perspective has variously been called postpositivistic, ethnographic, phenomenological, subjective, qualitative, hermeneutic, humanistic, heuristic, naturalistic, or constructivist (Guba and Lincoln, 1989; Lincoln and Guba, 1985; Guba, 1990). Regardless of the paradigm title, basic to the position is a belief in the relative nature of reality: that there are multiple socially constructed realities that cannot be understood by recourse to a concept of law, universal or otherwise. These realities can be studied only holistically. The inquiry into multiple realities will inevitably raise more questions than it answers. Prediction and control are unlikely outcomes.

The goal, instead, is to understand the fundamental, emergent nature of the social world at the subjective, experiential level. The outcome of inquiry is understanding, or verstehen, a concept introduced by Dilthey (Rickman, 1976) and elaborated by Weber (1949). Verstehen, or placing oneself in the role of the actor under investigation, is seen as a means of relating inner experience to outward actions. Instead of dealing with the study of external processes in a material world, verstehen is concerned with interpretive understanding of the world of human affairs, the internal and intangible processes of human minds. The aim is to develop an idiographic, personalized, body of knowledge: the meaning given by people to their own situation.

This position rejects the assumption of the temporal and contextual independence of observations: that what is true at one time and place may, under appropriate circumstances, also be necessarily true at another time and place. From this perspective then, it would be impossible to establish control and standardization, because what is true for one person at one time will probably never be true for another person at another time, since reality is multiple and constructed. Evaluations, then, completed from the quantitative perspective cannot help but produce results lacking in relevance to at least some segment of the evaluation consumer group, because whatever is produced will not reflect the constructions of some stakeholders or consumers of the research product.

Further, from the constructivist perspective, causality, where it concerns human relationships, is so enmeshed in mutual and simultaneous interactions as to be unlikely to be discovered in any important or practical sense. Instead, an action may be explainable in terms of multiple interaction factors, events, and processes that shape it and are part of it. The idea of linear causality is rejected; cause and effect cannot be determined. The idea that there are no effects without causes and no causes without effects is put aside. Instead, at best, plausible inferences about the pattern of shaping in a given case may be possible. It is no wonder then that it would seem impossible to develop programs that produce effects in desired directions, because what might have been labeled a cause may really be an effect or a part of a hopelessly enmeshed interaction. Evaluations cannot be expected to deal with causes and effects, only with the webs of relationships related to the program under investigation.

In addition, inquiry is fundamentally bounded by the context of the investigation, thus generalizability is not a primary concern of inquiry. At most, a series of working hypotheses can be developed to describe the individual case. From this perspective, the differences that emerge are as inherently interesting as the similarities that, in another paradigm, might be hoped to lead to generalizations. This is why evaluation processes that count on aggregate data can be assumed to be insensitive to differences. This perspective explains why evaluations are likely to be criticized for producing findings that are not useful, i.e., quantitative data produced from the positivist perspective will not apply to the uniqueness of a given context.

Arguments Regarding the Nature of Research

As one might guess, different assumptions about the nature of reality and ways of knowing lead to different methodological assumptions and expectations for the research enterprise. If the researcher believes in the reality of universal scientific law, then the objectives of research are those we think of as traditionally scientific: i.e., to analyze relationships and regularities between various elements, to identify and define elements and how the relationships are expressed, etc. The methodological issues would concern operationalization of concepts, measurement, and identification of underlying themes (looking for laws). Research would be systematic regarding both protocol and technique. Hypothesis testing would proceed with scientific rigor.

In other words, the experimental field is to be controlled so as to eliminate contaminating influences. Controlling for alternative explanations allows the process to reveal the truth of the matter. Further, whatever exists does so in some measurable amount. All problems are empirical, measurable, quantifiable, operationalizable, simplifiable, and resolvable. It is the responsibility of the scientist to develop tools and protocols sufficiently calibrated to measure the phenomenon. If it cannot be measured there must be doubt about the phenomenon's existence for any scientific purpose.

If, on the other hand, the researcher believed in the relativistic nature of the world, then the focus of research would be on the subjective experience of the individual in the creation of the social world. The goal of inquiry would be understanding ways in which the individual uniquely creates, modifies, and interprets the world. The methodological emphasis would be on understanding the unique and particular in the individual rather than the general and universal. Research would have an individualistic, idiographic approach (no search for laws), looking for firsthand knowledge of the subject under investigation and analysis of subjective accounts, letting the subject unfold its nature and characteristics during the process of investigation. Intuition, tacit understanding, and holistic impressions would become practical sources of information. The effort would be more focused on capturing the fullness of the reality, rather than measuring parts of it.

The context toward which inquiry is directed is precisely what is important to understand. The context gives the important meaning to what is observed in detail. It is for this reason that understanding of the interactive mutual simultaneous nature of the relationship between the context and the phenomenon under study must be undertaken. This understanding must recognize the tacit nature of some realities and the importance of intuition in capturing the holistic fullness of a phenomenon.

Polanyi (1966) has drawn the distinction between propositional knowledge that can be stated in language form, and tacit knowledge (intuitions, feelings) that cannot be stated in words but is somehow known to the subject. Scientific knowledge limits itself exclusively to propositional knowledge. The alternative paradigm permits or encourages connotative or tacit knowledge that will lead to the description and understanding of phenomena as wholes or in ways that reflect their complexity. Measurability is not at issue; understanding is. In fact, according to Guba (1987, p. 35), "Constructions exist only in the minds of constructors and cannot be divided into measurable entities; if it can be measured it is probably trivial."

Different perspectives about the nature of reality and the nature of the research enterprise also lead to different assumptions concerning the relationship between the researcher and the phenomena under study. From the positivist perspective, there is a subject-object dualism. The observer and the observed are distinct and independent. There is a certain "twoness" or "separateness" that characterizes the investigator-investigated relationship.

The inquirer is thus able to maintain a discrete distance from the object of inquiry. In doing so, he or she neither disturbs nor is disturbed by it. It is as if the objective independent scientist can stand on his or her own scientific platform while orchestrating the world and arranging, through methodology, that the data should sing for themselves without essential change to either the orchestrator or the music. The observer observes, never disturbs. Thus, an observer is able to know a reality independent of the effect of the observation process. Maintaining a discrete distance between investigator and object is sufficient to guarantee objectivity because of the discrete dualism between the inquirer and the object of inquiry.

The alternative perspective rejects the assumption about the possibility of the separation of the observer from the observed, the knower from the known. He or she believes instead that the inquirer and the object of inquiry interact to influence one another. The scientific paradigm assumes that the inquirer will have no effect on the phenomenon being studied and that the phenomenon will have no effect on the inquirer. It is believed that, given reasonable precautions such as adequate controls against the reactivity of the subject to the inquirer, it is possible for the inquirer to keep a suitable distance removed from the phenomenon. Conversely, the alternative paradigm assumes that all phenomena are characterized by interactivity.

Therefore, efforts to control or reduce reactivity, indeterminacy, or interaction reduce the wholeness of the inquiry process. From this position it is fruitless to pretend that interactivity is not there. The observer and the observed interact so that the research process must take that into account, making explicit the perceptions of the investigator and the effect of those perceptions on the developing information. The uniqueness of this in every research encounter means that the observations are unique to that observational encounter and conclusions are then precisely the creation of the process of observation. In fact, the inquirer and the phenomenon are so interlocked that the findings of any investigation are really the creation of the inquiry process.

One final, and perhaps most important, distinguishing premise between the conventional posture and its alternative concerns beliefs about the relationship between facts and values. It is most important because it serves to shape the expectation of knowledge building. The positivist or conventional paradigm asserts that inquiry is value-free. It can be maintained as such by virtue of the methodology employed because appropriate scientific methods are designed to isolate and remove all subjective elements from the inquiry process. From this perspective values can be separated from facts in the research process where methods screen out values to allow a focus on true facts. Social science is value neutral, and its conclusions are objective in the sense of being value-free. This objectivity aids in the discovery of truth. For the truth of a fact can be determined by empirical testing. Facts speak for themselves. Objective truth arrived at through empirical testing creates the only range of scientifically admissible knowledge.

The alternative paradigm takes the position that, far from being value-free, inquiry is affected by values of all kinds. Indeed, descriptions of reality are never value-free. Inquiry is value bound in at least five ways. The personal values of the inquirer shape the choice of the problem for study. Values not only guide the framing, bounding, and focusing of the problem, but influence the methods of data collection and analysis to be employed and the analysis and interpretations to be made from the findings. Recognition and articulation of the influence of personal values provides the consumer of the research a perspective from which to judge the research product which is more honest and probably more useful than the practice of hiding predispositions from the reader, as in "objective" work.

Value influences the choice of the substantive theory that guides the investigation into the problem. The theory is the lens through which the researcher observes and understands the phenomena under study. Facts are read differently, and interpretations provided based on how those facts meld with the researcher's theory.

Just as value undergirds the theory, so too does it undergird the inquiry paradigm that guides the investigation into the problem. Acceptance of the very assumptions under consideration here in dealing with the nature of reality, the interaction of observer and observed, the phenomenon of mutual shaping, and the impact of value means a shifting from the traditional stance vis-à-vis investigation into any problem. This shift means the expectations related to the research process and research product would shift depending upon which paradigm is preferred.

The general cultural values of the context within which the inquiry is undertaken also shape the inquiry. The social and cultural norms influence what is seen and heard and how it is interpreted. Overidentification (such as "going native") or underidentification (such as remaining "at a distance") with the contextual values will lead to errors in understanding and errors in the description of reality. Lack of attention to these possibilities can result in the generation of findings contrary to the needs of science and destructive to research participants.

Finally, from the constructivist position, an inquiry is either value-resonant or value-dissonant. The problem, the substantive theory, the inquiry paradigm, and the context must have value resonance if the inquiry is to have meaningful results. To the extent that all values are consistent and reinforcing, the inquiry can proceed meaningfully and will produce findings and interpretations that are agreeable from all perspectives. Inquiry is value-bounded and should be related to as such in the constructivist paradigm. The process of knowledge building should focus on exposing and explicating values. It is necessary to recognize that what counts as a description of reality is not objective facts, but is based on values and interests. Truth and objectivity, from this perspective, are not only a social construction, but are matters of social agreement.

Conclusions

The test of a paradigm is its utility in the arena in which one wishes to apply it. Based on the criticisms leveled in this chapter regarding the traditional paradigm for evaluation practices, it is evident that the utility of evaluation as it is currently conceived is in question, and, therefore, so is the utility of the assumptions underlying evaluation practices. Various efforts have been undertaken to enhance effectiveness and utility. Instead of utilization-focused quantitative evaluation, Patton (1980) offers utilization-focused qualitative data for evaluation research. Dorr-Bremme (1985) suggests ethnographic evaluation. Chen and Rossi (1980) link basic and applied social science through a multi-goal theory-driven approach to evaluation. Subjective and objective methods of evaluating social programs and their trade-offs have been pursued (Alemi, 1988), and attempts have been made to reconcile qualitative and quantitative analyses (Trend, 1978). But these efforts, such as combining qualitative with quantitative evaluation methods, looking at evaluation beyond program impact, and other such twists, are doomed to confusion unless we continue to look at the paradigmatic level. It is not necessarily with the methods, qualitative or quantitative, that evaluation research experiences its difficulties. Those from the constructivist perspective would suggest that the problem is deeper. The problem is not whether to use quantitative or qualitative methods in evaluation. The problem is what should evaluation research be expected to produce. This is a difference at the paradigm level.

It has been frequently argued that the difference between the conventional paradigm and the constructivist paradigm is more apparent than real and that a compromise position should be devised that takes advantage of their complementarity. But, as this discussion reveals, the assumptions of the conventional posture are fundamentally at odds with those of the alternative paradigm. One may be able to combine both quantitative and qualitative methods in one evaluation process, but how does one assume both singular and multiple realities at the same time? How can one believe in the separation between the investigator and the object of inquiry while also allowing for their mutual interaction? How can one work toward both an idiographic and nomothetic body of knowledge? From this vantage point, no manner of accommodation and shifting will eliminate the difficulty as described.

Unfortunately, at this stage in the evolution of the philosophy of science, it is also not possible to prove the superiority of one paradigm's beliefs over another. Now, the issue becomes deciding how well the assumptions of each approach fit the phenomena being investigated. Some would argue that another important decision criteria would be dependent upon the stage of the inquiry, i.e., the constructivist/qualitative perspective has no peer in the early stages of exploration, description, or discovery in inquiry, where the researcher/evaluator does not even know the names of the variables, but is not useful for real "scientific" evaluation. To allow the reader to determine more easily which model of evaluation is most appropriate, the next chapter will provide a thorough view of the constructivist evaluation methods that are generated by the alternative paradigm. It will then be for the reader to decide if constructivism and the inquiry processes that derive from it are more in keeping with the goals of evaluation research. Constructivist inquiry's utility in evaluation practice will then be the true test.

Endnotes

1. We are grateful to Madaus, G. F., Scriven, M. S., and Stufflebeam, D. L., for the category titles utilized in this section. Their discussion can be found in (1983) *Evaluation models*. Boston, MA: Kluwer-Nijhoff Publishing, p. 4.

2. There are a few major exceptions to this. The Westinghouse studies of Headstart, the National Guaranteed Annual Income studies, and the Medicaid-waiver studies were large scale programs with immense, long-term commitment to evaluation. Though not without problems in implementation, monitoring, evaluation, and interpretation, it must be noted that each program has shown positive effects upon evaluation.

3. Due, in part, to the findings mentioned above, there are some exceptions for social programs delivering other kinds of benefits, such as income-transfers and the like.

4. Until the publication of *Fourth generation evaluation* (Guba and Lincoln, 1989), this alternative perspective was known as *naturalism*. The change in terminology was made to more accurately reflect the interpretive nature of the perspective and to avoid confusion with traditional inquiry done in the natural (non-laboratory) setting.

References

Alemi, F. (1987). Subjective and objective methods of evaluating social programs. *Evaluation Review, 11*(6), 765–774.

Back, K. W. (1956). The well-informed informant. *Human Organization, 14*(4), 30–33.

Birdwhistle, R. L. (1952). Body motions research and interviewing. *Human Organization, 11*, 37.

Bloom, M. (1978). Challenges to the helping profession and the response of scientific practice. *Social Service Review, 25*, 584–495.

Campbell, D. T. (1969). Reforms as experiments. *American Psychologist, 24*, 409–429.

Campbell, D. T., & Stanley, J. C. (1966). *Experimental and quasi-experimental designs for research*. Chicago: Rand McNally.

Chen, H., & Rossi, P. H. (1980). The multi-goal, theory-driven approach to evaluation: A model linking basic and applied social science. *Social Forces, 59*, 106–122.

Cronbach, L. J., Ambron, S. R., Dornbusch, S. M., Hess, R. D., Hornik, R. C., Phillips, D. C., Walker, D. F., & Weiner, S. S. (1980). *Toward reform of program evaluation: Aims, methods, and institutional arrangements*. San Francisco: Jossey Bass.

Dorr-Bremme, D. W. (1985). Ethnographic evaluation: A theory and method. *Educational Evaluation and Policy Analysis, 7*(1), 65–83.

Festinger, E., & Katz, D. (1953). *Research methods in the behavioral sciences*. New York: Dryden Press.

Fischer, J., & Hudson, W. (1983). Measurement of client problems for improved practice. In A. Rosenblatt and D. Waldfoger (Eds.), *Handbook of clinical social work* (pp. 673–693). San Francisco, CA: Jossey-Bass.

Guba, E. G. (1987). Naturalistic evaluation. *New Directions for Program Evaluation, 34*, 23–43.

Guba, E. G. (ed.). (1990). *The paradigm dialogue*. Newbury Park, CA: Sage.

Guba, E. G., & Lincoln, Y. S. (1983). *Effective evaluation*. (Third printing). San Francisco: Jossey-Bass.

Guba, E. G., & Lincoln, Y. S. (1989). *Fourth generation evaluation*. Newbury Park, CA: Sage.

Haworth, G. O. (1984, September). Social work research, practice, and paradigms. *Social Service Review*, 343–357.

House, E. R. (1983). Assumptions underlying evaluation models. In C. F. Madaus, M. S. Scriven, & D. L. Stufflebeam (Eds.). *Evaluation models: Viewpoints on educational and human services evaluation*. Boston, MA: Kluwer-Nijhoff Publishing.

Jahoda, M., Deutsch, M., & Cood, S. W. (1951a). *Research methods in social relations. Volume 1: Basic processes.* New York: Dryden Press.

Jahoda, M., Deutsch, M., & Cood, S. W. (1951b). *Research methods in social relations. Volume 2: Selected Techniques.* New York: Dryden Press.

Lincoln, Y. S., & Guba, E. G. (1985). *Naturalistic inquiry.* Beverly Hills: Sage.

Madaus, G. F., Scriven, M.S., & Stufflebeam, D. L. (Eds.). (1983). *Evaluation models: Viewpoints on educational and human services evaluation.* Boston, MA: Kluwer-Nijhoff Publishing.

Merwin, J. C. (1969). Historical review of changing concepts of evaluation. In R. W. Tyler (Ed.) *Educational evaluation: New roles, new means.* Chicago: University of Chicago Press.

Morgan, G. (Ed.). (1983). *Beyond method: Strategies for social research.* Beverly Hills, CA: Sage.

Patton, M. Q. (1980). *Qualitative evaluation methods.* Beverly Hills, CA: Sage.

Polanyi, M. (1966). *The tacit dimension.* Garden City, NY: Doubleday.

Reason, P., & Rowan, J. (Eds.). (1981). *Human inquiry: A sourcebook of new paradigm research.* New York: John Wiley.

Rickman, H. P. (Ed. and Trans.). (1976). *W. Dilthey selected writings.* Cambridge: Cambridge University Press.

Ritzer, G. (1980). *Sociology: A multiple paradigm science* (rev. ed.). Boston, MA: Allyn and Bacon.

Rosen, A. (1978). Issues in educating for the knowledge-building research doctorate. *Social Service Review, 52,* 437–448.

Rossi, P. H., & Wright, J. D. (1986). Evaluation Research: An Assessment. *Evaluation Studies Review Annual, 11,* 48–69.

Schwartz, P., & Ogilvy, J. (1979). *The emergent paradigm: Changing patterns of thought and belief.* Analytical Report 7, Values and Lifestyles Program. Menlo Park, CA: SRI International.

Stufflebeam, D. L., & Webster, W. J. (1983). An analysis of alternative approaches to evaluation. In C. F. Madaus, M. S.Scriven, & D. L. Stufflebeam (Eds.), *Evaluation models: Viewpoints on educational and human services evaluation.* Boston, MA: Kluwer-Nijhoff Publishing.

Trend, M. G. (1978). On the reconciliation of qualitative and quantitative analyses: A case study. *Human Organization, 37*(4), 345–256.

Tripodi, T., & Epstein, I. (1978). Incorporating knowledge of research methodology into social work practice. *Journal of Social Service Research, 2,* 65–78.

Weber, M. (1949). *The methodology of the social sciences.* Glencoe, IL: Free Press.

Weiss, C. H. (Ed.). (1977). *Using social research in public policy making.* Lexington, MA: Lexington Books.

CHAPTER THIRTEEN

Qualitative Research Methods and the Constructivist Paradigm in the Evaluation of Social Programs and Policies

Introduction

Constructivist (formerly naturalistic) evaluation is an intensely personal, introspective experience that provides a fit between the science and the art of inquiry, while allowing for divergent values and personal styles. This by no means is meant to suggest that the process is not without unique challenges. Most constructivist evaluators will agree with Berreth's (1986) discoveries: Naturalistic (constructivist) evaluation is an intellectual process of convergence punctuated by periods of divergence. Along with this ebb and flow, there is a constant, rhythmic loss of focus, so that the process is permeated with feelings of uncertainty, and loss of an internal standard by which to judge the work. Because the process is ever emerging, there is a consistent lack of clarity. At the same time the evaluator can be overwhelmed and frustrated by the wealth of information. Often there is a need for distance from the enveloping experience for sense-making, sometimes resulting in expanded time frames for the evaluation process.

The evaluation process and product should be found to be full, live entities that continue to grow at every stage of the inquiry, including the final member check (discussed in detail later) and revision. Every stage allows for new insight and meaning, hopefully moving to more profound sophistication about the phenomena under study. The process and product provide a tangible means of regarding the web of relationships involved not only in the evaluation process but also in any social program response. It should be fascinating.

The methodology, by its very nature, seems to prevent escape into pure research because it practically and theoretically eliminates the distinction between a phenomenon and the context within which it is found. The methodology forces attention to the issues of the implication of that which is being understood on the parts of evaluator and participants. This means that the results of the process will probably always have not only evaluative but also policy implications for both the evaluator and the evaluation participants.

It would be naive to overlook the socio-political implications of constructivist evaluation. The participants are real people, not a data set. The findings have real contextual meaning and therefore real political consequences. Constructivist evaluation redistributes power in the evaluation process. The participants own their own data and they know it. This creates a more active and reactive interchange during the data gathering and interpretation phases. This kind of research is never finished because the consequences of the evaluation process itself continue to reverberate. The methodology produces change. It is developmental and educational for all involved. It is also enjoyable.

Before moving to a more detailed accounting of the philosophical and methodological issues that make this type of evaluation possible, let us first return to the question of some type of compromise between the positivist and the constructivist paradigms. Many have suggested that the answer to some of the thorny problems in evaluation research can be achieved by taking advantage somehow of the merits of both the positivist and the constructivist perspective. Though the compromise idea seems innately attractive, it represents much more complexity than appears at the surface. Gareth Morgan (1983) in *Beyond Method* nicely outlines five possible approaches toward this type of accommodation. The reader will note that each is not without major difficulties:

Supremacy

This approach seeks to establish one of the approaches as "best." Morgan finds, as we have, that this approach is impossible in principle. Our argument came from a values/beliefs perspective. Morgan, on the other hand, attacks the logic involved: No criteria for determination of the best can be identified that are not already a part of one of the assumptions of the paradigmatic position and, therefore, must be part of the argument in favor of the particular paradigmatic approach, not part of the analysis of which paradigm is best.

Synthesis

In attempting to combine the strengths and minimize the weaknesses of the paradigms, this approach would attempt to be eclectic. Morgan suggests that "attempts to find an all-embracing paradigm or metaphor for framing inquiry, to translate different strategies into common language, or to find ways of overcoming traditional dichotomies, provide good examples of such integrative effort" (p. 378). Cook and Reichardt (1979) would seem to agree with this position, asserting that accepting only one or the other paradigm means accepting non-comprehensive evaluation because neither position alone is sufficient for all the diverse requirements of evaluation research. But others have rejected the idea of synthesis as not only reductionistic but impossible to achieve (Hofstadter, 1979). For example, in his unique work, *Godel, Escher, Bach: An eternal golden braid*, to avoid the reductionist problem, Hofstadter found it necessary to present new concepts twice, once metaphorically to serve as an intuitive background for a more "serious and abstract presentation" (p. 28) of the same concept in order to present a full and understandable accounting of his ideas.

Contingency

This approach suggests, as we have in the prior chapter, that the inquirer must examine the contingencies, such as the people and material resources, logistics, etc., in the context and with the phenomena under study and select that paradigm which provides the best fit to those contingencies. Guba and Lincoln (1989) and others, however, would suggest that the constructivist paradigm can be the only paradigm of choice when human inquiry, such as evaluation research, is undertaken. This is because it is the only approach that can look at the relative interactive holistic nature of the human condition without reducing it or removing uniqueness and multiple perspectives.

Dialectic

This approach "attempts to use the difference among competing perspectives as a means of constructing new modes of understanding" (Morgan, 1983, p. 379). This volume may indeed represent just such a struggle. This is certainly what Schon (1984) alludes to in his discussion of the crisis of professional knowledge and "reflection-in-action" as an important step in the pursuit of an epistemology of practice. It may also be at the core of Guba and Lincoln's (1986; 1989) "fourth-generation" evaluation that focuses on value pluralism and negotiated outcomes.

Anything Goes

Morgan calls this *radical epistemology* and cites Feyerabend in saying that "there is no idea, however ancient or absurd, that is not capable of improving our knowledge. Approaches to research that are complementary, contradictory, or proceed counterintuitively are all acceptable because they may generate some form of insight and understanding that cannot be achieved in any other way" (p. 380). This position clearly allows for proponents and opponents of every position, including the new, never-before imagined. Unfortunately, it may also allow for the new to be overlooked and disregarded, leaving the old and the outmoded free from criticism because anything goes. More acceptance might lead to less critical analysis.

It is our position that a volume such as this cannot be expected to put the discussion to rest, nor are we actually advocating any one of Morgan's positions, because much more thought and dialogue is necessary (Guba, 1990). This era of reconceptualization, one that looks at alternatives to the classic social science paradigm, may be just beginning. Our best hope at this stage is that we are able to clearly offer the reader several dimensions from which to judge conceptions of evaluation.

We can also attempt to lend more clarity to two important segments of the positivist/constructivist question. First, the quantitative/qualitative or positivist/constructivist argument is fraught with confusion between paradigm and method (see Cronbach and Associates, 1980; Cook and Reichardt, 1979; Miles and Huberman, 1984; Smith, 1986). Terms are used interchangeably. From some perspectives, the choice of quantitative or qualitative evaluation practices indicates a choice between a quantitative or qualitative view of the world. Others who choose between quantitative and qualitative practices do so within a positivist frame of reference with all that it assumes, while for others, the choice of quantitative or qualitative methods indicates a choice between a positivist or constructivist paradigm.

To get beyond this terminology problem, recall that a paradigm represents the general organizing principles governing perceptions, and, according to Ritzer (1980), this includes beliefs, values, and techniques that describe what exists, where to look, and what the scientist can expect to discover. A paradigm, then, defines fundamentally different perspectives for the analysis of social phenomena, generating different concepts and analytical tools, but not necessarily demanding a choice of quantitative over qualitative methods or data. The paradigms reviewed in the last chapter are mutually exclusive, defining alternative views of the social world based on different meta-theoretical assumptions regarding the nature of science and of society. But it must be clear that both quantitative and qualitative techniques can be used with either paradigm.

Data can be gathered and manipulated from either frame of reference. The data can be numbers or words from either frame of reference. The difference is whether the expectation of the research/evaluation process is to provide essentially rational explanations of social affairs (the positivist position) or to understand the fundamental nature of the social world at the level of intersubjectively shared meaning of experience (the constructivist). Quantitative methods, which through research design controls, attempt prediction and control for generalizability, fit more comfortably with the positivist position focusing on prediction and control. The at-a-distance quantitative methods that remove the observer from the observed will more likely meet standards of objectivity that are required for generalizability. Qualitative methods that use the observer as the research instrument and focus on the process to gain understanding of a naturally occurring phenomenon represent a better match for the constructivist position. Clearly, qualitative methods that tend to mitigate against objectivity are much more likely to be viewed as successful in adhering to standards of rigor that do not require objectivity. However, either qualitative or quantitative methods of data collection and analysis can be useful in either paradigm (probably with the exception of quantitative methods using causally inferential statistics in the constructivist framework), as long as the expectations for the research process and product based on the paradigmatic perspective guide the use of the method.

The second area of confusion is related to the concept of constructivist né naturalistic evaluation. There seems to be no agreement about what naturalistic evaluation really is. Aside from the confusion that comes from positivistic research undertaken in a natural setting, Guba (1987) has shown that two forms of naturalistic evaluation have appeared in the literature within the past decade. One form treats naturalistic evaluation as a collection of qualitative techniques that are complementary with conventional quantitative methods. From this position, it is interchangeable with qualitative evaluation that, indeed, is a variation of ethnographic evaluation: a collection of tools and techniques at the methods level. These techniques have been used for the purposes of exploration, description, illustration, realization, and testing, but within the confines and expectations of the conventional, scientific paradigm.

The other, less utilized form of naturalistic evaluation (now called constructionist) is the one we shall pursue more directly in this chapter. This form emphasizes naturalistic evaluation as an alternative paradigm, a wholly different way of viewing the world, so that "thinking naturalistically" (Biklen and Bogdan, 1986) is an alternative way of thinking about reality, research, and evaluation. According to Guba (1987) this approach to naturalism and to constructivism (Guba, 1990) represents an alternative view of evaluation, one emphasizing negotiation of results that present multiple constructions of reality, the interdependence of facts, beliefs, and values, and the emergent nature of the evaluation process.

In what follows we will discuss various important qualitative methods that were selected based on their ability to support naturalistic thinking. Emphasis will be on those methods that enhance negotiation of multiple socially-constructed realities, have the capacity to recognize, articulate, and interpret the interdependence of facts and values, and are supportive of the view of the emergent character of the evaluation process. Of course, some of these methods can be found both in the conventional posture of evaluation and in constructivist research, while other methods are derived from the constructivist posture solely. The effort in the following sections will be to provide a broad view of this different paradigmatic approach, since our purpose is to help the reader determine if it has utility for evaluation and evaluators.

Evaluation Research Implications Based on a Paradigm Choice

The constructivist evaluation focuses on "the methods and techniques of observing, documenting, and interpreting attributes, patterns, characteristics, and meanings of specific contextual or gestaltic features under study" (Leninger, 1985, p. 5). It is an evaluation methodology that can address multiple perceptions—multiple realities of the social context (Guba and Lincoln, 1984). The goal of constructivist evaluation is to observe, document, interpret, and analyze as fully as possible the multiple realities of the problem in particular social contexts from the participant's point of view or frame of reference.

This includes the identification, study, and analysis of subjective and objective data in order to know and understand the internal and external world of the participants (Guba and Lincoln, 1983). Verbatim statements, thoughts, and action or non-action patterns are studied critically to discover patterns and themes within particular life settings (Spradley, 1979). At no time does the constructivist evaluator control or manipulate participants; for, natural events within their contexts are the point of the inquiry (Lincoln and Guba, 1985; Reinharz, 1979; Stern, 1985). Removing experiences and ideas from situations, interactions, or environmental sources is avoided (Mishler, 1978). The social context containing cultural, physical, social, and historical elements provides the data for documentation, interpretation, and analysis (Leninger, 1985).

Doing evaluation activities within the constructivist paradigm requires the inquirer to be open to the environment and to be subject to and shaped by it. Evaluation research, then, is interactive in that the direction of inquiry is shaped through involvement with the participants. Both propositional knowledge (stated and expressed in language form) and tacit knowledge (not voiced or expressed) are recognized and utilized in the inquiry process and product.

But notice that, different from other evaluation processes, changes, adjustments, and refinements in the focus of the inquiry and the cognitive and affective growth of the investigator are valued, expected, recorded, and reported (Lincoln and Guba, 1985; Reinharz, 1979; VanMaanen, Dabbs and Faulkner, 1982).

Methodologic Consequences of the Constructivist Paradigm

There are fourteen logical methodologic derivations of the constructivist position (Guba and Lincoln, 1983; Lincoln and Guba, 1986; Skrtic, 1985) that have direct impact on the process of doing a constructivist evaluation. This section will define each and develop practice principles of interest to the program evaluator. Subsequent sections will address the distinctive features of constructivist evaluations and suggest ways of assuring that these methodologic consequences are thoroughly addressed in the evaluation process. Figure 13–1 graphically illustrates how these methodologic consequences establish the flow of a constructivist inquiry.

Natural Setting   Field Study

Evaluation must occur in the context of the program to be evaluated. Unlike evaluation framed from the positivist perspective, it is never acceptable to utilize a laboratory removed from the location of the phenomena of interest. Inquiry must proceed in the organizational or community environment because reality cannot be understood in isolation from its context, nor separated into fragments or parts. Instead, attention should be given to the factors that shape the environment, the patterns of influence that are accepted and rejected, and the values that are chosen, and for what reasons. All this is considered to shape actors and events into specific configurations. The evaluator must be in constant interaction with the setting and its inhabitants in order to understand them and to present reasonable reconstructions of their realities. It is those reconstructions that are the results of the research process.

Attention to the natural setting consequence would mean that a constructivist evaluation of a particular program in a local social service agency would require the evaluator not only to attend to, but to be knowledgeable about the program, its components, goals, objectives, and the like. Likewise, the larger agency context within which the program operates, not only at the local, but at the state and, perhaps, the federal level, must be understood and considered. Meaning derived from context would also require that knowledge be developed about the community within which the program is operating.

FIGURE 13–1 • *The Flow of the Program Evaluation Process Under the Assumptions of Naturalistics Inquiry**

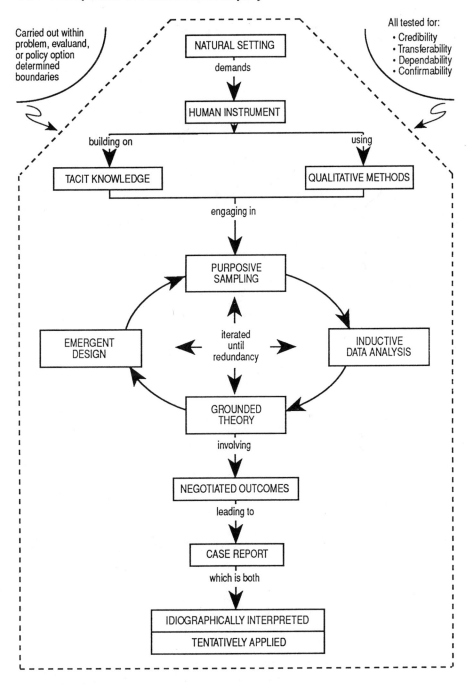

Carried out within problem, evaluand, or policy option determined boundaries

All tested for:
• Credibility
• Transferability
• Dependability
• Confirmability

NATURAL SETTING

demands

HUMAN INSTRUMENT

building on

using

TACIT KNOWLEDGE

QUALITATIVE METHODS

engaging in

PURPOSIVE SAMPLING

EMERGENT DESIGN

iterated until redundancy

INDUCTIVE DATA ANALYSIS

GROUNDED THEORY

involving

NEGOTIATED OUTCOMES

leading to

CASE REPORT

which is both

IDIOGRAPHICALLY INTERPRETED

TENTATIVELY APPLIED

*This depiction of the flow of constructivist inquiry is borrowed from Lincoln, Y. S., and Guba, E. G. (1985), *Naturalistic Inquiry*. Beverly Hills, CA: Sage, p. 188. Reprinted by permission of Sage Publications, Inc.

Without this information, the evaluator would have no way of understanding the complex web of relationships that shape the program intent, the program processes, including results, and even the evaluation itself.

Emergent Design

In marked contrast to traditional evaluation, the constructivist evaluation, or research design, emerges from the experience of doing the evaluation, rather than being totally developed a priori. Because constructivists are committed to the concept of multiple and constructed realities, it is impossible to project these ahead of time. No one knows enough in advance about the circumstances involved in the multiple realities to devise a design that can adequately tap into the unpredictable interaction that will determine what is interesting or important. These will be revealed as the multiple realities are exerted on one another and on the researchers. The actors, the values, the uniqueness of the setting all serve to shape the research process. Thus it is not only unwise but impossible to plan for outcomes or design processes that are largely products of an unpredictable interaction. In constructivist inquiry, therefore, the research design is an emergent social process created by the individuals concerned (Burrell and Morgan, 1979).

The emergent design of an agency social service program would mean that not only the precise questions for the evaluation, but also the decision about those who would be asked to participate in answering the questions, would be determined as the evaluation process unfolds. Increased understanding of the context within which the program is operating would help to hone and shape the questions. Clearer understanding of the context would also inform the evaluator about the major stakeholders in both the program and the evaluation and how those stakeholding perspectives can best be tapped.

Human Instrument

The evaluator is the primary data gathering instrument for constructivist evaluation. Instead of standardized tests, structured questionnaires, or other quantitative data collection tools, the choice is toward the human instrument and is based on its great adaptability. The researcher will be dealing with multiple realities. The data gathering instruments must be capable of recognizing, sorting, and honoring these multiple realities, distinguishing subtleties of meaning, and assessing the role of meaning in shaping behavior. No researcher can devise a priori a nonhuman instrument with sufficient adaptability to adjust to the various realities that will be encountered.

In addition, it is only the human instrument that is currently capable of understanding the role of the irrational as a powerful shaping device. Because human action is rarely rational, through acting with empathy to emotional, nonrational, spiritual, and affiliational issues of the research participants, the human instrument can truly enter into the exchange called *communication*. As Reinharz (1979) points out, "Personal knowledge requires emotional involvement, not merely logical and rational analysis" (p. 34). Only the human, not a survey or other information gathering tool, is capable of grasping the meaning of the communication interaction.

Tacit Knowledge

Unlike the positivist perspective—that if it is not operationalizable, it is not measurable, and if it is not measurable, it is probably not of interest for any scientific purpose—the constructivist perspective holds that it is not possible to describe or explain everything that one knows in language form; some things must be experienced to be understood. Polanyi (1966) has done much to conceptualize the distinction between knowledge that is *propositional* (can be stated verbally) and that is *tacit* (cannot be stated). Constructivism argues for the legitimacy of tacit intuitive felt knowledge in addition to propositional knowledge, which has been traditionally accepted as the only substantive knowledge. This position recognizes the utility of knowledge that is somehow known, but cannot be put into words.

The importance of tacit knowledge can be seen when one realizes that the many layers of realities and values that emerge in evaluation can, initially, only be known tacitly. Although nuances are only understood tacitly, they are important and can serve to amplify the understandings of the evaluator. As Schutz (cited in Weick, 1976) has pointed out:

> Through a combination of selective attention, activity, consensual validation and luck, organizational actors are able to stride into the streams of experience where things are mixed together in random fashion and unravel those streams sufficiently so that some kind of sensemaking is possible.

The constructivist position is that tacit knowledge is an indispensable part of the research process; it will be influential, whether or not its influence is recognized. It is the base upon which the human instrument builds many of the insights and hypotheses that develop through the evaluation process. In fact, the human instrument is the only data collection instrument that can build on tacit knowledge. Given the indeterminate, evolving nature of the initial form of the inquiry, it is essential that knowledge at the tacit level be given a clear and prominent place in data processing and analysis.

Qualitative Methods

These methods are more adaptable than the more structured methods of traditional evaluation. Qualitative methods are more capable of responding to the multiple, less aggregatable realities of interest in constructivist evaluation. Methods that rely on looking, listening, speaking, and reading present a better fit for the constructivistic inquiry process. Such qualitative methods as interviewing, observing, recording, and analysis of nonverbal communication, and artifactual analysis, including content analysis, documentary analysis, records usage, etc., are preferred. These methods are more capable of exposing more directly the nature of the transaction between the investigator and the respondent (see Bogdan and Taylor, 1975; Patton, 1987; Van Maanen, Dabbs, and Faulkner, 1982) than the at-a-distance methods, such as the standardized tests and structured survey instruments that are commonly used in traditional evaluation.

Qualitative methods can accommodate and explicate multiple, conflicting realities. They are also sensitive to interaction. In addition, these methods allow a more accurate assessment of the extent to which the phenomenon of interest is shaped by the inquirer's preferences and biases. They are more sensitive than quantitative methods to mutual shaping influences and have the potential of engendering larger holistic understandings. In the inquiry process these methods do not uproot the phenomena from their native contexts. Qualitative methods permit both teaching and learning to go on in increasingly sophisticated fashion without sacrificing to an a priori design or to imperfect and unchangeable instrumentation.

Grounded Theory

Just as the design emerges or unfolds from the context and the process, so, too, does the theory. Theory for the constructivist is not composed of a priori ideas that guide the collection of the data. Instead theory emerges from the inquiry. There may be some conceptual base that guides the initial stages of the inquiry, but this base becomes more fully developed as a result of the research process. There is no assumption here that evaluators have no biases or ideas of their own about the evaluation process. Indeed, theory grows out of the evaluator's understanding of the context-embedded data. Because of this, theory is less likely to constrain the inquirer's seeing and understanding process because it is likely to reflect more vividly and accurately the multiple constructions of reality that are a part of the context.

In addition, grounded theory is more likely to expose the values, beliefs, attitudes, prejudices, and biases of all the participants because it is less amenable to disguise by the inquirer. The constructivist position rejects the notion of a priori theory determining a research design to obtain data that is congruent with a theory (Guba and Lincoln, 1982). Instead the theory is generated from the collected data, and the theoretical design unfolds as the inquiry proceeds (Lincoln and Guba, 1985; Reinharz, 1979; Stern, 1985). Theory emerges from, is grounded in (Glasser and Strauss, 1967), the data on the assumption that no a priori theory could encompass the multiple realities that are likely to be encountered. Grounded theory, theory that follows from data rather than preceding them, is indicated by the data under study, and must be meaningfully relevant to and be able to explain the behavior under study (Glasser and Strauss, 1967, p. 3). Grounded theory is a necessary consequence of multiple perspectives and is essential to the concept of the emergent research design. Grounded theory produces discrete hypotheses, not a general theory. According to Guba and Lincoln (1984):

> *The naturalist seeks continuously to refine and extend the design of the study—to help it unfold. As each sample element is selected, each datum recorded, and each element of theory devised, the design can itself become more specific and more focused (p.27).*

Regarding monitoring from the point of view of the constructivist paradigm, the reader can see how the assumption that helping with human problems is unique to each person, group, or circumstance leads to a belief that social programs will be guided by as many different theories of the problem or of helping as there are people, groups, and circumstances to be helped. It should be obvious that monitoring program activities from that perspective on helping will be quite different from monitoring them under the quantitative/positivistic perspective that prescribes the commitment of a program to an a priori theoretical perspective and implies that this commitment is to be followed (in its main outlines) by all program staff.

Since criteria for satisfactory implementation are based on stated program theory, in the constructivist case, theory is replaced with, most likely, multiple working hypotheses. That is not to say that from the constructivist perspective just any implementation is satisfactory, since program activities must be logically linked to the working hypotheses, however unique they may be. And, note, that imposing objectives and activities that obscure both client uniqueness and the helping process is a bad implementation because it will necessarily violate the fundamental assumptions of the perspective. On the other hand, to say that program activities and criteria for satisfactory implementation are multiple and that they must arise out of (be unique to) the unique characteristics of the individuals and their situations within which help is offered is, in no way, to say that they cannot be described or measured.

Grounded theory as a result of an emergent evaluation design also has implications for subsequent research about the same, or similar, phenomena. The degree to which working hypotheses hold outside the time and context within which they were found depends upon the degree of similarity between the sending and the receiving contexts (Lincoln and Guba, 1985, p. 316; Skrtic, 1985, p. 200). What is determined about the agency social service program in a certain community in a state may or may not hold in a similar social service program in another community in the state. It may or may not hold in another agency or another state. If the descriptions of the multiple constructions of reality in one location provide sufficient information about that context, then the informed reader/researcher who knows his or her own context should be able to reach a conclusion about whether transfer to another context is possible.

Purposive Sampling

No matter the research/evaluation paradigm, all sampling is done with some purpose in mind. Using the conventional frame for evaluation research, sampling is done to get a representation of the population to which it is desired to generalize (Patton, 1980). Constructivist investigation is tied to contextual factors, and, because of this, uses a strategy of purposeful or purposive sampling. According to Patton (1980, p. 107) this is the strategy of choice when "one wants to learn something and come to understand something about certain select cases without needing to generalize to all such cases." Constructivist evaluators use purposive sampling to increase the scope and range of the data exposed, looking for multiple realities.

Patton suggests several strategies for this type of sampling, including: (1) sampling extreme or deviant cases (such as the most and least dissatisfied or the most and least difficult clients), (2)sampling typical cases (the most common type of client or problem), (3) sampling for maximum variation (all the various types of clients or problems), (4) sampling critical cases (such as those that were most difficult to serve or those that were most costly to the agency and/or the practitioner), and (5) sampling politically important cases (such as those that made the newspaper or those in litigation) (1980, p. 104). These strategies can be useful not only for sampling respondents, but also for sampling sites and units within sites. Moreover, according to Skrtic (1985, p. 187), the purpose of the sampling may change as the research progresses. Thus, different sampling strategies might be appropriate at different points in the process. Remaining open to the different sampling possibilities maintains responsiveness to local conditions, mutual shapings, values, the emerging design, and grounded theory.

Inductive Data Analysis

Inductive data analysis, from the specific to the general, is preferred to *deductive data analysis,* from the general to the specific, at least in the early stages of a constructivist inquiry. The data is analyzed from the specific raw units of information to subsuming categories. Inductive analysis is in keeping with an emergent design that attempts to reflect multiple realities constructed out of the context. The investigator moves from varying degrees of a discovery mode to varying emphasis on a verification mode in attempting to understand the real world of the various stakeholders in the phenomena under investigation.

In the early stages the investigator is open to whatever emerges from the data, and utilizes an inductive constant comparison method of data analysis where each data unit is compared with every other (Rosengren, 1981). Later, as the inquiry reveals patterns and major dimensions of interest, the investigator focuses on verifying what appears to emerge—a more deductive approach to data collection and analysis. This process requires that the evaluator consciously work back and forth between parts and wholes, separate variables, and complex interwoven constellations of variables in a "sorting-out" and then "putting-back-together" process (Patton, 1980).

Problem-Determined Boundaries

Participants, not the evaluator, bound the inquiry in constructivist research. Factors that emerge from the respondents' realities set the limits to, or expand the margins of, the questions brought to the inquiry process. Factors in the minds of the inquirers and factors in the environments in which problems are found determine the focus and boundaries of the inquiry—unlike in conventional research, where the null hypothesis or the research question provides the focus. In constructivist inquiry the final boundaries of the research are based on an emergent focus informed by the values, conditions, and important shaping structures of the environment. This permits multiple realities to define the focus of the inquiry.

In the example of an evaluation of an agency social service program, the initial evaluation question might have been related to the effectiveness of their child neglect investigation processes. As the research unfolded, it became apparent that the Child Protective Service (CPS) worker's effectiveness as viewed by supervisors and parents of children under investigation was dependent upon the attitude and skills of the judges and the law enforcement officials who determined if the information provided was sufficient for a court case. Further, investigations of incidents of suspected neglect could only be investigated if suspicions were reported to CPS, and medical professionals, as well as preschool, grammar school, and high school personnel, were reluctant to become involved in reporting. CPS effectiveness could not be assessed without considering the contextual systems and human resources upon which the program was dependent.

As the inquirer comes to know what is important to all the stakeholders in the investigation, the participants and the evaluator together will come to know when the inquiry should stop. Ideally, it should not stop until the point where information becomes redundant. In the case of the evaluation of the neglect investigation program, the evaluation stopped when no new perspective or information was being uncovered.

Idiographic Interpretations

Constructivist evaluators interpret the data produced in an inquiry in terms of the particulars of that case (*idiographic* interpretations), rather than in terms of overarching, lawlike generalizations (called *nomothetic*). The assumption is that the particulars of any given context or site shape their data interpretations and conclusions. Different interpretations are meaningful for different realities. What is important in the interpreting is that the conclusions are embedded in the realities of the participants who live them, that they are reflective of the value systems involved, that they are faithful to the nature of the inquirer/participant relationship, and that they honestly portray the perspectives of all stakeholders.

The inquirer learns about the idiographic perspectives, but he or she also teaches participants about the mutual shaping and influences that occur. An expectation is that this teaching can lead to new insights and understandings on the part of all the participants, not only about the bounding and shaping of their own perspectives, but of those of the other stakeholders. In terms of our neglect evaluation example, the social workers began to understand the requirements of law enforcement and became less inclined to assume that an officer was insensitive and incompetent. The law enforcement officers came to understand the requirements of the CPS worker and saw them less as overreacting and more as focusing on other elements of the protection system. Judges came to understand why social workers would use "feeling" words in court when observations and evidence were what was needed. Parents began to understand why they were investigated in the first place and why the process unfolded as it did.

Participants are not necessarily expected to adopt this new perspective. And all participants in the neglect evaluation certainly did not change their personal view of the effectiveness of the neglect evaluation process. However, it is hoped that the evaluation results lead the stakeholders to understand the reasoning process and how interpretations are achieved, accepted, and transmitted, and, in our case example, this did occur.

Tentative Application

Constructivist evaluation makes no broad application of data results and interpretations, believing that realities are multiple and different. Because of these differences, sweeping application of findings may not be duplicated elsewhere. There will always be a tentativeness about large-scale applicability of inquiry findings. From this perspective, the best the constructivist can provide are descriptions that are sufficiently rich to enable judgment of similarities between contexts. In fact, foregoing the concept of generalizability, constructivist research and evaluation, at most, expects judgments of transferability, or how well the tentative hypotheses hold in other contexts. It is for the consumer of the findings, provided with sufficient information about the local conditions that shaped and influenced findings, to determine if such situation-specific information has applicability elsewhere. Final transferability judgment between the sending context and any receiving contexts must be made by the reader who is well grounded in a receiving context (Lincoln and Guba, 1985; Skrtic, 1985).

Negotiated Results

The constructivist evaluator negotiates meanings and interpretations from the inquiry process with the human sources of data, because it is their construction of reality that the inquirer is seeking to accurately reconstruct, instead of interpreting findings based on the presence or absence of statistical significance, such as in the traditional evaluation mode. The final product in constructivist evaluation is based on negotiated outcomes. The final case report is subjected to the scrutiny of the participants, so that from an insider's perspective, the reconstruction of the processed data is consistent with and credible to the multiple realities of the social context (Guba and Lincoln, 1984; Guba and Lincoln, 1989; Lincoln and Guba, 1985).

Logistics and sample size may prohibit negotiations with all participants. At a minimum, representatives of all stakeholding groups must have an opportunity to provide feedback. Here, stakeholding groups are seen to be those distinct groups with an interest in the results of the inquiry process, either because they are involved in the phenomena or activities under study, affected by the phenomena or activities, or must make decisions about the phenomena or activities based on research results (Gold, 1983). This will guarantee at least minimal attention to assurances that the multiple perspectives have been honestly portrayed.

Case Study Reporting Mode

The case study is written as a comprehensive description that depicts the emergent concepts and theories. It chronicles the documentation of the inquiry process, communicates the insiders' view, and recounts the local understanding (Guba and Lincoln, 1982; Leininger, 1985; Reinharz, 1979). The study covers the information in what has been termed a *thick description* (Geertz, 1973; Guba and Lincoln, 1983). Thick description is the "malange of descriptors" (Lincoln and Guba, 1985; Zeller, 1984) that involves the literal description of the entity being studied, the circumstances and people involved, and the nature of the community in which the entity under investigation is located. It involves interpretation of the demographic and descriptive data in terms of cultural norms and mores, community values, deep-seated attitudes, and motives. The primary goal of a thick description is to provide *emic* understanding (the local or native view derived directly from the people's language, beliefs, and experiences), rather than an *etic* view, which would be the external, more universal, and generalized view (Pike, 1954). To be adequate, the description must contain everything a reader may need to know in order to understand the findings (Lincoln and Guba, 1985) and make informed decisions about their applicability in other contexts (Skrtic, 1985). Unfortunately, for the evaluator, no real metric has been developed against which to measure how thick this description must be to be considered thick enough.

The case study reporting mode with a thick description is aimed at providing the essential judgmental information about the context under investigation. The case study is the mode of choice because it is not as reductionistic as other reporting methods. It is more adapted to multiple realities and is capable of capturing the wholeness of the phenomenon as it naturally occurs, absent stability, control, or manipulation. It is the mode of choice because it can reveal more easily the inquirer's interaction in the process, which also enables the reader to determine the degree to which the inquirer's biases may have unduly influenced the results. Not surprisingly, however, good creative writing skills are necessary in addition to good constructivist evaluation skills in order to create the full, engaging story that is the goal of the case study.

Trustworthiness

Guba and Lincoln (1985) have developed special criteria for rigor that are analogous to the traditional trustworthiness criteria for scientific rigor of internal and external validity, reliability, and objectivity. These criteria are: (1) credibility, activities aimed at increasing the probability of credible findings; (2) transferability (mentioned earlier in the context of tentative application of findings), measures of how well the working hypotheses hold in other contexts; (3) dependability, accounting for instability and design induced changes and reflecting the appropriateness of inquiry decisions and methodological shifts; and (4) confirmability, proof that the results are linked to the data themselves. Techniques to increase the probability that these criteria can be met, or to test the extent to which they have been met, will be discussed in a subsequent section.

Authenticity, a more recently developed criterion for rigor, is directly implied by the constructivist assumptions. It does not continue the analogous nature of trustworthiness; instead authenticity taps the interactive result of the evaluative process, not the product of the evaluation. It is an intrinsic constructivist criterion related to the integrity and quality of the inquiry. Five aspects of authenticity have been identified but not yet fully developed (Guba and Lincoln, 1989; Lincoln and Guba, 1986): (1) fairness, a balanced view that presents all constructions and the values that undergird them; (2) ontological authentication, evidence of improvement in the participant's conscious experiencing of the world—consciousness raising; (3) educative authentication, evidence of an increase in appreciation of the constructions that are made by others and understanding how those constructions are rooted in the different value systems of others; (4) catalytic authentication, the degree to which the inquiry process facilitates and stimulates action; and (5) tactical authenticity, or stimulation to effective action. As with trustworthiness criteria, techniques to increase the probability that these criteria can be met, or to test the extent to which they have been met, will be discussed in a subsequent section.

Principles of Constructivist Evaluation Practice

Practice principles prescribe what a practitioner should do in a given situation (Blythe and Briar, 1987, p. 495; Chambers, 1975, p. 37). Practice principles, therefore, are the dimensions an evaluator keeps in mind during the evaluation process. They explain how the evaluator might understand the nature of the evaluation relationships and, most importantly, the nature of the required action. Clear practice principles can consistently guide one's work. They also allow for flexibility and for self-correction when the principles' strengths and weaknesses become clear in the evaluation context. In addition, principles should guide the evaluator in making evaluative recommendations.

We derive nine principles of evaluation practice from the constructivist perspective. These principles should provide assistance in thinking naturalistically in the evaluation process.

1. A social program under evaluation is to be understood as a social world and explained (primarily) from the point of view of the actors directly involved in the social process. No useful understanding can be derived by an evaluator without experiencing the context and stakeholders of the social process under investigation. Evaluation cannot be carried out except with field based methods, taking full account of the local context. Note especially that a change in the social context of a program changes judgments of both the needs it "should" address and the worth of its product.

2. The evaluator, using good communication and empathic skills, is the main instrument used to gather evaluation data. Only an evaluator acting as the "person-in-situation" data collector can assure that the process leads to accurate understanding of the context and the various stakeholders of the social process under investigation.

3. In the conduct of the evaluation, the evaluator is both a student of the stakeholders' particular construction of social program realities and a teacher, aiding others toward new insights about the constructions of other stakeholders.

4. Conflict rather than consensus is the expected condition surrounding an evaluation in process. Multiple, sometimes conflicting, perspectives will appear when the goal is the study of multiple meanings or perceptions of participants. The role of the evaluator is to utilize the learning/teaching process to manage the conflict and maximize the potential for consensus. The point is respectful negotiation among equal participants. In those cases where consensus is not possible, maximization of the contenders' understanding of their opponents' point of view should be the focus.

5. The evaluator's tacit knowledge must be permitted to be used full strength in the evaluation process to achieve the full value of the inquiry. Conversely, tacit knowledge of all stakeholders in the evaluation process must be converted to propositional knowledge so that the evaluator can both think about it explicitly and communicate it to others.

6. The evaluation research design and the theory within which to frame and understand the data collected must be allowed and encouraged to emerge from the inquiry process in order to encompass the multiple constructed realities encountered in the evaluation process.

7. Parties holding a variety of value postures must be involved in every part of the planning of the evaluation process and its product to assure that value pluralism and stakeholder constructions are fairly preserved. The evaluator is taking a collaborative rather than controlling posture.

8. The evaluator is duty bound to collect information relevant to all stakeholders, to collect information in ways that expose facts useful to all sides, and to release findings continuously and openly so that their credibility can be examined by all.

9. Generalizability of findings is not a matter of fundamental concern. Instead, negotiation between the stakeholders will determine evaluation conclusions. The role of the evaluator is to mediate that process with equity and fairness. The evaluator is not the judge but the mediator of the judgmental process.

Each of these practice principles is consistent with the constructivist paradigm and directly related to the research implications that derive from the constructivist point of view. When evaluation research is undertaken with these practice principles in mind, the evaluator will be "thinking naturalistically" (Biklen and Bogdan, 1986). The reader by now should be able to note the marked difference between the spirit of these practice principles and those that derive from the requirements of a controlled setting, objective instrumentation, and randomly selected and assigned sampling—required for discovery and verification in a traditional evaluation design. These above principles should seem contrary to conventional practice. They do, however, support the perspective that constructivism is an alternative way of thinking about reality, and of implementing and consuming research and evaluation.

These principles can be further refined into specific evaluator behaviors. The next section will describe some methods that are necessary in order to deliberately apply the constructivist assumptions and research implications in an evaluation process.

Methods of Constructivist Evaluation

As you will see, a variety of qualitative methods are utilized during the emerging constructivist evaluation process. What is presented here is the translation of the constructivist paradigm's assumptions and implications into the actual doing of constructivist evaluations. To aid in presentation, this section has clustered constructivist implications and related evaluation methods into five sets that correspond roughly to the sequence of how an evaluation should be conducted. Table 13–1 shows the five sets of methods and the clustering of the constructivist implications.

TABLE 13–1 • Clustering of Constructivist Inquiry Implications*

Aspect of Inquiry	Cluster
Research design	Emergent design Problem-determined boundaries Purposive sampling
Data collection	Qualitative methods Human instrument Tacit knowledge
Data analysis	Grounded theory Inductive data analysis
Reporting	Case study reporting mode Idiographic interpretation Temtative application
Rigor	Trustworthiness Negotiated outcomes Authenticity

Note: The natural setting is implied in all clusters.
*This conceptual clustering is borrowed from Skrtic, T. M. (1985), Doing naturalistic research into educational organizations, in Y. S. Lincoln (Ed.), Organizational Theory and Inquiry: The Paradigni Revolution. Beverly Hills, CA: Sage, 187. Reprinted by permission of Sage Publications, Inc.

Research Design: Emergent Design, Problem-Determined Boundaries, Purposive Sampling

Even though the research design must emerge from the context of the evaluation process and tends to be changed resulting from new insights, the design will also emerge as a part of a planned process. Two points where the design can be expected to emerge are during the initial discussion with key actors in planning the evaluation and from subsequent data collection and analysis. It should be clear that these processes have the potential to reveal aspects of the context and additional evaluation questions that were not initially obvious.

The sampling plan is another example of how the design, though planned, continues to be emergent. The purpose of the sampling both regarding the sites of the evaluation and the participants in the process continues to evolve as the evaluation unfolds. The purpose of sampling itself may change as the research progresses; thus, Patton's (1980) purposive sampling strategies for sampling the extremes, the typical, the critical, the politically important cases, or to gain maximum variation might appropriately serve all stakeholders' purposes at different points in time. In their fourth book on this alternative evaluation process, Guba and Lincoln (1989), in emphasizing the key dynamic in evaluation as negotiation, underscore the belief that all stakeholders, the bureaucrats, the practitioners, the beneficiaries, or the recipients of service share a rightful role in articulating claims, concerns, and issues that create the agenda for the evaluation process, and should, therefore, have a role in determining the boundaries and design of the evaluation.

In addition, the constructivist evaluation can be expected to go through several predictable phases in order to identify the salient questions (what one needs to find out about); to understand and find meaning resulting from the process of answering the questions; to check the findings in accordance with trustworthiness procedures (analogous to measures of rigor in conventional evaluation); and to gain closure (Guba and Lincoln, 1989; Lincoln and Guba, 1985). These phases roughly mirror Kirk and Miller's (1986) phases of ethnographic field work: *invention* (designing a plan of action), *discovery* (information collection), *interpretation* (understanding), and *explanation* (closure and departure from the field). A constructivist evaluator might find objections to the terminology found in the last phase, but inasmuch as Kirk and Miller's intent in this explanation phase of "communication, or packaging . . . a message" (p. 60) is congruent with the constructivist perspective, their model has been included as a helpful tool for conceptualizing the work of constructivist evaluation.

Phase I orientation and overview Even if the evaluator has a good deal of prior knowledge about the situation under investigation, the initial site visit should involve open-ended approaches to respondents. No predetermined questions allowing for only predetermined responses such as those found in "Yes/No" questionnaires should be undertaken. Instead, questions should be largely of the "grand tour" type (Spradley, 1979), aimed at helping participants tell the evaluator what he or she ought to know about the phenomena under study. The object of the questions here is to discover what is salient, to begin to ponder what the whole is and where the parts are that are needed to complete it. The object of this first phase is to obtain sufficient information to identify what is important enough to follow up in detail.

Returning to our example of the evaluation of neglect investigations, at this phase of the process, the evaluator would focus on discovering details about the agency, community, and larger environmental contexts that impact on the neglect investigation process. In doing so, the evaluator would begin to identify the important stakeholding groups other than the CPS workers, such as parents, educators, mental health professionals, law enforcement personnel, etc., to be tapped in later phases of the evaluation. Initial questions would be geared at identifying the differing ideas about what the evaluator should know about neglect investigations, from the trauma of the investigation process to the anger law enforcement has regarding the "soft hearted" nature of the social work investigation process.

Phase II focused exploration This phase moves away from the general discovery of Phase I to more targeted probing. Time should be allowed between Phases I and II for Phase I data to be analyzed. Time should also be allowed between the completion of phases between sites for data analysis, if more than one site is part of the evaluation. In order to manage data overload during the analysis process and to continue to allow the process to emerge from the data, data from each phase and from each site should be analyzed serially before moving to the next site or phase of the process. This is particularly true if only one evaluator is involved in the evaluation. Team evaluation processes will require that some level of data analysis occur before moving from phase or site, but evaluator style and strategies may mitigate against teams working in unison across phases and sites.

In this stage of data analysis general themes will begin to emerge that require further investigation for greater meaning. As in our neglect example, themes such as "poverty," "parents' rights," "professional liability," "the local protection system," and "system neglect" are bound to emerge. These themes, to be more thoroughly developed and to accurately reflect the constructions of all stakeholders, may require follow-up questioning, which might require more structured interviewing and observation techniques. It is in this phase that a structured interview protocol with established questions might be developed. Other types of structured information gathering mechanisms ranging from standardized tests to questionnaires might be useful. All structured tools, not unlike the grand tour type questions in the earlier phase, should be based on what emerges from the process and the data, and should serve to obtain information in depth about those elements determined to be salient during Phase I interviews.

Phase III comprehensive member check   Time should be allowed between Phases II and III to analyze the information from Phase II and to write the case studies. During Phase III the provisional report is sent back to the study sites and subjected to the scrutiny of the persons who provided information. The task is "to obtain confirmation that the report has captured the data as constructed by the informants, or to correct, amend, or extend it, that is, to establish the credibility of the case" (Lincoln and Guba, 1985, p. 236). The reader should not fail to realize the importance of this phase to the overall spirit of constructivist evaluation. If the stakeholders reject the rough drafts of the case studies, modifications based on true negotiation must be made. Note that we are not calling for the creation of a consensus document. Negotiations among all stakeholders must occur until an appropriate, acceptable compromise is achieved. This must be seen to include the possibility of "agreeing to disagree," with the areas of disagreement becoming part of the case study. This must be seen as possible because the report itself, as well as the data of the evaluation, is fundamentally the property of the people who give the data, not the data compiler/interpreter (the evaluator).

The more dissatisfaction there is with the report, the more iterations will exist in this phase of the process. We have found, however, that an evaluator, thinking naturalistically, rarely has major problems with the substance of the reports when reviewed by the stakeholders. The evaluator who fails to respect, and therefore accurately capture, a perspective is the one who will encounter difficulty. If the evaluator has established full participative involvement such that the stakeholders and others have been drawn into the evaluation and welcomed as equal partners in the design, implementation, and interpretation of an evaluation, then this phase should present no challenge to the evaluator or participant other than the challenges presented by greater insight and understanding about the program being evaluated.[1]

Clearly, it is only with this total negotiation of the drafted case studies that the evaluator can move to complete the final case study after the closure of Phase III. You will see in later sections that closure of Phase III is not really the end of an evaluation. The teaching/learning process that occurs during evaluation will continue with unpredictable outcomes. Shared knowledge and new insights are sure to be associated with improved sophistication in program delivery.

Data Collection and Recording: Qualitative Methods, Human Instrument, Tacit Knowledge

Qualitative methods including techniques such as interviews, observation, use of nonverbal cues and unobtrusive measures, and documentary and records analysis, because of their flexibility, are better suited to the study of complex human and organizational interactions than those more structured quantitative methods of traditional evaluation. The evaluators themselves are the main instrument to gather evaluation data. The human instrument is better equipped than instruments created a priori for taking data from a complex, living system like an organization delivering social services of one kind or another.

The trained evaluator, with the exquisite human attributes of intelligence, creativity, and humor, is capable of processing and combining intuitive hunches with great amounts of factual information. The human instrument is adaptable to the emergent nature of the constructivist evaluation. The evaluator is capable of combining the past experience of the evaluator and the experiences of others he or she has heard about, learned about, or read about, with the experiences of the other stakeholders in the evaluation, using tacit as well as propositional knowledge to ascribe meaning to the verbal and nonverbal data that is uncovered.

The techniques of data collection and recording that follow take the best advantage of the human instrument and tacit knowledge potentials.

Interviews   An interview, according to Dexter (1970), is a conversation with a purpose. In constructivist inquiry, those purposes are:

- *Obtaining here-and-now constructions of persons, events, activities, organizations, feelings, motivations, claims, concerns, and other entities*
- *Reconstructions of such entities as experienced in the past*
- *Projections of such entities as they are expected to be experienced in the future*
- *Verification, emendation, and extension of information obtained from other sources, human and non human (triangulation)*
- *Verification, emendation, and extension of constructions developed by the inquirer (member checking) (Lincoln and Guba, 1985, p. 268)*

The interview as utilized in constructivist inquiry can be structured or unstructured (Dexter, 1970). In the structured interview, the problem is defined by the evaluator before the interview, and the respondent is expected to answer in terms of the interviewer's framework and definition of the problem. In an unstructured interview, the format is non-standardized, and the interviewer does not seek normative responses. The interviewee's definition, structure, and account of what is relevant is stressed because the interviewer is concerned with the unique, the idiosyncratic, and the wholly individual viewpoint (Guba and Lincoln, 1981). For the most part, unstructured interviews that have both the questions and answers provided by the respondent are preferred. Grand tour questions like, "Please tell me what you think I need to know about neglect investigation," or, "What do you think are the main questions that should be answered in this evaluation of neglect investigations?" are the type of questions used to begin an unstructured interview. Follow-up questions would be geared at achieving clear evaluator understanding of the participant's individual viewpoint.

In latter stages of the inquiry (particularly for triangulation or member-checking purposes), more structured forms of interviewing can be utilized (Lincoln and Guba, 1985). Follow-up interviews that consistently check for all participants' meanings for concepts such as "poverty," "parents' rights," "professional liability," "the local protection system," and "system neglect" are examples of a more structured approach to interviewing for the purposes of data collection.

Active listening is the foundation of the interview process, whether the interview is structured or unstructured (Corimer and Corimer, 1979). It is a nonjudgmental, here and now reflection to the respondent of his or her feeling state as perceived by him/herself (Compton and Galaway, 1975). Active listening increases the respondents' willingness to talk and does not shut off communication. The investigator who actively listens demonstrates the skill of understanding what the participant is saying and feeling by communicating to the participant, in his/her own words, what the investigator thinks the participant is saying and feeling (Gerrard, Boniface, and Love, 1980). Active listening encourages the participant to help with the pace and content of the interviews. It can lay the foundation of building a trusting relationship between the participant and the investigator (Gerrard, Boniface, and Love, 1980). According to Inberg (1975), through active listening it is often possible to get much data without having to ask numerous questions that might create discomfort. At the same time, it demonstrates to the respondent that what is being said is worth listening to, an ultimate expression of human dignity and respect (Inberg, 1975).

Total or complete listening involves not only listening to and interpreting the respondents' verbal messages, but also observing and interpreting the respondents' nonverbal behavior (posture, facial expressions, movement, tone of voice, etc.) (Egan, 1982). This other aspect of active listening will be discussed in the next section on observation.

The interview should involve the following general steps (Lincoln and Guba, 1985):

1. Deciding whom to interview. In addition to sampling and selection of participants, negotiating fully informed consent is necessary.

2. Preparing for the interview. Becoming as fully informed as possible about the participant is necessary. Also important are: practicing the interview; deciding the general content and sequence of questions; deciding on the

evaluator's appropriate role, dress, level of formality, etc.; confirming the time and place of the interview with each participant.

3. Setting tone. Broad, universal, overview questions, called *grand tour* by Spradley (1979) should be used to give participants practice in talking in a relaxed atmosphere while providing information about how the participants view the general characteristics of the community and the phenomena or program under study.

4. Establishing pacing and productivity. More and more specific questioning occurs as the interview moves along to gain development of points; probes and directed cues should be used for more information; "pumps" should be utilized to encourage more information: calls for examples, when they do not come spontaneously, calls for reactions, or questions to embellish or extend information also should occur.

5. Termination and closure. When the interview has ceased to be productive, the information is redundant, both evaluator and participant display fatigue, or the responses begin to seem guarded or distracted, the interview should be terminated. Closure occurs with the evaluator summarizing what he or she believes has been said, while asking the participant to verify, amend, and extend the constructions of the evaluator. Here, the participant can also be asked to provide questions that might be asked of other participants. Before interview completion, each participant should assess the precision and faithfulness of the interviewer's construction of the reality (member check for trustworthiness). When necessary, participants can add new and/or refined elements. With all this, participants are put on record as to the confirmation and verification of data.

As the evaluation proceeds, the evaluator may find it helpful to develop an interview guide to extend and focus the data collection process. The form and content of the guide emerges from the inquiry data produced by the evaluator and the participants. An interview guide, grounded in inquiry data and not designed a priori, is consistent with constructivist methodology and can be found to be helpful in the collection of data from participants for recording and analysis by the evaluator (Guba and Lincoln, 1985).

Observation Observation and interpretation of the participants' nonverbal behavior during the interview process is essential, since sometimes the nonverbal messages of facial expressions, bodily motions, voice quality, and autonomic physiological responses can provide more important data than the verbal messages (Egan, 1982). According to Knapp (1972), nonverbal behavior can punctuate or modify interpersonal communication in at least four ways: (1) confirming or repeating what is being said verbally, (2) denying or confusing what is being said verbally, (3) strengthening or emphasizing what is being said, and (4) regulating or controlling what is happening. Data from nonverbal behavior should be recorded along with the verbal data.

Interpretation of the nonverbal behavior should be in the entire context of the interview, and integrated with all other information so as not to distort the evaluator's reading of the situation (Egan, 1982). In dealing with nonverbal behavior, the investigator either notes and records it, and explores it more fully at another time (Lincoln and Guba, 1985), or describes the behavior to the participant when it happens (Corimer and Corimer, 1979). In deciding which option to implement, the evaluator should consider the physical and psychosocial dynamics of the participant, the time, and the environment; the pace and productivity of the interview/observation; and the general or focused purpose of data collection. The evaluator may wish to follow both the pattern established by Lincoln and Guba (1985, p. 276), to use nonverbal cues "in a supplementary fashion to flag items of information that require more detailed attention later," and the suggestion of Corimer and Corimer (1979), to use nonverbal cues to highlight an item of information for amplification and clarification when it occurs and seems appropriate to do so.

At another level, observation (sometimes called *persistent observation*) is the act of noting, watching, and taking into account the physical and psychosocial dynamics of the time and place of the observation, in order to learn from participants in their environment and to allow the evaluator another opportunity for synthesis. These observations are overt, planned, scheduled, and require the same informed consent and practices of interviews. In most cases in constructivist evaluation, observation and interview are concurrent activities. But Guba and Lincoln suggest (1981) that observation in connection with interviewing is less full because it is difficult for the investigator to see and note all the aspects that are occurring while involved in another data collection technique. This concern, however, does not prevent them from supporting interviewing and observation as concurrent processes. Rather, it serves to underscore the highly developed skills necessary for the human instrument to record data thoroughly and accurately.

Documents and records   *Records,* according to Lincoln and Guba (1985), are "any written or recorded statement prepared by or for an individual or organization for the purpose of attesting to an event or providing an accounting" (p. 277). Lincoln and Guba (1985, p. 277) use the term *document* "to denote any written or recorded material *other than a record* that was not prepared specifically in response to a request from the inquirer (such as a test or set of interview notes)." A report of a meeting or a case record would be an example of record. Written policies and procedures for the investigation of instances of suspected neglect are examples of documents.

Lincoln and Guba (1985, p. 276) recommend documents and records as "singularly useful" collateral data in constructivist inquiry because they are available from the social context at relatively low costs. Although both vary in quality, their content reflects the general language of the time and the specific idioms of the social context. They are non-reactive, and can be stable sources of information in that their content is settled and positioned and is not subject to the change processes of time, place, and people. Some records (as in children's cases) are maintained with specific responsibility and accountability requirements that can withstand legal scrutiny and procedures. However, because of this they are also much more difficult to access than other types of records and documents.

In addition, interpretation of the meaning of the words contained in both records and documents can change with linguistic and cultural changes. Without efforts of member checking or other forms of triangulation, it may be difficult for a person outside an organization, who is not a part of the information chain and the organization history, such as an outside evaluator, to capture and understand the full meaning of records and documents. Even the use of interpreters will shape meaning, based on the interpreter's knowledge, frame of reference, and position in the organization and their spot in the organization's history.

Baily (1978) presents several other disadvantages to the use of documents and records in any evaluation effort. Many records and documents were not originally intended for inquiry purposes and, therefore, may present biased information. The purpose for which they were written might mean that the information contained is exaggerated, omitted, deleted, altered, or fabricated, to serve the goals for which they were written. Also, documents and records are subject to selective survival. Archiving of day-to-day materials does not generally occur. If archiving has occurred, written material does not withstand the elements well. What remains may provide an incomplete account of events or behaviors.

Further, the problem of sampling bias by educational level is acute in document and record analysis. Poorly educated people are much less likely than well educated people to write documents or records. In addition, the poorly educated read much less frequently than the well educated. Therefore, mass media are not aimed at them, and it is less likely that their viewpoints are well represented in such publications.

Some documents and records are kept according to a system. When the system is changed or varied, the kind, quantity, quality, inclusiveness, exclusiveness, categories, and continuity may change, making evaluation over time impossible. Documents and records also tend to be without standard format. Analysis and comparison is difficult because salient information contained in documents and records at one point in time may be entirely lacking in earlier or later ones.

Validity of document and record analysis may be increased by the fact that the documents and records are often first-person accounts of events or feeling experienced by the writer, and thus have face validity (Carmines and Zeller, 1979). Tending to mar validity is the likelihood that the writer did not write the document or record for inquiry and may have had ulterior motives unrelated to the inquiry process. Also, the time lag between the occurrence of the event and the writing may have led to memory failures and inaccuracies (Carmines and Zeller, 1979). Further, due to selective survival, the documents and records that remain provide an intentional or unintentional biased sample, which does not provide an accurate picture.

Dissimilarities of content, variety of sources, multiple purposes, lack of standardized formats, and lack of consistent recording systems make it necessary for the investigator to consider a variety of analytical methods to identify and describe data within the texts of documents and records. Lincoln and Guba (1985) give the following directions for the analysis of documents.

> *The analytic process itself varies depending upon both whether the analytic categories are specific a priori and whether the documents to be analyzed are similar (for example, a series of annual reports or five year plans) or different. The naturalistic inquirer will rarely enjoy the luxury of an a priori taxonomy, but when it occurs the analytic modes are well spelled out in such standard content analysis source works as Holsti (1969), Krippendorf (1980), and Rosengren (1981). If the documents are dissimilar, an especially useful approach is the case aggregation method outlined by Lucas (1974a; 1974b). An extended illustration of the latter is given in Guba and Lincoln (1981). When a taxonomy is to emerge in (be grounded in) the data themselves, the method of constant comparison outlined by Glaser and Strauss (1967) is applicable (p. 278).*

Lincoln and Guba offer these directions for the analysis of records:

> *The analysis of records is a somewhat different matter. As a first principle, the inquirer should begin on the assumption that if an event happened, some record of it exists. . . . To put it another way, every human action "leaves tracks." The second relevant principle is that if one "knows how the world works," one can imagine the tracks that must have been left by the action. A third principle is that, if one knows one's way around the world of records, one knows where to look for the tracks. Possibly the most useful metaphor for the "tracking" inquirer is that of the investigative journalist, a metaphor that has been explored in detail by Guba (1981b), who provides several examples of application. (p. 278).*

Reflecting on the validity issues mentioned earlier, Lincoln and Guba (1985) present the following arguments regarding ways of counteracting threats to validity. The claim of ulterior motive can be substantiated or refuted by checking the reputation of the writer in terms of believability and corruptibility. This can be done in the organizational context or in the context of the greater environment. Superiors, peers, and acquaintances can be approached directly or indirectly regarding the writer's competence and character. The time lag, memory failure inaccuracies can be matched with other known facts. The plausibility of the document or record can be tested against other known facts (a kind of triangulation). Assessing consistency of word patterns, language, writing style, and record accessibility supports internal consistency and coherence. Further, one must keep in mind that, from the constructivist perspective, the interest is maximizing information, not facilitating generalizations; therefore, selective survival and bias do not impede the efforts of analysis of available documents and records.

Unobtrusive measures Lincoln and Guba (1985) define unobtrusive information residue as "information that accumulates without intent on the part of either the investigator or the respondent(s) to whom the information applies" (p. 279). For them, the focus is on physical traces that can be collected in the absence of the participant who provided them, thus providing a nonreactive data source unlike observation or nonverbal cues (Campbell and Stanley, 1963; Webb, Campbell, Schwartz, and Sechrest, 1966; Webb, Campbell, Schwartz, Sechrest, and Grove, 1981). Examples of such traces include shortcuts across lawns as indicators of preferred traffic patterns, worn and smudged conditions of books as indicators of their use, or the amount of paperwork that accumulates in the "in" basket as an indicator of work load.

According to Lincoln and Guba (1985), unobtrusive traces or residues have the following strengths: (1) they often have face validity; (2) they are simple, direct, and usually, noninterventional; (3) they are stable; (4) they are independent of language; (5) they are nonreactive. However, the weaknesses are: (1) they are sometimes heavily inferential; (2) they are found in bits and pieces that are difficult to aggregate and to interpret holistically; (3) they are serendipitous, thus making it difficult to identify a measure to fit a particular investigative situation; (4) they cannot be directly manipulated; and (5) their trustworthiness is difficult to establish.

Recording modes for data collection Data collected from interviews, observations, and documents and records should be recorded by the evaluator in two field journals (condensed and expanded), a personal log, a log of activities, and a document and record file.

The field journals require the evaluator to describe in detail the events, interactions, thoughts, and feeling of the participants as they occur in the social context (Punch, 1986). Field journals contain an account of what occurred at each interview and/or observation. Lofland (1971) suggests that the accounts of the interview and/or observations include a concrete running description of what occurred, recorded at the lowest possible level of inference, along with impressions of the participants, analytic ideas, and thoughts of both participant and investigator, and notes regarding further needed information.

Spradley (1980) suggests the use of condensed and expanded journals for data collected during participant interviews and/or observations. The condensed journal is used by the evaluator during the actual interview and/or observation. It contains direct quotes, specific behaviors, specific words, key phrases, chronologs, and significant ideas, such as evaluator reactions and questions to jog the memory of the investigator when preparing the expanded account.

The expanded journal is used to record the full account of the interview or observation within twenty-four hours to ensure recall and accuracy. Investigator notes about personal reactions, analytical ideas and thoughts, and needs for further information are included, as well as a complete running account of what transpired during the interview and/or observation. Lofland (1971) recommends including information originally regarded as important, but not recorded because of the need for speed in recording even more important information. It may occur that an earlier happening, which at the time seemed too unimportant to record, takes on additional significance with additional interviews and as the inquiry process unfolds. Spradley (1979) suggests that the inclusion of analytical ideas and thoughts about the information, organization, and categorization of information, and present and future informational needs, can facilitate subsequent collection and analysis of data.

The personal log is a log of the evaluator's own feelings and reactions. According to Spradley (1979, p. 71), "like a diary, this journal will contain a record of experiences, ideas, fears, mistakes, confusion, breakthroughs, and problems that arise during fieldwork." It is a record of the investigator's feelings and reactions to the participants and the social context (Punch, 1986). For Lincoln and Guba (1985), the log includes several kinds of entries:

> *Reflexive and introspective notations about the state of one's mind in relation to what is happening in the field (developing constructions, commentary on the perceived influence of one's own biases, expectations about what will happen next . . .); a record of hypotheses and questions that will be useful to follow up and/or discuss with one's fellow inquirers; and a cathartic section in which one can vent one's frustrations and anxieties (p. 281).*

The log of activities is similar to a calendar of appointments. Each entry includes the date, time, place, people involved, and scheduled event (Lincoln and Guba, 1985). This log should be maintained throughout the evaluation.

Finally, as a means of maintaining order to aid in data analysis and creation of an audit trail (to be discussed later), a separate filing system should be designed for the documents and records used as sources of information for the inquiry. Each record and document should be coded and identified with regard to its source and date of acquisition. Other identification strategies, such as listing by title with a brief description, can aid data analysis at a later stage of the process.

Data Analysis: Grounded Theory, Inductive Data Analytic Procedures

Data collection and data analysis are interactive elements of a cyclical process in constructivist inquiry (Lincoln and Guba, 1985). Data analysis begins with the first data collection in order to facilitate emerging design development, grounding of theory, and more structured data collection from a more focused sample element. The method used to process data for analysis is the constant comparative method provided by Glasser and Strauss (1967) for discovering theory from data by means of the constant comparison of every datum with every other datum.

It is important to note, however, that the original intent of the Glasser and Strauss method was not to process data for analysis, but to provide a means for deriving grounded theory in data "to enable prediction and explanation of behavior" (p. 3). Lincoln and Guba (1985) reconceptualized the method for inductive data analysis. Unlike Glasser and Strauss, this reconceptualization does not have as a goal the development of theory. Their procedure used for the processing of data for analysis includes:

1. *Unitizing.* Unitizing is a persistent search in the accumulated data for units of information that are relevant and applicable to the focus of inquiry. The units focus on an understanding or action the evaluator needs to have or take, and are the smallest piece of information that can be understood by someone with minimal knowledge or experience in the particular social context. The unit can be as short as a phrase or as long as several paragraphs, but it must stand alone and be relevant and applicable to the focus of the inquiry.

2. *Categorizing.* Categorizing begins with the first set of data units produced and continued as the inquiry continues and the data collection and data analysis become more focused. Using the method of constant comparison, of comparing each data unit against all the other units of data, the task is to bring together into provisional categories those data units that apparently relate to the same content and to devise rules that describe category properties that are non-redundant and exclusive. These decision rules can, ultimately, be used to justify the inclusion of each data unit that remains assigned to the category as well as to provide a basis for later tests of replicability; and to render the category set internally consistent (Bulmer, 1979). The goal is to provide a reasonable construction of the data that might be tested subsequently for logic and replicability by the auditor reviewing the process.

3. *Filling in patterns.* When it becomes evident by the logic of the category system as a whole that some categories are missing, several strategies are available to enrich the overall construction: (1) extension—the investigator begins with a known item or items and builds on them as bases for other questions or as guides in the examination of documents; (2) bridging—the investigator begins with several known, but apparently disconnected, items using them as points of reference for further inquiry in an effort to identify the connections and understand them; and (3) surfacing—the investigator proposes new information that ought to have been found in the field and then verifies its existence or lack thereof.

4. *Member checks.* The investigator returns the analytic categories, interpretations, and conclusions to the participants who were the human sources of the data, for examination and reaction.

Sadler (1981), viewing qualitative data collection from the positivist perspective, suggests some constraints or limitations the constructivist data processor might encounter:

1. *Data overload.* "An informational bottleneck . . . which places severe limitations on the amount of data able to be received, processed, and remembered by the human mind" (p. 27).

2. *First impressions.* Persistence on the first information received so that later revision is resisted.

3. *Availability of information.* Information that is difficult to unearth or retrieve receives less attention than that which is easier to unearth or retrieve.

4. *Positive and negative instances.* A tendency to ignore information that conflicts with already-held hypotheses and to emphasize only that which confirms them.

5. *Internal consistency, redundancy, and novelty of information.* A tendency to discount more extreme information; what is novel may be seen as unimportant.

6. *Uneven reliability of information.* A tendency to ignore the fact that some sources are more credible than others.

7. *Missing information.* A tendency to devalue something for which some information may be missing or incomplete.

8. *Revision of a Tentative Hypothesis, Evaluation, or Diagnosis.* Reacting to new information either conservatively or by overreacting.

9. *Base-rate proportion.* A tendency to assume some average base rate when no actual base-rate data are available, or to suppress concrete base-rate information in favor of clinical information.

10. *Sampling considerations.* A tendency to be "less sensitive to the absolute size of the sample than to the ratio of sample size to population" (p. 30).

11. *Confidence in judgment.* A tendency "to have an almost unshakeable confidence in the correctness of their decisions, even in the face of considerable relevant, contrary evidence" (p. 30).

12. *Co-occurrences and correlation.* A tendency to interpret observed occurrences as evidence of a strong correlation.

13. *Consistency in judgments.* A tendency for repeated evaluation of the same data to be different.

While many of Sadler's points could be considered less important under the constructivist paradigm that looks at multiple constructions of reality than under more nomothetic paradigms focusing on "truth," there is little doubt that his concerns are generally meaningful and should be kept in mind during data processing. Most concerns, with the possible exception of base-rate proportion and co-occurrence and correlation should be attended to and potential problems overcome through the devices of member checking and other methods used to establish trustworthiness (to be discussed in detail later).

As an additional safeguard, the evaluator should establish a methodological log in which all codes used and all methodological decisions made during sampling, data collection, data analysis, emerging design, grounded theory, and case study construction are recorded. This information will become a part of documentation to support the rigor of the evaluation process.

Reporting: Case Study Reporting Mode, Idiographic Interpretations, Tentative Application

The final stage of the data analytic procedure is the development of the case study (Lincoln and Guba, 1985). Following Lincoln and Guba's (1985) suggestions, the data categories and index of documents can be the source for a provisional, overall outline for the study. The study should reflect what has been seen and heard so that it will make the same sense to the reader as it does to the evaluator. The writer's understanding should be grounded in the data, interpreted idiographically rather than in terms of broad generalizations.

Because the interpretations depend so heavily for their validity on local particulars, constructivist evaluators are tentative about making broad applications of their findings. The extent to which the findings may be applicable elsewhere depends on the similarity between both a sending and a receiving context. Because the evaluator cannot possibly know all the contexts to which the evaluation interpretations might be applied, the best the evaluator can do is maintain diligence in describing the sending context. Therefore, the outline of the case report should, at a minimum, consist of three parts: (1) site description, (2) problems/issues, and (3) lessons to be learned. Support material, such as data units, records, documents, etc., should be cross referenced to this outline.

The first draft of the cases should be completed and shared with the peer reviewer (to be discussed later) with attention to (Lincoln and Guba, 1985): (1) the adequacy of the representation of what the context was like; (2) the existence of errors of fact or interpretation; (3) omissions; (4) the clarity of the writer's interpretations as distinct from the respondents; (5) the degree of confidentiality and anonymity protections; and (6) the need to eliminate irrelevant, controversial issues. Revisions are made prior to the submission of each case report for its comprehensive member check (discussion follows). All suggested revisions, actions taken regarding the revision, and pertinent comments should be recorded on case study revision sheets in order that revisions also become a part to the data tracking process (Skrtic, Guba, and Knowlton, 1985). A complete interview, document, and record audit master list becomes a part of the text of the final report to link statements and assertions to the original data on which they are based or to pre-revision case studies.

Rigor: Trustworthiness, Negotiated Outcomes, Authenticity

Trustworthiness is the constructivist criteria for testing the rigor of constructivist studies and parallels criteria for rigor found in the conventional approach to evaluation. Trustworthiness depends on inquiry activities increasing the probability that credible findings and interpretations (an analogue to internal validity) will be produced; that dependability (an analogue to reliability) is established; that the data, findings, interpretations, and recommendations are confirmable (an analogue to objectivity); and that there is potential for transferability (an analogue to external validity). Efforts to establish trustworthiness are intended to establish the truth value, applicability, consistency, and neutrality of the results (Lincoln and Guba, 1985; Lincoln and Guba, 1986; Schwandt and Halpern, 1988).

Dependability or consistency can be established, according to Schwandt and Halpern (1988), if the procedures employed to gather, analyze, and interpret data fall within generally accepted constructivist practice and have been carefully documented. They also note that confirmability or neutrality is established when findings are supported in the data and inferences are not illogical or unreasonable, given the data. For them, credibility is assured when findings and interpretations are perceived as credible by those who supplied the original data. Participants must verify the findings. Finally, transferability or applicability occurs when sufficient description is provided "to enable someone interested in making a transfer of findings to reach a conclusion about whether transfer can be contemplated as a possibility" (p. 76).

To establish credibility or the truth value of the findings, the evaluation should include prolonged engagement, persistent observation, triangulation, peer debriefing, and member checks. An audit trail (Schwandt and Halpern, 1988) should be developed and maintained throughout the process. The audit trail structure usually consists of physical evidence, such as raw data files; documentary evidence, including interview summaries, records of data analyses, and written review of the literature; internal control evidence documented in the methodological log; computations; and oral evidence provided by the inquirer during interviews conducted by the auditor (to be discussed later). Dependability is established through a dependability audit of the inquiry process to determine the degree to which the criteria used in conducting the inquiry and analyzing the data were consistent with good methodological practice. A confirmability audit assesses the degree to which the findings are grounded in the data. Potential for transferability is established through the thick descriptive narrative about the context of the inquiry. The level of transferability will be determined by the readers of the final product who must make judgments about the similarities of the findings with other contexts.

Credibility Credibility includes activities that increase the probability of credible findings. Credibility is established through the implementation of the following processes:

Prolonged engagement of participants in their environment is meant to provide the evaluator with an opportunity to learn the working, living, and interacting patterns of the participants; to discern and attend to distortions and inaccuracies introduced by the evaluator and the participants; and to engage in the developmental process of building trust (Lincoln and Guba, 1985). In our neglect evaluation, the evaluator should find ways to "hang out" with the major stakeholders to watch not only how they act, react, and interact during the neglect investigation process, but also to better understand the greater picture of the system of protection and the community within which it operates. Not insignificantly, this evaluator availability to the process will allow stakeholders to both formally and informally get to know the evaluator's skills, perspectives, and agendas.

Trust builds over time and can begin when the evaluator demonstrates to the participants that confidentiality and anonymity will be maintained; their confidences will not be used against them; there is no hidden agenda; and their input will influence the inquiry process. The field journals should contain notation of the investigator's inner biases and conflicts and the strategies used to cope and reach resolutions. The journals should also chronicle the development of different or deeper insights and understandings of the life-styles and constructions of the participants.

Persistent observation, or the act of noting, watching, and taking into account the physical and psychosocial dynamics of the time and place, enables the evaluator to recognize prevalent and persistent qualities as well as unusual and atypical characteristics, and to assess what is fundamental and vital (Lincoln and Guba, 1985). For Lincoln and Guba (1985), "if prolonged engagement provides scope, persistent observation provides depth" (p. 304). Through persistent observation, the investigator learns to eliminate aspects that are irrelevant while continuing to address those that, while atypical, are critical to the inquiry (Eisner, 1979). The reflexive journal should reflect the evaluator's grappling with what is and what is not relevant and persistent.

Triangulation uses different modes of data collection to cross check data collected and data analyzed (Lincoln and Guba, 1985). As the inquiry progresses and pieces of information are recognized, the evaluator should take steps to verify each piece of information with another source (a second interview) or another method (an observation in addition to an interview). The neglect investigation evaluator might check the observed process of investigation against the agency policies and procedures or the state laws on investigation, because "No single item of information (unless coming from an elite and unimpeachable source) should ever be given serious consideration unless it can be triangulated" (Lincoln and Guba, 1985, p. 283). In a later work, Guba and Lincoln (1989) suggest that triangulation carries too positivist an implication by implying that there is some sort of unchanging phenomena out there that can be checked. We, on the other hand, believe that triangulation remains a useful check on stakeholder manipulation and lying.

Peer debriefing establishes a connection between the evaluator and a professional peer who is not part of the inquiry process but has knowledge of the focus of the inquiry and is familiar with the methodology (Lincoln and Guba, 1985).

> *The purposes of debriefing are multiple: to ask the difficult questions which the inquirer might otherwise avoid ("to keep the inquirer honest"), to explore methodological next steps with someone who has no axe to grind, and to provide a sympathetic listening point for personal catharsis (Lincoln and Guba, 1985, p. 283).*

The neglect evaluator might choose another person familiar with the processes of constructivist evaluation and knowledgeable about child welfare and neglect investigations as the peer evaluator. Both the evaluator and the debriefer should keep a journal. These journals should contain a record of the content and process of each session. The expanded field journals will reflect the influence of these sessions on the investigator's thinking, inquiry decisions, and inquiry activities. Other selected peer debriefers can be utilized when their content expertise is felt to be important to the evaluation process.

The member check is a formal and informal process whereby the collected data and the analyzed data are continuously tested, as they are derived, with the participants from whom the data were obtained (Lincoln and Guba, 1985). These opportunities provide participant correction of data, challenge of interpretations, provision of new data, assessment of overall adequacy, and confirmation of the evaluator's reconstruction of their constructions. The neglect investigation evaluator might check the accuracy of his or her understanding about the information gathered from one protective service worker about agency expectations with that worker. The evaluator might test this same material with another service worker or supervisor or even the judge. The field and reflexive journals document not only when and with whom member checking is done, but detail how the inquiry emerged or unfolded as a result of the participants' input.

The final comprehensive member check has the same general purpose as this ongoing member checking process, but is specifically focused on the final case report. Respondents are invited to participate in this final attempt at assessing the overall adequacy of the portrayals. Member selection should depend on the emergent nature of the evaluation process. Criteria for selection may include: membership in an important stakeholding category, ability to articulate support or objections, and willingness to expend further time with the inquiry. Other criteria may be found to be important in a particular evaluation setting.

Each participant in a member check process should be provided, at a minimum, with a written case study of the evaluation process. Members may be provided with a set of member check questions and be asked to complete the questionnaire and make whatever marginal notes they feel necessary. Other situations will be conducive to face-to-face discussion among the various stakeholding participants, with negotiation of the final report the goal of this discussion. The process must be selected that will be supportive of securing comments as to the accuracy of the case study portrayal from their perspective and offer the best opportunity for a final teaching/learning process. The input from this negotiation provides the basis for the final case study report.

Dependability and confirmability Though credibility demonstrates dependability, there are additional processes that serve to account for instability and design induced change. These practices can allow for the determination of the appropriateness of inquiry decisions and methodological shifts (Greene, Doughty, Marquart, Ray, and Roberts, 1988; Schwandt and Halpern, 1988). Many of these same practices will support efforts to determine that the data are confirmable, if the results are linked to the data themselves (Greene, Doughty, Marquart, Ray, and Roberts, 1988; Schwandt and Halpern, 1988). A discussion of the major practices for both dependability and confirmability follows.

Audit trail. While the inquiry is in progress, the evaluator should maintain records of data collected, data analyzed, decision rules, analytic categories, interpretations, and conclusions for a dependability and confirmability audit. This audit involves a formal examination and checking of the record to verify consistency, appropriateness, and accuracy of the content and the procedures for analysis (Lincoln and Guba, 1985). Source material for the audit is all journals, logs, and files. These records containing raw data, data reduction and analysis products, data reconstruction and synthesis products, process notes, material relating to intentions and dispositions, and concepts for triangulation comprise the audit trail (Halpern, 1983).

The dependability and confirmability audit. The audit trail is made available to an external agent to perform the external audit. The auditor's role is to assess the quality of the inquiry process and product. The auditor must be familiar with the methods and techniques employed in the inquiry process in order to be technically competent to perform the audit. It would also do well to have the auditor be sufficiently familiar with the substantive, theoretical, and conceptual issues surrounding the evaluation (Schwandt and Halpern, 1988) to attest to the integrity and quality of the inquiry.

The auditor undertakes a systematic and planned review of the evidence using the framework of an audit suggested by Schwandt and Halpern (1988; Halpern, 1983). Comments on the degree to which the procedures used fall into generally accepted constructivist inquiry practice are a part of an audit report. The auditor's examination of the record of the evaluation process results in a dependability judgment. The examination of the data and the investigator's reconstructions result in a confirmability judgment of the final report of the evaluation process (the thick descriptive product). The auditor's function is to examine the process used in the inquiry and affirm acceptability and internal cohesiveness of the inquiry product (Lincoln and Guba, 1985). In doing so the auditor attests to the degree of rigor, technical accuracy, and trustworthiness of the evaluation. The audit report should serve to bolster the defensibility of the study results.

Additional unique constructivist criteria: Authenticity   In an attempt to divorce rigor in constructivist inquiry from the tests of rigor in the conventional, scientific sense, Lincoln and Guba (1986; Guba and Lincoln, 1989) are in the process of developing an intrinsic constructivist criteria, *authenticity*. Authenticity has at its core the very nature of the differences in constructivist evaluation: multiple constructions of reality heavily shaped by context and values; full participative involvement in the evaluation process by all stakeholders; and an action orientation of the teaching/learning process. Five aspects of authenticity have been identified. To judge the authentic quality of the constructivist evaluation among the participants in the process and product of the evaluation, it must be determined the degree to which there is:

- Evenhanded representation of all viewpoints (*fairness*)
- Increased awareness of the complexity of the program's social environment (*ontological authenticity*)
- Increased understanding of and respect for the value systems of others and their impact on the other stakeholder constructions (*educative authenticity*)
- Change (reshaping) of the program (*catalytic authenticity*)
- Empowerment or redistribution of power among stakeholders (*tactical authenticity*)

In an effort to aid in the practical development of a useful conceptual framework, the following is a discussion of how the process and the results of an evaluation can be assessed related to authenticity.

Evenhanded representation of all viewpoints exists when the case study reflects a balanced view that presents all constructions and the values that undergird them. Fairness is achieved through the ascertaining and presentation of different value and belief systems represented by conflict over issues and the negotiation of recommendations and subsequent action carried out with stakeholders to the inquiry.

Multiple perspectives should be the focus of the evaluation process and should also be the goal of the final product. Honest adherence to the various perspectives in the construction of the case studies should be attempted with an eye to the values undergirding the conflicts that become evident in data gathering and data analysis.

Negotiation should occur around the final case study, with preparation on the part of the evaluator in ways of dealing with strong objections to the material as written. Efforts should be made to further enhance perspectives other than in the way originally presented, if it becomes necessary. This negotiation should follow the minimum rules for negotiation as described by Lincoln and Guba (1986): The process, when possible, should be carried out in full view of the parties. It should occur between equally skilled bargainers operating from equal positions of power. All sides should have the same information, and negotiation should be carried out in accordance with rules that have been established through negotiation beforehand. Appellate mechanisms should be developed for those who might object to the negotiation process. Strong, unresolved objections to the report should be dealt with in a minority report addended to the final report. All participants should be made fully aware that a minority report always remains an option open to them in the final report.

Fully informed consent should be obtained from all participants in the inquiry and renegotiated and reaffirmed as the process unfolds, through the establishment and maintenance of trust and integrity between the participants and the investigator. Constant use of the member-check process should also occur, with specific calls for comments on fairness.

Increased awareness of the complexity of the program's social environment occurs with the improvement in the participant's conscious experiencing of the world. The evaluation process (based on feedback from most participants) should increase participant appreciation of the complexities of phenomena under study. Participants may report never having thought about the phenomena in the same way before. Others may find the simple act of the evaluator questioning procedures or positions to be enough to rethink what has been happening over time. This type of authenticity can be achieved by raising the consciousness of most participants.

Increased understanding of and respect for the value systems of others and their impact on the other stakeholder constructions is achieved when participants gain appreciation of the constructions that are made by others and an understanding of how those constructions are rooted in the different value systems of others. All stakeholders should have the opportunity to appreciate fully the positions of all other stakeholders. There should be an increased appreciation (even if grudgingly given) of the challenges and opportunities of each stakeholding group. The emphasis is not on determining which difference is better, but in coming to an understanding that each difference has merit worthy of consideration. The goal is a greater understanding of the persons in the system being evaluated and a greater empathy, including respect for a differing perspective borne out of differing responsibilities. Education and increased understanding should be one of the consequences of the evaluation process.

Change (reshaping) of the program can be seen in the degree to which the inquiry process facilitates and stimulates action. The evaluation should result in change. Some degree of rethinking or reshaping as a result of the teaching/learning process should occur. In many cases it is impossible to claim that an activity is a direct result of an inquiry process; however, an evaluation posture that involves all stakeholders from the start, that honors their inputs and provides them with decision-making and negotiation power in guiding the evaluation, enhances possibilities for change.

Empowerment or redistribution of power among stakeholders is achieved through stimulation to effective action. Power redistribution or efforts toward empowerment provide educational opportunities for all stakeholders that can help to assure that the actions resulting from the evaluation process achieve desired results. Lincoln and Guba (1986; Guba and Lincoln, 1989) suggest that a way of projecting the possibility of desired change is through determining if the inquiry process was empowering or impoverishing and to whom. All subjects should be seen as equal participants in the process. They should be treated with honesty and respect. No one should be consciously manipulated or diminished as a result of the evaluator's behavior. Subsequent contacts in the evaluation sites will probably be necessary to determine the degree of success with the last two types of authenticity. Failing that possibility, the ethical and ideological basis of the evaluation should be supportive to both types of authenticity.

Distinctive Features of the Constructivist Evaluation and the Constructivist Evaluator

Evaluation based on the assumptions and value premises of the constructivist paradigm has several distinctive features that serve to dramatically change the evaluation process and the role of the evaluator in evaluation. The following is a brief discussion of the special features of constructivist evaluations and the changed evaluator role as a result of these features.

1. Evaluation is a social political process within and between the stakeholders, mediated and furthered by the evaluator. The evaluator understands the need for judgment in the evaluation process, but instead of judging, the evaluator mediates the judgmental process. The judgmental process itself is essentially a political process because it is embedded in value pluralism.

2. Evaluation is a learning/teaching process which is continuous, recursive, divergent, and never finalized. The evaluator participates in the process from a collaborative rather than controlling posture. Not only does the evaluator learn about the different value positions and perspectives, he or she also teaches the stakeholders about the positions of others and how to ask better

questions of one another. As teaching occurs, more questions emerge in an all but unending, recursive, divergent process.

3. Evaluation is a process that creates a new reality from which the negotiated understandings about what a program is emerges. The evaluator is the reality shaper. While the constructions emerge from the various stakeholding groups and initially reflect only their values, when the evaluator teaches these constructions to others, the evaluator inevitably infuses these with his or her own reconstructions. Essentially, the evaluator and the stakeholders literally produce the outcomes of the evaluation by their continuous mutual shaping.

4. Evaluation designs and, for that matter, program designs can never be specified in advance. The designs emerge as the evaluation proceeds. Structure emerges only as the evaluation unfolds. Results also emerge out of the negotiated understanding. It is a collaborative process, open to choice. Evaluation results are not only unpredictable, they represent only a frozen point in time. What holds for the future remains unknown, but the results of this type of collaborative evaluation may serve as an agenda for negotiation of that future. The evaluator's role inevitably emerges as mediator and change agent in this agenda for negotiation.

Evaluators who can successfully participate in constructivist evaluations also are quite distinctive. The constructivist evaluator appreciates diversity, respects the rights of individuals to hold different values and to make different constructions, and welcomes the opportunity to air and clarify these differences. The constructivist evaluator is not threatened by differences, but embraces them.

Guba and Lincoln (1986, p. 85) have described the personal qualities necessary in a constructivist evaluator. The evaluator must possess the personal qualities of honesty, respect, and courtesy, and his or her integrity must be above suspicion. The evaluator must be able to engender trust not only in his or her own ethics, but also in his or her professional competence. Training and experience must provide a grounding in the technical qualitative methodologic skills and, in addition, social, political and interpersonal skills must be clearly demonstrable. The individual must have high tolerance for ambiguity and frustration, as well as possess the capacity to distance him or herself from processes to avoid undue influence. The evaluator must be able to maintain genuine involvement to engender trust and enhance understanding, while maintaining healthy skepticism to guard against lies, deceptions, and other manipulations by stakeholders. Finally, the evaluator must be willing to be changed by the evaluation process both personally and professionally. The evaluator must be open to the risks involved in participating in an all-encompassing, unpredictable, unending process of becoming.

Given this discussion, it is now for you, the evaluator, to decide if this type of evaluation should achieve acceptance and legitimation in the evaluation community. Does it have potential to move the evaluation process to higher levels of sophistication and utility? Does it have the potential to overcome the major criticism of the traditional approach to evaluation? Can constructivist evaluation make a difference?

Endnote

1. The seriousness with which this approach takes the involvement of the stakeholders is dramatically detailed in *Fourth generation evaluation* (Guba & Lincoln, 1989). We direct the reader to their discussion of full participative involvement, including political parity, control, and conceptual parity in Chapter 7.

References

Bailey, K. D. (1978). *Methods of social research* (2nd ed.). (Chaps. 1 & 2). New York: Free Press.

Berreth, D. G. (1986). *Experiences of naturalistic inquirers during inquiry.* Unpublished doctoral dissertation, Indiana University.

Biklen, S. K., & Bogdan, R. (1986). On your own with naturalistic evaluation. In D. D. Williams (Ed.), *Naturalistic evaluation.* New Directions for Program Evaluation, No. 30. San Francisco: Jossey-Bass.

Blythe, B. J., & Briar, S. (1987). Direct practice effectiveness. In A. Minahan (Ed.-in-chief), *Encyclopedia of social work* (18th ed.) (Vol I, pp. 399–407). Silver Spring, MD: National Association of Social Workers.

Bogdan, R., & Taylor, S. J. (1975). *Introduction to qualitative research methods: A phenomenological approach to the social sciences.* New York: John Wiley.

Bulmer, H. (1979). Concepts in the analysis of qualitative data. *The Sociological Review, 27,* 651–677.

Burrell, G., & Morgan, G. (1979). *Sociological paradigms and organisational analysis: Elements of the sociology of corporate life.* London: Heinemann.

Campbell, D. T., & Stanley, J. C. (1963). Experimental and quasi-experimental designs for research on teaching. In N. L. Gage (Ed.), *Handbook of research on teaching.* Chicago, IL: Rand McNally. (Also published as *Experimental and quasi-experimental designs for research.* Chicago, IL: Rand McNally, 1966).

Carmines, E. G., & Zeller, R. A. (1979). *Reliability and validity assessment.* Beverly Hills, CA: Sage.

Chambers, D. E. (1975). Three principles of a knowledge guided social work practice. *Journal of Social Welfare, 2*(1), 35–43.

Cook, T., & Reichardt, C. (Eds.). (1979). *Qualitative and quantitative methods in evaluation research* (Vol. 1). Beverly Hills, CA: Sage.

Corimer, W. H., & Corimer, L. S. (1979). *Interviewing strategies for helpers.* Monterey, CA: Brooks/Cole.

Cronbach, L. J., Ambron, S. R., Dornbusch, S. M., Hess, R. D., Hornik, R. C., Phillips, D. C., Walker, D. F., & Weiner, S. S. (1980). *Toward reform of program evaluation: Aims, methods and institutional arrangements.* San Francisco: Jossey-Bass.

Compton, B. R., & Galaway, B. (Eds.). (1975). *Social work processes.* Homewood, IL: The Dorsey Press.

Dexter, L. A. (1970). *Elite and specialized interviewing.* Evanston, IL: Northwestern University.

Egan, G. (1982). *The skilled helper* (2nd ed.). Monterey, CA: Brooks/Cole.

Eisner, E. W. (1979). *The educational imagination.* New York: Macmillan.

Gerrard, B. A., Boneface, W. J., & Love, B. H. (1980). *Interpersonal skills for health professionals.* Reston, VA: Reston.

Geertz, C. (1973). Thick description: Toward an interpretive theory of culture. In C. Geertz (Ed.), *The interpretation of cultures.* New York: Basic Books.

Glasser, B. G., & Strauss, A. L. (1967). *The discovery of grounded theory.* Chicago, IL: Aldine.

Gold, N. (1983). Stakeholders and program evaluations: Characterizations and reflections. In A. Bryk (Ed.), *Stakeholder-based evaluation.* San Francisco: Jossey-Bass.

Greene, J. C., Doughty, J., Marquart, J. M., Ray, M. L., & Roberts, L. (1988). Qualitative evaluation audits in practice. *Evaluation Review, 12*(4), 352–375.

Guba, E. G. (1981). Investigative journalism. In N. L. Smith (Ed.). *New techniques for evaluation.* Beverly Hills, CA: Sage.

Guba, E. G. (1987). Naturalistic evaluation. *New Directions for Program Evaluation, 34,* 23–43.

Guba, E. G. (ed.).(1990). *The paradigm dialogue.* Newbury Park, CA: Sage.

Guba, E. G., & Lincoln, Y. S. (1983). *Effective evaluation* (3rd printing). San Francisco, CA: Jossey-Bass.

Guba, E. G., & Lincoln, Y. S. (1982). Epistemological and methodological bases of naturalistic inquiry. *Educational Communication and Technology Journal, 30,* 233–252.

Guba, E. G., & Lincoln, Y. S. (1984). Do inquiry paradigms imply inquiry methodologies? In D. L. Fetterman (Ed.), *Ethnography in educational evaluation.* Beverly Hills, CA: Sage.

Guba, E. G., & Lincoln, Y. S. (1986). The countenances of fourth-generation evaluation: Description, judgment, and negotiation. *Evaluation Studies Review Annual, 11,* 70–78.

Guba, E. G., & Lincoln, Y. S. (1989). *Fourth generation evaluation.* Newbury Park, CA: Sage.

Halpern, E. S. (1983). *Auditing naturalistic inquiries: The development and application of a model.* Unpublished doctoral dissertation, Indiana University.

Hofstadter, D. R. (1979). *Godel, Escher, Bach.* New York: Basic Books.

Holsti, O. R. (1969). *Content analysis for the social sciences and humanities.* Reading, MA: Addison-Wesley.

Inberg, A. C. (1975). A student's view of social work. In B. R. Compton and B. Galaway (Eds.), *Social work processes* (pp. 516–523). Homewood, IL: The Dorsey Press.

Kirk, J., & Miller, M. L. (1986). *Reliability and validity in qualitative research.* Beverly Hills, CA: Sage.

Knapp, M. L. (1972). *Nonverbal communication in human interaction.* New York: Holt, Rinehart & Winston.

Krippendorf, K. (1980). *Content analysis.* Beverly Hills, CA: Sage.

Leininger, M. M. (1985). *Qualitative research methods in nursing.* (Chaps. 1, 5). New York: Grune & Stratton.

Lincoln, Y., & Guba, E. (1985). *Naturalistic inquiry.* Beverly Hills, CA: Sage.

Lincoln, Y., & Guba, E. (1986). But is it rigorous?: Trustworthiness and authenticity in naturalistic evaluation. In D. D. Williams (Ed.), *Naturalistic evaluation.* New Directions for Program Evaluation, No. 30. San Francisco: Jossey-Bass.

Lofland, J. (1971). Styles of reporting qualitative field research. *American Sociologist, 9,* 101–111.

Lucas, W. (1974a). *The case survey and alternative methods for research aggregation.* Santa Monica, CA: Rand.

Lucas, W. (1974b). *The case survey method: Aggregating case experience.* Santa Monica, CA: Rand.

Miles, M. B., & Hubberman, A. M. (1984). *Qualitative data analysis: A sourcebook of new methods.* Beverly Hills, CA: Sage.

Mischler, E. (1978). Meaning in context: Is there any other kind? *Educational Review,* 19(1), 1–19.

Morgan, G. (Ed.). (1983). *Beyond method: Strategies for social research.* Beverly Hills, CA: Sage.

Patton, M. Q. (1980). *Qualitative evaluation methods.* Beverly Hills, CA: Sage.

Patton, M. Q. (1987). *Creative evaluation* (2nd ed.). Beverly Hills, CA: Sage.

Pike, D. (1954). *Language in relation to a unified theory of the structure of human behavior* (Vol. 1). Glendale, CA: Summer Institute of Linguistics.

Polanyi, M. (1966). *The tacit dimension.* Garden City, NY: Doubleday.

Punch, M. (1986). *The politics and ethics of fieldwork.* Beverly Hills, CA: Sage.

Reinharz, S. (1979). *On becoming a social scientist.* San Francisco, CA: Jossey-Bass.

Ritzer, G. (1980). *Sociology: A multiple paradigm science* (rev. ed.). Boston, PA: Allyn and Bacon.

Rosengren, K. E. (Ed.). (1981). *Advances in content analysis.* Beverly Hills, CA: Sage.

Sadler, D. R. (1981). Intuitive data processing as a potential source of bias in educational evaluations. *Educational Evaluation and Policy Analysis, 3,* 25–31.

Schon, D. A. (1984). *The crisis of professional knowledge and the pursuit of an epistemology of practice.* Paper presented for the Harvard Business School, 75th Anniversary Colloquium on Teaching by the Case Method.

Schwandt, T. S. & Halpern, E. S. (1988). *Linking auditing and metaevaluation: Enhancing quality in applied inquiry.* Beverly Hills, CA: Sage.

Skrtic, T. M. (1985). Doing naturalistic research into educational organizations. In Y. S. Lincoln (Ed.), *Organizational theory and inquiry: The paradigm revolution.* Beverly Hills, CA: Sage.

Skrtic, T. M., Guba, E. G., Knowlton, H. E. (1985). *Interorganizational special education programming in rural areas: Technical report on the multisite naturalistic field study* (Vol. I). Washington, DC: National Institute of Education.

Smith, M. L. (1986). The whole is greater: Combining qualitative and quantitative approaches in evaluation studies. *New Directions for Program Evaluation, 30,* 37–54.

Spradley, J. (1979). *The ethnographic interviews.* New York: Holt, Rinehart, & Winston.

Spradley, J. (1980). *Participant observation.* New York: Holt, Rinehart, & Winston.

Stern, P. N. (1985). Using grounded theory method in nursing research. In M. M. Leininger (Ed.), *Qualitative research methods in nursing* (pp. 149–160). New York: Grune & Stratton.

VanMaanen, J., Dabbs, J. M., & Faulkner, R. R. (1982). *Varieties of qualitative research.* Beverly Hills, CA: Sage.

Webb, E., Campbell, N., Schwartz, R., & Sechrest, L. (1966). *Unobtrusive measures: Nonreactive research in the social sciences.* Chicago, IL: Rand McNally.

Webb, E., Campbell, E., Schwartz, R., Sechrest, L., & Grove, J.B. (1981). *Nonreactive measures in the social sciences.* Boston, MA: Houghton Mifflin.

Weick, K. E. (1976). Educational organizations as loosely coupled systems. *Administrative Science Quarterly, 21,* 1–19.

Zeller, N. (1984). *Writing the case report.* Unpublished manuscript, Indiana University.

INDEX

Abt Associates, 5
Accounting method, 245–247
Achenbach, T. M., 203
Acquiescence response set, 196
Active listening, 312
Adoption programs, 169
Advertising, 3
Advocacy role, of evaluator, 60
Age of Efficiency and Testing,
    272–273
Age of Expansion, 273–274
Age of Innocence, 273
Age of Professionalization, 274
Age of Reform, 272
Aggregate measures, 89
AIDS, 166–167
Aid to Families of Dependent
    Children (AFDC), 7
Alcohol research, 200, 250–255
Alemi, F., 285
Alpha, 192
Altman, D. G., 69
American Evaluation Association,
    1, 29
American National Standards
    Institute (ANSI), 47
Anchoring, 196
Anderson, B., 158
Anderson, L. G., 258, 270

Anonymity
    in monitoring program
        utilization, 163
    in needs assessment surveys,
        96–97
    trust and, 323
Antecedents, 115
Aslanian, C. B., 69
Attention placebos, 198
Attkisson, C. C., 208
Audit
    confirmability, 322, 325–326
    program audit vs., 156
Audit trail, 318, 322, 325
Authenticity, 304, 326–327
Autonomy of persons, 40, 42
Availability of information, 320

B

Babbie, E. R., 95, 97
Back, K. W., 273
Bailey, K. D., 315
Balkin, S., 152, 153
Barbano, J. D., 90
Barlow, D. H., 209
Baron, J. B., 34–35
Baron, R. M., 34–35

L

Laboratory research, 37–38, 43–44
Landefeld, J. S., 257
Latent organizational objectives, 24
Lavrakas, P. J., 95
Legal issues, 30, 62–66
  breach of confidentiality, 64–65.
    See also Confidentiality
  contract performance, 63–64
  defamation of character, 65–66
  legality, 123
  malpractice, 64–65
  rise of litigation, 62–63
Leininger, M. M., 293, 303
Length of questionnaire, 95, 194
Lesage, J. P., 260–263, 266
Levin, H. M., 239, 240, 243, 268
Libel, 65
Lincoln, Y. S., 14, 15, 19, 49, 53,
    121, 139, 272, 279, 280, 290,
    293, 294, 295, 298, 299,
    302–304, 307, 308, 310–314,
    316–319, 321–329
Lindblom, C., 150
Lindenberg, R. E., 98
Linstone, H. A., 86
Lipsey, M., 19
Local molar causal validity, 235
Lofland, J., 317, 318
Logan, S., 174
Logs, 318, 321
Longabaugh, R., 250, 254
Love, B. H., 312
Lt. Kiji Error, 149
Lucas, W., 316
Lynch, M. M., 98

M

Madaus, G. F., 272, 276
Maeterninck, 149
Magura, S., 177, 197, 203

Mailed questionnaires
  amount of time required for, 96
  for key informants, 75–76
  in needs assessment surveys, 93
Malpractice, ERS Standards for,
    64–65
Management-by-objectives (MBO),
    3–4
Mark, M., 218
Market pricing, 241–242
Market research, 3
Marsh, J., 233
Mass communications, 3
Mathematica Inc., 5
MAUA. *See* Multiattribute utility
    analysis
Maximizing good outcomes, 37
Mayer, R., 70, 71
Maynard-Moody, S., 149
McClintock, C., 116, 200
McCrady, B., 250–254
McGuire, D., 56
McKillip, J., 69, 86, 89, 91, 100, 101,
    162
McLeod, K., 247
McNamara, Robert, 3–4
Measurement
  ERS Standards for, 51, 58–59
  evaluation vs., 273
  impression management in,
    20–21
  issues of, 213–214
  problems of, 19–21
  reactivity and, 20
  validity and, 196–198
Measurement error, reliability
    and, 193–194
Measurement tools, 201–203
  global assessments, 202
  hard-data measurements,
    201–202
  reliability of, 51, 58–59
  standardized instruments,
    202–203